UNREVISED AND UNREPENTED

From a recent portrait of ARTHUR MEIGHEN
by Ernest Fosbery

UNREVISED AND UNREPENTED

DEBATING SPEECHES
AND OTHERS

BY

THE RIGHT HONOURABLE
ARTHUR MEIGHEN

WITH A FOREWORD BY
M. GRATTAN O'LEARY

Toronto
CLARKE, IRWIN & COMPANY LIMITED
1949

CONTENTS

(Speeches are printed in chronological order)

PREFACE

THE AUTHOR OF THIS BOOK cannot claim that it is being published in response to an irresistible, or even numerous, popular demand. The impelling incentive has been self-evolved. He wishes to make available in permanent form, for those who may desire to read it, a record of the position he has taken on public issues during the past four decades of Canadian history, and of his reasons therefor. The latter, it is hoped, will be found worthy of perusal and perhaps of adoption.

Arising as they do out of a life devoted largely to controversy, it is inevitable that many of the speeches appearing here partake of that character. The majority were delivered in one of our two Houses of Parliament or in election campaigns. A number of special addresses are included. These will relieve the atmosphere of contention which otherwise might become wearisome.

Unrevised and Unrepented—the title chosen—will be found in its original context on page 434. The word "Unrevised" requires explanation. Most of the contents of this book are debating speeches. In the heat and clash of battle across the floor of Parliament, where no text or notes are at hand, construction sometimes falters, and clarity is obscured. Listeners on both sides have heard previous speakers, and the significance of every sentence is more easily appreciated by them than is possible on the part of readers who come on the scene years later. Further, repetition for emphasis is employed, and employed legitimately— more than would be welcomed by a reader of cold print. The fullest freedom has been exercised throughout in repairing these infirmities, but there has been no revision in substance and opinion. The word "Unrepented" stands intact, and the views presented in this volume, as well as the arguments by which they are fortified, are again earnestly commended to the people of Canada.

October, 1949.   A. M.

vii

Of the speeches in this volume *The Greatest Englishman in History* has been previously published. The author and the publishers wish to acknowledge with thanks permission from the Oxford University Press, Canadian Branch, to include this speech in the present collection.

FOREWORD

CARDINAL NEWMAN ONCE SAID that the true life of a public man is contained in his letters and speeches, and that "not only for the interests of a biography, but for arriving at the inside of things, the publication of letters and speeches is the true method. Biographers (he continued) varnish, they assign motives, they conjecture feelings, they interpret Lord Burleigh's nod, but contemporary letters and speeches are facts."

It seems to me that these words apply especially to the speeches of Arthur Meighen here collected. Mostly spoken red-hot in the House of Commons or on electioneering platforms, or amid the hurry of a crowded life, they are the spontaneous presentation of the man himself. And, to my thinking, a particular merit of that unconscious presentation lies in the fact that never a word, whether spoken in defeat or victory, shows the nature and acts of the man to have been other than faithful to his principles. Appropriately, I think, is this volume entitled "Unrevised and Unrepented."

Arthur Meighen grew, with age and experience, in maturity and power, but though his opinions on many questions may have changed with years and circumstances, his principles remained fixed. Mr. Gladstone once condemned scornfully "changes which are systematically timed and turned to the interest of personal advancement, changes which are hooded, slurred over or denied." Never can it be said of Arthur Meighen that his opinions were moulded by any such considerations. So far from gaining "personal advancement" through any such devices, he sacrificed a great career and incurred tremendous obloquy for the sake of fidelity to principles to which he became pledged. In this volume we may read the speeches it contains with the certainty that whether we agree with the opinions expressed or not,

ix

the man who uttered them meant exactly what he said because he was honest and unafraid.

Arthur Meighen was that sort of leader. As I saw him in our public life—many of the speeches in this volume I had the privilege of hearing—he had two outstanding qualities. One was determination, reinforced by a brilliant, questing mind, to get at the truth. The other was determination, reinforced by character, to fight for the truth as he found it, regardless of consequences. In a world pitifully all signposts and no destination, he always knew where he was going, always knew where he was leading. In a world of "light half-believers in their casual creeds," his faith in his own beliefs was sharp and shining. Faith he had, deep and abiding, in the ultimate splendour of human achievement; but he knew, and was never afraid to proclaim, that the way wasn't easy—that it could never be a track for sheep, but a path beset by trials, challenging the best in man's nature.

And to that integrity—integrity of mind and soul—Arthur Meighen added a reverence for the integrity of speech. For great words—

"Words that have drawn transcendent meanings up
From the best passions of all by-gone time,
Steeped through with tears of triumph or remorse,
Sweet with all sainthood, cleansed in martyr-fires . . ."

he had, indeed, a passion. To them he gave often the sheen of a fresh glory.

My privilege it has been, through forty years of journalism, to have heard all the great masters of our speech on both sides of the Atlantic: Our own Sir Wilfrid Laurier on great occasions; America's Franklin Roosevelt; France's Viviani; Britain's Birkenhead, Balfour and Churchill in Parliament and on the platform, and Lloyd George exhorting the multitude in the passion of a general election. I write here deliberately that Arthur Meighen, at his highest and best, was an arrow's flight beyond them all. In our own country, only Laurier, Howe and McGee dwelt on the same plane with him.

Lord Curzon, in his great lecture on "Modern Parliamentary Eloquence," said of Asquith:

"Whenever I have heard him on a first-rate occasion, there arose in my mind the image of some great military parade. The words, the arguments, the points, follow each other with the steady tramp of regiments across the field; each unit is in its place, the whole marching in rhythmical order; the sunlight glints on the bayonets, and ever and anon is heard the roll of the drum."

That could have been said of Arthur Meighen. In clearness, in logic, in cogent and relentless reasoning, he was without an equal. He could state his case, argue it, illustrate it and prove it with a persuasiveness that was irresistible.

Like Bacon, he had to have the "dry light" of reason on whatever subject he dealt with—the truth, the whole truth, and nothing but the truth, unaffected by any distorting or discolouring rays of passion, prejudice or emotion. I have seen him work himself into new questions, feel his way to the heart of them, then gradually marshal the facts with relation to some fundamental principle or some significant circumstance until the whole subject became luminous even to the mind of a layman.

And Arthur Meighen was more than a matchless debater. It has been said of him by critics that he was too passionless and austere to attain to the highest in oratory. The truth is that while it was as a debater and advocate that he excelled, there were times when, stirred by deep feeling, he became neighbour to the sun, reached to the purest and noblest eloquence. His speech on such occasions may have lacked the combination of "cloud, whirlwind and flame" which somebody once ascribed to the oratory of Grattan, but the anthologies of eloquence will be searched long for anything of more stately grandeur than the passage with which, at Winnipeg, he closed his defence of his famous "Hamilton Speech," or for something finer than his tribute to Thomas D'Arcy McGee, or for more of solemn beauty than his words of dedication of the Cross of Vimy. Whenever I go back to those lines on Vimy there comes a reminder of Lincoln, of his beauty and sublimity, while no one of Irish extraction can read the eulogy of McGee without memory of the magnificent words which the orator Patrick Collins spoke at the grave of Boyle O'Reilly: "By the great mysterious Rath, over one sanctified spot dearer than all others to him . . . the spirit of O'Reilly hovered, and shook the stillness of the Irish dawn on its journey to the stars."

"The exigencies of politics," Arthur Meighen once said, "are merciless and inscrutable." The exigencies of politics, with that baffling caprice of democracy which forever is crowning and crucifying its kings, robbed us of the full gain of his own genius.

Rosebery in his life of Pitt wrote that "time and circumstances and opportunity paint with heedless hands and garish colours on the canvas of a man's life; so that the result is less frequently a finished picture than a palette of squeezed tints." In Arthur Meighen's parliamentary life there was, alas, no finished picture, and in the political misfortunes which engulfed him he well could have quoted with Asquith the lines of James Shirley:

> "The glories of our blood and state
> Are shadows, not substantial things;
> There is no armour against fate."

Yet something remained. Remained the knowledge, proudly for his fame and his friends, that never in his political career had he paltered with truth, nor denied for the sake of his political fortune what he believed to be right for his country. In adversity he remained to Canada—

> "As true as the dial to the sun,
> Although it be not shined upon."

Here a brief digression. One speech in this volume I recommend beyond others: That speech in which Arthur Meighen exposes in all its meanness and falsity the issue which once was raised against him, and which became notorious as the "Byng Incident." All history, it has been said, is collective memory. If that be true, it is well then to have revealed in all of its duplicity an issue which, for those who were near to it, and who knew well the truth behind it, was perhaps the most dishonest and cruel in our political story, but which yet, through sustained propaganda, took on the danger of passing from myth into accepted reality. Here, in clarity, in logic, in expository power, and above all in fidelity to truth, we have Arthur Meighen at his best. Here we have, beyond challenge, the naked facts of an episode discreditable to our political history.

Arthur Meighen's public life will be judged by posterity on its merits. I believe that judgment will be more favourable than that passed by his contemporaries; that history will be more kind to him than the times in which he lived. Be that as it may, here in these speeches we at any rate are permitted to see what manner of man he was, the things which he believed, the loyalties for which he fought, the principles which he loved; may judge him better from the words he uttered than from any of those memoirs—those creations of vanity, of malice, and sometimes of garrulous old age—in which the picture of a public man becomes more of the artist than the model. We may agree or disagree with what we read, but we can have the satisfaction of knowing that it is the man himself who speaks to us and not the hollow voice of some actor behind a mask—that here from a great man are the words with which his tongue and heart stirred and enriched our country.

M. GRATTAN O'LEARY.

Ottawa,
October,
1949.

UNREVISED AND UNREPENTED

FARM IMPLEMENT DUTIES

This speech was made in the House of Commons on January 18, 1911 *during the Laurier regime, in support of the following resolution:*

That in the opinion of this House, a substantial reduction in the import duties on agricultural implements is now due the agriculturists of Canada, and is in just accord with the true ends of a protective tariff.

The debate was continued by other members the same afternoon, but no opportunity for its resumption later was accorded and no vote on the resolution took place.

THE SUBJECT LAUNCHED IN THE resolution which I now have the honour to move occupies a position of supreme importance in the commercial life of this country. For close upon a third of a century, the basic principle which should govern our fiscal system and the application of that principle to details of our importations has been canvassed more thoroughly than has any other subject in the political history of Canada. Throughout that time, the party with which I am associated has planted its faith on those articles of economic belief laid down by its founder and now recognized as the National Policy, and to that fiscal system it has, in my humble opinion, consistently throughout all these years adhered. To the National Policy fully stated, stated in the language of Sir John Macdonald himself and repeated in the words and illustrated by the practices of his successors, to that policy, stated wholly and not partially, I am still proud to adhere.

What has been the course of the party now in office, and what has been its fiscal theory, I shall not trust myself to define. But you will agree with me, Mr. Speaker, from occurrences, particularly of the last few months, that no argument will appeal, at this time, to either side of the House which has not its footing in a sane and reasonable protective policy. I say that because, in

3

my judgment, there is no member on either side of the House today who would not be compelled to acknowledge, to himself at least, that, under conditions now obtaining on this continent, a protective policy is the only one possible for Canada. Perhaps in that statement I could have excepted the hon. member for Red Deer (Mr. Clark), who is yet a fiscal exotic in this country, and who, I sincerely think, still manages by assiduous care to keep alive his free trade theories. But with that exception, it is not too much to say that the mask is now pretty largely thrown off, and that every member, even on the other side, actually does acknowledge in his inmost heart that nothing but a tariff protective in principle is practicable under present continental conditions.

It may be possible, and I think it is a fact, that there are some hon. gentlemen opposite who have no fiscal belief of any kind, and it is not surprising that men who have followed that party have been confused by its tortuous course through these later years, and, in despair at the double life it has been leading, consorting with protection while under marital vows to free trade, have become economic atheists. For my part I conclude there is only one assumption on which an argument can possibly be based in seeking to make a case for tariff change. This has been impressed upon me by events during the last few months. A short time ago we had one thousand or more agriculturists waiting upon this Government, and at considerable length assailing the First Minister and his cabinet for continuing, as they contended, in a more pronounced form than ever before, the principle of protection in our fiscal system. Without a dissenting voice they asserted as a fact which could not be denied that protection, whether it be good or bad, was more pronounced in the present tariff than it had been in that of the Conservative Government. On the other hand, what did we see later? A delegation representing manufacturers of Canada came to Ottawa, and in a well-matured presentation of their case they assumed, as a basis, that the same fiscal system which now prevails had been in effect for thirty years. To neither one contention nor the other did the Prime Minister, who replied, offer any word of resentment or dispute. He did not dare to tell those thousand agriculturists that he had eliminated the protective principle; he did not even dare to say that he had moved one hair's breadth towards doing so. Nor did he resent the statement of that body of manufacturers that the very same system prevails now as has prevailed for thirty years. Consequently, I am not out of the way when I assume as a starting point that the only argument which can influence either side is an argument based on the inescapable necessity of a fair and reasonable protection.

Now, Sir, the charge I have to make against the Government in this connection is not the gravest charge that can be laid at their door. The gravest charge which history will always hold against them is that they preached a doctrine in which they had no real belief; that they professed in infidelity hostility to a policy which they knew was the only one practicable for this country, and thereby acquired office by false pretence and deceit; and that for fourteen years they have worn the mask of hypocrisy, ever getting thinner and thinner, until now it is literally blown away. But the indictment I have to make, and which I hope to bring home to the Government this afternoon is not that one, though it is the most serious; it is this, that in their attempts to continue the National Policy which had been in effect for years before, they have neglected one essential feature; they have quite forgotten its guiding principle, namely, that as our industrial institutions advanced in strength and as they became able with every advance to acquire a greater share of the home market, the import duties were to be adjusted in order to meet evolving and changing conditions. It is that restraining, guiding principle which I claim this Government has entirely overlooked, and, as a consequence, in the class of goods I am discussing this afternoon, they have allowed protection to run rampant; and have, for reasons which are only too obvious, become the slaves of those who helped them into power and who now maintain them there behind ramparts of gold.

Permit me in support to lay certain facts on the record. I first quote briefly from the language of that distinguished statesman whose title to greatness is becoming clearer and stronger as the fruits of his labours multiply; I quote the words of Sir John A. Macdonald, in a speech made in this House in 1878, at page 857 of Hansard. Speaking on March 8th, Sir John A. Macdonald said:

> If we had a protective system in this country, if we had a developed capital, we could, by giving our manufacturers a reasonable hold on our home trade, attain a higher position among the nations.

Further on:—

> I do not mean that we should adopt a tariff like that of the United States, but one such as the necessities of Canada demand.

And still further:—

> It can be well understood that a judicious tariff may, on the whole, be a moderate tariff.

Thus, the basic rule laid down, in so far as the feature I am now emphasizing goes, was that the object of a tariff was to give manufacturing industries of Canada a reasonable hold on the home market. The same principle was supported by Sir Leonard Tilley at page 429 of Hansard, 1879, when, on 14th March, he made his budget speech introducing the National Policy. With a consistency of which we are proud Finance Ministers who succeeded in office carried into effect the same doctrine thus expressed. I quote now words of the present hon. member for North Toronto (Mr. Foster), who at the time they were uttered was Finance Minister of Canada. They are from Hansard 1894, page 194. I do not know how far he may agree with me as to the application of the principle there expressed, but I do know that the principle itself which he there defined he is not the man to fall away from now.

> If there is to be a protective system at all, everybody knows that it must be higher in its inception than as the years gradually pass, when industries have become established and when the industrial development of the country grows apace.

And further, at page 234:

> The reduction in agricultural implements—

This has a very particular bearing on the present discussion.

—from 35 per cent to 20 per cent, is one under which it would tax the ingenuity of the manufacturer to keep the field against what is now keen competition especially in the North-west.

Thus did he postulate that the standard by which these duties were to be judged was such a rate as would tax the ingenuity of our manufacturers to keep the field against foreign competition and clearly indicate that as conditions of production improved and as their hold became stronger, the principle thus defined would compel a reduction. At page 202, the following remarks were also made by the same hon. gentleman:

Our industries have not yet overtaken the home consumption of the people, but are gradually growing up to the point of meeting the consumptive demand in the country.

In those words he implied support of the same clear test— that is, whether these manufacturers had what Sir John A. Macdonald called a reasonable hold on the home market. I refer also, because the words are particularly in point, to remarks made by the present member for South Lanark (Hon. J. Haggart) who was at the time Minister of Railways and Canals in the government of Sir John Thompson. The hon. member for South Lanark, at page 347 of Hansard, 1894, made the statement that, as evidenced by vastly growing exports abroad, our manufacturers had demonstrated their ability to stand reductions. Further, and this is a quotation I wish to emphasize, the hon. gentleman said:

For the last fourteen years, protection in Canada has so developed our manufactures that the government now think that a fair reduction in the tariff can be ventured on. They believe that our people can compete with less protection than formerly, and to prove that, it can be pointed out that we are now sending agricultural implements to many portions of the world.

There the hon. member clearly laid it down that the gauge to be applied as to whether the purpose of a protective system was being served and as to the measure in which it had been served was the relative size of export trade to home consumption. I ask the House to bear especially in mind Mr. Haggart's reference to agricultural implement export, because later I will be able to convince simply and by the fewest figures that our export of these goods at that date, when the duty was reduced by 15 per cent, was almost as nothing compared to what it later became under the protection afforded by former apostles of free trade.

What is the present situation in agricultural implements? I have chosen this field not because there is no other which could be the subject of attack, but because investigation has persuaded me that a very strong argument can be made in it, and because also a better purpose is served by a clear-cut and definite discussion of one class of business than by a rambling one over the whole field of our tariff schedules. In the phrase "agricultural implements" I mean to include only larger articles. My argument will not, indeed, apply with equal force to all of these. There are, however, certain implement manufacturers who, by reason of the protection afforded by this Government, have in their expansion gone away beyond the point at which reductions should have been applied. I refer particularly to makers of binders and mowers.

As everybody knows, in 1896 and for two years previously, the duty on agricultural implements of all kinds stood at 20 per cent and the same rate was maintained by this government for eleven years longer, or until 1907. In the meantime the insidious work of departmental officials in increasing valuations for duty had got into play, and while a nominal tariff was maintained at 20 per cent, the actual rate was appreciably higher. Other regulations were made which afforded manufacturers a greater protection than the 20 per cent set out in the Customs Act. Up to 1896, the nominal valuation placed on five and six foot binders was $80, and 20 per cent of this valuation compelled the purchaser to pay $16 duty. I have proof here of what the exact valuations were, but it may be taken for practical purposes that the average for a number of years was around $80. In tables which I have prepared I give the average duty and the average valuation from Canadian Trade and Navigation returns. These show that advanced valuations made under regulations of the Customs Department had the effect of throwing round the manufacturer—

entirely aside from still more help afforded him by a drawback privilege—a materially higher protection.

IMPORTATION OF BINDERS
Year ending June 30, 1897.

Number of binders imported	1,946
Total valuation	$203,537.00
Average valuation per binder	104.00
Total duty	40,647.39
Average duty per binder	20.35

Next will come similar statistics for the year ending March 31, 1907—which is ten years later, and before the 17½ per cent duty line was drawn:

IMPORTATION OF BINDERS

Number of binders imported	2,878
Total valuation	$315,744.00
Average valuation per binder	144.44
Average duty per binder	21.87

For the year 1910, after the 17½ per cent came into effect, the following figures apply:

IMPORTATION OF BINDERS
Year ending March 31, 1910.

Number of binders imported	1,481
Total valuation	$165,759.00
Average valuation per binder	111.92
Total duty	29,052.34
Average duty per binder	19.61

MR. FOSTER: What was the average valuation for 1907?

MR. MEIGHEN: $144.44. The House should note that this gives the duty actually paid and it is only one constituent of the protection afforded, because in that year the manufacturer in addition to tariff levy enjoyed a drawback on duties paid on his raw material.

I have before me similar detail covering importation of mowers for the same periods. From these it is clear that the Government have, by merely raising valuation from $34.20 to $44.00, increased protection from $6.56 per mower to $7.70, notwithstanding a much-vaunted reduction in rate of duty from

20 per cent to $17\frac{1}{2}$ per cent. That again is entirely aside from further help afforded by drawback privileges which also applied to the manufacture of mowers. These drawbacks on steel and pig iron, and to some extent on malleables, apply only to production of binders, mowers and reapers, and, of course, it is only on these implements that the duty was reduced from 20 to $17\frac{1}{2}$ per cent.

Let me endeavour to illustrate the effect of these drawbacks. To the following concerns, namely, Massey-Harris & Co., the International Harvester Co., Noxon & Co., and Frost & Wood, the total drawback payable last year was $207,458.99. That works out on each mower and each binder in the following way: on a five foot mower the 99 per cent rebate on cast iron at $2.50 per ton comes to 49 cents; 99 per cent on rolled iron and steel at $7 per ton makes the rebate on each mower 43 cents, and $2\frac{1}{2}$ per cent on malleables makes the rebate on each mower 7 cents, or a total of 99 cents. From this should be deducted an increase on cold drawn steel, 27 cents, which deducted from the 99 cents leaves a balance of drawback amounting to 72 cents per mower. Similar figures apply to binders in the following measure: 99 per cent on cast iron gives 28 cents on each binder, 99 per cent on rolled iron and steel gives $2.17 more, and the rebate on the malleables is 21 cents, making a total of $2.66 from which should be deducted the increase on cold drawn steel 41 cents, leaving a net drawback per binder of $2.25.

MR. KNOWLES: Was there any drawback prior to 1896?

MR. MEIGHEN: None, except what I have stated in the table, and that applied only to export. It now applies to both home and export business.

The average duty actually paid on mowers in 1896 was, as I have shown, $6.56. This, without drawback advantages, was increased by the mere artifice of added valuation to $7.70. This with 72 cents net drawback makes the present protection per mower $8.42, notwithstanding the diminution in duty from 20 to $17\frac{1}{2}$ per cent. It would be interesting to know how the Prime Minister feels when he reflects that his Government, pledged through the mouth of the hon. member for Brandon (Mr. Sifton) not merely to reduce the duty on agricultural implements, but absolutely to abolish it, has been responsible for raising the protection on every mower from $6.56 to $8.42, an increase of 24 per cent.

Applying the same accurate calculation to binders, we have the following:

Average duty paid in the year ending March 31, 1907, $20.35. Average duty last year, notwithstanding 2½ per cent reduction, $19.61. Add to that $2.25 which the manufacturer gets as rebate and his protection per binder is found to be $21.86. So the hon. member for Brandon saw to it that his pledge was implemented—a pledge for which no doubt he had full authority from the First Minister, a pledge justified by the statement of the First Minister in Winnipeg when he proclaimed the doctrine of free trade as they had it in England—by working out an ingenious elevation of the protection on every binder from $20.35 to $21.86. If hon. gentlemen tell me I have selected last year because it shows the Government at a disadvantage, I answer by going back a few years. The figures for 1908 would be much worse for them. Valuation then was so high that actual protection afforded the manufacturer on binders was equal to 25⅕ per cent under the conditions which obtained in 1896 during Conservative rule.

What is the reason for all this? If it could be argued that these industries had retreated from manhood to infancy, that they had got younger instead of older, that competition had lately been more severe than it was before, that relative cost of labour has been higher, there might be some excuse. If the Government could show that manufacturers of these implements had receded from wealth to comparative poverty, that they had removed from a concentrated monopolistic area, widened out into a diversified multiplicity of plants, there might be some defence; but in every respect the very opposite has taken place, in every respect those conditions which call for a reduction have operated, those conditions that demand an increase have been consistently absent. From 1897 to 1898 export was comparatively small. At present it is large. But before going into that phase, let me give a few facts to show that costs of production at the present time do not warrant a very material duty, particularly as respects binders, mowers and reapers, articles made by the International Harvester Company. My proof is gathered from what may be called the very camp of the enemy, from the officers of the International Harvester Company, from its own official, Mr. Metcalfe. I quote his evidence given before the Committee of Ways and Means of, the House of Representatives last year, and it will convince hon. members that there is very little, if any, difference in the cost of manufacture of these machines on this side of the border and in the United States. At pages 7323-4 of the U.S. Tariff Hearings, I find the following:

> MR. CUMPACKER. Do you manufacture any cheaper in Canada than in the United States?
> MR. METCALFE. They do not.
> MR. CUMPACKER. As cheaply?
> MR. METCALFE. Comparatively.
> MR. CUMPACKER. Can you manufacture cheaper than the English manufacturer or the German manufacturer?
> MR. METCALFE. I think they can, otherwise they could not compete with them in Germany and England.

Mr. Metcalfe is thus on record as admitting that there is comparatively no difference in production cost on the other side of the line and on this. He further admitted that the relative cost of manufacturing on this side of the border and in England and France is in favour of Canada.

Mr. Metcalfe is further on record as stating, in the plainest language, that his company produces in this country for export ·abroad. It is, therefore, reasonable to argue that it is just as cheap to produce those articles on this side as on the other, because otherwise they would manufacture for export on the U.S. side and not on this, for they have factories on both.

On page 738 of those tariff hearings, Mr. Metcalfe answered the chairman as follows:

> MR. CHAIRMAN. Are you exporting from Canada?
> MR. METCALFE. They are.
> THE CHAIRMAN. To what countries?
> MR. METCALFE. All the foreign countries and particularly to France. We are very much interested at the present time in the treaty between Canada and France.

Mr. Lafollette, senator from the State of Wisconsin, arguing on this very evidence, used the following language:—

> I would call the attention of the senators from Michigan that representatives of the International Harvester Company, who were present before the Committee of Ways and Means, said that with respect to their manufacture in Canada it cost them just as much to manufacture here. That the price of labour was the same.

A clear implication is that conditions and cost of production are practically the same on both sides of the boundary.

From that source, therefore, very little defence can be found for the conduct of this Government. Can they get any comfort from developments in the industry itself? In a moment it will be made clear that for many years these factories, instead of being multiplied in numbers and thus having to meet that healthy competition which keeps down profits, have gradually become concentrated. The Government has failed to become alive to that circumstance and to deprive them of undue protection. The following table shows the number of agricultural implement factories in successive years:—

In 1881	234
In 1891	221
In 1901	114
In 1905	70

For more than two decades there has been going on a continual process of concentration, and this movement has been allowed to proceed under the very eyes of the Government. But though these establishments have weakened in numbers, have they weakened in financial strength? Has their capitalization gone down? Has money been lacking? Have they been driven by stress of poverty to demand this higher protection which the Government has afforded? The facts show the reverse. In 1891 total capital invested in them was $9,116,000. It rose in 1901 to $18,307,342. In 1905 it increased to $28,304,970. And these increases took place notwithstanding a continual reduction in their number. A moderate estimate for 1910, assuming the same rate of growth, indicates that today they have a capitalization of

about $40,000,000. That is the picture which presents itself.
Investigation in every direction confirms the view that all circumstances which demand a reduction in tariff have been present
in increasing degree throughout this century, and that every
consideration which would call for additional protection has been
eliminated.

I wish to treat of another circumstance which shows quite
strikingly what a contrast there is in the position now occupied
by the agricultural implement industry and its position in 1896.
From statistics showing imports relative to exports— the talisman
by which in great measure scales of duties are fixed—a very
instructive lesson can be drawn. In the last fiscal year we
exported as follows:

Mowing machines	$ 614,912
Reapers	202,618
Binders and harvesters	1,371,543
Ploughs	328,000
Harrows	72,589
Hay rakes	150,690
Seeders	6,811

Sales abroad of other implements amounted to $1,220,105, mak-
ing a total of $4,319,385. Let us deduct, for a purpose which
will appear later, the item of ploughs. If we deduct that item,
total sales are left at $3,991,295.

Next we look at imports. The same statistical source shows a
total importation of $1,679,737 of all agricultural implements,
and a total duty of $283,633.99. If we deduct again the single
article of ploughs, we have the comparatively insignificant
imports of $734,391, and the comparatively insignificant duty of
$92,954.72. Now, place these sales against purchases and what
happens? Our sales were, as I have shown, $4,319,385 and our
purchases only $1,679,737. But if we leave out ploughs, the single
article which has not enjoyed the same protection as others and
has, therefore, not thriven in the same degree, we find the result
to be, exports $3,991,295, imports $734,391, or a proportion of
about 5 to 1. Such is the position in which the policy of
"eliminating protection" has placed manufacturers of these
implements as compared with where they were in 1896 when

their total exports amounted only to some $400,000. They have reached an absolutely unique position among manufacturers in Canada, sending abroad $5 worth of products for every $2 imported, if we include them all; and if we exclude ploughs, exporting $5 in goods for every dollar's worth brought into this country.

Let us as well contrast the position which producers of these implements have attained with the position reached by other manufacturers. I make the statement that if we survey the whole field of manufacturing in Canada we can find no class which has risen to a position in any way comparable to that reached by the makers of agricultural implements. I go further and say that in no instance of any important manufacture, except one, have I been able to find that exports exceed or even approach imports. If hon. gentlemen will but look at Trade and Navigation returns for the year ending March 31, 1907, they will find that our total imports last year of all manufactures of iron and steel, excepting agricultural implements, were $48,180,521; and our total exports, excepting agricultural implements, were $3,506,307; over $48,000,000 of imports of productions of iron and steel outside of agricultural implements, and a little over $3,500,000 of exports. Compare this situation with the very reverse position which has just been proved to exist with reference to makers of farm implements and ask yourselves: Could anything more clearly show the unique position which these favoured manufacturers have been able to attain under the increased protection afforded them by this once free trade Government?

It has been contended on behalf of our hon. friends opposite that they are imposing duties with a view to revenue only. I do not accept for a moment, nor do I think they believe, that this is the main purpose of their tariff. That there may be no argument left, that there may be nothing remaining on which to hang a defence of the policy they have pursued, I wish to dwell upon this point for a moment—the effect on revenue. Why, Sir, we have in respect of farm implements no tariff for revenue at all. They have so added to protection afforded manufacturers that the effect has been almost to shut out importations altogether. Today total revenue which this Government derives is, as I have

shown, some $283,634, even including ploughs; and, if we omit
that one article, the total revenue which this tariff-for-revenue
Government has gathered from importations of agricultural
implements sinks to the insignificant sum of $92,955.

What, Sir, are makers of these implements enabled to do?
They are able, under this tariff, to exact a higher price than they
could exact if the rate were lower. It may be that a reduction
will not, to any very important extent, affect the price. It will,
however, render some relief, particularly to farmers of the West,
many of whom, notwithstanding statements made here, are
struggling between success and failure every hour. It will accord
some relief to them, and I believe it is the bounden duty of the
Government so to assist them. In my hand is a table showing
relative prices of these implements now prevailing in this country
and in the United States. I can place it on Hansard if desired.
At a moderate estimate, there is at least an addition of 10% in
Canada. Our people generally would be ready to pay that, if
conditions so demanded. In days gone by, they did decide that
it was in the best interest of the whole of Canada that consumers
should be taxed in order that Canadian industries might not
be overrun by foreign products, and might attain a reasonable
command of our own home trade. They are, I feel sure, still
willing to co-operate in reaching that great end, in order that
our country may grow into a full-statured nation with diversified
industries and occupations which all nations must have, but
I do not know when or where it was agreed that this principle
should be carried farther. It has been left for this Government
to carry it farther. I do not know where it was agreed that
for the purpose of obtaining foreign markets duties should be
increased or even maintained. I do not deplore—on the contrary, I rejoice—that our manufacturers have gained an entry
into foreign markets. This is good in itself. It is something
devoutly to be wished, and in their success I rejoice. But, Sir,
it never was accepted by the people of this country that to
attain this end, very desirable as it is, the consumer should be
taxed. If we increase our tariff, doubtless command of foreign
markets will strengthen. That in itself would be desirable, but
the line has to be drawn somewhere. The Conservative party

traced the line, declaring that once a reasonable hold of the home market had been attained, then was the time for a stay and a diminution. It has remained for this Government to push the boundary far beyond, and they have not only given our manufacturers a grip on the home business but have practically given them a monopoly, and have taxed the consumer in order to push these products successfully into foreign lands.

A moment ago I referred to the effect on our revenue. To my mind this tariff is designed to benefit revenues of other countries rather than revenues of our own. As at present constituted, we have not so much a tariff for the revenue of Canada as a tariff for the revenue of Spain, a tariff for the revenue of Austria. In entering Austria, our manufacturers of binders and mowers are able to take in their stride a duty of some $33 on every binder, and yet they sell binders there at a profit. We have, Sir, a tariff for the revenue of Roumania, a tariff for the revenue of Russia, a tariff for the revenue of France, rather than a tariff for the revenue of Canada. I have before me a table which shows the duties these countries levy against our importation of binders and mowers. Notwithstanding those duties, our manufacturers, because of the protection afforded them here and the profits they are enabled to make by reason thereof, are strong enough to leap over tariff walls of foreign nations and to sell at a profit in the four quarters of the globe. Strong indeed must an industry have become within its own well-fortified home when it is able to launch out into far-distant fields, scale these tariff barriers and sell against the world.

There has been consolidated in my resolution a clause which declares that a reduction in these duties now is consistent with the true ends of a protective tariff. My remarks have been directed to support every term of the resolution, and none more firmly than that clause. From both sides of this House, though, I invite concurrence and help. And, Mr. Speaker, if the debate this afternoon has to be cut short under our rules, I invite the Government to give an opportunity, as they have power to do, for a further discussion and vote, at an early date in the session.

THE CASE OF R. C. MILLER

POWERS OF PARLIAMENT TO COMMIT TO JAIL

Early in 1912 *the Public Accounts Committee of the House of Commons was investigating certain payments appearing in the Auditor General's Report for the year ending March 31, 1911, as having been made by the Canadian Government to a certain Company headed by one, R. C. Miller. Others connected with the company had testified that its Board of Directors, by vote, placed in Mr. Miller's hands the sum of $41,026 to be used in procuring business. Because the business obtained was almost entirely Government business, Mr. Miller was summoned to give particulars as to those to whom he paid the money. He refused to appear. The Speaker, upon order of the House, issued his warrant, but was not able to locate Miller and serve him until the Session had prorogued.*

When the Committee on Public Accounts met again early in 1913, *Mr. Miller was a second time ordered to attend, was questioned and refused to answer. He was ordered to appear at the Bar of the House of Commons, and upon again insisting on his refusal, a Motion was made for his commitment to the common jail. This was finally passed and the offender was sent to Carleton County jail in Ottawa.*

The following speech was made on February 20, 1913 in course of a debate which ensued on the Motion; its importance is due entirely to the light it may throw on the question of Parliament's power to make effective inquisition into public accounts:

THERE CAN READILY BE SEEN in the more moderate tone of the hon. member for Carleton (Mr. Carvell) since eight o'clock, as compared with his much stronger language before adjournment,

18

a softening of his conviction that there is something which can reasonably be opposed in the resolution before the House. Before he had spoken, however, the hon. member for St. John (Mr. Pugsley) advanced and supported vigorously an argument which merits refutation. He took serious objection to the form of the question asked of the witness, Mr. Miller. He said there is incorporated in it a statement that Mr. Miller had testified before the Public Accounts Committee that he had paid $41,026 to secure some $117,000 worth of government business. This statement the hon. member claims is not correct, and, therefore, that the question is unfair and should not be answered. One would think that even if this contention be right the witness could quite easily deny the assertion himself and then proceed to make his reply.

There appears to be no dispute on the other side of the House that this money, whether spent or not, was paid to Mr. Miller by his company for the purpose of getting government business.

SOME HON. MEMBERS: No, no.

MR. CARVELL: Getting business generally, he said.

MR. MEIGHEN: The hon. member for Carleton, in the very first minute of his own speech, cited Mr. Miller as having sworn that the money had been voted him for the purpose of getting government business. I noted it in his remarks, and gave him credit for not wanting to quibble over the inconsequential fact that an utterly trifling amount of business had been secured elsewhere. Miller confirmed the evidence of Bain[1] that in all the years following receipt by him of this money, and up to Miller's severance from the company in June, 1911, total orders secured by the company, aside from those from the late Government, did not exceed $2,000, and that its orders from the late Government amounted to $117,000. Surely, therefore, it is doing no justice to the intelligence of hon. members to argue that the money was voted for any other purpose than to secure government business. This was what they were after; such was the evidence of Bain, and such was the evidence of Miller. I quote from the latter when I say that practically all business the

[1] A Director of Mr. Miller's company.

company had during his presidency, and subsequent to being voted the money, was government business. It was the one end to which they directed their efforts.

But the hon. member for St. John says: "Be it so, there is no evidence that Miller ever paid out the money." He says further that Harvey, Miller's counsel, came to the Bar of this House and asserted that there is embodied in the question put to the witness a false allegation, in that the question assumes a statement of Miller's that he paid the money somewhere. This, I presume, expresses fairly the position of the hon. member for St. John; if it fails, he is not so modest as to refrain from interrupting me.

MR. PUGSLEY: It is not exactly as my hon. friend puts it. The question makes an assertion to the witness that: "You swore that you paid the sum of $41,026 for the purpose of securing government business." My statement was that there is no evidence before the Public Accounts Committee which warrants that statement in the question.

MR. MEIGHEN: The hon. member stood in his place and said the allegation that Miller paid the money at all, or said he paid it, was false, and in this he was supported by the hon. member for Carleton.

MR. CARVELL: Will the hon. gentleman show me any part of the evidence in which Miller says he ever paid out a dollar of it?

MR. MEIGHEN: I will come to that too soon for the comfort of my hon. friend. The hon. member for St. John was, in his statement, corroborated by the hon. member for Carleton. No reasonable man can read the evidence before the Public Accounts Committee and come to any other conclusion than that the allegation of the money being paid is perfectly justified. In the first place, every question there was built upon an assumption that the money was paid, and, when Mr. Miller declined repeatedly to deny that it had been, common sense would certainly lead to a conclusion that it had been, and that such was the impression he desired to leave with the committee. Let me call attention to a question put by myself and answered by Mr. Miller. This is now a part of the House records; the whole evidence was laid on the table on Friday last and has been before hon. members for almost a week.

Q. Your travelling expenses and other expenses were paid besides that? A. Yes.

Q. And you gave vouchers for them? A. Yes.

Q. But for this money that you spent to get business you gave no vouchers? A. I initialled only in the cash book of the company.

From these statements, who could draw any other conclusion than that Mr. Miller intended the committee to believe that the money was disbursed as alleged in the question? Otherwise, what notations could he have made in the cash book? Also, Mr. Miller's counsel came before the Public Accounts Committee and distinctly repudiated any allegation that the money was not spent. Further, Mr. Miller came before the House of Commons today and repeated this repudiation, because he declared that he had been guilty of nothing criminal. If he had not spent the money, he would have appropriated to himself what was not his own. Besides, Miller said in his last remarks to the committee:

In connection with the litigation now on in Montreal, my reason—or rather an additional reason—for not giving the destination of that money is this:

He proceeded to give a reason why he would not give the destination. If the money had no destination, how could he have referred to it in such a manner?

The issue is in two parts: First, was the money voted Miller for securing business? Was that ever denied by him, or did he assume it was true? He assumed it was true, distinctly, and said so in his evidence on page 5. On this the hon. member for St. John touched, and went on to discuss whether or not there was evidence to support the allegation in the question that Mr. Miller had actually used the funds. I clearly understood the hon. member to deny that there was evidence of such use for any purpose and to rely on Harvey as his authority. Very certainly the hon. member for Carleton asserted definitely today that Miller had never sworn to having paid out to anyone the money voted him. I have taken the trouble to procure from Hansard a transcript of Harvey's statement this afternoon and shall read it just as it comes from the reporter:

MR. HARVEY: What Mr. Miller did state before the committee and what he stated in court was that during the four or five years that these transactions with the Diamond Light and Heating Company were going on he had paid the sum of $41,026 in connection with getting business for the company.

He had paid the money; so with what a thud does the contention of hon. members drop to the hard earth!—the contention that there is no evidence of the money having been paid for getting business from anyone.

This also answers the second phase, because it must be repeated—particularly in the hearing of the hon. member for St. John—that if Mr. Miller swore, as his counsel, Harvey, admits, that he paid the money for getting business, he must have paid it for getting government business, for that was all the business he got. The statement in the question was true. It was misleading in no way whatever.

There is another and important consideration. On the 17th of this month we passed a resolution that Mr. R. C. Miller be asked a specific question, namely, the one he has been asked today. Then was the time for his counsel or for any hon. member to object to the form of the query, if he had objection; and any hon. member who sat in his seat and voted for that resolution, as all did, is estopped by rules of law and of common sense from afterwards saying that he objects to the form. Hon. members then gave assent to it, both to its purpose and its form. Surely now, three days after, when the witness comes and refuses to give answer, is not the time to object to the form, even could valid objection be made. I submit that hon. gentlemen and Mr. Miller as well are too late, and moreover, that had they raised their objection in time, there is obviously nothing in it at all.

We are now called upon to discharge a serious duty in deciding whether we shall proceed further with this man, at the Bar of Parliament. What is Mr. Miller's record? A year ago he was summoned as a witness, after other members of his company had given testimony to the effect that some $41,026 had been paid to him for the purpose of securing government orders. The summons was served upon him. He refused to come. In his own words, he ignored the summons of our committee, and remained somewhere where process could not reach him. This was reported to Parliament. A warrant was issued, and during all the remaining time Parliament sat it was impossible for its officers to find Mr. Miller to serve him. Such was his conduct during our session of a year ago. The matter is now resumed; he is brought before the Public Accounts Committee; he declines to give evidence—evidence which that committee has a right to receive. I contend that the Public Accounts Committee is beyond all cavil and doubt entitled, and in the public interest is bound, to trace the destination of that $41,026 and that it is not enough to be told, in the bald language of Mr. Miller, that he did not pay a dollar to a member of Parliament, a senator, or an officer of either House. It would be possible for Miller to have paid that money in a thousand ways which would be a breach of privilege, which would be corrupt, and still leave his statement true, and it is further possible that cross-examination might establish that his evidence was not true.

I was astonished this evening to hear the hon. member for Carleton (Mr. Carvell) argue that it was the duty of this Parliament to discharge Miller from custody and await the result of litigation in Montreal. I was astonished beyond measure to hear it, and why? Because the hon. member, lawyer as he is, is the very gentleman who stood before the Public Accounts Committee and asserted that this litigation of Mr. Miller's had nothing to do with his obligation to answer questions. His statement is found on page 8 of the Committee's report. Mr. Carvell had argued at some length that Miller was bound to answer, quite irrespective of litigation. Then the report goes on:

MR. MEIGHEN: Your position is that the litigation in the courts of Montreal does not affect us, but the whole province of this committee is to inquire whether or not public servants get money.

MR. CARVELL: Public servants or public men, or whether there has been anything wrong in connection with obtaining this business.

MR. MEIGHEN: Regardless of litigation.

MR. CARVELL: That is the ground.

And this is the hon. gentleman who tonight stands in this

Parliament and asks that the request of Mr. Harvey be granted, and who calls upon the Prime Minister to discharge the prisoner at the Bar, to let him go and to await the event some time in an indefinite future when he gets through with his litigation in Montreal. It was argued before the Public Accounts Committee this session and again tonight by the hon. member that all we are concerned with is to ascertain whether or not senators or members of Parliament or servants of either Chamber were corrupt. But a year ago, when the matter was first under investigation, the hon. member for Carleton was the very gentleman who asserted that a general inquiry—not a restricted, a general inquiry—into the destination of this money was a function of the Public Accounts Committee. I shall quote what he said. It is found on page 38 of the evidence in the report for 30th March, 1912:

> We have not any objection whatever to getting all the evidence you can bring, or all the witnesses you can bring, who know about the paying of this money.

It could not have been proclaimed in clearer or stronger language than this used by the hon. member for Carleton, a year ago, that our committee had undoubtedly power to inquire broadly into the distination of this money.

MR. CARVELL: Was there any evidence at that time of any litigation pending?

MR. MEIGHEN: The hon. member for Carleton is himself authority for the statement that any litigation does not affect the matter. So we come to this point, with no shadow of doubt that the Public Accounts Committee has not only a right, but has a duty cast upon it, to find where this money went.

There is something I almost forgot: The hon. member for St. John, ex-attorney-general of New Brunswick says: I object to this question, I object to forcing the witness, Miller, to answer, because it is a leading question. And he referred in terms of scorn—

MR. PUGSLEY: I said a leading one and a false one.

MR. MEIGHEN: There are many members of this House who are practitioners at the Bar. I do not address myself to them; they would consider the point too ridiculous for discussion. I address myself to the laymen of this House; and, indeed, who of them does not know why a leading question is objectionable? There is a rule against leading questions put by a lawyer to his own witness, and the ground of objection is that it suggests to the witness an answer; it makes an answer easy for the witness, and leads him to understand what counsel wants him to say. Is that an objection to this question? We have had the spectacle of an ex-attorney-general of New Brunswick, a distinguished lawyer, without a doubt, standing in this Parliament and asking us to exonerate a recalcitrant witness because, forsooth, the question is too easy for him and the answer too plainly suggested.

MR. PUGSLEY: I rise to a point of order.

SOME HON. MEMBERS: Order, sit down.

MR. PUGSLEY: I rise to correct my hon. friend. I did not say that the question was objectionable simply because it was leading. I said it was objectionable because it was leading, and also because it contained a statement purporting to be a statement of fact, which was false.

MR. MEIGHEN: That is exactly what I stated the hon. gentleman said. I have dealt with both his contentions; first, with his argument that the question was improper in its statement of fact, and next, with his complaint that it was leading. What measure of success I have had will be left to the House to judge.

It is affirmed in rather hesitating language, but none the less affirmed by hon. members opposite, that we have no power to act as we are now asked to act by this motion; that we have no power to commit this man to the common jail of the county of Carleton. It is quite true that in the history of Canada since Confederation there has not been a precedent for committal to jail. Not since 1867 has there been a case of committal, for the simple and obvious reason that there has been no instance of a witness defying this House. But Parliaments of the provinces of Canada before Confederation without question had power to commit to jail witnesses who refused to answer questions. After being given every opportunity, they were, I say, repeatedly committed to jail by Parliaments which preceded the present House of Commons. Further, in the Imperial House, from earliest days to the present, each time a case such as this has arisen the witness has been first of all committed to custody and afterwards committed to jail. In some cases he has been sent to the tower, in other cases to His Majesty's jail at Newgate or to some other public prison. Authorities definitely prove that the Imperial Parliament has always had power to commit a prisoner such as this to any common, or as it is usually expressed, to any public jail. I quote first an author most frequently referred to in Canada, Bourinot. At page 158 he says:

> It is clearly established that the power of commitment for contempt is incident to every court of justice, and more especially belongs to the Houses of Parliament as essential to the maintenance of their undoubted rights and privileges;— that it is incompetent for other courts to question the exercise of the privileges of the Houses of Parliament in a commitment for an offence which they have adjudged to be a contempt of those privileges.

If we have power to commit, we necessarily have power to commit to a place. The question is—what place? In the Criminal Code, a statute of this Parliament, we have throughout our history directed Courts to commit persons convicted of offences to the Common Jail of the District where the Court is held. We, therefore, must have power to send this convicted man to the Common Jail of this District, and that is what is being done under the Motion we are discussing.

Even more specifically I refer to another authority on parliamentary powers and procedure, *The Law and Practice of Legislative Assemblies* by L. S. Cushing, at page 401:

> When a witness refuses to answer the questions which he is directed to answer, or to produce a paper or other document, the proceeding against him is intended not only as a punishment for his contempt, but also to compel him to obey the order. For these purposes a contumacious witness is usually committed, in the first instance, to the custody of the Sergeant-at-Arms.

That is the course we are taking.

> If this fails to induce him to submit himself to the order, he may then be committed to Newgate, or some other public prison.

Could words be more clear and unequivocal? This proceeding, then, is undoubtedly in the power of and is the usage of Britain's Parliament. Next, has this Commons of Canada jurisdiction commensurate with that exercised by the Commons of Britain? It has. By section 18 of the British North America Act, this House is authorized to establish by Statute its immunities and privileges on any standard it chooses, provided that it cannot establish them higher than those enjoyed by the Imperial House. And by section 4 of our Parliament Act, it has been enacted that the House of Commons of Canada shall thereafter enjoy all immunities and privileges possessed by the Imperial House. Our Parliament is, therefore, clothed with every privilege vested in the Imperial Parliament. I accordingly ask this House to come to the conclusion that it is the undoubted right of Parliament to commit this man and to commit him to the common jail.

To do so is not only within our competence but it is our duty. Surely we must have regard for the stature of Parliament and the respect it must command in the minds of Canadian citizens. Here a witness stands defying this House, saying that we can order what we like and he is not bound to submit, and his counsel comes and asks that, after such conduct, he be discharged from custody and this high Tribunal surrender to the pert dictum of its own prisoner.

Mr. Miller made a plea for deferring his case. Did he give sufficient reason to warrant us in adjourning this matter? What was his argument? When we strip his statement of its verbiage, when we strip it of its self-adulation, when we get down to the bare residue, what is it? Because, he says, I have litigation pending in Montreal where civil rights are in dispute, I ask this House, the highest court in Canada in respect of its own procedure and prerogatives, to wait until I have disposed of these actions. If such is to become, by precedent, a rule of Parliament, then all a witness would have to do at any time when he is summoned would be to start suit against somebody in relation to the matter in question and forthwith he would be sheltered and removed from any obligation here. A more absurd proposition could scarcely be imagined. To cite authority again, I refer to Cushing, page 397:

> A witness before either House of Parliament cannot excuse himself from answering any question that may be put to him on the ground that the answer would subject him to an action; or expose him to a criminal proceeding; or be the means of divulging the secrets of his client; or etc., etc. . . . some of which would be sufficient grounds of excuse in a court of justice. This difference, between proceedings in Parliament, and in the ordinary courts, has been established upon grounds of public policy, and is considered to be fundamentally essential to the efficiency of a parliamentary inquiry.

In other words, even what would be an excuse in a court of justice is no excuse before this House. Would the reason advanced by Mr. Miller be taken cognizance of even in a court of justice? Why, in any court it would be looked upon as ridiculous to say that because a witness has a civil suit pending somewhere, he should be excused from giving evidence elsewhere. Such a plea would not be heard even in a court of justice, but what I have just read is authority for the conclusion that even if such a plea could be considered there, it cannot be presented before Parliament, the grand inquest of our Nation.

The hon. member for Carleton, having exhausted what he could say on points already reviewed, comes to his final phase with an assertion that, though we may have this power, it is an antiquated one, a relic of the barbarism of a century ago. He calls upon us to rise in our dignity and absolve ourselves from its shame. A century ago, he says, is the last time this thing was done. I affirm that it has been done repeatedly, done in the lifetime of the hon. member for Carleton himself. Commitment to jail has been executed on a number of occasions by the Commons of Great Britain. The last case was in 1879, when one, Grissell, was committed for contempt and was subjected to imprisonment in Newgate. That is not so very long ago. More important, though: there never was a shrinking from duty when need arose. I stand here and challenge contradiction when I say that there has been no case at any time when a man appeared and refused to answer, and after having been directed to answer still refused, who was not committed. What will be the consequence, where are we headed for, if by our pending vote we announce that a man can bid defiance to this House, can commit the plainest possible breach of privilege, can be guilty of the most open and flagrant contempt and still be absolved from punishment? The meanest court in this country—if it can be said that any court is mean—the court in this country of smallest jurisdiction has power to commit to prison for contempt. We have vested our county courts, even our police courts, just as we have vested our higher courts, with full authority to commit for contempt of the privileges and dignities of those courts. All this is right and necessary and has been done in every country. Is the Parliament of Canada to take the position that this power is an indispensable prerogative of every tribunal of its own creation but is not possessed by Parliament itself? If there is any way in which this House could more clearly abdicate functions which constitute the first reason of its being, any way that we could more shamefully abandon a duty we owe the people, any way more flagrant and more disastrous than would be a yielding to Mr. Miller tonight, then I would like to have it suggested. It would mean the dissolution of our powers of inquest altogether.

We have no recourse left but imprisonment. We must either imprison this man or say to him: "Go your way in victory and in peace. Our resources are exhausted. We thought we were the High Court of Parliament, but it was all a delusion. We find we cannot even compel a witness to testify. With our hands above our heads we confess your supremacy. You are above Parliament itself."

Mr. Speaker, this is the pass into which hon. gentlemen opposite would lead us. The course they urge upon us would only exhibit to the world the helplessness of this House. We would simply be exposing ourselves as swirling around here in aimless impotence instead of conducting manfully our peculiar and proper tasks, preserving our privileges and thus vindicating the sacred rights of those whom we are sworn to serve.

Lastly, there has been an appeal for delay. It has been argued

that notice has not been given of this motion, and that hon. gentlemen would like time to think out what more can be done on the prisoner's behalf. Very plainly no notice could be given until Mr. Miller would make his decision for a second and last time as to whether he would obey our order. This afternoon he said, "No." Not a rule has been cited calling for notice in a matter of privilege, which this is. No such rule can be cited. If two days' notice were required of a motion to commit where the witness has defied, then also two days' notice would be necessary of a motion to discharge where the witness has complied. How absurd that would be! We must remember as well that in either case, while notice is running, the witness is still a prisoner. Delay where there is definite guilt, continuous unrepentant guilt, is futile and unworthy. The Manxe incident in England referred to by the hon. member for St. John is as yet unreported but we do know it was very different from this. Manxe had without warrant lampooned a Minister. There was no refusal to submit to the judgment of a committee or of the House itself. The offence was completed and done with and it may well have been considered a case for compassion. This man, Miller, on the contrary, has been in defiance for a long period of time: he is in defiance at this very moment, his offence continues until he chooses to obey or purges his guilt by punishment.

It may be worth while, before closing, to summarize categorically what has been established, definitely established, and how. First, $41,026 was voted to Miller by his company to be used in getting business. This is latent in every phase of the evidence and was specifically declared to be a fact this very day by the hon. member for Carleton himself. Second, the money was paid out—and necessarily must have been paid out in getting business. This is proved by Mr. Miller who swore that he initialled such payments in the company's cash book. It is also frankly asserted to be a fact by his own lawyer, Harvey, in a quotation I read to the House. Third, the $41,026 was paid Miller to get Government business. It must have been, because that is all the business his company got—all but $2,000 out of $119,000. The query put to our witness on the floor this afternoon embodies as a basis that final conclusion and nothing else.

From that final conclusion, as I have shown step by step, there is no possibility of escape. The long, laboured argument about the question containing a misstatement of fact just crashes to the ground.

Around and about these findings of fact, and sustaining the House in acting on them, there has been adduced abundant precedent and authority that we have ample power to give effect to every line and word of the resolution under debate. When the time comes to vote, it is impossible to think that hon. members can mistake their duty.

CLOSURE

In the House of Commons' Session of 1913, the Government of Sir Robert Borden submitted to Parliament a Bill providing for certain naval construction designed to strengthen the Royal Navy against what then appeared to be a possible war with Germany.

Up to this time the Code of Rules of the Canadian House had contained no provision enabling a majority to put an end to debate. The Naval Bill, as it was called, was resisted with great energy and tenacity by the Opposition of that day, headed by Sir Wilfrid Laurier. What had been generally known as a blockade was set up. For many weeks no progress whatever could be made. The House over long periods sat night and day in Committee of the Whole.

If this blockade was to be broken, new and carefully thought-out amendments to the Rules had first to be devised, submitted to Parliament and enacted. Further, a method of introducing these amendments on the floor had to be found, such as would prevent an interminable blockade being set up against them just in the same manner as it had been set up against the Naval Bill. To effect this necessary purpose any motion for the adoption of new rules had to be made free itself from all possibility of amendment.

Such a plan having been worked out, Sir Robert Borden, on April 10, 1913, introduced three amendments to the House of Commons' Rules and moved their adoption. In the speech re-printed here will be found an account and a defence of the method used, and, as well, a general justification of the principle of Closure.

The plan proved successful. All three amendments were passed: they were employed first to terminate the original Naval Bill blockade, and anything in the nature of permanent obstruction, forcing dissolution, has ever since been impossible in Canada.

I DO NOT REMEMBER having ever risen in this House with greater satisfaction that I do tonight; not that I feel in any degree more

32

competent than other members to discuss this issue, but because
we are now actually at grips with a reform which has been much,
and with increasing insistence, on my mind since first entering
Parliament. The necessity for it has been borne in upon me,
not only while my seat has been with the Government party,
but earlier while with the Opposition. And, Sir, if anything I
can say may contribute in the least measure towards realization
of a reform in our procedure, I shall be well employed. Legislation which flows from Parliament must, not only in its extent,
but far more importantly in its quality, have a direct relation to
the competence of the mechanism by which that legislation is
produced, and, therefore, when we engage in improving the
efficiency of that mechanism, we are performing an essential
duty.

Very considerable complaint has been heard from across the
floor with respect to certain proceedings which immediately followed the Prime Minister's speech of yesterday, introducing and
moving these amendments to our Rules. Be this said, though,
for all hon. gentlemen opposite who have spoken, that however
they have stated or mis-stated their case, none descended so far
and degraded so lamentably the whole plane of discussion as has
a prominent newspaper in its issue today. The complaint is that
the right hon. leader of the Opposition was not permitted
immediately to follow the Prime Minister. He was not permitted immediately to follow, and for a very sufficient reason.
He was not howled down by this side of the House, and there is
no hon. gentleman opposite so lost to a sense of truth as to say
that he was, or even that anyone on this side was discourteous.
The right hon. gentleman was delayed for a minute and a half,
and no longer, in order that under Rule 17 the Minister of
Marine and Fisheries (Mr. J. D. Hazen) might be given the
floor for the single purpose of moving the previous question and
directly taking his seat. Then it was within the power of the
Opposition leader to rise at once and discuss as freely and as long
as he desired every issue that is before this House. He did not do
so; he was refused permission to rise at once, and by whom? By
that master of many wiles, the hon. member for the city of St.
John (Mr. Pugsley) who conceived that our business would not

be properly conducted unless he appeared on the scene to move an adjournment and make a speech thereon.

Why was the previous question moved? As every member knows, the purpose of the previous question is to prevent amendments to the main motion.

Mr. Devlin: That was not done in the British House.

Mr. Meighen: That is the only purpose of the previous question. The hon. member for Wright (Mr. Devlin) states it was not done in the British House. No, and for the very reason that conditions which made it imperative here, if we were to have any chance of ever getting the debate on the Prime Minister's motion over and thereafter proceeding to a vote, did not exist in the British House. Unless the previous question is moved, the main motion is subject to amendment after amendment so long as an Opposition wishes to move one. When the avowed policy of an Opposition is obstruction, who can imagine a Government so foolish as to throw its proposed amendments to the Rules into the camp of the enemy to be mauled forevermore. I am told—perhaps not correctly as to number—that Opposition members, in pursuance of their well-defined blocking policy so manfully avowed yesterday by their right hon. leader, had framed and ready to present all in due time, extending over days and nights *ad infinitum,* not less than ninety-six amendments. If the previous question had not been moved, no one could truthfully say that within the circumference of our present Code and in the face of an Opposition admittedly bent on obstruction, there would be any possibility of reaching a vote on these amendments. This means that after having proposed a plan of closure we would have found ourselves stifled and frustrated just as we had been for many months before. We would indeed only have fed the flames of obstruction.

The previous question is within our Code as now devised. It has been for many years one of the Rules of this House and of the British House. It has been exercised times without number in Britain. Our Canadian Rules, including No. 17, are those which have just been proclaimed by the Opposition leader as the very consummation of justice, as reason reduced to writing. You, Mr. Speaker, when the Minister of Marine and Fisheries

(Mr. Hazen) rose at the same time as the leader of the Opposition, saw the right hon. gentleman oppostie. It is and has been a custom in this House that the Opposition leader follows the leader of the Government; and as a consequence, you, Sir, were amply justified in seeing him first; but the Government, in a manly way, assuming full responsibility, took the only step available to it and had a motion made under Rule 17 that the Minister of Marine and Fisheries be heard, only for the purpose of moving the previous question. Unless that step had been taken when it was taken, the previous question could not have been moved at any time and this whole plan of closure would have been thrown into the maelstrom of indefinite and irremovable obstruction. Oh, this was a vicious thing; this was the very guillotine itself, say hon. gentlemen opposite, to dare to rise under Rule 17 and move that anybody be heard in place of the leader of the Opposition. Let me say with all emphasis that this was not done in order that anybody might be heard instead of him. He had a perfect right to rise two minutes after and reply fully to the Government leader. There was no intention, either manifest or concealed, to limit in any degree the liberty of speech of the right hon. the leader of the Opposition, much less to do him a discourtesy.

What is the history of this Rule 17? It is one of a Code of Rules of this House of Commons because it was placed there by the right hon. the leader of the Opposition himself on July 9, 1906, when Sir Wilfrid Laurier was Prime Minister of this country. He, in pursuance of a long evolution leading to that perfection which he now says our Code of Rules enjoys, placed No. 17 there on his own motion, just in the form in which it is today. Did he place it there in the thought that if ever it was acted upon for a perfectly legitimate and necessary purpose, as it was yesterday, hon. members opposite should howl themselves hoarse shouting Shame?

Mr. Lemieux: Does my hon. friend mean to say that the inventor of the previous question was the right hon. the leader of the Opposition?

Mr. Meighen: I say that Rule 17, which this Government availed itself of in order to permit the previous question to be moved was made a law of Parliament on motion of the right hon. the leader of the Opposition. The previous question is as old as I am. It was the use of Rule 17 which raised pandemonium yesterday. I ask the hon. member for Rouville (Mr. Lemieux) if it is a shame and a disgrace to this House to act within the authority of Rule 17. . . .

MR. LEMIEUX: It is half a century old.

MR. MEIGHEN: No, six years—If it is a shame and a disgrace to act within the authority of Rule 17, was it not also a shame and a disgrace to move its adoption? Will not the hon. member admit that both steps were honourable and right? The only purpose, and it was a necessary purpose, if we are not to remain bound hand and foot as a Parliament, was to see to it that this discussion got before the House in a form in which there would be some certainty of its termination.

We come now to a close examination of these proposed amendments. There are three in all. The first commences by reciting classes of motions which shall hereafter be open for debate just as they have been in the past. These classes are intended, and carefully drafted, to embrace all that can by any possibility be called substantial. They include all those which a member on either side could heretofore place upon the Order Paper, and as well they include any motion which, though one of substance, does not ordinarily appear upon the Order Paper. It goes without saying that when a motion, or resolution, remains debatable, any and all amendments thereto also remain debatable. This first clause thereafter goes on to forbid discussion and to require immediate vote on purely formal motions, that is, motions upon which discussion is wholly unnecessary and can be indulged in only for purposes of delay. Surely there is nothing unfair or impracticable in such a provision.

Now, we are told by the hon. member for Carleton: Why, you shut off debate on adjournment, and in that way you clip the wings of discussion, you gag the Opposition, you paralyze them more than the Opposition are paralyzed in the British House. He says it has been a practice in this House for years to move an adjournment when we like, and on that motion to discuss all manner of subjects. We know it has been. We know

also, though, that under Rule 39, when an hon. member wants
to move adjournment for the purpose of discussing a matter of
public importance, he may do so. And he is still able to do this
under the first clause of these amendments. The hon. gentleman
says, however, that, after these amendments pass, a member cannot discuss anything he wishes on an ordinary adjournment
motion. True, he cannot. But would we have closure at all if he
could? The hon. gentleman says such a thing can be done in
England. I could not believe my ears when he told us that in
England a member may move the simple adjournment and discuss thereon any subject he chooses. He proceeded to read the
British Rules. But did you notice where he stopped? Did you see
the stone wall he ran up against and from which he bounded
back? Here is the English Rule; it is Standing Order number 22:

> When a motion is made for the adjournment of a debate, or
> of the House during any debate, or that the chairman of a
> committee do report progress, or do leave the Chair, the
> debate thereupon shall be confined to the matter of such
> motion; and no member, having moved or seconded any such
> motion, shall be entitled to move, or second, any similar
> motion during the same debate.

That is to say, in England, any speaker moving the adjournment must confine his remarks to reasons why adjournment
should be taken. Why does the hon. member for Carleton, as a
responsible member of this House, get up with the Rule-book in
his hand and tell hon. members that in England they can do still
what we have been doing up to now—move the adjournment and
discuss anything and everything? In England a member cannot
talk at all for one minute unless the majority permit, for no
sooner is adjournment moved in that Parliament, either adjournment of the debate or adjournment of the House, than any one,
whether in Opposition or on the Government side may rise and
call upon the House to apply closure by immediate vote. Even
before there has been a word spoken, a majority can thus compel
the stoppage of debate.

Mr. Marcil: Will the hon. gentleman, before he leaves that
point, tell us why the discretion was not left with the Speaker of
the House?

MR. MEIGHEN: I was intending to come to that later, but out of courtesy to the hon. member (Mr. Marcil) who himself for many years occupied with distinction your place, Mr. Speaker, I will make answer now. Following the great legislative bodies of the world, we must place responsibility for choosing the time when closure shall be applied either on the Speaker or on the Government; under any rational conception of constitutional procedure it cannot be placed elsewhere. In England, for several years, responsibility for application of closure was placed on the Speaker. The result was that between 1882 and 1887 closure was very seldom acted upon, because the Speaker was diffident about taking the initiative himself. Their new Rules were, in effect, a failure. The hon. member for Richmond said that they abandoned them altogether—that they ran away from closure. But such is not the case. The remarks of the hon. member for Carleton on this point had very considerable truth—if we except three or four sentences which were quite uncalled for. He explained that, by reason of the method of electing a Speaker in the British House, the office has a somewhat different and more permanent status in that House than it has in this. As a consequence, if responsibility for bringing closure into effect had been placed upon the Speaker, it would have been open to hon. gentlemen opposite to complain. They would have cried: "Our Speaker is elected by the majority, he is a creature of the majority, and consequently he is prone to follow the will of the majority." Therefore, instead, under this amendment, the Government takes the manly position of accepting responsibility and abiding by it. But the conditions attached are such that reasonable notice in all cases must be given; and as a result we put it out of the power of Government to do what is, and has been for many years, in the power of the British House—to apply closure suddenly at any time. In England, as I have said, it was found impracticable to have closure; the measure was proved abortive so long as initiative was left to the Speaker. Consequently about 1888 their Rules were changed so that responsibility was lifted from the Speaker and placed upon a member of the House, which, of course, in its working out, means the majority. While responsibility for moving closure was extended to any member, the Speaker was left a discretion to say whether and when it should be exercised. If we were to take that course, we would be open to the same objection as has been brought to our attention by the hon. member for Carleton. The Government, therefore, takes responsibility itself, but under conditions that they must give at least twenty-four hours' notice. After discussion has proceeded for such length of time as in the judgment of the Government is sufficient, then if obstruction develops all it can do is to move adjournment of the debate, give notice of closure, and after that is done, the Opposition have the following day and until two o'clock the next morning to organize their attack and discuss the matter to their hearts' content.

MR. DEVLIN: I would like to ask a question before the hon. gentleman leaves that point. Does he maintain that the Opposition may expect that a minister of the Crown will be more impartial than the Speaker of the House in exercising closure?

MR. MEIGHEN: I do not think the hon. gentleman seriously thought that I was so maintaining. I have never challenged the impartiality of a Speaker.

MR. DEVLIN: I am not asking merely to interrupt, I am asking for information.

MR. MEIGHEN: I was saying that under these proposed rules, the responsibility is on the Government who are answerable to the people, and not on the Speaker, who, as such, is not answerable to the people.

MR. DEVLIN: Why did not the English Government of the day, Mr. Gladstone at its head, place upon a minister of the Crown or the Government of the day the duty of imposing closure, rather than leaving it to an individual member of the House?

MR. MEIGHEN: The hon. gentleman does not seem to appreciate the English Rules. The duty of imposing closure over there is on the majority of members in the House of Commons, always.

MR. DEVLIN: Exactly; that is what we want here.

MR. MEIGHEN: And exactly what you are getting. But in Britain, any member of the House, however humble he may be, can at any time, on his own responsibility, demand that closure be applied immediately (unless the Speaker forbids) and put it to a vote; not even the Government can do so in this House under these amendments.

Some time ago I intimated that this first amendment was objected to on the ground that it did not provide the cherished liberty of debating, without limit, a motion to adjourn. There was, though, another objection, raised by the hon. member for St. John (Mr. Pugsley), seconded with very great eloquence by the right hon. leader of the Opposition, affirmed by the hon. member for Richmond (Mr. Kyte) and reaffirmed, but in faltering tones, by the hon. member for Carleton (Mr. Carvell) who has looked into the subject; namely, that, if we pass these Rules in their present form, it will be impossible for any hon. member, as a matter of privilege, to make a charge against an hon. member of this House, move for its reference to a committee and have his motion debated. The hon. member for Richmond, in answer to a question of mine, stated that if these Rules had been in force the hon. member for St. Hyacinthe (Mr. Gauthier) would not have been able to prefer his recent charge against, and make his motion in respect of, the Secretary of State. That is what the hon. member said, is it not?

Mr. Kyte: What I had intended to say was that it could not be discussed. A motion is of no consequence if we are not permitted to discuss it.

Mr. Meighen: The hon. member has a very frail ability to say what he intends to say, if such is the case. What he said—and it will appear in Hansard tomorrow—was that the motion of the hon. member for St. Hyacinthe, levelling a charge against the Secretary of State, could not have been made if these rules had been in force at the time. The same thing was said earlier by the hon. member for the city of St. John. There might possibly have been some excuse for him; he had only two days to study the subject, but the hon. member for Richmond had three. The hon. member for Carleton this afternoon—I watched him carefully—in order to establish unwavering loyalty to his leader made a like declaration. I affirm, Mr. Speaker, that this question is away beyond the pale of being even a subject for debate. I stand here to prove by the records of every charge made in this

House for twenty years gone by, that the hon. member for St. Hyacinthe will have just the same liberty to make such a motion after these rules go through as he had before, and further, the motion will be open to discussion in the same way; all discussion, of course, being subject to a general rule that there will be power to terminate it—it cannot be endless. What will such a motion come under? It will come, as it has always come, under "routine proceedings." The first clause of these amendments says that every motion heretofore debatable made upon routine proceedings—except adjournment motions—shall be debatable; so that, providing the hon. member for St. Hyacinthe could heretofore make his charge and motion under routine proceedings it can be made and will be debatable in the future just as it has been in the past. The question is, can he or can he not make it now under that heading? The right hon. leader of the Opposition said, "No." "It is true," he said, "we have the privilege of making motions under routine proceedings, but such privilege does not mean motions of this kind—it means only such as appertain to procedure; it does not comprise such motions as that made by the hon. member for St. Hyacinthe." That is actually what the right hon. leader of the Opposition, once Prime Minister of this country, said, and that is what was first adduced by the ingenious and fertile brain of the hon. member for St. John. What are the facts? Back in 1890, Sir Richard Cartwright, who was for many years a colleague of the right hon. the leader of the Opposition, and who now, unfortunately for the happiness of some hon. members, is in some sense his biographer—Sir Richard Cartwright in March 1890, made a charge against, and a motion in respect of, the hon. member for Lincoln, Mr. Rykert. When did Sir Richard Cartwright make his motion? He made it under routine proceedings, right under the eye of his leader. At what stage did he make it? He made it immediately after prayers—the first item in routine proceedings. The records of Hansard and our Votes and Proceedings show that, after he made it, Senate Bills were reported, and Senate Bills are always reported under routine proceedings, so that there is no possible way of arguing that the Cartwright motion was not made under that heading.

We come next to a motion made by Mr. M. C. Cameron on August 20, 1891, levelling a charge against a Mr. Cochrane, then a member of this House. This was also made under routine proceedings and was made by a follower of the right hon. leader of the Opposition, under his very eye. Passing to the 23rd day of September, 1891, for these motions were very frequent about that time, under the same leadership, Mr. Lister made a charge against the late lamented Hon. John Haggart. He also laid his charge under routine proceedings just half a page after prayers and before several reports of committees were adopted, reports which are always dealt with under the same heading. Passing on to a later date in 1899 the present leader of the Government rose as a matter of privilege and moved a reference to the Committee on Privileges and Elections of certain charges against officers of this House operating in the constituencies of Huron and Brockville. Only two years ago, the present Deputy Speaker, Mr. Blondin, in exactly the form used by the hon. member for St. Hyacinthe, stated that upon his responsibility as a member he was prepared to make and prove certain charges against another member and moved that those charges be referred to the Committee on Privileges and Elections. These things took place under the Premiership of the Right Hon. Sir Wilfrid Laurier and were recorded in routine proceedings, immediately after prayers. Yet, so destitute are the Opposition of grounds for their attack upon these amendments that they have had the hardihood to declare to this House that under them a charge against, say, the Minister of Public Works could not be levelled and discussed.

MR. NESBITT: Were not all the quotations made questions of privilege?

MR. MEIGHEN: Certainly they were. Any man at any time can rise to a question of privilege and consequently he can rise under routine proceedings.

MR. NESBITT: At any time if he is allowed by the House.

MR. MEIGHEN: No, a man has a right to rise to a question of privilege and if these amendments go through he will still have that right. But if he wants his question debated, he makes a motion. His motion appears next day on the Order Paper and there is nothing in this amendment to change that. No man has a right to say to an hon. member that if he gives notice he cannot make a motion and it is the same with motions which affect the privileges of a member of Parliament.

We come now to amendment No. 2. Without No. 2 the whole machinery of progress would be in no wise improved. We can pass 1 and 3 but if we do not put in amendment 2 there is no machinery at all for stopping discussion. It is No. 2 which provides the method, upon reasonable notice, of doing so. Amendments 1 and 3 are for the purpose of putting it out of the power of purely loquacious and obstructionist members to defeat the purpose of amendment 2. What is No. 2? It provides that whether in committee or in the House, any subject that is before Parliament may be discussed as it has always been, but when it has been discussed for such length of time as the Government take the responsibility for saying is sufficient, a minister of the Crown may, after moving postponement of the debate, give notice that on some day following he will move that the debate be not further adjourned. If the House is in committee he must add that it be hereafter the first business of committee. Hon. gentlemen should note that even the Government is not empowered by this amendment to put a stop to discussion the way it can be done in England. A majority in this House can not sharply and without notice say that the guillotine falls. No, there is power only to say this: We bind ourselves to submit this matter to you again on some future day; you shall have that day for a continuation of this discussion up to two o'clock of the following morning, when it must cease. Surely that is fair.

There is still another objection dwelt upon, particularly by the hon. member for Carleton. Why, he says, this is worse than the British closure; this is something shocking! I am against closure of every kind, closure is Russianizing our country; nobody up to three years ago ever thought of this monstrous thing; and he adds: If we are going to pass these amendments, then discussion in Committee of Supply will be smothered. I tell him first that in committee of the British House, just the same as in the House proper, closure may be applied at any time under their Rule 133. They can close a debate in a minute there; they can close it even before it starts. Oh! says the member for Carleton: even though they can do that they have twenty days for Supply; you cannot shut them out of twenty days because their Rule forbids. In the first place, it is utterly inconceivable that in twenty days we could get through Supply in this House of Commons even under these Rules. But I answer the hon. member: in the British Commons there is no rule whatever which says there must be twenty days for Committee of Supply. What their Rule says—and I asked the hon. gentleman to read it when he was on his feet but he did not—what their Rule says is there shall not be more than twenty days for Supply. The maximum is fixed, the minimum is not.

Mr. German: As this resolution is not going into committee, some latitude might be allowed in asking questions, and I wish to put another question to the hon. member.

Mr. Speaker: It is quite in order for any hon. member to ask a question, so long as the hon. member who has the floor is willing to be interrupted.

Mr. Meighen: I will be glad to hear the hon. gentleman's question.

Mr. German: The resolution says:

> Any minister of the Crown who, standing in his place, shall have given notice at a previous sitting of his intention so to do, may move that the debate shall not be further adjourned, or that the further consideration of any resolution, or resolutions, clause or clauses, section or sections, preamble or preambles, title or titles, shall be the first business of the committee, and shall not further be postponed.

Now, the second clause of the Naval Aid Act is under discussion. If a motion is made that the debate be not further continued, does the hon. gentleman understand that that simply adjourns the debate on that clause, or does he think that it terminates the debate on the whole Bill?

Mr. Meighen: No, just on that clause—

Mr. German: That is what I understand.

Mr. Marcil: But it says: clause or clauses.

Mr. German: Could they not give notice as to the whole Bill and stop the discussion on every clause?

Mr. Meighen: This is what can be done: clause 2 is under discussion, say for two weeks or three weeks or five weeks, as would better suit hon. gentlemen opposite, and a motion to postpone its consideration is made and carried. Then it would be in order for the committee to pass on to clause 3; clause 3 would be discussed and a separate postponement motion would have to be made as to clause 3.

Mr. German: In the same way on the twenty-four hours' notice?

Mr. Meighen: Yes.

Mr. German: As to each clause.

Mr. Meighen: Exactly. After all, or a substantial group, have been so dealt with, notice is given that the clauses so postponed be on a certain day considered and not further postponed. At two o'clock on the following morning the debate on these clauses must be concluded and a vote taken.

Mr. German: It is worse than I thought it was.

Mr. Henderson: You mean it is better than you thought it was.

Mr. Meighen: I have been describing what would be within the power of a Government. Even that, the extreme exercise of its power, would be to give a day's discussion beyond what is permitted under the British Rules. Within that day, the Opposition have opportunity to organize their forces and to debate the subject within that time to the best possible advantage.

There is another safeguard inserted in this second amendment, because, presumably, it was anticipated that hon. gentlemen opposite would say: "Why, on the last day you have us right in your grip; you can put up some Government supporter and he can hold the floor until two o'clock." It is on that account provided that no hon. member shall speak during this period longer than twenty minutes, or more than once; so that there can be no possibility of either side monopolizing the time.

Mr. Marcil: Does the same rule apply to a discussion of the estimates? As the rule now stands, the estimates are taken up one after the other. Would it be possible for a minister of the

Crown to give notice that on a certain day the whole estimates of one department or of all departments might be called automatically or put to the House?

MR. MEIGHEN: When estimates are before committee, a resolution on each item is moved or understood to be moved. Consequently the procedure set out in amendment 2 applies to estimates in the same way as to clauses of a Bill.

MR. MARCIL: What about the resolutions that have not been discussed?

MR. MEIGHEN: They must all be discussed and the discussion on each postponed before they can be brought up on this last day. I am sure that the hon. member for Bonaventure will acknowledge that, consistently with making rules which cannot be circumvented, the Government has done everything in its power to be generous to an Opposition.

Clause No. 3 of these amendments provides that on Thursdays and Fridays when the Order of the Day for the House to go into Committee of Supply or Ways and Means is called, you, Mr. Speaker, shall leave the Chair without putting any question. If no question is put, there can be no amendment and therefore no discussion. The House, on Thursdays and Fridays, if the relevant Order of the Day is reached, will go at once into Committee. Hon. gentlemen opposite are almost pale with terror at the effect of clause 3. "Oh!" they say, "it is a time-honoured privilege of the people's representatives, before they vote a dollar of Supply to the Crown, to insist that all public grievances be redressed." Yes! It has also been for many years, not a time-honoured, but an ill-starred privilege of an Opposition whenever obstruction is thought good tactics, to take advantage of motions to go into Committee to move any amendment of whatever frivolous character it may desire. Unless it is put within the power of a Government to get into Committee on certain days without motion, a determined minority can by means of an amendment utterly frustrate the processes of Parliament by "talking out" the motion. I invite hon. gentlemen opposite to tell me how, without such restriction as is here provided, a House of Commons confronted with resolute obstruction can ever get into Supply. We impose this restriction or recede from closure, and to recede from closure is to expose to the world the impotence of Parliament.

Is this new rule really as terrible as it has been painted? There are at least three working days besides Thursday and Friday, and on these, particularly after the first four weeks of a Session, the House often goes into Committee. On these days a motion is necessary and an amendment is in order; the administration of any and all ministers can be challenged and vigorous debate ensue. Further, each department must first present its estimates on one of the other days and thus subject itself to unlimited criticism. True, a minister may first present his estimates to Committee on Thursday or Friday by consent. "Oh," say hon. gentlemen opposite, "that means the consent of the majority." I invite the hon. member for Bonaventure (Mr. Marcil), I invite any hon. member opposite to stand now and name me an instance in the whole history of this House or in the history of the British House where the term "consent of the House" has been held to mean "consent of the majority." These words have always been interpreted to mean "unanimous consent of the House," just as stated by the right hon. leader of the Government. Hon. gentlemen opposite, when this strange idea was first advanced, were offered opportunity to have the word "unanimous" inserted, but the right hon. leader of the Opposition said: "I am too old a bird for that." His reception of the prompt proposal of the Government leader was equivalent to saying, "I am not here to make these rules perfect; I am here to debate them." Or in other words: I want to make even this discussion serve the ends of obstruction. Since the point was raised, I have referred it to officers of this House, and they give the same opinion I had arrived at myself and which earlier the right hon. leader of the Government had expressed. The Prime Minister added that if in the face of his own opinion and the advice of officers, the Speaker should decide that this phrase meant consent of the majority, he would bind himself to move that the Rules be amended by inserting the word "unanimous." Nothing more could be asked. It is quite clear that certain hon. gentlemen do not desire these Rules perfected, they want to debate them without end.

MR. MARCIL: Rule 25 provides that Government business has precedence for the first four weeks of the session only on Tuesday, Thursday and Friday. That would mean that for that time Monday and Wednesday would not count.

MR. MEIGHEN: As the hon. member knows—probably no one knows better— the House is very rarely in Committee of Supply during the first four weeks of a session. If it should be, even during that time, they have always Tuesday, and then and thereafter they have a right to move an amendment and debate anything they choose. They can move want of confidence or that the moon is made of green cheese, before they permit a minister to get his estimates into Committee. Surely then opportunities are ample. But the hon. member for Carleton objects to being confined to any particular days; he demands this privilege at all times. If he gets his way, he has defeated the whole purpose of these amendments. That is what some hon. gentlemen want— they want rules that can be over-ruled, or cross-ruled, or by-ruled; they want amendments that do not amend, they want closure that does not close.

It was not always thus. Hon. gentlemen opposite are recent converts to these extraordinary views. I am sorry the member for Carleton is not in his seat. He is the man who tonight declared that there was no reason for closure in Canada and never had been; that we are introducing Russian methods, Polish methods; that we are worse than Russia and Poland in ever thinking of closure. He said: "I was on a committee three years ago, and up to that time nobody even thought of closure; we never contemplated such an extraordinary and vicious principle." He declared that to think of such a thing in this free country appalled him; that European countries might suffer it, for there they do not know what freedom means, but that we can never get a Canadian to put up with it.

SOME HON. MEMBERS: Hear, hear.

MR. MEIGHEN: Hon. members opposite say "Hear, hear." Presumably these hon. gentlemen never gave outlet to any other opinion than that which they now express. But has the hon. member for Carleton always been of this mind? Has he never thought of closure until now? Let me quote his words. Here is what he said—and the House should remember now his assertion that up to three years ago neither he nor others had ever been polluted with the idea of closure—here is the way in which the hon. gentleman dealt with this question on June 5, 1908, nearly five years past:

> The action of these hon. gentlemen—

That is, the Opposition of that day—

> —raises the question fair and square: Can the Government of this country, whether Liberal or Conservative, afford to be placed in such a position as that? Can any government afford to place itself at the mercy of an Opposition and virtually declare that, if the Opposition do not like anything contained in legislation that is introduced, all the Opposition has to do is to withhold Supply and the Government will back down? Carried out in practice and you have a country ruled not by the majority but by the minority.

And again:

> I say there is only one solution to this question; if this Opposition, or any other Opposition, choose to pursue such a course, the inevitable consequence will be the closure. I am not the first one to advocate the closure.

He certainly was not.

> Closure began in the French Parliament. It was adopted by that of Great Britain. It exists in the Congress of the United States. These are in their way the three leading parliamentary bodies in the world. What they have agreed to accept may be expected to come in other popularly ruled countries. . . . To my mind that is the proper doctrine.

And the hon. member for Carleton added:

> Let the Government start in at once to change the rules of this House, if it takes months to do it in order to adopt the closure.

These are the words of a man who now thinks his province is disgraced because a minister from New Brunswick[1] had something to do with the introduction of this resolution!

[1] Hon. Mr. Hazen

The hon. member for Carleton was not alone in the expression of these views in days past. Who was first in this House to ridicule the idea of closure? Who was first to defy the Government to bring in such an iniquitous measure? Who was first, after closure was introduced, to throw all his cards on the table and to proclaim obstruction as the only means of countering this calamity? It was the hon. member for St. John, was it not? The hon. member for St. John could not fight closure to his satisfaction on its merits; he had to get up and move an adjournment in order to discuss bad roads in the Province of New Brunswick, woman suffrage and other topics, so that he might obstruct and, by obstruction, prevent, if possible, the passage of closure. He conceived that to expound leisurely the wrongs of women in England was an appropriate method of shielding Canada from the contamination of these amendments. Has the hon. member for St. John always been of that mind? How is it his eyes are now so pure that they cannot behold the iniquity of closure, when they cast a very different gleam but a short time ago? Here is a quotation from the hon. member which I take from page 10070 of Hansard, July 24, 1911—he can certainly outclass his friend from Carleton when it comes to turning himself upside down. He said:

> I ask hon. gentlemen opposite whether, after hon. gentlemen have had a full opportunity, as they have had during the time that this question has been under discussion, of expressing their views, it is not tending to destroy free parliamentary institutions for hon. gentlemen to rise as they have risen today and threaten that this question shall not be allowed to come to a vote.

Here we have a statement of the hon. member that the actual program of this Opposition, as avowed by its own leader yesterday, is nothing less than an attempt to upset the whole structure of our Parliamentary institutions! On the occasion of his so speaking, he was asked, "What about 1896?"—when the Liberal party obstructed—and he answered:

> I do not care what took place in 1896; I was not here in 1896. I say it is not in harmony with the principles which ought to govern parliamentary institutions that gentlemen

should rise in their places and threaten, simply because their
views are not the views of the majority, that there shall be no
opportunity to vote upon this question, and no opportunity, in
a constitutional way, of giving expression to the views of the
majority of this House. That is revolutionary; it is not in
harmony with the principles of constitutional government.

Will the hon. member for St. John be good enough now to
tell the House whether he is prepared to see the legislative
institutions of this country subverted rather than accept a reasonable limit of debate?

The right hon. leader of the Opposition informed us yesterday that no matter how far others may have erred and strayed
from the narrow path, he has always been true to the gospel of
freedom of speech. He at least has never renounced his allegiance
to the liberalism of Charles Fox. No matter how the Hon.
William Paterson differed from him on this subject in 1909 and
in 1911, he was always, he said, on the other side. No matter
what the Hon. Sydney Fisher had said, he himself had stood
true to the doctrine of unlimitable speech. I would never introduce closure, said Sir Wilfrid Laurier, I would rather go into
Opposition. Notwithstanding what Sir Allen Aylesworth[1] had
said, he (Sir Allan) was all wrong, false to the principles of
Liberalism; notwithstanding what the Hon. Rodolphe Lemieux
had said at St. Hyacinthe, notwithstanding what the Hon. Wm.
Pugsley had declared and repeated in this House; notwithstanding
that the opinions of these five members of his Cabinet had been
re-echoed and reaffirmed by the Hon. Charles Murphy who was
his Secretary of State; notwithstanding these six Cabinet ministers who were piling on his back to pass closure, he had stood
true; and now he has all of them behind him and not one has any
use for closure. It is true, he tells us, that Gladstone introduced
this wicked law; it is true that he, Sir Wilfrid, has up to now
proclaimed himself a Liberal of the Gladstone school; but he
has changed, he has found a higher model: He is a Liberal of
the school of Fox.

Yes, Gladstone introduced closure, why? In order to defeat
the obstruction of forty Irishmen in the British House, and the

[1] Minister of Justice in Sir Wilfrid Laurier's Cabinet.

leader of the Opposition says that was quite legitimate; the Opposition then believed it was the duty of Government, it was a duty which both parties owed the country, to see to it that the wheels of Parliament were not clogged, that the arteries of legislation were not stopped, that it was not possible for a small minority to thwart and throttle the whole Parliamentary system. And the hon. member for Carleton, by some circuitous route, got around to the same idea and he also says that was right and proper. Therefore, so long as it is forty Irishmen who are obstructing it is all wrong, but when eighty members of Parliament do so it is perfectly right and just. It is all wrong for forty men, and entirely right for eighty men, to subvert free institutions; so long as the official Opposition joins in the conspiracy, obstruction becomes a virtue instead of a vice. "Ah!" says the right hon. leader of the Opposition, "even though Mr. Gladstone did introduce closure, that was only the first page of his political career, and to that page I do not subscribe. I subscribe to the second page when he gave adhesion to the cause of those Irish members and endeavoured to bring it to fruition." But will the leader of the Opposition not recall a fact affirmed by every member in the British House at that time, by every historian of any party, that it was impossible for Gladstone or any statesman to have ever succeeded in putting through the realization of his dream of Irish self-government except by the instrument of closure? Gladstone, it is true, never did succeed in bringing to actual legislation the dream of Home Rule in Ireland, but whatever be the merits of Home Rule, Gladstone would never have been able to get his Bill through the House of Commons except by the application of closure. The leader of the Opposition cannot therefore subscribe to the second page of Gladstone's life unless he also subscribes to the first. When he finds he cannot quote his own ministers or even the Toronto *Globe,* where does he go for comfort? His authorities today against closure are Edmund Burke, Fox and the Ottawa *Citizen.* The names of Fox and Burke should not be mentioned in any British Parliament without emotion. Burke and Fox were men of great talents, great virtues and great errors. But hon. gentlemen can search the long catalogue of endowments possessed by Fox and Burke and they will never find in either of them a capacity to prolong a speech away beyond the boundary of the speaker's ideas. To do so was a practice unknown to either Fox or Burke and is the very element and essence of obstruction. Neither of these men would have been guilty of so much as a trace of the wasteful performance which has for months been rampant in this House, nor would either of them have countenanced it had it been attempted then in the Parliament of Britain.

How is it that the right hon. gentleman had to go so far back? Are we to look for authorities against closure a century and a half ago when the business of the British Parliament bore no comparison in magnitude to its business now and before the monster obstruction had ever reared its head? We cannot find a prescription for cure of an evil before the evil exists. How is it that the authority of British Liberalism has so degenerated since the days of Fox and Burke? How is it that in this special matter of perfecting and evolving rules of procedure to meet advancing conditions we must look to British statesmen only of the long ago, back of 1867, and shut our eyes to the experience and enlightenment they gained in later years? On this the hon. member for Carleton is still more arbitrary than his leader. He says we can look to them for justification back in the early Nineteenth Century and farther still, but that the moment we amend our Rules in the light of what they have learned in Britain since 1867, that moment our family of provinces and especially Quebec have an unanswerable grievance and may shake the citadel of Confederation! Surely we are bound to gain all we can of light and leading from what has taken place in the British House both before and after 1867, and having done so we have sovereign freedom to do as we think best.

We have, more than once since that date, availed ourselves of what they have more recently learned and practised. No later than 1910 we enacted into our code of procedure a Rule of the British House. This one provided that the Speaker might interrupt a member who was tediously repeating himself, and call upon him to cease. We took it verbatim from the Rules of

Westminster enacted there since 1867, and we adopted it on motion of the right hon. leader of the Opposition and with approval of the hon. member for Carleton.

We are told by the hon. member for Richmond that Liberalism has turned with disgust from these things in Great Britain and that closure there has become a Tory device. What do returns brought down in the Imperial House show? As we will remember, there was a Tory government in power in the Motherland from 1900 to 1905. The following statement discloses how often closure was applied during the ten years starting with 1900.

Under Tory Government

1900	17
1901	57
1902	70
1903	20
1904	69

Under Liberal Government

1905	61
1906	112
1907	66
1908	63
1909	156

This record of the Liberal Government proves—and I make no criticism of them—that they applied closure nearly double the number of times that the Tory Government did in an equal period of time. The Prime Minister of Great Britain—a Liberal—within two weeks of the present hour, introduced an amendment stiffening their Rules and making them even more drastic than they have ever been. In speaking to his motion he affirmed that there is no member of either party who would contend that progress of legislation, even without deliberate obstruction, would today be possible in the British House were it not for closure Rules. We have framed ours with a more limited objective, not to meet unnecessary but legitimate discussion—because in this country we have time for all legitimate discussion—but to meet obstruction and obstruction alone.

I urge upon hon. gentlemen in all seriousness that we come, at this juncture, to an intelligent and adequate realization of our duties. There is no one who will not agree that a very large proportion of the time of Parliament is not occupied as effectively as it should be and that energies devoted merely to party warfare are energies wasted to the nation. Let us rise above the conception espoused by one hon. member, that we are here as two sets of gladiators on a political theatre, or two strutters in a prize ring each trying to win under certain Rules. The party system is good, but purely party warfare can be overdone. We are here, sworn servants of the Canadian people, and, if we carry out our obligations under our oaths of office, we will make certain that to the best of our capacities we utilize time in this House to the advantage of those people. To do so we must without any doubt or question amend the mechanism of Parliamentary procedure so as to make it impossible for hon. members who may not have that conception of their duty to thwart the purposes of the majority who have.

In years gone by no party has been free from this infirmity. Human nature being what it is, an Opposition is almost certain, so long as we have the party system, to seize upon Rules, and loopholes in Rules, to gain advantage in its upward struggle. But in this crisis the voice of duty is clear. We have to decide whether or not we shall proclaim our situation as hopeless at the hands of an Opposition hungry for office and burning with lust for power—an Opposition whose weapon is an antiquated Code of Procedure which substitutes license for order and has been abandoned in every enlightened country; whether we are reconciled to lying here bogged down in cold obstruction or whether we shall purge this House of that "obstruction which begins to stop our very veins of life." Let us look at what has been accomplished in a greater Parliament than ours after its members had witnessed what we have witnessed and turned the way this Parliament is now about to turn. Let us look at the volume of legislation so massive and so splendid now stored in history to the credit of the British House. Let us look also at the path, the constantly developing procedural path along which this ponderous burden has been carried, a path blazed first by a great chieftain of the Liberal party, perhaps the most illustrious of its leaders, and travelled later by both his successors and his foes.

THE PANAMA TOLLS

Delivered before The Canadian Club at Ottawa, March 7, 1914, in attack upon The Panama Canal Act which had recently been passed by the United States Congress. This Act authorized the President (Mr. Taft) to fix tolls on shipping passing through the newly-constructed Panama Canal, sufficient to provide upkeep and maintenance, but required him to exempt United States' Coast-wise shipping, and empowered him, if he thought fit, to exempt as well foreign shipping of that country. The U.S. position was subsequently reversed and this Act did not go into effect.

I AM NATURALLY SENSIBLE of the high honour paid me by your Executive in asking me to speak before the Canadian Club of Ottawa, and doubly so by reason of the character of the subject which they have entrusted to me. The pleasure I would otherwise feel, though, is more or less overcome by a sense of responsibility when I think of the importance of the topic and of the crisis through which its discussion is passing at the present time. There are none present who do not know that at almost the hour at which we meet there has been added to the British-Canadian side of the case the most powerful advocate on earth.[1]

"THE PANAMA TOLLS"—that is how your announcement of title reads; but to be more specific, I am to present the objections taken by this country to the tolls provisions of the Panama Canal Act passed by the U. S. Congress, and if I can, to substantiate those objections by good reasons. From the first word to the last of what I say, there must be kept steadfastly in mind as a first and paramount consideration, that toward us the United States is friendly even beyond the sense in which that word is customarily applied, and that however erroneous we believe their views to be, those views have so far been pressed by methods and in

[1] President Wilson of the United States

56

language befitting a great nation. And, having especial regard to the course pursued by those brave men among them, who on this question have set themselves against the current of feeling in that country, among whom we now number their President himself, it becomes abundantly clear that this is no time for words of bitterness, or of impatience, or of international distrust. Strong arguments will do good; strong language will do harm. Our every word must carry the force of a sincere conviction. It will need no other force.

Just a sentence as to the plan of these remarks. In January last this Club was favoured with a presentation of the Panama Tolls Case from the standpoint of the United States, made by Mr. Samuel J. Elder, an eminent American jurist. In what reading on the subject I have been able to do, I have not found the U.S. side of the controversy more ably stated than it was by Mr. Elder, and it may safely be assumed that his arguments then advanced constitute the American case. I, therefore, put my presentation mainly in the form of a reply to that address.

By way of approach, I may state the case like this: The sea is a common highway of mankind; upon it there can be no proscriptive right. That is a maxim of civilization. The water of the whole world must be as free to the vessels of commerce as to the winds that sweep its bosom. But against the movement of sea-borne trade nature opposed two narrow barriers of land. One blocked its pathway to the east at Suez and the other obstructed its course westward at the Isthmus of Panama. Sea transport in the last century doubled and multiplied. Britain led, and all maritime nations took their part. But the two narrow barriers stood, every year more obstinate, and every year more costly. To hew them out and thus control these passageways round the globe, became recognized as, in each case, a franchise, not to be appropriated by any person, company or country, but as a great outstanding world franchise, still unseized, and when seized, to be held in trust for mankind. And so the Suez Canal was built, and became, by the Convention of Constantinople, a world utility, operated by a company on terms fixed by the Powers, where all are treated alike. The Panama project was of more colossal proportions and slower of maturing.

But, at last, it too is all but complete. The dream of four centuries becomes a fact, and next year will see in operation the greatest canal on this planet. The United States has built it, and controls it, and the question is: Does the trust subsist? . . . the trust which in the Suez case provides for its use, on equal terms, by all nations. Or, is that trust impaired? Is the United States, besides controlling the canal, able to use it for the advantage of its own commerce as against that of other Powers?

This right is claimed by the Republic and the facts urged by Mr. Taft and Mr. Elder in support are these: "We built the works with our good money, and it cost us $400,000,000." That is true. "We own the canal, and the whole canal zone, ten miles wide, across the Isthmus; we bought the land alone for $10,000,000, and an annuity of $250,000 soon to commence, and we had to promise ships of the Panama Republic free transport as well." And all that is true. "Not only do we own the canal zone in fee simple, but we are sovereign there and can legislate for the whole ten-mile strip." That is also in a measure true. "We became owners and sovereign and built the canal without violating any treaty." That again is undenied. And so as owners and sovereign they passed the Panama Canal Act; they author-ized their President to fix tolls on shipping through that artery, which tolls were not to be less than sufficient to pay for up-keep and maintenance, but they bound him to exempt from those tolls the coast-wise shipping of the United States, and authorized him, if he thought fit, to exempt their foreign shipping as well. President Taft, in the exercise of that authority, fixed one dollar and twenty cents per ton as toll on all foreign shipping, and, of course, exempted United States coast-wise shipping as the Act bound him to do. He refrained from exempting United States foreign shipping, though the statute empowered him so to exempt it. Great Britain has lodged a protest against the exempting clauses of this statute. The United States are owners and sovereign, so the burden is on us to show that their power thus to legislate has been restrained. We rely on the Hay-Pauncefote Treaty of 1901, and as we rely chiefly on the preamble and on Article III, Rule 1, I quote them. Here we reach the very heart of the controversy. A clear understanding of these provisions makes the whole argument plain.

> PREAMBLE. His Majesty, Edward the Seventh, of the United Kingdom . . ., and the United States of America, being desirous to facilitate the construction of a ship-canal to connect the Atlantic and Pacific Oceans, by whatever route may be considered expedient, and to that end to remove any objection which may arise out of the convention of the nineteenth of April, 1850, commonly called the Clayton-Bulwer Treaty, to the construction of such canal under the auspices of the Government of the United States, without impairing the "general principle of neutralization" established in Article VIII of that convention, have for that purpose appointed as their plenipotentiaries; etc.

> ARTICLE III. The United States adopts, as the basis of the neutralization of such ship-canal, the following rules, substantially as embodied in the Convention of Constantinople, signed the 28th of October, 1888, for the free navigation of the Suez Canal, that is to say:
>
>> 1. The canal shall be free and open to the vessels of commerce and of war of all nations observing these rules, on terms of entire equality, so that there shall be no discrimination against any such nation or its citizens or subjects, in respect of the conditions or charges of traffic, or otherwise. Such conditions and charges of traffic shall be just and equitable.

You observe the purpose, and the only purpose, of this treaty, which superseded the Clayton-Bulwer Treaty, is "to facilitate the construction of a ship canal . . . by whatever route . . . and to that end to remove any objection which may arise out of the Clayton-Bulwer Treaty of 1850 to the construction of that canal under the auspices of the United States," but to do so, "without impairing the general principle of neutralization established in Article VIII of that convention." Note carefully the reservation. Now the Clayton-Bulwer Treaty provided that Great Britain and the United States would give support and encouragement to any company that would undertake to build the canal and would jointly guarantee its protection, provided:

> That the parties constructing or owning the same shall impose no other charges or conditions of traffic thereupon,

than the aforesaid Governments shall approve of as just and equitable, and that the said canal or railway being open to the subjects and citizens of Great Britain and the United States on equal terms, shall also be open on like terms to the subjects and citizens of every other state which is willing to grant thereto such protection as Great Britain and the United States engage to afford.

There is quoted verbatim the "general principle of neutralization" provided for in Article VIII of the Clayton-Bulwer Treaty, indeed, the only principle of neutralization mentioned in Article VIII. And remember, this is the "general principle of neutralization" which the Hay-Pauncefote Treaty undertook in its very preamble to preserve, and preserve "unimpaired." Pardon me if I impress upon you again the very words that clothe this principle, the principle which was to survive all change, which has been the chief corner-stone of all these negotiations for seventy years, which was to stand whatever else might fall, the principle, namely, "of the canal being open to the subjects and citizens of the United States and Great Britain on equal terms," and on like terms to all other countries who came into the burden of protection. Subject to maintaining that traditional feature of policy intact, the United States were to be at liberty to have the canal constructed "under the auspices of their Government" and to control it; which liberty they were denied by the Clayton-Bulwer Convention. So there you have the intention of both parties to perpetuate this equality of treatment as to tolls and terms set out in the preamble to the Hay-Pauncefote Treaty, and surely in language as plain as language ever was.

Then Article III comes in, and adopting the words of the Suez Canal Convention, demands that:

The Canal shall be free and open to the vessels of commerce and of war of all nations observing these rules, on terms of entire equality, so that there shall be no discrimination against any such nation or its citizens or subjects, in respect of the conditions or charges of traffic, or otherwise. Such conditions and charges of traffic shall be just and equitable.

You remember Mr. Elder argued that, "all nations" meant all nations but the United States. They, he said, must be understood as excepted because they were to build the canal. I answer: He cannot argue that, in the light of the preamble. The general principle of neutralization established in Article VIII of the Clayton-Bulwer Treaty was to be preserved unimpaired. If you exclude the United States from the meaning of "all nations," you cannot preserve that principle "unimpaired." You cannot preserve it at all. Right there seems to me the stone wall in the path of this American contention, and able indeed would be the arguments which could ever surmount it.

What are those arguments? "We are not only owners but sovereign," says Mr. Elder, "and it is a rule of interpretation that if you can reasonably interpret the words of a treaty so as not to take away sovereign rights, you must give them that interpretation. For such must be considered the intention of the parties, and it is the intention that governs." So, he contends, the United States being sovereign, the parties to the treaty must have intended not to include that nation in the words "all nations."

The trouble about this argument is that the United States was not sovereign when the treaty was made, nor for two years afterwards. How then can he say that the intention of the parties to the treaty was governed by a consideration which did not exist? So on that ground there is no merit in arguing that the expression "all nations" means anything but what it says.

Mr. Elder next invites us to look at the other five rules of Article III. These rules deal with blockade and re-victualling and the embarkation of troops at the canal. "Now," says Mr. Elder, "these rules cannot apply to the United States because the territory is ours and we can do what we please with it. And, as these remaining five rules do not apply to us, why do you say that 'all nations' in Rule 1 should include us?" That sounds very plausible, but, on reflection, this argument vanishes too. When the treaty was made the U.S. was not sovereign and did not own the territory. So the intention then was that the whole six rules should bind both nations. Some may now, on account of a move made since, a changed condition effected, by one Power, have a different application, but surely not to the prejudice of the other contracting party. The United States has since become sovereign of the canal zone and the British Government does

not question its title to exercise belligerent rights for protection. But why should that affect Rule 1, which treats of tolls
and terms? With Rule 1 it is not a question of changed effect.
It is question of original construction. The United States does
not claim that Rule 1 has by its Act, two years afterwards, a
changed effect—changed to our great prejudice. That would be
absurd. The argument is that Rule 1 never did and never was
intended to include that country. Then how can a subsequent
changed effect of Rules 2 to 6 alter the original construction of
Rule 1? If anything further were required to eliminate this
argument as to sovereignty we should read Article IV:

> It is agreed that no change of territorial sovereignty or of
> international relations of the country or countries traversed
> by the before-mentioned canal shall effect the general prin-
> ciple of neutralization or the obligation of the High Con-
> tracting Parties under the present treaty.

Mr. Elder omitted all reference to this provision. I am at a loss
to understand how Article IV and the American contention as to
sovereign rights can live together.

"But," says Mr. Elder, "we have succeeded to the rights of
New Grenada, as it were. New Grenada was sovereign and
owner in 1850, and there is not a whisper in the Clayton-Bulwer
Treaty of that date to prevent New Grenada building the canal
and exempting her ships from tolls. We have now got into the
shoes of New Grenada and have all her rights." The answer is—
there is not a whisper in the 1850 convention about any country
building the canal; all they ever thought of then was that a
company might build it, as every article of the treaty shows.
But even if New Grenada could have built the canal and
exempted her own ships, the United States could not, under the
old treaty, acquire such a right from New Grenada, for both
parties agreed therein as follows:

> Nor will Great Britain or the United States take advantage
> of any intimacy or use any alliance, connection, or influence,
> that either may possess with any state or government,
> through whose territory the said canal may pass, for the pur-
> pose of acquiring or holding, directly or indirectly, for the
> subjects or citizens of the one, any rights or advantages in

regard to commerce or navigation through said canal, which shall not be offered, on the same terms, to the subjects or citizens of the other.

So the trouble is again that the United States acquired its sovereignty in the canal zone by virtue, not of the Clayton-Bulwer Treaty, but of the Hay-Pauncefote Treaty, and while under the obligations of the Hay-Pauncefote Treaty. That sovereignty is a conditional sovereignty. It is restrained and abbreviated by the terms of that convention. How, then, can it be used to modify those terms?

Mr. Elder also argues at some length that in other treaties where the words "vessels of commerce" or "vessels of nations" have been used, coast-wise shipping was assumed to be excepted and that, therefore, it should be excepted in this case. Even if this assertion and deduction be correct, the argument would be of limited value to the advocates of the American contention, because they all insist that United States foreign shipping and United States coast-wise shipping are on the same footing, and stand or fall together. On this Senator Lodge is particularly emphatic. But is either the assertion or deduction correct? I can find only one such treaty where coast-wise shipping was not excepted by express words. So that all but this one tell against Mr. Elder rather than in his favour. The one exception is the Convention of Commerce of 1815 between England and the United States. In this we find the following clause:

> No higher or other duties or charges shall be imposed in any of the ports of the United States on British vessels, than those payable in the same ports by vessels of the United States; nor in the ports of any of his Britannic Majesty's territories in Europe, on the vessels of the United States, than shall be payable in the same ports on British vessels.

Notwithstanding this clause, says Mr. Elder, in spite of the general words "British vessels" and "vessels of the United States," the coast-wise shipping of both countries has been considered as not included. Very true, is the answer, but why? For the plainest possible reason; because that convention was made with the one single purpose, "to regulate commerce between the territories of the United States and of his Britannic Majesty." This is expressed as the sole object of the convention no less than three times in the convention itself. How then could that treaty possibly apply to coast-wise shipping? But in the present case the reverse is the fact. Unless coast-wise shipping is held to be included, an expressed purpose of the Hay-Pauncefote Treaty is in large measure defeated.

Again, Mr. Elder claims that if the words "vessels of all nations" mean literally what they say, then the treaty was broken in 1903, and without protest from England. In 1903, he says, the United States agreed to exempt the ships of the Panama Republic, when they bought the territory from that state, and England never protested. This is a rather dangerous argument. It has a reverse action. If it is any good at all, it strikes one case as hard as the other. We say that "all nations" means really "all nations." Our adversaries say that "all nations" means all nations except themselves. If, therefore, to exempt Panama shipping is inconsistent with the contention of Great Britain, is it not equally inconsistent with the contention of the United States? But, I submit, the argument has no force against either position. The Panama people were owners of the zone and masters of the situation, and they fixed their price. Exemption of their shipping was a part of that price. It is now an element of the cost of the canal to the United States, and has a right to be considered as well as the rest of the cost, in estimating a return on capital invested. For a fair return on capital invested is undoubtedly due the builders of the Panama Canal.

But our American cousins have still another resource, and here Mr. Taft, Mr. Knox, Mr. Olney, Senator Lodge and Mr. Elder make a final stand. They say, "After all, you are fighting about very little or nothing, inasmuch as only our coast-wise shipping has been actually exempted, and under our laws you cannot compete in that trade anyway." So, they conclude, nobody is hurt. Well, coast-wise shipping means one thing in one country and another thing in another country, just as each chooses to define the term in its own legislation. In the United States it includes vessels plying between New York and Seattle, though they go around by Cape Horn; also between New York and the Philippines; between San Fransciso and Hawaii. If our neighbours are right about this thing, they can give free passage to ships loading at Tacoma and discharging at Portland, and at the same time can tax Canadian vessels passing from Victoria to St. John. They could so exercise that right as to force Canadian traffic over American railroads from our eastern provinces to their Atlantic ports, thence in American bottoms to their Pacific ports, and over American railroads again to destination in the Canadian West. Our traffic between British Columbia and the Maritime Provinces in 1911 was 118,417 tons, and that went all the way around the Straits of Magellan. Carloads across the continent cost thirty dollars per ton and up, and should, by way of the Panama, cost six to nine dollars per ton. That alone would represent a saving of $2,500,000 per year. What then might not such a traffic become? Would there not be a fatal discrimination between, for instance, a Canadian line running from Vancouver to New Orleans, and an American line from Tacoma to the same port? New England merchants would have another big advantage over British merchants in competing for trade of the Pacific states. Again, supposing British Columbia timber or Alberta wheat is wanted at Rio de Janeiro, or at an old world Atlantic port, a Canadian vessel must pay the canal tolls, while an American vessel can escape them by the simple expedient of trans-shipping at New Orleans. Indeed, coast-wise ships may engage in foreign commerce according to United States law. And, if they wish, they can extend still further the scope of coast-wise traffic. We will know what discrimination means if the Tolls Act goes into operation. We are not fighting for nothing.

"Anyway," says Mr. Elder, "we have exempted only our coast-wise shipping, and we could do the same thing by a subsidy." That argument goes too far. If a subsidy, in the actual working out, means the same thing as an exemption, then they can undoubtedly subsidize their foreign commerce also; Britain can do the same and all other countries as well. So the treaty as to tolls is thereby repealed. Such is the absurdity into which that argument leads us. As a matter of fact, we do not dispute the right of the United States to subsidize shipping, though a method of subsidizing might be chosen that would amount to a violation of their covenant. But a subsidy, as a subsidy, must be justified to their tax-payers on its own merits. Paid in the ordinary way, it comes out of American pockets. But if the United States is right on this question, it can give a subsidy by the mere device of exempting its nationals; it can add to the tolls of others to make up the exemption and thus tax the rest of the world to pay the subsidy. Right there is the great difference. "Oh," says Mr. Elder, "we are not doing that though. Mr. Taft has imposed on you only one dollar and twenty cents per ton, and this will do little more than pay for upkeep." Yes, but our trade will suffer and theirs profit by the discrimination itself. Besides, they have asserted in their statute a right to go farther. If their statute is valid under our treaty, they can add to those tolls, and they can exempt their foreign shipping also, any time they like. Our whole protection is levelled to the ground; we are disarmed for the future; therefore, we act now.

It was a surprise to me to find in Mr. Elder's speech the assertion that no one, at the time of the Hay-Pauncefote Treaty, ever thought of the provisions as to the equality of tolls applying to the United States. Time—my allotment has already gone by—time will not permit me to call the multitude of witnesses from his own country to disprove that statement. I appeal hurriedly to the most direct and potent evidence. John Hay, their Secretary of State at the time, and an able man he was, both as diplomat and as a writer of surpassing excellence, negotiated the treaty for them. Joseph H. Choate still adorns their citizenship, and respect for his authority, like the fascination of his personality, grows with the weight of years. He was their ambassador at London, and was a signatory to the treaty. What, first, is his testimony as to its meaning and intent?

The great design of both treaties, that of 1850 and that of 1901, was to promote the construction and maintenance of a ship-canal between the two oceans, for "the benefit of mankind, on equal terms to all," and to protect the neutralized canal effectively when built. In urging on the British Government the making of the Clayton-Bulwer Treaty, the American negotiator said to Lord Palmerston: The United States sought no exclusive privilege or preferential right of any kind in regard to the proposed communication (that is, a canal or railroad), and their sincere wish, if it should be found practicable, was to see it dedicated to the common use of all nations on the most liberal terms and a footing of perfect equality for all. That the United States would not, if they could, obtain any exclusive right or privilege in a great highway which naturally belonged to all mankind.

This statement expresses accurately the avowed intention and resolve of the United States from 1850 to 1912 concerning the Panama Canal. All treaties on the subject are based on this intention and resolve, many times reiterated by official representatives of the American Government.

John Hay has testified to the same effect. His lips are silent now, but on January 15, 1904, two years after the treaty, he thus described its effect:

> The Clayton-Bulwer Treaty was conceived to form an obstacle, and the British Government, therefore, agreed to abrogate it, the United States only promising in return to protect the canal and keep it open on equal terms to all nations in accordance with our traditional policy.

That "traditional policy," who can mistake it? From the early years of the Ninteenth Century almost to the present hour it has been attested over and over again by American presidents and secretaries of state, by resolutions of their Senate and House of Representatives, and by their ambassadors in foreign lands. It was declared by Henry Clay in 1826, and more fully pronounced by resolution of their Senate in 1835:

> Resolved, that the President of the United States be respect-fully asked to consider the expediency of opening negotiations with the governments of other nations, and particularly with the Government of Central America and New Grenada, for the purpose of effectually protecting, by suitable treaty stipulations with them, such individuals or companies as may undertake to open a communication between the Atlantic and Pacific Oceans by the construction of a ship-canal across the Isthmus which connects North and South America, and of securing forever, by such stipulations, the free and equal right of navigating such canal to all such nations, on the payment of such reasonable tolls as may be established to compensate the capitalists who may engage in such under-taking and complete the work.

In 1839 the House of Representatives unanimously passed a similar resolution. Again it was affirmed by President Polk in 1846, who said, in commenting on the treaty with New Grenada:

> The ultimate object, as presented by the Senate of the United States in their resolution, to which I have already referred, is to secure to all nations the free and equal rights of passage over the Isthmus.

To this array may be added Mr. Clayton, Ambassador at London in 1849, and later on James G. Blaine. Mr. Blaine's words are most emphatic and significant:

> Nor does the United States seek any exclusive or narrow commercial advantage. It frankly agrees, and will by public proclamation declare, at the proper time, in conjunction with the Republic on whose soil the canal may be located, that the same rights and privileges, the same tolls and obligations for the use of the canal shall apply with absolute impartiality to the merchant marine of every nation on the globe; and equally in time of peace the harmless use of the canal shall be freely granted to the war vessels of other nations.

That does not read consistently with any idea of discriminatory rights in favour of the "republic on whose soil the canal may be located." But it is in harmony with the Suez Convention, in which Turkey and Egypt, who are sovereigns of the territory, are on an equality with all others as to tolls. I hurry through the list of witnesses to quote the words of Senator Davis, Chairman of the Committee on Foreign Relations, presenting his report on the Hay-Pauncefote Treaty. After lauding the large and generous views of those statesmen of Europe who conceived the Suez Canal Convention of 1888, he says:

> The United States cannot take an attitude of opposition to the great Act of October 22, 1888, without discrediting the official declarations of our Government for fifty years on the neutrality of an isthmian canal and its equal use by all nations, without discrimination.

> The Suez Canal makes no discrimination in its tolls in favour of its stockholders, and taking the profits or the half of them as our basis of calculation, we will never find it necessary to differentiate our rates of toll in favour of our own people in order to secure a very great profit on the investment.

Then again:

> To set up a selfish motive of gain by establishing a monopoly
> of a highway that must derive its income from the patronage
> of all maritime nations, would be unworthy of the United
> States if we owned the country through which the canal was
> to be built.

More is not necessary, but I conclude by reading an amendment
moved in the United States Senate by Senator Bard, of California,
as an alteration of the Hay-Pauncefote Treaty:

> "The United States *reserves the right* in the regulation and
> management of the canal, to discriminate in respect of the
> charges of traffic in favour of vessels of its own citizens
> engaged in the coast-wise trade."

This amendment was defeated by a decisive majority. It is true
that it applies to the 1900 Treaty, which was not ratified, but the
final text of 1901 was in the same language regarding tolls.

Two generations have passed since both countries commenced
to treat on this great subject. They started from a footing of
comparative equality, for both had influence in the territory and
stake in the project, far beyond those of other Powers. These
mutual rights were cordially acknowledged, and, on a high plane
which does credit to civilization, the negotiations have all along
been maintained. So it must be to the end.

Great Britain, in the name of her subjects everywhere, is
prepared to abide by the event of arbitration. In that event, or
on an earlier settlement, as now happily seems probable, she is
prepared to contribute her full share on a parity with the world
under whatever tariff may be necessary to provide maintenance
and a fair return on capital. Such would be the due of a company. Such is the due of the Republic.

Even then the world will owe much to the United States.
Theirs was the initiative, theirs the capital, theirs the courage,
theirs the resource which brought success where others failed.
Those of their number, and indeed of many countries, who
assert that if the British position be vindicated it will mean that
there lies upon the rest of the world an obligation to the United
States not to be wiped away, are beyond all doubt asserting what

is true. That country has indeed made the world a debtor. But to make the world a debtor is the privilege and mission of great powers as it is the privilege and mission of great men. None the less it is in direct line with self-interest; it is the highest conception of self-interest. The United States have more than once in their history risen to that honour. They have done so in Cuba, in Hawaii and in the Philippines. They have done so by their very dedication to democracy on Plymouth Rock. In a task of like character they are engaged to-day in Mexico, we all hope with success. But those of us who have read well the life-story of the parent state, who remember the plight of civilization a century ago, and can picture still an island kingdom that counted her blood as water and her gold as dust, as she stood between Europe and a conqueror; those of us who know of an Egypt rescued from chaos and re-animated for the world's work, of a South Africa regenerated and an India redeemed; those of us, best of all, who know the full meaning of a Canada, a New Zealand, an Australia, sheltered through a hundred years of peace and progress to renew the youth of an Empire, will dare to believe that Britain too has a store of service at her credit on the balance sheet of nations.

THE MILITARY SERVICE ACT

CONSCRIPTION

After the First Great War had been raging for more than two years, the Prime Minister of Canada, Sir Robert Borden, approached the Leader of the Opposition, Sir Wilfrid Laurier, in an effort to bring about Coalition. .. The Liberal-Conservative Government then in office had, after long trial, found it impossible to provide adequate reinforcements for the Canadian Overseas Army by the voluntary system. Sir Robert's proposal was that the primary purpose of Coalition should be a Compulsory Selective Service Law in terms to be agreed upon by representatives of both parties entering the new Government. Representation in the new Government was to be on a fifty-fifty basis. Having given the subject some days' consideration, Sir Wilfrid declined to co-operate.

Later, on June 11, 1917, some time before the personnel of his Cabinet had been altered by the inclusion of many Liberals, the Prime Minister introduced a compulsory measure known as The Military Service Act and explained fully its provisions. When motion for second reading was made later on, Sir Wilfrid Laurier moved in amendment:

> That the further consideration of this Bill be deferred until
> the principle thereof has, by means of a referendum, been
> submitted to and approved of by the electors of Canada.

The following speech was delivered on June 21, 1917 in debate on the above amendment:

No ONE COULD BE PRESENT during this debate, or, if not present, could look out with intelligent mind on manifestations of sentiment everywhere appearing, without being conscious of the momentous importance of our pending decision. This is said not because there is any doubt as to what the verdict of the House will be. Substantial unanimity—not necessarily entire unanimity—on this side alone would probably carry the Bill. But

the courage of certain hon. gentlemen across the floor—courage
amid real difficulties and, therefore, creditable in high degree—
has placed the issue beyond all question. What we must keep in
mind, though, is not merely the present, but what is of final,
lasting consequence: in a word, we must so conduct ourselves as
to insure that the largest possible preponderance of public support accompanies the enforcement of this measure. Enactment
of law is only a beginning; it is obedience to law which determines its value. That is why this Bill of all Bills should be
thoroughly considered and why this debate should be conducted
in such a spirit and upon such a plane as will afford an example
and inspiration to our people everywhere. The right and
honourable thing must be done. The right and honourable thing
will be done, and in our view it is embodied in this measure.
The highest duty of members of Parliament is to spare no effort
to make plain to every reasonable man and woman in all parts
of Canada that we pass this measure and enforce it only because
it is right and honourable; that we do so for no unworthy
reason or out of any spirit of vindictiveness, but because in this
crisis of our country it is the only course we can take which has
the sanction of both mind and conscience.

I regard the forwarding of troops to the front on the scale
now being undertaken as an all-essential, as something we cannot
shirk. Does anybody really think otherwise? Whatever means
are necessary to procure these men, they must be sent; and whatever action is necessary on our part to support our army at
present in France, we must take. No one has seriously argued
in this House—and in solemn truth no one seriously believes—
that we can despatch, as we have done, 350,000 men overseas,
commissioned by us to stand between our country and destruction, pledge them the undying fidelity of a grateful people, watch
them through harrowing years of suffering, bathe ourselves in
the reflected glory of their gallantry and devotion, and then
leave them to be decimated and destroyed. Surely, surely, an
obligation of honour is upon us, and fortifying that obligation
of honour is the primal, instinctive, eternal urge of every nation
to protect its own security. There is no other way in which the
security of our state can be to a maximum ensured, and certainly

no other way in which its honour can be preserved.

In the next place, we are able to send these men; we have them here to send. Does anybody dispute that? It is argued feebly by some that we require all our men for industrial, commercial and agricultural pursuits. True we can use them all at home; there are opportunities in Canada to occupy them. But, Mr. Speaker, a reasonable mind must agree that we need them far more sorely in France. It is true we cannot send them without some inconvenience. The soldiers—millions of them—who represent France on that 350-mile battle line are not there without inconvenience to their people at home; neither are the soldiers who represent Great Britain. When men are sent away, necessarily more women will be employed in factories, more elderly persons will be employed on street cars, more boys will be employed on farms during summer instead of passing their time at lake resorts. There might even be a small diminution of production. But all this we can afford infinitely better than we can afford to allow our lines in France to be abandoned, weakened or destroyed. We can afford the men; we must send them. What way is there of securing them other than that provided here?

Some have suggested that if we withdraw this Bill we can sustain our forces by a continuation of the voluntary system. The hon. gentleman who has just sat down (Mr. Pardee) and who has delivered an address which will long live in our records, has indicated that without compulsion and merely beneath the shadow of this Bill more volunteers may be enrolled. I do not doubt that what he has in mind is true: quite probably beneath the shadow of this measure more men will enlist, under a sort of voluntary system. But that emphasizes—it does not destroy— the necessity for the Bill. Withdraw the Bill and its shadow vanishes; on the other hand, enact it into law, and, before an organization can be set up to give it effect over the length and breadth of Canada, thousands upon thousands will flock to the colours, knowing what is certain to come.

Who can contend, with justification, that the voluntary system has not been adequately tried, both in the way of vigorous effort and of length of time? The hon. member for St. John

(Mr. Pugsley), if I understood correctly an interruption he made yesterday, feels that the voluntary system is now doing enough. Well, for one year it has produced an average of 6,000 to 7,000 men a month, while wastage in Canada and in England amounted to a very substantial portion of that total. In the two months through which we have just passed, the voluntary system yielded us not one man for four of those who were casualties among our troops in France. Add casualties in France and wastage in England to wastage in Canada, and it is as plain as a rule of arithmetic that further reliance on the voluntary system will in time—perhaps in a very short time—so reduce our forces that we shall have no substantial representation in the war.

We are told over and over that everything has not been done which might have been done. Perhaps that is so; all I know is that we have done everything that we were able to devise, that the resources of the Administration were able to evolve, to make voluntary enlistment successful. Has there been, during the whole course of this debate, a suggestion of any practical step which might have been taken and which was not taken? I have not heard one. Was there not a sufficient number of recruiting officers? Were the recruiting officers not the proper men? In some cases, quite possibly, they were not; no Government and no Minister who ever existed could select in every particular case the proper man. There may have been—there no doubt was— an English recruiting officer in Montreal, and such an appointment has been scornfully attacked. If memory serves me aright, there is a considerable English population there, and from it has come a creditable supply of troops. But there were French recruiting officers as well in Montreal. One would think, listening to the hon. member for Rouville (Mr. Lemieux) that the only man commissioned to recruit in that area was the Methodist minister of whom he complained. I asked from the Militia Department a list of recruiting officers in the province of Quebec and in the city of Montreal. When I received today a long tabulation, I really thought for a moment they had sent me a list of French-Canadian recruits; the number was almost legion. Any hon. member can have these names copied for himself, and if he examines them he will admit that of those willing to serve the best were chosen. There was no way of forcing men to act.

If ever ministers of the Crown have been anxious about anything, present ministers have been anxious to retain the voluntary system, rather than disturb domestic unanimity, and no one has been more intensely in earnest about this than the Prime Minister himself. It is simply not true to say that at any time he made promise or pledge that compulsory service would never come. What he did do—and more than once—was to deny any present intention of resorting to that system and to express a most ardent hope that compulsion would never be necessary. To have that hope, that anxious hope fulfilled, I can think of no resource which was not exploited, no honourable appeal which was not made, no worthy exhortation that was left unuttered, no decent pressure that was not applied. Yes, I know, or can imagine, what is in the mind of hon. members. They are thinking of extremes resorted to which went away beyond these limits and, truth to tell, their thinking is absolutely right. The system became, at last, one which could be called voluntary enlistment only in a corrupted and attenuated sense. It became a system rather of conscription by cajolery—and not creditable to Canada. This so-called voluntary principle is illogical, it is unjust, it is cruelly unjust to many who volunteer to go; it is shamefully unjust to many who decide to stay. It provides no tribunal authorized to separate in public view two classes of men, the eligibles and the ineligibles, for a fighting war. It leaves everything to caprice. There is method and rationality in the plan before us now.

In objection it is urged that, however essential this plan may be, however ample may be the means at our disposal to carry it to success, we are restrained by constitutional limitations. There is no need of a long, wire-drawn argument as to our powers. Every one who wants to face this issue rather than evade it will admit that there is no question whatever of jurisdiction; all talk of doubt is pusillanimous. If jurisdiction is not with us it is either in the Imperial Parliament or in the provinces. To suggest the first is an affront to Canada; to suggest the second is nonsense. What hon. gentlemen have really intended to argue is not that jurisdiction is lacking, but that we have never heretofore exercised this power, never declared by Statute that the armed forces of our country, no matter how enrolled, whether by conscription or otherwise, could be despatched overseas. Even in this they are wrong, totally and obviously wrong. Sir George Etienne Cartier was our first Minister of Militia. Under his guidance the first Militia Act following Confederation was passed. It provides that all males between 18 and 60 shall be "liable" to service. It sets out clearly the manner in which they can be compulsorily enrolled, and the same Act as amended in 1904 goes on to say that the armed forces of this country having been enrolled may be sent anywhere "within or beyond Canada for the defence thereof." This Statute as so amended is still in force in those very terms and could be used today. It is laid aside not because the powers it gives the Government are inadequate—that is to say powers in respect of compulsory enrollment and compulsory despatch overseas. These are quite ample. What is lacking is the right to select, the right to establish boards of inquiry who can make selections on a basis of facts. If the Militia Act is used there is indeed nothing that can be called Selection. The men, after reporting, are chosen by lot, by chance, by hit and miss—a method abounding in inefficiency and injustice.

The hon. member for Kamouraska (Mr. Ernest Lapointe) in a well-constructed speech struggled manfully to uphold an idea which he and his leader have been cultivating—that it was the intention of The Militia Act to limit compulsion to defence within this country, or at most, to defence within this continent. The hon. member's speech was plainly designed for distribution in his province, and I address these words in reply particularly to my French-Canadian friends. A moment ago I quoted from clauses of the Act words which made all males between 18 and 60 "liable" to service and which authorized the Minister of Militia to send them anywhere "within or beyond Canada for the defence thereof." You are being asked to conclude, first, that the word "beyond" has no meaning, or if it has a meaning, its scope is restricted to North America. True, North America is not mentioned, any more than is Mesopotamia but the hon. member argues that those words have been interpreted as not to authorize a despatch of troops overseas. True, he quoted in support two distinguished public figures—Sir Frederick Borden, the Minister of Militia in 1904 when the amended Act was passed, and Sir Sam Hughes. Then somewhat over-inspired by the prestige of these authorities in matters of legal interpretation, he went on to make the following astonishing pronouncement:

> Until a few days ago, I do not think that anybody who has studied the constitutional history of Canada ever expressed the opinion that her militia could be sent overseas by virtue of that Act.

It is unfortunate that the hon. member forgot to inform his hearers that Sir Frederick Borden had at another place in Hansard used language indicating a directly opposite opinion and that Sir Sam Hughes after further study had completely altered his view and declared that under our Militia Act troops can undoubtedly be sent overseas. It is worth explaining also that neither of these two men was a lawyer. Sir Frederick Borden was a Physician and Sir Sam Hughes an Editor.

Let us examine further this edict or verdict of the hon. member for Kamouraska. Nobody, he says, who has studied constitutional history ever expressed an opinion that Canada's troops enrolled under the Militia Act could be sent overseas— not until a few days ago. To whom, I ask, when the amended Act was going through in 1904, would questioners look for guidance in matters of law—to the Minister of Militia, Sir Frederick Borden, or to the Minister of Justice, Sir Charles Fitzpatrick? And Sir Charles Fitzpatrick was asked for guidance and Sir Charles Fitzpatrick responded. He told the House in unmistakable terms, in language limpid clear that under the Act then being debated troops of this country compulsorily enlisted could be sent overseas, even to India, if in the judgment of the Governor General in Council the defence of Canada was being fought overseas. Sir Charles Fitzpatrick stated at that time that the discretion resided solely in the Governor General in Council (that is, the Government) until Parliament later on could pass upon his decision. Yet, in the face of that declaration by the constituted legal authority of Canada when the Act was passed in 1904, and almost in the hearing of that distinguished man, the hon. member told this House that no one ever asserted such a thing until a few days ago.

Mr. Carroll: Does the Solicitor General make a distinction between the power of the Government to send conscripted troops overseas and the power of the Government to send voluntarily enlisted troops overseas?

Mr. Meighen: I make no distinction whatever. The Act makes no distinction; it says that we may enlist troops voluntarily or by conscription, and that after we have enlisted them, we can send them beyond Canada for the defence of Canada. Sir Charles Fitzpatrick said, as any one after a careful reading would have said, that it was a matter for the Government, in the exercise of its discretion, to decide whether it believed the war being fought overseas was a war involving the defence of Canada.

Now I ask, and earnestly ask, hon. members seated around me—I ask particularly hon. members from Quebec—"Do you think that statement of the member for Kamouraska was a fair statement?" And further—"Do you think it was a true statement?" You will find it in days to come scattered through the homes and laneways of your province in the hope that it will incite your compatriots against the Military Service Act. No one, he said, who had studied constitutional history had ever, until now, expressed an opinion that our troops could be sent overseas under the old or the revised Militia Act! That is what the hon. member said no less than three times in his speech. I affirm, and challenge contradiction either right now or later from anyone within sound of my voice, that from the time our first Militia Act was passed in 1868 up to the present hour no student of constitutional history and no constituted legal authority in our country has ever said anything else.

We are told, however, that, even if we have always had, and have today, power to despatch our troops beyond Canada for the defence of Canada, we should not exercise that power. Why? The leader of the Opposition assures us that he is not afraid of an invasion of Canada. The hon. member for Bonaventure (Mr. Marcil) is also brave; he is not afraid of an invasion either. These hon. gentlemen in their predictions—because at best they are only prophecies—are either right or wrong. Whether they are right or wrong I don't know and they don't know, and, as a certainty, no human being knows. But let us come to grips on this question. One or the other is true: either we are in danger of invasion now or later as a result of this war, or we are not in danger. If the first is true, then no question arises; all agree that we should send our men and send them at once. If the second is true, then our defence is being fought out over there, and it is because the right hon. gentleman (Sir Wilfrid Laurier) believes that the armed forces of Britain and of France, Italy and Russia will emerge victorious that he sits comfortably in his seat, untroubled by fears of invasion. That means those nations are fighting out there the defence of Canada. How, then, can he shrink from the duty, which he must surely feel upon his heart, of sending the troops of Canada to sustain our own defence?

I pass on to examine some contentions advanced in support of the amendment moved by the right hon. Opposition leader. It has been a matter of much interest, and indeed of curiosity, to observe the wonderful variety of opinions collected behind this referendum amendment. A referendum amendment is really not an amendment at all. Very definitely it is not a policy: it is a negation of policy. Why has it been adopted as party tactics? Merely as an expedient to avoid facing the issue, and to gather behind the Opposition leader all support, however incongruous, that can be got together. What kind of opinions are behind the amendment? It is moved by the leader of the Opposition, who complains that we have dashed this Bill upon the House too suddenly and too soon. It is seconded by the hon. member for Edmonton (Mr. Oliver), who complains that we have already waited too long; that we should have taken this course and held a referendum a year ago. The leader of the Opposition argues that the Bill will be met with opposition, if not with resistance, on the part of French Canada and will bring about disunion in our country. His seconder, the hon. member for Edmonton, wants in place of this Bill another one which will take all of these 100,000 men out of French Canada alone.

MR. OLIVER: I would like my hon. friend to keep closer to the facts than that. Hansard is my record.

MR. MEIGHEN: I would not have said so if it had not been on

Hansard. The hon. gentleman's words are capable of that interpretation, and of no other. I know he did not employ his language with an intention that that interpretation be applied.

MR. OLIVER: Thank you.

MR. MEIGHEN: He took the ground that this Bill would take men out of Alberta, out of Edmonton constituency, from which enough men had already gone, his idea being to make the Bill unpopular in the constituency of Edmonton. This is what he said, as reported in Unrevised Hansard, page 2520:

> We have been led to believe that a conscription measure would be fair to the country, and as we have done our duty, in a measure, so it would compel the people in other parts of the country to do their duty. Now, that is the kind of conscription measure I want to see, but that is not the kind of conscription measure my hon. friend has brought down.

MR. OLIVER: Hear, hear.

MR. MEIGHEN: He wants to compel those who have not done their duty to do it.

MR. OLIVER: Hear, hear.

MR. MEIGHEN: What does he say on the previous page?

> Given a proper measure of universal military service, and there is equality in the distribution of the burden, an equality that does not exist in the case of voluntary service. . . . If there is not equality of service under the compulsory principle, then, instead of it being a democratic method of meeting a great emergency, it becomes an instrument of tyranny and unfairness in every particular.

Those are his words: "I want a conscription measure," said he, "that provides for equality of service." And how? By taking from areas which have not enlisted voluntarily until we bring about an equality.

MR. OLIVER: Hear, hear.

MR. MEIGHEN: How are we going to get an equality in this country unless in addition to the 8,000 of French-Canadian extraction already enlisted in the province of Quebec we take 100,000 more?

MR. OLIVER: If it requires 100,000 men from the province of Quebec for the province of Quebec to do its share, then certainly take the 100,000 but my hon. friend does not suggest that it does require that.

MR. MEIGHEN: Would 108,000 from French Canada be any more, proportionately, than the present contribution from Alberta, and how can we get an equality unless the contributions are proportionately equal?

MR. OLIVER: I could not say without a pencil and paper. When my hon. friend attempts to make it appear to this House that I said anything which could be construed as stating that all the further military requirements of Canada should be supplied from the province of Quebec, he is using language which has absolutely no foundation, and which is absurd on the face of it.

MR. MEIGHEN: I will leave the House and country to figure out how equality is going to be reached unless contributions are proportionately equal.

MR. OLIVER: Equality is what we want.

MR. MEIGHEN: What I have expressed is an inescapable conclusion from the hon. gentleman's words, and I do not intend that he shall shy away from that conclusion. He used those words for the purpose of currying favour in his own province.

MR. OLIVER: Will the hon. member be good enough not to impute motives to other hon. members of this House?

MR. MEIGHEN: I will not impute dishonourable motives but I have a right to impute motives not dishonourable.

MR. OLIVER: I rise to a point of order. My point of order is that the Solicitor General, or any other hon. member of this House, must take the statements of other hon. members as they are uttered and he has no right to impute any motives.

MR. MEIGHEN: I took the statement as it was uttered. I do not want to change the statement but surely I have a right to argue from it what I believe to be its inevitable conclusion.

MR. PUGSLEY: The Solicitor General entirely ignores what my hon. friend from Edmonton says he said and alleges that my hon. friend from Edmonton made a statement in order to curry favour with the district of Edmonton. I understand that is what my hon. friend complains of?

MR. OLIVER: Yes.

MR. PUGSLEY: Is that in order, Mr. Speaker?

THE DEPUTY SPEAKER: I do not think that the hon. the Solicitor General has imputed motives or has said anything to which the attention of the Speaker should be called.

MR. MEIGHEN: Yes, Mr. Speaker, the reasons presented to hon. members for the purpose of urging adoption of this amendment are incongruous and conflicting. Here is an amendment moved by the leader of the Opposition because he himself is against conscription. It is seconded by the hon. member for Edmonton because he is in favour of conscription. And its first sponsor is the hon. member for Bonaventure (Mr. Marcil) who does not know whether he is in favour of conscription or against it. It must be clear to everyone its purpose is to evade, and not to face manfully, a very great issue at this time. It is to avoid rather than to enforce the performance of duty. The amendment is a refuge of discord—a haven of the disunited. It is not a declaration of faith, it is a declaration of despair. We cannot win a war by referendums.

Do hon. gentlemen realize where they are when they support this proposal? Do they recognize the company they are in? I make appeal to hon. gentlemen opposite, who at other times and under brighter skies may have felt there was some principle behind a referendum, to argue out for themselves whether that principle has any application in a crisis like this. Is the referendum peculiarly suited for war? Is it suited to a time when the best and most deserving of our electorate are overseas, shifting and surging along a battlefront of continental scale, and when only a mere fraction of their number may possibly be counted in the vote? Results of twelve months and more have proved that recruits in numbers anything like those required cannot be obtained by methods of the past. The Toronto *Globe* has said that the voluntary system is as dead as Julius Caesar. Months ago the Liberal press of English-speaking Canada proclaimed that under it we could not get absolutely necessary troops. We have waited until we thought the public of Canada generally had realized that truth, and realized it with such overmastering conviction as to mean general consent to the enactment of a compulsory law. Why confuse the situation by a tricky referendum? Do not hon. gentlemen in their hearts admit that the passing of this amendment would bring joy to friends of Germany in every part of the world? It would be welcomed at Potsdam. It would be supported, were he here, by the head of the German nation himself. It would make headlines of elation in every German newspaper on this and other continents. Such is the company hon. gentlemen are in who support this proposal. Its passing would be a cause of rejoicing to every pool-room loafer, to every movie veteran, to every sporting fan, to all who have shrunk from duty; but it would be a subject of resentment, regret and pain to men who have nobly done their part to preserve the liberty, and uphold the honour, of Canada.

What does this proposal really mean? A referendum on the principle of the Bill! What does that mean? Is it intended that one interrogation shall appear on the ballot:—are you in favour of conscription? Well, first, a conscription law has been in our statutes throughout our history, and for fifty years no Party has uttered a word against it—not even a voice from the wilderness. But think—if only that bald question is to be put, have not voters a right to say, "Tell us what kind of conscription; we cannot answer intelligently until you do: What is to be your method of selection? What classes are going to be called? In what order will you call them? Are you going to insert a provision that there must be equality by provinces?" That last question would be hurled at us by the hon. member for Edmonton himself. There would scarcely be a man entering the poll who would not have some such protest. And they would all be right. We would, therefore, have to submit the entire Bill to a vote. Then a situation just as bad arises. Everyone opposed to conscription votes "No." And scores of thousands who favour conscription vote "No" as well. The hon. member for Edmonton would be first: "Not until you have equality by provinces," is his cry. Another sincerely believes that the classes start too young; another that they start too old. Do hon. gentlemen really suggest that this great measure, on the success of which depends the sustenance of our army in France, depends the support of those who have appealed to us in language we can never forget, appealed to us for months, yes for years, to add to their numbers, to reduce their burdens, if possible to limit their perils—that this Bill, on which so largely depends the honour and security of our country—should be exposed to such improper hazards, to such unfair opposition, as it would encounter under a conscription referendum? We as a people have a right to deliberate, and in a constitutional way to vote, to negative, if we so desire, any policy which is still open for us to decide. But surely the prosecution of this war with the whole might of Canada is not in that category. That question has been passed upon. If there ever was a time for a referendum—which I deny—it was in August, 1914; it is not now. We have committed ourselves as a nation, we have signed the bond, it is for us to discharge the obligation. The prosecution of this war by every effective and honourable means is now a matter only of good faith: 300,000 living men and 20,000 dead are over there, hostages of our good faith. All that remains for us is a choice between fidelity and desertion, between courage and poltroonery, between honour and everlasting shame.

We must rise to the level of our responsibilities. We must not be afraid to lead. Ministers of the Crown have been execrated from end to end of Canada for failure of leadership and all the rest. Many of those who have skulked at home, but who should be at the front, have lampooned the able and overburdened head of this Government, crying out tiresome jargon about failure to lead. Newspaper after newspaper has done the same. Well, here is leadership. Let those who lagged behind and comforted themselves with this monotonous complaint—let them walk up now, close the gap and stand beside the Prime Minister. The people of Canada, we have oft been told, call out to Parliament, to members of this House, for strong and fearless leadership. Are we going to answer that call with our hands in the air crying back to those people: "For heaven's sake, lead us." Such is the amendment we are now asked to support.

Lastly, the shadow of disunion is raised and we are pressed to turn back. One cannot help but observe that those who hold over us this threat are, one and all, opposed to the measure anyway, on other grounds. There will inevitably be difference of opinion, but quite plainly there will be nothing in the nature of schism unless hon. gentlemen are determined to create it. I am as confident as I have ever been of anything in my life that if members of this House, reading and studying this measure, and hearing it debated, will go to their constituents and tell them the meaning, purpose and spirit of this Bill, there will be no possibility whatever of discord or resistance. Why should there be? There is not a clause that is unjust as between provinces, or races, or creeds. Very positively, and very obviously, there is neither intent, nor possibility, of unfairness to the province of Quebec. Never was more anxious care taken in drafting a law. The Minister of Justice, whose home is in Montreal, will be in charge of its administration.

Let us use our reason:—We went into war by resolution of Parliament and we were a unit—not a negative vote! Over there, three years after, the same war still rages, week by week and month by month, with greater and greater intensity. The enemy is adding to his strength. On our sectors reinforcements are failing. The Prime Minister has faithfully portrayed the situation, and his analysis, dependable to a last detail, shows that without this law our divisions will sink before our eyes from four to three, from three to two and perhaps from two to one. Can hon. members in sight of such a prospect threaten to split this nation unless we hold our hand and calmly witness the abandoning of our defenders and the humiliation of our country? One can hardly contemplate anything more wicked, and I cannot believe it will occur. But only by such conduct can there come the disunion of which we are warned by hon. members across the floor.

There is another consideration. If we retrace our steps as these hon. members, under threat of schism demand, and suffer, as we must, consequences which no man can measure, are we not destined to be a divided people then? There may be danger of disunion growing out of a great issue, even when our decision is right; but may there not be still greater danger when our decision is wrong? Regrettable, and worse than regrettable, would be disunion on any line and for any cause, but lamentable beyond parallel and beyond forgiveness would be a disunion born of infidelity to the nation's defenders and the nation's life.

I appeal to our friends opposite, and to those around me as well—for party divisions as we once had them are not just the same today—I appeal to all of every political faith to take the course which alone will command our self-respect, and which will entitle us to the regard of our own people, of our allies, and of generations to come.

CANADA'S NATURAL RESOURCES

Delivered before the Royal Geographical Society, London, England, on June 24, 1918. The author at that time was Canadian Minister of the Interior. The President was in the Chair, and at the close of this speech the Rt. Hon. Walter Long addressed the meeting and expressed thanks on behalf of the Society and of its many guests.

THIS AUDIENCE IS GATHERED under the auspices of an institution of long and distinguished history, and I gratefully acknowledge the kindness by which I am permitted to appear upon its programme. The normal activities of this Society have, as your Secretary has informed me, been interrupted and in important directions suspended by the rude clang of war. It is not the part of Britons, though, to surrender to naked force what has been found to be good, and for that reason your organization keeps its strength and lends its resources to the great cause. "By these things men live," and long may the Royal Geographical Society survive the agony of this conflict and the accursed system which brought it on.

I have had the advantage of a perusal of several issues of your *Journal*—a precaution undertaken, unfortunately, after instead of before my acceptance of the invitation to address you. This perusal has emphatically convinced me of my inability to contribute any material of that scientific and informative character which distinguishes past performances from this platform, and I am free to say that had my inquiry and study preceded my rather hasty acquiescence in your kind proposal, you would have been spared the digression on which I now am launched.

It will be impossible for me to add anything of value or very much of interest to the knowledge of those who hear me in respect of the geography of Canada. Our Governmental activities

87

have been commercial rather than explorative. Our country is young, our territory is vast. The Dominion is indeed in extent something akin to a continent, and in its 3,729,000 square miles of area approximates closely to the dimensions of Europe.

Its more accessible and productive regions have offered such obvious and distinct advantage to the settler that these portions have almost wholly absorbed the attention of our population, so much so that definite information as to our great hinterland is meagre in the extreme. The unexplored area in 1916 is estimated by Mr. Camsell at 900,000 square miles, or 25 per cent. of our entire domain. It stretches with casual interruptions from Hudson's Bay westward to the Yukon and eastward to the Labrador coast. The best I can do is to present with what clearness I may a brief topography of the Dominion and a partial sketch of her possessions. There may be much in what I say characterized by indefiniteness and of the nature rather of indications than of positive ascertainment, but such is necessarily unavoidable in the present state of Canadian prospecting and exploration.

Canada may be likened to a monstrous torso resting on the American Continent, both arms being severed by political divisions. Alaska on the west has gone to the United States, and Newfoundland, the oldest British possession, is still aloof on the east. Nevertheless the area remaining is somewhat larger than the United States, Alaska included.

Speaking broadly, the general slope of the country is northward, nearly two million square miles—or over half—draining into the Arctic Ocean and Hudson's Bay. About one and a half million square miles fall towards the east, draining into the North Atlantic, and something less than half a million square miles on the western coast beyond the Rocky Mountain range drain into the Pacific. Only a comparatively negligible basin, less than 13,000 square miles at the south-west end of the prairies, drains into the Gulf of Mexico.

To obtain a systematized view of Canada's general physical features, and consequently of her mineral contents, it is convenient to make a few bold divisions. In geological formation the maritime provinces of Prince Edward Island, Nova Scotia, New Brunswick and the south-east portion of Quebec constitute the northern end of the Appalachian mountain system. The chief basic constituent is pre-Cambrian rock—covered of course in the main with later and more fertile deposits—and within this geological province are found minerals which inhabit the Appalachian system along the Atlantic States and which have added so much to their wealth. Coal, iron, and gold predominate, the first-named being, up to the present, of greatest importance commercially. Their significance in the national balance-sheet I will call attention to later. The next geological province is the lowlands of the St. Lawrence basin, draining from south, north, and west into this mighty river. This formation is Palæozoic. Minerals found and the nature and productiveness of the surface generally are true to the record everywhere of that formation. Over this territory is now spread the larger portion of Canada's population.

What I might describe as the main framework geographically and geologically of the Dominion is the Laurentian Plateau. This is a tremendous V-shaped territory stretching from Newfoundland and Labrador on the Atlantic coast across Quebec and Ontario around the southern basin of Hudson's Bay, and thence northerly, and to some extent westerly, toward the vast northland. As every one knows, the rock formation of this plateau is of granite character and of pre-Cambrian age. It is widely believed that at one time the great mass, if not all, of North America was constituted by this formation, the overlying strata and deposit now existing being a product of succeeding ages of erosion, volcanic action and vegetation. This pre-Cambrian granite abounds throughout Canada in minerals, viz., in copper-nickel, cobalt, silver, zinc, lead, and iron. A tongue of these rocks projects southerly into the State of New York, and supports there large and varied mineral industries of that State. Another tongue crosses southerly from Canada into Michigan, Wisconsin, and Minnesota, and contributes to these States the Michigan copper mines and their great Lake Superior iron ranges. It may be of interest to know that products of these mines, though they are out of Canada, contribute more as yet to the traffic of our great lakes than even the tremendous western wheatfields. Within this plateau in Canada are found the great nickel mines of Sudbury in Central Ontario, from which mines the British Empire and our Allies in this war have drawn almost all their nickel supply, so vital now to military and naval equipment. Close by are the great Cobalt silver deposits, and further east are corundum deposits of Ontario and molybdenite and asbestos deposits of Quebec. These latter, and as well the nickel, are respectively the world's largest reserves. On the extreme east, though in Newfoundland, are the world's greatest iron mines— mines which, in furnishing material for our steel production, have contributed vastly to the war effort of Canada. All great minerals known to occur in the developed southern edge of this plateau have been noted by explorers in northern reaches of the same formation. Copper in particular seems to be abundantly prevalent in our northern and western expanses, so much so that discoveries are heard of from almost every quarter, wherever the prospector travels. Eskimos, who are located at various points north-westerly from Hudson's Bay to the Arctic, have their spears, snow-knives, ice-chisels, fishhooks, and arrow-heads beaten out of pure native copper, and even use copper tops for their smoking pipes. Their stories agree with the explorers' as to vast quantities of native copper along our Arctic coast and on neighbouring islands. Within the present populated area, however, there have recently been discovered deposits of this metal of present commercial importance. One mine lately opened at Scist Lake, north-west of The Pas, is so rich in copper that ore has been shipped in substantial quantities, 40 miles drawn by wagons to the Saskatchewan River, 190 miles taken by barges to The Pas, and thence 1500 miles by rail to a smelter in British Columbia; and after carrying this burden of transportation so rich is the ore that it yields a profit.

The Atikokan iron range just west of Lake Superior, and the Michipicoten mining district north of the same lake, are con- clusive evidence of the presence of commercial iron in northern as well as southern reaches of this plateau. Immense deposits of these various minerals will in good time be uncovered.

The meagre character of our information as to earth contents of our country, may be judged from the fact that our nickel mines just referred to were unknown until about twenty years ago, when they were accidentally discovered in the construction of a railway. The premier silver camp of Canada at Cobalt, although only a few miles from one of the earliest routes of travel and from silver-lead deposits known for 150 years, remained undiscovered until fifteen years ago.

West and south of the Laurentian Plateau is a great interior plain constituting the larger portion of Manitoba, Saskatchewan, and Alberta. This territory is principally agricultural and rests upon a rock formation of later Cretaceous age. It contains coal in great abundance, as well as mineral clays and cement material.

On our farthest west comes the fifth and last geological province: the Cordillera. This is a northern projection of the great Cordillera range which extends over the whole western coast of North America and covers a territory in Canada 1300 miles north and south by about 400 miles in width. Included in it is the mountainous region of British Columbia and the Yukon. This entire range stands unparalleled anywhere for the continuity and extent of its mineral resources, and in Canada as well as in Alaska are to be found within its folds the same deposits of gold, coal, copper, lead, and zinc which characterize the entire system throughout its continental length. Values of production are constantly growing, but possibly in no portion of Canada is the extent of the unprospected so vast as in this territory. This range has given to the Dominion its majestic system of mountains which constitutes one of the great tourist attractions of the world. The Rockies range in height from 10,000 to 13,700 feet, but the highest known point in Canada is Mount Logan of the St. Elias Range in the Yukon, which rises to an altitude of 19,539 feet, or three and two-third miles.

It may interest some to recall that 100 miles west of the Cordillera, and only 25 to 30 north of the Peace River, is a plateau 10,000 square miles in area and about 2500 feet higher than surrounding land. Though close to a much-navigated river, only one white man has ever crossed this plateau. There is a lake on it 60 miles long, never yet even mapped. The heights swarm with caribou, and it is called Caribou Plateau. There is another north of Lake Athabasca. It is 47,000 square miles in extent. One point in it at the north is a paradise for Indian hunters, who gather there every fall. This plateau also only one white man has ever crossed; he was Samuel Stearne, who traversed it twice 145 years ago.

It is a tendency of people far removed in point of distance to form exaggerated notions of the outstanding physical features of a country, and as a consequence I find that our Dominion suffers somewhat in the eyes of strangers from erroneous ideas as to its rigorous climate. Canada is indeed a northern land, and there are undoubtedly large portions of its Arctic and sub-Arctic territory within which by reason of shortness of seasons and extremity of climate ordinary pursuits of life cannot be followed, but the proportion of this territory and its effect in an estimation of the capital assets of the country are not nearly so great as is the prevailing impression. While the atmosphere as a rule grows colder as one proceeds northward, it must be remembered that elevation as well as latitude must be taken into account in arriving at natural conditions governing climate. The elevation of the great body of our western country, for example, is thousands of feet lower than it is south of the United States boundary, and climate moderates as lower levels are reached. It is stated on competent authority after careful study, that spring in the Peace River district—a territory of vast extent and fertility—in Central and Northern British Columbia and in Alberta, begins earlier than it does further south, and indeed advances south-east at a rate of 250 miles per day. Summers in the north-west are warm, and, as civilization advances, are not unduly short. Not only is elevation lower—accounting in part for this phenomenon—but mountains on the north as a rule are also much lower, and through their passes blow Chinook breezes from the Pacific. The presence of almost innumerable lakes, many of them of great extent, throughout our north-west, exercises as well a moderating influence on climate.

The value of Canadian agricultural production, as well as its promise, is too well known to justify elaboration by me. It is my purpose, though, to say a word as to certain of our resources with regard to which less definite impressions exist.

Coal deposits while very far indeed from being fully explored, may now be estimated on a reasonably safe basis. So far as discovery has yet proceeded, we do not appear to possess anthracite coal in quantities comparable with those enjoyed, for example, by Great Britain or by the United States. We have, however, even of this variety, quite substantial quantities. Located in Western Alberta, in the basin of Cascade River, are deposits of anthracite estimated at 400 million tons. Total tonnage of anthracite in Canada appears to be approximately two thousand one hundred million. This is less than 20 per cent. of anthracite tonnage estimated to be in reserve in the British Isles.

Coming to bituminous coal, our reserves are undoubtedly immense. The Province of Alberta alone, which is indeed a territory veritably charged with this mineral, is underlain to the extent of about 30,000 square miles with bituminous and semi-bituminous coal. Nova Scotia is, of course—now at all events—our greatest coal-producing province; and indeed, Canada, measured by the standard of production rather than of reserve, cannot be said to stand as yet in the front rank of coal countries. War conditions, or war necessities, are proving the mother of invention, and there can be little doubt that the not distant future will see a marked advance in coal mining. For the present it may be worth while, although by no means in the nature of new information to members of this Society, for me to emphasize the stupendous reserves which lie in the bosom of our Dominion. Including only anthracite and bituminous coals, the best estimate available places our reserves at 285,000 million tons. Including lignite, which is already in use, and for greater use of which the Provincial and Dominion Governments are organizing, the total deposit may be placed at 1,234,000 million tons. This constitutes about 70 per cent. of the entire coal reserves of the British Empire, and of this more than four-fifths is in the single province of Alberta. The British Empire is said to contain one quarter of the world's coal reserves. Much of this great natural wealth in Canada is inland, and may not experience rapid development, but, on the other hand, there are vast supplies close to water transportation on both east and west shores which will share more and more in foreign trade. Another feature of importance is that not a single province is without some supply, and only a limited though thickly populated territory in Central Canada is far removed from larger sources of this fuel.

Closely allied in modern commercial calculations with coal is water-power. Here the Dominion stands in a position of great natural advantage, and what is perhaps of more immediate consequence, in a position of relatively rapid present development. It is a matter of much interest, as well as of stupendous importance, that the great hydrodynamic powers of Canada are located profusely throughout the very territory which does not enjoy the advantage of coal deposits. Throughout Southern Ontario and Quebec, and Manitoba as well, are to be found as superbly placed and as mighty water-powers as exist in the world. It is not worth while in our time to discuss all water-power resources of the Dominion, for many of them are situate in districts which at present are without substantial population; but confining ourselves to the peopled parts of Canada, a fairly thorough survey has been made by competent engineers under the Water Power Branch of the Federal Interior Department, and this survey places our potential commercial water-powers at a capacity of 18,805,000 H.P. Of this total there has already been developed 1,735,600 H.P., or a little less than 10 per cent. Such an achievement is, in my humble judgment, creditable to Canadian resource and Governmental activity, especially when regard is had to paucity of population and to the short period over which operations have proceeded. Water-power development in Ontario and its control are something from which every Canadian can take confidence and hope. Of this 18 million odd potential H.P. in settled portions of Canada, a little less than 6 million is in Ontario, and 6 million is in Quebec. The falls are all within easy transmission distance of great industrial centres, and, properly directed and co-ordinated with our other fuel resources, constitute a magnificent basis upon which the future industrial progress of these great provinces rests. A single horse-power is estimated for power purposes as of the fuel value of ten tons of coal. There is being used in Canada in water-power the equivalent of an annual consumption of 14,600,000 tons of coal, or not far below our present coal importation. Coal is destructible and exhaustible; water-power is indestructible. Among exports of Canada to-day is an item of 275,000 H.P. or the equivalent of practically three million tons of coal, which amount almost represents total anthracite importations into the Dominion. Exported power is being utilized by United States industries for war purposes.

Perhaps I might be permitted to place on your records a table showing available and developed power in settled portions of each of our respective provinces, viz.:

Province	Power available	Power developed
Ontario	5,800,000	789,466
Quebec	6,000,000	520,000
Nova Scotia	100,000	21,412
New Brunswick	300,000	13,390
Prince Edward Island	3,000	500
Manitoba		76,250
Saskatchewan	3,500,000	100
Alberta		32,860
British Columbia	3,000,000	269,620
Yukon	100,000	12,000
Total	18,803,000	1,735,598

An interesting feature is that 78 per cent. of total water-power now in use is publicly controlled. Of the balance, 14 per cent. is consumed by pulp and paper manufacturers situated mainly at points more remote from industrial centres, and the remaining 8 per cent. is used in electro-chemical and similar processes. The electro-chemical industry appears to be due for rapid advancement in Canada. Its products at present are, I believe, almost wholly used for war purposes. Indeed, through Provincial and Dominion control, priority is given to war productions in allotment of all our developed water-power. The Dominion stands second in the world, and not far below the United States, in the wealth of its hydrodynamic natural resources. There are no three countries in Europe whose water-power potentialities added together would equal those of Canada. When it is considered that one-fifth of our railway tonnage consists now in haulage of coal, some idea may be obtained of the importance of water resources in the commercial expansion of our country.

I would not venture to discuss before scientific men any explanation of the extraordinary abundance of waterfalls, but, briefly put, my rough understanding is this: the phenomena of the glacial age in their retreat from the earth's surface necessarily lingered last in its northern zones, and these waterfalls are the immediate progeny of those phenomena—a liaison between us and those far distant times.

If there is one possession more than another the value of which we have failed to realize ourselves, it is our forest wealth. There are no good guesses as to the extent of this resource, for the reason that forest exploration even to this day is singularly incomplete. The best qualified experts we have, while reluctant to hazard an estimate, place the extent of tree-covered territory at between 500 million and 600 million acres, of which perhaps 300 million acres are covered with merchantable lumber. Ravages of fire accompanying settlement have devastated vast areas and destroyed a deplorably large proportion of this element of our national capital. It is true burnt-over mileage is in process of reforestation, but progress is slow. However, through the activities of provincial and federal authorities, organization for control, conservation, and proper utilization of our forests is becoming more and more efficient. Forest area is spread over the length and breadth of the Dominion, except perhaps in the very farthest north, and is everywhere except there in quantities and locations commercially valuable. It is noteworthy that even in the older provinces of Nova Scotia and New Brunswick the greater portion of land is still tree-covered, such area in Nova Scotia being two-thirds of the whole, and in New Brunswick about four-fifths. The Province of Quebec is the most richly endowed; and so great is the entire supply that utilization of our forests for lumber, fuel, pulp, and paper, though substantial and great enough to constitute one of the foremost of our exports and source of wealth, is, even under present conditions of administration, very substantially less than their annual increase from natural causes alone. The pulp industry of Quebec in particular is extending with great rapidity, but as yet it is estimated—though with a degree of uncertainty due to inadequacy of our investigations—that depletion by use is not more than one-sixth of natural growth. In farther western provinces the proportion will be less. British Columbia has, as is well known, an empire of forest wealth. The trees in that province reach majestic proportions and attain a venerable age. Douglas fir, which is the principal variety, grows at times to a height of 300 feet and to a diameter of 15 feet. It is true that these dimensions are exceptional, but elevations of 250 feet and diameters of from 6 to 10 feet are common. Sitka spruce—a variety which flourishes along the coast—has proven of superior value for aeroplane production, and is now being utilized in substantial quantities for that purpose. Large islands on the Pacific coast are especially fortunate, and annual growth in that region, due to climatic and soil conditions, is much more rapid than in other portions of the Dominion. For purposes of preservation, silviculture and re-forestation, forestry branches have been established by the Dominion Government and by most provincial administrations. A total of 159 million acres have been allocated to forest reserves, and over these areas organizations of the various Governmental branches exercise supervision. Their activities are directed first to protection of their respective reserves from forest fires, and in this respect have, particularly in recent years, achieved a con-siderable degree of success. The total number of fires during 1916 was 891 as compared with 1455 in 1915 and 1986 in 1914. The total area burnt over in the last fully recorded year was 116,310 acres, of which area only 2000 acres could be classed as merchantable timber. The Dominion organization also oversees lumber operations and wood cutting within other areas, and in established reserves has commenced a system of reforestation, though as yet on a modest scale. Nurseries have been instituted, and last year some seven million trees were distributed for planting free of cost to farmers on the western plains.

If one of my listeners takes up a railway map of Canada he will be impressed with the comparative narrowness of the belt of settlement which stretches across 3500 miles from ocean to ocean. There appears to be an almost illimitable area of barren land— and indeed barren land it is geographically called—stretching away toward the vastness of the Arctic. There is, however, one feature of this territory to which it is fitting now to call attention. The land is by no means barren. It supports a wealth of plant and animal life, and no barren land can do that. The few explorers who have visited these regions, commencing with Stearne in the latter half of the eighteenth century, report very enthusiastically not only on the splendour of its summer climate, but on the richness in many parts of its plant and animal production. Its fur resources are enormous, and it is not improbable that the animal product of this territory will yet become commercially valuable. All explorers unite in affirming that the country is literally covered with enormous flocks of caribou. Mr. Thompson Seton declares that at a most conservative estimate there must be 30 millions of these animals inhabiting those western northlands. They are said to be easily domesticated. They weigh from 100 lbs. to 400 lbs., and when slaughtered their meat equals the best of beef. It is not impossible that post-war conditions as to meat supply and as to transportation will direct attention to this resource. Musk ox also are present in large numbers. The black fox is, of course, already a subject of domestic production, and fur-farming promises to constitute a stable industry.

A word now as to Governmental control. Canadian industrial expansion has proceeded chiefly along lines of private initiative and enterprise. The stimulus of individual profit remains, in almost every field, the most potent force in our development. Every motive of honour and of interest enjoins that that stimulus be not blighted or destroyed. There is no spirit of confiscation abroad among Canadian people or Canadian public men. Such of our resources as from time to time pass from public ownership into private hands are thereafter subjected to control, only that waste and a locking-up for selfish and speculative ends may be avoided, and by no means that their legitimate earning power may be checked. Dictates of wise policy have suggested that our invaluable water-powers—an asset of a clearly distinctive character—should be to the utmost possible extent not only state-owned and controlled, but state-developed and operated. All arguments that go anywhere to support Government monopoly apply with peculiar force to water-powers. The long years required in production of a forest crop render forest supervision also a proper sphere of Government activity. But private enterprise has and will have in Canada abundant opportunity. No just right of invested capital is now being disturbed or will be disturbed. While our people realize that in the evolution of industry the tendency is, in some spheres at least, for units to collect and grow larger and larger, ultimately maturing by slow degrees into a single unit and into state proprietorship and operation, still, while that is realized, there is no spirit of rampant or headlong socialism in possession of the Canadian mind. There will always be British fair play. Capital is as safe in Canada as in any country on earth.

I have recounted some material resources to which the Dominion is heir, but I would fail indeed to represent that country if I did not tell you of another inheritance which she prizes most of all: the full free stature of nationhood, with equality of citizenship and equality of opportunity into which she has grown under the ægis of the British Crown. That heritage is the Ark of the Covenant to Canada as to every British community, and every piece and pillar, every line and letter of it she will guard with her life. And let me say this more, and I am a proud man to say it now at this very hour of destiny when the truth which I express means the most: Canada is a faithful child of these islands. Crossed with the blood of your great ally France, and influenced industrially by the almost overwhelming current of the vast Republic that surges to the south, Canada none the less is British, sternly, dependably British. In feeling and in thought, in sentiment, in aspiration, in the sense of her mission in this world, Canada is British—never more British than now. She believes and always wants to believe that Britain stands for real democracy. Our country is unitedly, determinately democratic. She hopes and expects that out of the welter of this war of democracy, a war in which she strains, as in honour she must, every fibre and muscle of her half-grown frame—she hopes that out of it all there will come not so much avenues to greater masses of wealth, but a wider area of opportunity, an improvement of living conditions, a higher general conception of public duty, a releasing of human energy for the pursuits of science and art—an advance for democracy all round over the whole universal line, and an advance commensurate with the cost.

RESPONSE TO A WELCOME HOME

Delivered before a large outdoor gathering in the Town of St. Marys, Ontario, on August 16, 1920, in response to a number of addresses. The occasion was a welcome back of the speaker, as Prime Minister, to his home surroundings, by the people of St. Marys and neighbouring countryside.

VERY OFTEN IT HAS BEEN MY LOT to address audiences of my fellow-citizens, but so different is this occasion from any other within my experience, and so profoundly am I moved by what has been said and done today, that there is danger of emotions becoming stronger than will, and the discharge of duty next to impossible. It is not wholly a constraint born of knowledge that the path I must travel in my remarks is necessarily narrow, not just a feeling that most fields of discussion are forbidden; indeed, not so much a barrenness of topic as a sense of fullness of memory, a crowding to the front of all the past seeking room in one's mind at once out of the vista of these twenty, thirty, yes forty years.

When accepting the invitation of your Mayor and the Reeve of Blanshard and the President of your Board of Trade to be their guests, I had no conception at all that anything so magnificent as this was in contemplation. The extent of your preparations, the vast amount of organization and hard work it has entailed, the very dimensions of this event and the overwhelming kindness of it all quite overpower me.

I have met this afternoon playmates of some decades ago, boys with whom I shared a desk at school, neighbours of the old days on the farm. Everything seems to have been ordered, and everybody seems to have come, necessary to bring back into one great day all the happy associations of youth.

No one is prouder than I to be a British subject, no one more thrilled by the splendid history and heritage that is ours as a member of the great British Commonwealth—and no one more resolved that we never lose our attachment to the "sceptred Isle" and "happy breed of men." Nevertheless, I am glad above all things today in being born a Canadian, nor could one have conceived of a more fortunate birth or a bringing-up more healthful and wholesome than was provided for me in this garden spot of old Ontario. How very little you and I reared in this countryside have been denied at the hands of a bountiful Nature.

The hardships of the pioneer had been well overcome before my time. Privations of life had been removed. The stubborn turf had been cleared, the woods had fallen and good old British stock had planted themselves and turned a forest into a smiling land. Schools and churches were as numerous as they are today. Libraries were available for all, not perhaps in convenience but within reach and good in quality and teaching. Every home had its quota of books; there was no plethora, but there was sufficient real literature to wake the hunger of the mind. It is in truth better that there was not so much as to dissipate the conviction that books are a prize and a treasure. These circumstances, linked with the supreme advantage of a good home, are about all of value that a youth can hope to possess, could he choose for himself his nativity and environment—those things which go so far to determine his destiny in life.

It has been said by the Provincial Treasurer[1], the honour and generosity of whose presence I want publicly to acknowledge, that a tendency exists today unfair in its hostility to men in public office. Just previous to his utterance I was giving inward expression to the opinion that no human being, and certainly not myself, could ever hope to be worthy of the tribute being paid me here and the words of eulogy employed. There is not so vast a chasm between one man and another in this world as many people think. Only a short distance, bridged mainly by harder work, and sometimes by better fortune, separates those who occupy positions of distinction from those who perform tasks of undoubted worth in humbler walks of life. Never could

[1] Hon. Peter Smith.

I hope to reach any pinnacle of achievement which would for a moment entitle me to the sentiments spoken this afternoon; but if that is true it is just as true, as stated by our friend, the Treasurer, that while we who can be called, for the time being, fortunate, merit not many of the good things said about us, we are just as innocent of a large proportion of the frailties and misdemeanours charged against us.

These are days of censoriousness, unrest, discontent and even disorder, a condition which has become epidemic the world over. As yet it reflects itself here in Canada in only a minor and lighter form, but in such times it is particularly true that grave results are bound to flow from an attitude of antagonism of one class of the community toward another and of all classes toward those in authority. It is a phenomenon which has followed in the wake of every great war in the past and has precipitated itself upon this afflicted generation to a degree unparalleled for many years. I hope I am not speaking words of delusion in expressing a belief that as respects Canada the crest of this evil wave has been passed. With good reason it may be hoped that here in our country, a veritable land of Canaan in a troubled world, we shall be first to taste the sweets of a return to a better harmony and sanity. I believe that already softer winds are blowing and a brighter sun is shining, and that if each in his own sphere holds high his head and keeps steady his thinking, we will not suffer, as it looked a short time ago we might, the agony which other nations have so long and so bitterly endured.

One thing upon which we can rely is the intellectual health and moral stability of our people. If this foundation holds—and it never was better in comparison with other populations than now—we need have no fears as to our future. Out of the goodness and greatness of our country and the preponderating wisdom of her councils, out of the hard, dependable common sense of our citizens, out of the zeal and pluck of a dauntless breed of men, there will come triumph over the infection of unrest and disorder and all vicissitudes that beset an advancing civilization, just as certainly as there has come triumph over the forces of war.

My last word must be one of simple thanks to the people of

this town and the townships around, and particularly of the old Anderson neighbourhood where childhood days were spent; to all from far and near I extend my deep and lasting gratitude. Do take home the assurance that the toil you have expended so liberally and the kindness you have shown so lavishly have made an indelible impression upon me.

There are many faces we miss in this throng—many who in the years since I lived among you have passed to the Beyond. Some have surrendered their lives in the war lately closed— surrendered them in the same gallant way as did the young man[1] named in honour by Mr. Martin[2], who truly was one of my treasured friends. Their names and their deeds we never can forget. But none the less, St. Marys is St. Marys still. It is the old family home, and there cling to it endearing recollections which can circle around no other place on earth. This is the home of boyhood and young manhood, the home where first were learned those simple truths last to fade from the mind, the home of earliest friendships the most sacred and inseverable of all, the home around which linger memories of brothers and sisters now far away and of one generation which has gone forever. Time changes much. It destroys and builds again, but the attachments and affections I have described abide to the end.

> Love is not love
> Which alters when it alteration finds.

This event will be an inspiration to me, a new starting point from which will date another season of labour, another and better effort, which if it does not result—and it will not—in achievement that wins the approval of all my fellow-citizens, should at least merit a fair measure of assent and be such, I trust, as to deserve general recognition that my motives were unselfish, my labour unstinted, my conduct unstained, and that at all times I was animated only by a desire to serve my native land.

[1] Lieut. W. J. Wright, B.A., late Principal of St. Marys Collegiate Institute.

[2] S. K. Martin, B.A., formerly Principal of St. Marys Collegiate Institute.

LIBERTY AND LAW

Delivered in London, England, at Gray's Inn Hall, at a Dinner given by the Treasurer and Benchers of Gray's Inn, June 20, 1921.

EVER SINCE I RECEIVED an invitation of this Society to meet here His Majesty's Judges and Lords of Appeal, I have looked forward with unusual pleasure to the event. No honour could be more prized by one who has spent some years in practice at the Bar—and my years were arduous though far too few—than that which you are conferring upon me tonight. This learned and honourable Society has been a bright palace of the lawyer's vision in every British country from the days of Bacon until now. To its Bench and membership I feel a sense of lasting gratitude, but the institution itself has a significance and a dignity apart wholly from the respect which must attach to the fleeting incumbents of the one or the transient tenants of the other. It is your desire, I know, that the distinction you offer shall be held to come from this ancient foundation, as it is mine to receive it as filling the high office which for the time is mine.

A few years ago the then Prime Minister of the United Kingdom (Mr. Asquith), addressing an assembly similar to this, remarked that a hundred years had passed since a practising barrister had reached, in this country, the post of highest responsibility in politics. At the same time he commented upon the large number of gentlemen of the long robe who, through all of England's history, had served the State in other offices with fidelity and success. In the Dominion of Canada, in other Dominions, in the United States, as indeed, in all countries where Parliamentary Government or its prototype prevails,—and Parliamentary Government is a British development and legacy— we have witnessed the same contribution of lawyers to public service as has been characteristic of the Motherland. Perhaps the most conspicuous illustration is the United States. It may be doubted whether any nation in the world has ever been served by a long line of chief executives of such unfailing capacity and patriotism as the Presidents of the Republic. A great majority of them have been drawn from the legal profession. In Canada five of my eight predecessors—and this is not said as an incentive to migration to the Dominion—five of my eight predecessors were in active practice at the Bar before being called to office.

It would be presumption to imply that professional attainments are indispensable, or nearly indispensable, to usefulness in public life,—a score of great names chiselled not far from here would repel such an assertion forever—but it is not easy to understand British institutions without some knowledge of the history of British law. The two streams of law and politics have flowed commingled, all through the centuries. They started from the same fount and have expanded by the same accretions; they have encountered with the same spirit varying currents of time and circumstance; their course has been directed less by considerations of symmetry and logic than by wise regard for the stern lessons of experience. The body of law thus developed, of living growing common law and of statute law, and the political institutions thus matured, have become an inestimable boon to mankind.

People of other countries who misunderstand British traditions tell us that we have no constitution. Canada, they admit, has the British North America Act; Australia, the Commonwealth Act; and South Africa, the South Africa Act; and these may be called constitutions; but Great Britain has none, they say, and the Empire has none. Well, there is more in the constitution of Canada than is contained in the British North America Act, and the fabric of this Empire is held in place by vital, and to us perfectly understandable, constitutional principles. What are constitutional principles? They are the common law of Parliaments. They bear something of the same relation to the charter of a State that common law bears to statute law. They are injunctions taught by experience, and matured by practice into authoritative conventions. They grow to have a more binding force, a higher sanction even than law. It is because of respect for the majesty of constitutional right—something incomprehensible to foreign critics of our system—that we of the British Commonwealth of Nations have been able to get along as one. We legislate each for ourselves unfettered; we advise through separate Councils a common Sovereign; we confer together in order better to understand the wider overriding common interest; we find that between a sense of independence and a sense of unity there is no clash, but harmony. On these principles our own league of nations has survived, and it has served the world wonderfully well.

I said that constitutional principles evolved until they attained an authority higher than law itself. If, for example, we must speak merely from the dictionary of law, we might say that the Parliament of the United Kingdom which passed the Canadian Act of Confederation could amend that Act of its own motion even to-day. If so it would be within its legal competence to impair, or indeed to destroy, the powers of our various legislatures and of the Parliament of Canada. But everyone knows that such a proceeding is as far beyond the constitutional right of your Parliament here as the Royal Veto is beyond effective revival. Everybody knows that such a step would never be dreamed of, and if taken would never be respected. The statutory translation of a Parliamentary Address from a self-governing Dominion, praying for a modification of its charter, is but a circuitous method of legislation, which, with our contempt for anomaly, we adopt until we find a better. The forms of law may remain after the spirit has departed, but the silent voice of constitutional right keeps every unit of our system in its proper place and orbit. That is why we are many nations but one Empire, an Empire that after a thousand years sees no westering sun, but is witnessing now what Victor Hugo called *la jeunesse de la vieillesse*.

As lawyers we are traditionists, but statesmanship knows no law of mortmain. If we neither miss nor misconceive their implications, there is wisdom in the *dicta* of an American jurist[1] that "the present has the right to govern itself so far as it can,"

[1] Mr. Justice Holmes, *Collected Legal Papers*, pp. 139, 211.

and that "continuity with the past is only a necessity and not a duty." Rashness and inconsequence are alien to the British tradition. "Reform," though, was the advice of him who was the glory of Gray's Inn[1], "reform without bravery or scandal of former times or persons"; and he advised us "as well to create good precedents as to follow them," and to remember to "ask counsel of both times; of the ancient time what is best, and of the latter time what is fittest." There could be no better precepts for British statesmanship.

[1] Bacon, *Essays*, Of Great Place. Bacon was successively Student, Ancient, Barrister, Bencher and Reader; and became Treasurer of Gray's Inn in 1608.

THE GLORIOUS DEAD

Delivered in France at Thelus Military Cemetery, Vimy Ridge, on the occasion of the unveiling of the Cross of Sacrifice, July 3, 1921.

THE GREAT WAR IS PAST; the war that tried through and through every quality and mystery of the human mind and the might of human spirit; the war that closed, we hope for ever, the long, ghastly story of the arbitrament of men's differences by force; the last clash and crash of earth's millions is over now. There can be heard only sporadic conflicts, the moan of prostrate nations, the cries of the bereaved and desolate, the struggling of exhausted peoples to rise and stand and move onward. We live among the ruins and echoes of Armageddon. Its shadow is receding slowly backward into history.

At this time the proper occupation of the living is, first, to honour our heroic dead; next, to repair the havoc, human and material, which surrounds us; and, lastly, to learn aright and apply with courage the lessons of the war.

Here in the heart of Europe we meet to unveil a memorial to our country's dead. In earth which has resounded to the drums and tramplings of many conquests, they rest in the quiet of God's acre with the brave of all the world. At death they sheathed in their hearts the sword of devotion, and now from oft-stricken fields they hold aloft its cross of sacrifice, mutely beckoning those who would share their immortality. No words can add to their fame, nor so long as gratitude holds a place in men's hearts can our forgetfulness be suffered to detract from their renown. For as the war dwarfed by its magnitude all contests of the past, so the wonder of human resource, the splendour of human heroism, reached a height never witnessed before.

Ours we thought prosaic days, when great causes of earlier times had lost their inspiration, leaving for attainment those things which demanded only the petty passing inconveniences of the hour. And yet the nobility of manhood had but to hear again the summons of duty and honour to make response which shook the world. Danger to the treasury of common things— for when challenged these are most sacred of all—danger to them ever stirred our fathers to action, and it has not lost its appeal to their sons.

France lives and France is free, and Canada is the nobler for her sacrifice to help free France to live. In many hundreds of plots throughout these hills and valleys, all the way from Flanders to Picardy, lie fifty thousand of our dead. Their resting-places have been dedicated to their memory forever by the kindly grateful heart of France, and will be tended and cared for by us in the measure of the love we bear them. Above them are being planted the maples of Canada, in the thought that her sons will rest the better in shade of trees they knew so well in life. Across the leagues of the Atlantic the heartstrings of our Canadian nation will reach through all time to these graves in France; we shall never let pass away the spirit bequeathed to us by those who fell; "their name liveth for evermore."

EDUCATIONAL VALUES AND IDEALS

Delivered before the University of Edinburgh, on receiving the honorary degree of Doctor of Laws, July 18, 1921.

I AM EAGER TO TELL YOU in simple words, and without undue superlatives, of the sense of pride and gratitude with which I accept this honour at your hands. There are many fine things which we have been forbidden to covet by the lawgiver at Sinai, but an honorary degree from Edinburgh was not included in the list. Nothing could have been more prized. Indeed, the only reason it was not coveted was that the possibility of receiving such a distinction had not entered my dreams. To know that it has actually come leads me to the conclusion that, after all, there is some advantage in living a long way off. There are not many amaranthine wreaths that come by way of unearned increment, but this surely is one.

Scottish Universities are ancient foundations, and we have had enough Scots among us in Canada to teach us why this should be so. Those intrepid adventurers, half warrior and half tillsman, who first raised the standard of civilization in this country, had to overcome almost every obstacle that man and nature could marshal. They found a rigorous climate and a rugged obstinate soil; they lived in the midst of enemies. But they and their descendants created out of a rough, defiant wilderness this marvel of industry, this land of learning, this home of culture. When the Scot transferred himself to Canada he repeated there what his ancestors had achieved at home. He did not choose the soil of easiest tillage, very often the reverse; but he was building for his children; his care was for generations to come. Some of our provinces owe their settlement in large degree to his courage. Nor was his mind centred on the pursuit of wealth and comfort. More perhaps than any other race the Scots of early days in Canada set their hearts on education, and it was a rule of their lives that, whatever else might be denied them, they would lay foundations upon which their children could erect in the new land that system of intellectual discipline and development which had been the pride of their fathers in the old. It was a custom of those families to select the son of greatest promise, or more than one if by any means they could, and at whatever cost, whatever sacrifice, to give those sons every advantage which Universities of their own, or even of this country, could afford. It is because of the stern idealism of such families that we have had good schools in the Dominion almost as long as we have had settlement. We are in the habit, as people are in every country, of pointing to increase of production and trade, to triumphs of engineering and construction, to the administration of our law; and nothing is easier than to find immediate causes or policies to which good results can be traced. But the simple and useful truth is this: whatever of moral and intellectual virility Canada enjoys, and she has much, not in her cities alone and around her cathedrals and colleges, but out on her frontiers and in her country homes,—whatever she enjoys of that moral and intellectual virility which is the real parent of every achievement, she owes to the severe self-discipline, the passion for education of her pioneers.

This explains a fact which already all of you know, all of you who take interest in the Dominion; it is the early growth of our seats of higher learning. Even before Canada received its present political institutions there were established several Universities. Those institutions were modelled pretty much after yours. My own Alma Mater, Toronto University, owes its inception to the energy and devotion to learning of a Scotsman. Compared with this ancient foundation its tradition is short, but when one remembers that the British flag has flown over Canada for only a hundred and sixty years, a University with a charter a century old is no longer juvenile. It has grown to extraordinary dimensions, and is now, I believe, if measured by the number of students within its pale, one of the largest in the Empire.

The preoccupations of a new country are, as you know, intensely practical; and institutions of learning like all other institutions, moulded as they are by national temper, have in such a country greater tendency to concentrate on the practical than they would have in older lands. I hope that tendency will not drive too far. I hope that the example of Edinburgh will again be contagious, that the example of other grand old Universities in these Islands will keep us right. I do trust that all this glamour of the practical will never be allowed to obscure the lofty but fundamental purpose of every seat of learning: the enlargement of the mind, the cultivation of the understanding, the purifying of taste. To these ends every branch of University studies should be subordinate. Only in that way can they cause the light to shine; only in that way can they diffuse those better things which interest and invigorate, which inspire and sustain, which comfort in adversity and temper in triumph; only in that way can they contribute to the production of those finer fruits of literature and art and science by which people of our own and future ages are wont to judge the human standard of a nation, and which survive without concern of time long after the nation itself may have passed away.

CHURCH UNION

In the House of Commons Session of 1924, a measure which became known as "The Church Union Bill" was before Parliament. This was a Bill to give necessary legislative sanction to a union effected to the full extent of their powers by the governing bodies of three Protestant denominations—the Presbyterian, the Methodist and the Congregational.

Throughout all three political parties, there was marked division of opinion. Both sympathy for and antagonism to the measure were intense. The speech hereunder was made on June 26, 1924, in the debate on Second Reading. The Bill was carried on division.

THE NATURE OF THE QUESTION under review tonight is such as has never in other years been before Parliament. The Prime Minister (Mr. Mackenzie King) is only expressing the real position when he says that there are wide differences of view accompanied by sunderings of sentiment, and that on both sides of a great controversy are ranged many of the best people of our country. Of course, we all respect the opinions of those who differ from us, and we must, in relation to a question such as now agitates us all, carry that respect to even greater lengths and depths than has been our habit. It is regrettable that words have been uttered impugning the motives or the personal conduct of any connected with either side of the controversy. For myself, I am in disagreement with very many of my best friends. My inclinations lead me naturally to cling to the Church with which my family for many generations has been associated. Personal ties bind me closely to those, both in this House and without, who seek earnestly, even passionately, to maintain in its present status the Church of our fathers. But I must say very frankly that, after the closest study possible for me to give any subject, compulsions of reason have drawn me the other way. It must be stated at once, so that there may be no misapprehension, that in my judgment the duty of Parliament is to pass this Bill and that Parliament cannot usefully evade that duty by any amendment, either such a one as is suggested by the hon. member for Skeena (Mr. Stork), supported by the Prime Minister, or that sponsored by the hon. member for Lunenburg (Mr. Duff), and now embodied in the Bill.

This is one of those questions which require most careful reasoning; where confusion of thought is not only possible, but almost inevitable; where men are easily driven from the straight path of logic by sentiments which are powerful and by passions which are deep. I do not claim to be in the least exempt from these influences myself; one can only try to dispel them to the best of his ability, and to reach a decision on what he ought to do by a route as simple and carefully chosen as he can find. Tonight I am not expressing my views with any lively hope of changing those of others. The most I aspire to accomplish is to lay down briefly and simply those considerations which guide me, and trust that in the future, when the result of our action now shall be reaped in all its fruits, these reasons may be looked back upon as adequate and appropriate.

We have a Bill before us, the purpose of which is, as I express it, to confirm the union of three great Church denominations, the Presbyterian, the Methodist and the Congregational. I find myself in agreement with the argument presented tonight in very clear and forcible form by the Minister of Railways and Canals (Mr. Graham). I do not think he fully explored the question, but to the extent he did I am unable to diverge from his line of thought. These three Churches come to Parliament, having stated their conclusions through those tribunals which alone are empowered to state them. Not only have they carried those conclusions to us, but they themselves have taken action. To the utmost of their power they have formed a union—indeed, they have in large measure consummated one—but, as all agree, legislation is necessary because of civil rights involved, because of properties over which in some cases a local Legislature, and in other cases the Federal Parliament, has jurisdiction, and because of the necessity of bringing those properties and corporations which control them into conformity with a new relation created by the union.

These Churches, appealing for legislation, say: "The question of union or non-union is ours, it is not yours. It is a matter for the exercise of our rights within our spheres. All we call upon Parliament to do is to consummate our action because of necessities arising from the existence of properties, and as well, because of the desirability of putting into corporate form the union we have effected." The Minister of Railways argues that these bodies have expressed their will through their definitely constituted courts. No one, indeed, disputes that to the extent to which those courts could accomplish their end they have acted in proper form. That is to say, if we admit that they had power to do what they have done, they have gone about it the proper way; they have taken all precautions; they have paid heed to all safeguards, and given effect to the will of their Churches. They now come to Parliament and claim that we have no right to deny them consummation of a union which they themselves have brought about.

It is contended on the other side that one of these Churches, namely, the Presbyterian, has exceeded its powers in taking those steps essential to union. It is curious enough to reflect that no such contention is levelled as respects either of the other denominations—the Methodist or the Congregational—and the reason given is that there is no dispute, no division of opinion in those two denominations. But does that reason really dispose of the question? If power to unite did not exist in the one, I as yet have not found any reason to conclude that it did exist in any of them. I have not found any possible disability affecting the Presbyterian Church, which did not equally affect the Methodist and the Congregational Church. If it appertained to one, it appertained to all, and merely because it has not been drawn to attention does not prove that Parliament should be troubled about the matter in one case and utterly ignore it in the case of others.

In our discussion a general contention has been that this Church—the Presbyterian—has not had power to take those steps necessary for union. It is not certain whether those using this expression intend always to say that the General Assembly of the Church did not have power delegated from the Church itself to take those steps. Usually persons who argue on this question of jurisdiction contend that the Assembly never received from the Church itself—presumably congregations and Presbyteries— authority to take the action which it did take. There is some difference between that and arguing that the people could not give to the Assembly such authority. Personally I am of opinion that not only had the Church inherent power but that it had validly delegated such power to its Assembly. As I proceed to discuss very briefly this point and buttress my opinion, I ask hon. gentlemen to remember that my support of the Bill does not necessarily rest on the foundation of this opinion. Others may have just as good and as strong a conviction the other way. I will contend later that it does not matter which is correct, that in any event the Bill ought to pass, but I do take the view that the Church inherently has the power, and, as well, that it has named the authority and created the court by which it may be exercised.

What, after all, is this power of union? Does it consist of anything more or less than a right to change doctrine? I most earnestly ask hon. gentlemen to reflect on that sentence. Does power to unite really embrace anything more than power to modify doctrine? If power to modify doctrine is conceded, what is there between that and authority to unite with any other Church holding the doctrine so modified? Surely it is obvious that once a Church is conceded power to modify doctrine we have ended discussion as far as its power of effecting union is concerned.

MR. MACLAREN: May it not be that one can change a doctrine to a limited extent, not being a fundamental or a radical change? No one questions the right to make minor changes, but I ask the right hon. leader if he asserts that it is possible for every General Assembly to change fundamentally while there is a basis of doctrine that is accepted by the Church?

MR. MEIGHEN: What is in the mind of the hon. gentleman is not a question of the right of a Church itself to change its tenets fundamentally, but whether there is power in the Assembly to change them fundamentally. I will discuss that, and, while probably my hon. friend whose views I respect profoundly will not be convinced, I will explain why I myself am convinced. Power to change, it seems to me, is inherent in the Church. The Assembly has power delegated to it to express and give effect to the will of the Church in this regard, and, subject to approval of Presbyteries in compliance with the Barrier Act, there is no limitation. I entirely dissent from the theory that there exists in the Parliament of Canada, or in any court in this country, a right to say what is fundamental in doctrine and what is not. What in Parliament would appear to one secular mind fundamental, would appear trifling to another. In a court of judges it would be just the same. Those prerogatives are the prerogatives of the Church. The Church must have power to determine how and to what extent it exercises those prerogatives, a power unrestrained by any secular authority, whether Parliament or civil court.

One reason for my contention that power must be inherent is that it is impossible to suppress or direct the conduct of any Church in this respect. If a Church exercises the right, who is to say it nay? If a Church exercises it through the tribunal it creates to exercise it, who can say halt, to such a tribunal? Who can dispute its jurisdiction? It is said that in England the courts did so in 1904. The courts did not decide in England in 1904 that the Church was without power. They decided that the Free Church of Scotland had not delegated power to its Assembly; because looking into practices, records and precedents of that Church, they found no case of its exercise, and no expression of its will such as would have empowered its Assembly. There is no need to argue whether, even on the grounds stated by those judges, their decision was right or wrong. I have my opinion, but it is not pertinent whether they were right or wrong. The basis upon which the House of Lords decided that there was not in the Assembly of the Free Church of Scotland a right to change its doctrine is wholly absent in the case of the Presbyterian Church in Canada. With all humility, but very firmly, I express that opinion—because both textually and by precedent there has been evidence of the existence and of the exercise of this power throughout the history of the Canadian church. It is true that such exercise has been in cases where it could not very well be said—at least where I would not say—that there was any fundamental or radical change. But this fact argues nothing. I do not think, indeed, there is ever likely to be at one stroke any fundamental or radical change. The whole tradition, the constraint of tradition and the safeguards which tradition imposes, protect a church against hasty or violent change. But if it wishes to alter doctrine through the authority it creates for that purpose, there is no higher tribunal to say it nay. Consequently the Church must have this power. The case decided in England in 1904 was decided on the conclusion of the judges, one and all, that, looking back at its practice and looking at constitutional records of the Free Church, there was nothing to indicate that that Church ever intended its General Assembly to exercise such power. Looking into our practice and constitutional records in Canada, there is indication in both that such intention has been manifested.

Referring to what is called the Blue Book, which is accepted certainly by the Assembly—and I think we can say by the Church—as constituting its code, sections 112 and 120 cannot be read in such a way as not to express both the inherent right of the Church, and the delegation of that right to its Assembly, to restate or to alter doctrine. Section 112 contains the procedure for restating doctrine; but in the case of change, section 120 applies, and provides an added safeguard ensuring that there cannot be alteration by a mere uncontrolled act of the Assembly. There must be a reference back to the Presbyteries, a series of bodies standing between the congregations and the Assembly, and an approval of any change by a majority of these Presbyteries, before it becomes effective. This safeguard is known as the Barrier Act. However, it does not really come into argument tonight. My point is that granted compliance with this Barrier Act, which is not denied, authority to change rests in the Assembly.

Again and again we are confronted with the question: Was all this intended to apply to fundamental change? I do not know where to draw the line, nor do I think that we have any business in trying to draw the line. It is for the Church to say what change is to be made, great or small; it is not for us to say yes or no; and very surely if Parliament adopts any other principle, we shall be launched upon a sea where storms will be heavier and dangers greater than those which surround us now.

I stated some moments ago that even if it were arguable that the Presbyterian Assembly, as it exists today, does not enjoy this power, such a state of affairs would mean only that the courts of Canada would decide as to the Presbyterian Church, as the Lords of England decided as to the Free Church. In this event it still seems to me it would be our duty to pass the Bill. Why so? Let us look back over the history of the Free Church case. As soon as judgment had been handed down, a condition arose where the intervention of Parliament became necessary. The condition was this: first, the Church, stripped of its membership to a very considerable degree, was deemed by Parliament incapable of administering trusts committed to it—trusts mainly of a property character—and the trustee being so incapable, the Church having been forsaken by its members, save to the extent of a remnant, Parliament was compelled to step in, take those trusts in large measure away, and repose them in another institution. Parliament as well by the same Act of 1905 went on to declare that certain rights in relation to alteration of doctrine were thereafter to be considered as belonging to the Church of Scotland.

I do not need to dwell on this Statute longer, but come to the Act of 1921. This was an Act passed by the Imperial House. It recited certain declaratory articles of faith of the Church of Scotland, declaratory articles which themselves affirmed the right of that Church through its Assembly to alter doctrine, and the Parliament of Britain placed upon those articles the seal of legislation. The significance of this conduct of the British Parliament is very great. It is very great when we remember that judgment of the Lords in 1904. It shows that the Parliament of England came to a conclusion that if, by reason of such judgment, there was imposed, or there remained, a restraint upon the power of the Church through its Assembly to alter its creed, such restraint should be removed; that it was not fit or right that Parliament should be in any position to supervise or censor alterations of doctrine made by the Church itself.

Now let me at this point ask: Must we witness a repetition of this performance in Canada? Are our people to be called on to struggle through a long legal process, whether on the lines indicated by the hon. member for Lunenburg or on the lines now approved by the Prime Minister, because one side hopes there will be handed down at the journey's end a conclusion of a court of law that the Presbyterian Church, through its Assembly, cannot alter doctrine—a result the same as what befell the Free Church of Scotland? If this verdict does come, what then would be the attitude of Parliament as respects the situation created? The Prime Minister says, "Well we could meet the situation whatever it might be." I have to say immediately, our position necessarily towards any Church in Canada in such circumstances would be the very position which the British Parliament took towards the Free Church of Scotland. This means that even if I have been entirely wrong in my contention as to the legal situation here today, and if our courts were to hold that an inherent right of change did not exist, this Parliament could not for a minute refuse an application from the Presbyterian Church to be given that amplitude of power which became vested in 1921 in the Free Church of Scotland. The Prime Minister brings in a condition and says that if a majority of members of the Church would come to us and ask for this power, we would grant it.

MR. MACKENZIE KING: I did not say a majority. I said if the constituted authorities of the Church came and asked for it.

MR. MEIGHEN: I am really very anxious not to get into a controversy with the Prime Minister over this.

MR. MACKENZIE KING: Will my right hon. friend take my word for it at the moment that that is what I meant?

MR. MEIGHEN: Certainly. I noticed he said the majority—

MR. MACKENZIE KING: Keep up the controversy.

MR. MEIGHEN: I am most anxious to avoid a controversy, only I noted the word and thought it was wrong. When the Prime Minister says "authorities," I agree with him. If the recognized authorities of the Church come and ask for it, we would comply at once. Very well, the recognized authorities of the Presbyterian Church are now right at the doors of this Parliament asking that we do this very thing. So I say, why throw the Church into litigation even though we pay the costs? Why prolong a racking controversy if it is bound to end after wearisome turmoil just where it will end if we pass this legislation now? Why add tedious years to what is truly a sad and shattering strife?

Before I pass from the subject, let me impress again upon the House the absolute necessity of our presuming from the beginning that we must concede to every Church, whether it is already possessed or not, a full and unrestrained right to alter its creed. How can we be so presumptuous as to say: "Bound as you are by a regimen of doctrine, you must remain in its coils, no matter what your own courts may feel to be right in the light of advancing years. Though you, through your constituted tribunals, decide that you desire to modify this article or modify that, you cannot do so. If you so alter, you are violating trusts, you are diverting to the teaching of other doctrines moneys or property committed to you for propagation of the doctrine of your fathers." I am referring now particularly to an argument of the hon. member for St. Lawrence-St. George (Mr. Marler). Can we possibly assume for a moment that sort of censorship over any denomination? If we say such a thing we merely condemn that Church to drift lifelessly on the reefs of time, while its children abandon its altar and its creed. A majority goes first and then a majority of the remnant goes, until finally the Church is left a shell. In this unhappy predicament we, a Parliament, would be compelled, as was the Parliament of Britain in the case of the Free Church, to invade the empty temple, disrobe the stranded Church of its trusts and allocate them somewhere else. This course is the only alternative to conceding at once to every denomination its full right to alter doctrine and to have its trusts follow the destiny of the Church itself. Between these two courses will hon. gentlemen reflect which they prefer to pursue— to hold the Church within a strict regimen, the rigid restraints of any statement of beliefs, which it had years before accepted, and say we must do such a thing because of trusts which that Church has under its care; or to hold that the Church itself shall be the author and master of its creed and that its trusts will follow its destiny. It is the latter course which I choose myself and which I commend earnestly to Parliament tonight.

We come now to the two amendments. I would prefer to oppose this Bill direct rather than to vote for either of them. It would be a more sensible treatment of those who come before this House. The amendment which is now part of the Bill and which was inserted on motion of the hon. member for Lunenburg provides that no legislation which we pass shall take effect until, as an outcome of certain litigation now launched in Ontario, our courts finally declare that the Presbyterian Assembly had power to enter into union upon the Basis of Union and the Appendix on Law. To this I take exception for the reason that even if the defendants succeed—succeed right to the last court of appeal—there is no certainty of any judgment on that question, yes or no. I call attention to the fact that this action is not between the General Assembly and the plaintiffs. The plaintiffs are not suing the General Assembly; they are suing a committee of the General Assembly, and the committee takes the ground in its defence that the pleading is not properly based and does not constitute a cause of action at all. If the committee win on this ground, then, of course, there can be no court decision as to what were the Assembly's powers. In this event we would have the Church committee winning against the plaintiffs and still no possibility of our legislation coming into effect. The committee might win its case on almost any other ground, but inasmuch as the Assembly is not a party to the action, it is very doubtful if the courts would give judgment as to what the powers of the Assembly were.

Moreover, I think that these plaintiffs should have moved sooner and not waited until hours before the opening of Parliament. They were in a position to launch their action two years ago. It is true they could give certain reasons for not doing so; for example, that they did not know the exact terms of this Bill. But they knew all those things to which chiefly they make objection in their Statement of Claim. They knew that the Church was negotiating for union on the Basis of Union and the Appendix on Law. Against this they direct their principal objection. They could have launched their action at that time and it would have been on just as strong a footing as it can possibly be on today. Next, when they did commence about the middle of January, 1924, they asked for an injunction to restrain further proceedings towards securing legislation. But we are now nearly four months in this session and there has been no motion for an interlocutory injunction, although such a step would have been the only way to get restraint. Application for interlocutory injunction was open to them, but they let time go by and were content to hold the sword of litigation over Parliament. There is a further fact that the plaintiffs could absolutely defeat this law by simply dropping their action. For these reasons I do not think we should be asked to abide the event of their lawsuit.

But again I emphasize: Above and beyond these arguments there stands the great dominating truth that no matter what the result of litigation, unless we are prepared to allow a condition to remain where a Church is denied a right to change its doctrine,—for that right alone is involved in the question of union—we would be certain to find ourselves back later in just the position we are in today, where we would be asked and bound to decide in the affirmative precisely what we are asked now to decide in the affirmative by passing this Bill. I, therefore, look upon the amendment under review as an evasion.

The Prime Minister has another motion pending, that this Bill shall take effect only to the extent of the powers of Parliament. Well, whether such motion passes or not I really do not care, because the result is exactly the same in either event; no Bill ever takes effect beyond the powers of Parliament. Parliament cannot do any more than it can do; so why inject mere surplusage into the language of a statute?

I want also to discuss briefly an amendment advanced today—though it is not technically before the House—by the hon. member for Skeena (Mr. Stork), an amendment to which the Prime Minister tonight gave his unqualified endorsement. This amendment is even more objectionable than the last; and I am at this advantage in discussing it, that its fatal features have been recognized already in questions put by the hon. member for Vancouver South (Mr. Ladner) and by the hon. member for Brandon (Mr.

Forke). The motion is that there be added at an appropriate place:

> Provided that as respects the Presbyterian Church in Canada, the provisions of this Act shall apply only when all doubt has been removed as to the power of the General Assembly of the Presbyterian Church in Canada, under its constitutions and rules, to agree to a union of the Presbyterian Church in Canada with the Methodist and Congregational Churches upon the basis of union as set out in schedule A of this Act; provided, further, that this question shall be submitted for decision to the Supreme Court of Canada by a reference by the Minister of Justice.

My objections are these: If a "stated case," as this is described by the Prime Minister, is submitted and the courts hold that in the Presbyterian Church there is no legal competence to unite, what results? We have then a union, effected by Parliament, of the Methodist and Congregational Churches alone, a union forced upon them by us against the expressed will of recognized authorities of both Churches. Does anyone dispute that this will be the outcome? Undoubtedly it will. Parliament has no right to do such a thing; and I venture to say that no person comprehending the full meaning of this amendment will be likely to give it support. There is also an objection presented by the hon. member for Vancouver South. I do not know who has advised the Prime Minister, and do not wish to pose as a great constitutional lawyer; but I agree with the hon. member that this clearly is not a matter for a "stated case." There would be no difficulty in framing a "question" for the Supreme Court of Canada. It could be put thus: "Had the General Assembly of the Presbyterian Church power to negotiate for or to effect a union upon authority of the Basis of Union and the Appendix on Law?" But that is not a stated case; a stated case involves setting out admitted facts. You cannot set out such facts because they are not admitted. On the other hand, if you put the bald question—not a stated case at all which is really intended by this amendment and what the Prime Minister had in mind—if you just put the bald question, what is the court going to do about it? The court then has to get to work and ascertain what are the facts upon which its judgment is to be based. These are in dispute, and there at once you have a law-suit. This subject, I repeat, is not appropriate for a stated case. One side will affirm, "Here is our Blue Book; this is our recognized authority, the discipline and law of the Presbyterian Church. Read what it says." The other side will say, "No, this Blue Book does not represent the law and the prophets of the Presbyterian Church." Which side is right? Your law-suit has already begun—a law-suit, remember, and not a stated case for decision by the Supreme Court. No matter how you go about to settle this matter in the courts, no matter which of these routes you take, that by way of the first amendment or this one, it is a law-suit, where facts are in dispute and where you have two sides ranged in battle array. Throughout all the controversy you will have opposing contentions; you will travel far over a long and stony road; you start in the lower courts and you land at length in the Privy Council before the law lords there.

Mr. MACKENZIE KING: Where does my right hon. friend get that opinion?

Mr. MEIGHEN: I so interpret the suggested amendment, although the Prime Minister may interpret it differently:

> Provided that as respects the Presbyterian Church in Canada, the provisions of this Act shall apply only when all doubt has been removed as to the power of the General Assembly of the Presbyterian Church in Canada.

You do not remove "all doubt" on such a point until you have persevered to the last court. This is my interpretation of these words. The Prime Minister may have intended to stop at the Supreme Court of Canada, but I do not think such is the legal effect of the amendment offered by the hon. member for Skeena.

Mr. MACKENZIE KING: I would wish to have it so worded at any rate.

Mr. MEIGHEN: Even so, it would only mean that the path to be travelled would be a little shorter. It would still be dangerous and expensive and finally inconclusive. For as a last word let me say that the end of the road no matter which route be taken is exactly that indicated by the hon. member for Lunenburg. If, therefore, as a final episode of either one journey or the other, the court finds that the power of the General Assembly does not exist, does any one fancy that the Church will not return to Parliament for that power? Does any one fancy that any Church will be content to live under such a conscious disability? Will any Church recognize the smallest assertion of authority in Parliament as respects its own articles of faith? No. Therefore, why delay?—I had almost said why evade, but wish to avoid every term that savours of offence. Why not, rather, face the real situation and end this matter now? Why not do now what, undoubtedly, in any event—as admitted even by the Prime Minister himself—we will later be compelled to do after months or years of confusion and estrangement, after all this litigation has been undergone, all this friction intensified, and all this agony endured? I ask hon. members to consider the reasons I have advanced and to give them such weight as they feel to be their merit.

THE SIR WILLIAM PETERSEN CONTRACT

OCEAN SHIPPING RATES

On December 11, 1924, the Dominion Government made a contract with Sir William Petersen, the object of which was to subsidize a line of ten ocean vessels to be built by him and operated in North Atlantic service. In return for a subsidy of $1,300,000 per year for ten years, Sir William agreed that the Government should have control of rates on these vessels.

Early in March, 1925, a Resolution ratifying this Agreement was moved in the House of Commons by the Prime Minister (Rt. Hon. Mackenzie King) and was strongly supported by him and by other Ministers in the ensuing debate. The Agreement itself was appended to the Resolution and made a part thereof.

The speech below, an attack on the entire arrangement, was made in the Commons on March 19, 1925.

(Very shortly after this debate, Sir William Petersen died. His Estate, of course, would still be liable, but nothing more was heard of the contract.)

THE MOTION UNDER DEBATE reads as follows:

> That to give the Government of Canada control over certain ocean rates it is expedient to ratify and confirm the agreement between His Majesty and Sir William Petersen, K.B.E., as set out in the schedule of this resolution, and dated the eleventh day of December, one thousand nine hundred and twenty-four, and that in view of the provisions of said agreement giving the Government control over such rates and of the services to be performed thereunder, the Governor in Council may authorize payment out of the consolidated revenue fund, to the said Sir William Petersen, K.B.E., of an annual amount of two hundred and seventy-five thousand pounds in the manner and for the period provided for in the said agreement.

Then follows the specific agreement. I read this so that hon. members, after being carried far and wide over the waters of controversy, may get some glimpse of the port towards which we are sailing. It is important that we know what is before us in its exact terms.

One would think from much of this debate, and certainly from the speech of the Prime Minister, that the motion under discussion was to appoint a committee of inquiry into a North Atlantic combine, which committee was, if possible, to devise some method whereby freight rates set by that combine could be controlled. The House has been instructed that a desire to control is a "principle," which we are to vote for or vote against. Those who favour control are advised that the only thing they can do is to support the resolution; of course, those who are against control and who like high rates are at liberty to oppose. How beautifully simple! If a government is authoritatively to instruct the House that the mere words of a motion are unimportant and as to what principle is to be considered as substituted therefor, then Parliament becomes a futile appendage, a mere servile register of the Administration's will. I think it is better for us to assume that we ourselves can read, and that we understand the English language; and when we are asked to ratify a contract, common sense dictates to me that what we are called upon to approve is the contract itself. When a Government gives us to understand, as has been done in this debate, that it is not at all particular about its concrete proposal, that all it wants is some way of reaching a goal, and that if the House will suggest some other method it will be gladly followed, then that Government simply abdicates its responsibilities, surrenders its functions, and becomes nothing better than surplusage in Parliament.

The motion before us is one to which this argument applies with double force. It asks us to ratify an agreement already entered into, signed and sealed by the parties thereto. The records of Parliament will be searched in vain for a case in which any Government in our history ever suggested that an agreement signed and sealed by itself and the other party and submitted to Parliament for approval was subject to anything save acceptance or rejection. Indeed, such was the stand first taken in this instance by the Prime Minister; in answer to interruptions by several hon. members, he declared that what Parliament had before it was the duty of deciding whether to reject or to approve the contract which his resolution embodies. In so speaking he followed every precedent. But, as difficulties loomed up, as clouds gathered around his head, as he looked across at gloomy faces among hon. gentlemen to my left,[1] he proceeded by a slow curve to alter his position. He altered it first to the extent of saying that the agreement must either be ratified as it is, or, if the House should decide on amendments, that the Government would take the amendments to Sir William Petersen and see whether he would agree to them. This is not a very dignified attitude for any government to assume. Every good citizen having made a contract feels that he should live up to it to the extent of his power. Having agreed that the terms are fair and reasonable, he does not like to submit to the humiliation of going back to his contractee and asking for a change. Well, what is binding on a citizen in that respect should be far more binding on a government. But this one we have here, having declared its belief that the terms of the bargain before us are fair and reasonable, is prepared to go back to Sir William Petersen and to say: A committee of Parliament does not like this contract, we possibly may face defeat; so we are ready to kneel at your feet and beg of you to change its terms. The Prime Minister said further that if Sir William refused to consent to any change, then it would be for the Government to stand or fall by the original agreement. But again, this altered attitude did not seem to appeal to hon. gentlemen whose votes he was seeking very eagerly. The hon. member for Red Deer (Mr. Speakman), encouraged by the receding attitude of the Prime Minister, made it clear that he would not consider the Government as acting in good faith unless the committee were to be free to devise some plan of control without subsidies—a wholly different idea from that embodied in this contract. The Prime Minister thereupon declared that all anyone would be voting for who supported the contract would be the "principle" of controlling ocean rates, and added that if the committee should favour some other method

[1] The Progressives

and suggest it, it would be for the Government to come back to the House and, as best it could, give expression in a new measure to the will of Parliament. In a word, the Prime Minister finally got around to a confession that his Government is prepared to change its much-heralded policy to the left or to the right, provided it can save its precious existence.

The right hon. leader opposite spent a considerable portion of his address in reciting conditions and circumstances which, I think, all of us know to exist; and it will contribute to definiteness in this discussion, as well as to a saving of time, if we can get together on what might be called conclusions from a large portion of his speech.

We can agree in the first place that there is a North Atlantic Steamship Conference—or "combine" if you wish so to describe it. We can agree that such Conference or combine fixes rates on goods its members transport. No one disputes these facts. Its officers did not dispute them before the committee presided over by the hon. member for Brome (Mr. McMaster).

MR. McMASTER: I think it only fair to state that the officers of the lines denied that there was a Conference, and the fact was only brought out with considerable difficulty.

MR. MEIGHEN: It will be left for the hon. gentleman to establish what he says. I have read the report and did not read that denial. Anyway, no hon. member of this House doubts for a minute that a Conference exists and has existed for many years, and that rates on commodities, with very few exceptions, are fixed by Conference. The argument has convinced me that grain rates are not so fixed. There may be an extent to which flour and cattle rates were fixed by it and possibly are today—that matter may be left for clarification—it is not material at the moment—but that rates are fixed generally, there is no question. It may be taken for granted also that rates have been materially advanced since pre-war days, and that such advance has had the effect of making difficult the export of goods; that it would be much better for Canadian industries if rates were lower; and that we would have more Canadian industries if there were no rates at all. It can be taken as accepted, as well, that repeated complaints have been made against these rates, back for six or eight years past—yes, for longer—and that these complaints still continue. In my view we can agree further still that the element of competition has been to some extent eliminated in respect of water-borne traffic. I do not think it has been eliminated nearly as far as it has been in land transport, nor does any other hon. member think so. It is impossible in the present stage of this industry to avoid competition, save to a limited degree.

Being at one on all these things does not get us very far towards enlightenment on the merits of this resolution; but it does dispose of at least three hours of the speech of the Prime Minister. I have stated that there is not now the same competition on water as in earlier days. I make a further affirmation for whatever hon. gentlemen accept it as worth—that when ocean steamship business develops to the extent that regular lines are inaugurated, then it is essential that there be something in the nature of Conference and fixing of rates for those lines. We must be candid in these matters. Is there any hon. member who really believes that when, in the evolution of ocean steamship business, regular sailings have been established, just as regular despatch of trains has been established on land, it is possible to maintain, save by some system of Conference, such a thing as uniformity of rates? I do not think the Prime Minister would say so. In a portion of his speech, towards the end, he clearly indicated the contrary. It cannot be done. If there is not some such system, there is going to be a reaching out after the big fellow's traffic, a giving of rebates and advantages to obtain it, and thereby discriminations will be produced which are far more serious than any discriminations complained of in this debate. The little fellow as a shipper will be penalized and crushed. Uniformity of rates established for liners ensures equal treatment to all shipments from all quarters, no matter whether those shipments be large or small. Further, as stated in the report of the American government commission, when regular transport lines are in operation, experience has proven that there is no middle road between peace and war; the big liner company has such advantage over the smaller that a crowding out process is sure to be successful, with consequent enthronement of monopoly, not only in rates but in service. The element of competition even in service is gone forever. These things follow if there is no Conference system; and consequently the Conference system is not necessarily an evil in itself.

Nevertheless, it cannot be argued that this practice, however necessary, of maintaining rate uniformity by internal regulation through a Conference, can go on indefinitely with no superimposed control. The principle is unsound. True, it is less dangerous than to suffer the absence of higher control on land—because, on land, competition in rates between railways is impossible, while on sea there is very substantial competition from a vast number of tramps. In respect of a large array of commodities, tramp competition is effective.

I agreed a moment ago that we had had in late years very material increases in ocean rates. The Prime Minister read letters from shippers, showing, in respect of certain commodities, rather startling percentages of increase. No doubt there are some large percentages, but the only way to establish what general advance there has been is by such a computation as takes all rates into account. I have before me a schedule prepared from the Index of Shipping Freights. This is an official index accepted everywhere as authoritative on this question. It indicates that the percentage increase shown last month over the average for fifteen years which ended in 1913, is 46.54 per cent. The percentage is, therefore, less than what was quoted by the Prime Minister as obtaining in relation to land transport. A complete table is before me and may be examined later by any hon. member.

MR. MACKENZIE KING: By whom was the table compiled?

MR. MEIGHEN: It is the Index of Shipping Freights and it appeared in an article in the *Economist* of very recent date. The table is completed to March, 1925.

MR. ROBB: In the rates quoted by the right hon. member, is any distinction made between Canadian ports and American ports?

MR. MEIGHEN: The North Atlantic is treated as one. I do not contend that this proves absence of discrimination as between Montreal and New York. But as the Acting Minister of Finance has raised the point, I quote from the same journal of 28th February of this year the following:

The fact is that the rates eastward are the same for all North Atlantic ports from Baltimore to Montreal, although insurance rates for ships entering Montreal are higher than for ships using American ports.

Returning now to the desirability of a superimposed control, we should first consider what necessarily must be the composition, what necessarily must be the status and representative character of a body before it can be in a position to exercise such powers. Surely a single country has not so much as a right to do so, and because it has not, it never can succeed in an attempt. I ask hon. gentlemen to reflect: Has Canada alone a right to supervise rates in and out between this Dominion and Great Britain? If she has, has not Great Britain also? And how can each country operate a separate control? I pause for a reply. Have we a right to fix or revise rates between here and Australia, or to dictate to Australia what shall be charged on goods shipped from that Dominion to Canada? Let us reverse the positions; let us suppose that Great Britain announces that her Government will control rates on wheat shipped from our shores to the British market; can any hon. gentleman imagine the speech the Prime Minister would deliver in this House? Can anybody conceive the campaign which would be launched against "Downing Street domination"? Well, if Great Britain has not that right, how then can we assert a corresponding prerogative for Canada? We are asserting an authority which inherently we do not and cannot possess.

What nature of board then, what is the smallest circumference in representation and power a board must possess which can even attempt to handle this situation? I venture to suggest, and it is embodied in our amendment as an affirmation, that no board of narrower compass than one on which are representatives of the whole Empire can even be considered. The Prime Minister himself in a portion of his address said it could not be effectively done except by a body agreed upon by all nations. Possibly for certain wider purposes that is true. But the shipping of this Empire is of so vast a magnitude that it cannot be boycotted, and its people have among themselves an undoubted collective right, if they choose to exercise it, to supervise shipping charges between its various ports. Therefore, the first step of any consequence not bound to end in disaster is to establish some body on which Britain and all Dominions are represented. If this can be accomplished, it may not be the last step in working out a system of co-operative control, but it will at least have a chance of succeeding within the wide range of inter-Empire ports.

Hon. gentlemen opposite who entered into this agreement very hastily—and some of whom I admit, by way of compliment, are exceedingly sorry—tell us: We cannot get any board in which the whole Empire is working together to take this matter in hand, so we have to splurge ahead and do something to attract attention and stir others to action. Well, what have been the attempts? According to the Minister of Railways (Mr. Graham) a first effort was made in 1910. He received a memorandum from Mr. Justice Mabee, then head of the railway commission. Now, I have had the highest opinion of Mr. Justice Mabee, but cannot be lost in admiration of his memorandum. It proceeds on an hypothesis that ocean transport is as susceptible of control by one country as is land transport within that country itself, and also on an hypothesis that competition has just as surely departed from ocean transport as from land. Both of these assumptions are manifestly wrong. His memorandum says also that in a few years—it was written in 1910—England would be importing 600,000,000 or 800,000,000 bushels of our wheat. Well, today, fifteen years after, there are only about 43,000,000 people in Great Britain, and all they can possibly consume would be 280,000,000 bushels. In a word, the memorandum was not carefully compiled. It was, however, forwarded to Great Britain with an expression of hope that some central body representative of the Empire might be created to take charge of ocean rates. Evidently the Canadian Government forgot that this question had already been investigated by a commission on which Canada had an appointee, and which reported that control on water, as distinct from control on land, was impracticable. This report declared that there were very great difficulties to be overcome which did not appear on land, and that especially a system which in its operation would necessarily put British shipping at a disadvantage with continental shipping would not redound to the benefit of any part of the Empire. These things were pointed out by British Ministers in their reply. They seem to me very sensible. There were, plainly, major difficulties to be surmounted, and the British Government suggested that the subject be still further explored to see if something could not be evolved to take care at least of this danger of discrimination. The Canadian Government stopped right there. The Minister of Railways says the reason was that they knew when they were turned down, and that, anyway, they knew the facts and needed no investigation. This was back in 1910. Well, if they knew the facts in 1910, why did they start to find them out again in 1923 and in 1924? They have started two investigations in the last two years.

The next move of importance—I am passing by various inquiries by British Governments—was an enquiry by the present hon. member for West York (Sir Henry Drayton, then Chairman of our Railway Commission). His report favoured supervision of Conference rates and proposed that the Dominion Royal Commission then sitting was a proper body to evolve a plan. This Royal Commission took the matter in hand and recommended creation of a co-operative British Empire tribunal. The war was on and throughout its duration, shipping was under command of the British Government. In 1918 representatives of Canada brought this matter forcibly to their attention. The British Government acquiesced to the extent of appointing what is known as the Imperial Shipping Committee on which all Dominions have members and to which certain definite powers have been given. These do not include powers specifically to fix rates; but the committee was invited to investigate and report on all matters concerning discriminations, harbour facilities, and in general the betterment of inter-Empire communications. Canada was not satisfied. Sir Robert Borden, in the spring of 1919, prepared a memorandum in which he strongly urged that powers of the Shipping Board be amplified and that this country continue its effort—and he invited the support of other Dominions as well—to have vested in this Imperial Shipping Board effective rate control. This was subsequently submitted to me, when I became Prime Minister, in a letter from Sir George Perley, who had been our representative on the Imperial Shipping Board. Sir George was of opinion that considerable good work was being done by that Board, but that he was not possessed adequately of information necessary to persuade the committee to request a grant of these control powers, and he asked us to have someone specially delegated to present this well-known Canadian view. We decided that Dr. Magill of Winnipeg was preëminently capable to do that work. Dr. Magill, however, declined. This was during the session of 1921. At its close I left for England on very important Imperial Conference duties, and immediately thereafter a general election was called.

Then came appointment of the committee under charge of the hon. member for Brome. This committee, however, was not authorized to investigate ocean freight rates, but to look generally into agricultural conditions. Mr. McMaster saw fit quite properly to give some attention to rates. His committee made its report in instalments, and in this debate we have been told that the Government bases the policy now submitted to Parliament upon that report. Well, one would never dream so, if he reads the document itself. The report found that there was a combine and that the combine controlled rates. Does the Prime Minister say that is the basis of his policy?

MR. MACKENZIE KING: Genesis was the word I used.

MR. MEIGHEN: The genesis of it? Be it so, the Prime Minister also said that the Government's policy had been adopted wholly irrespective of whether there is a combine or not. He said his policy had no relation to the combine, and in spite of that statement, now tells us it had its genesis in the report of a committee whose only finding in this respect was that there is a combine. Does he say now that the committee recommended any action of this kind? In so far as there is indication of any recommended course to be pursued, that course is directly contrary to the one the Government has taken. Here is what the committee said. It is found at page xxi of the Journals of the House for 1923:

> Your committee, in view of the foregoing and of the evidence adduced before them and referred to in a previous interim report, are of the opinion that action is desirable to control shipping rings or conferences.

What action?

> It is suggested that the Canadian representatives in attendance at the next meeting of the International Institute of Agriculture should be given authority to see that the matter is thoroughly discussed, in order to discover whether an international system of control is feasible through such agency.

Is there any family resemblance between that suggestion—which at least shows some enlightened understanding of the problem—and what is embodied in this resolution? The report goes on:

> In view of the fact that a very great deal of the shipping coming to Canadian ports is British shipping, concurrent action by the British authorities is respectfully suggested.

One would think that what had impressed the hon. member for Brome and his committee would have occurred to the mind of this Government, but not a move was even attempted to get British co-operation or concurrence. I quote further:

> The matter might well be made a subject for discussion and consideration at the next Imperial Economic Conference.

There end the suggestions.

Mr. McMaster: Oh, no.

Mr. Meighen: What was the other one?

Mr. McMaster: A little further on—several paragraphs.

Mr. Meighen: Where is it? I hope that any further suggestions are not contradictory to those just read?

Mr. McMaster: No, no.

Mr. Meighen: If they are in line with those just read, I do not see the purpose of this interruption. The committee did not feel that to understand the problem fully and to reach anything in the way of an expeditious and wise conclusion the facts were even yet well enough under command.

These recommendations the Government have flouted, and still they come to us and say they base their policy upon the committee's report! This "genesis" idea seems to me of very recent birth.

Mr. Preston's name is sometimes mentioned. The Government seem very sensitive as to the reputation of Mr. W. T. R. Preston, but no member on this side of the House has ever so reflected on that gentleman as has the Prime Minister himself. In March of 1924, Mr. Preston was sent across to investigate and report on this problem; such was the commission given him by Order in Council. It is, indeed, all the Order in Council says, except to specify his pay, which I venture to think was the most important part of the whole enterprise. After sending Preston over to investigate, the Government came upon a policy without waiting for his report. The Prime Minister stands now and says that it does not matter at all what is in Mr. Preston's report; that he is not basing his policy on Preston; he is basing his policy on Mr. McMaster's committee, which recommended movement and action in directly the opposite way.

Now what is this policy? It is embodied in a contract which we are asked to ratify. I am going to analyze this contract, and try to reveal to hon. members just what its contents are. Of course, the Prime Minister says: "Well, it does not matter; the Government is going to do so and so anyway." Mr. Speaker, there are some people in everyday life who, when they make a contract, do what they like irrespective of its terms, but I do not think Parliament should accept with placidity the declaration of a Prime Minister that he is going to follow in those footsteps.

By the way, one would think the Government was entitled to some special benediction because it did not make an agreement except "subject to ratification of Parliament." "We made it in this case," the Prime Minister said, "very clear to Sir William Petersen that the contract could not take effect till Parliament ratified it. That is the course we pursued." Well, there was no other course he could pursue. The Government had absolutely no power to make a contract save subject to approval of Parliament. No contract ever was made—not previously authorized by statute—except subject to ratification. When Sir Wilfrid Laurier in 1898 brought down the Yukon railway contract, he brought it down subject to ratification. When, in 1903, he entered into the Grand Trunk Pacific Agreement, it was signed and sealed, and he brought it here for ratification. When, in 1918, the Government of the day was obligated to take over the Grand Trunk Railway and made an Arbitration Agreement with its owners, this also was subject to ratification. All must be; the Prime Minister had no option. But there is this difference: In every one of those cases the Governments, under Sir Wilfrid Laurier, and under Sir Robert Borden, took full responsibility for their agreements; they each declared to Parliament: This contract embodies terms which in our judgment are fair and in the national interest; these terms are signed and sealed; Parliament can reject the contract if it will, but if it rejects the contract it rejects the Government. Sir Wilfrid Laurier and Sir Robert Borden—and at first the present Prime Minister— each of them said: The contract is here for approval or disapproval; it cannot be trimmed. But Sir Wilfrid Laurier and Sir Robert Borden stood by their assertions; stood by them in the face of opposition, stood up manfully and accepted their responsibility, and staked their Governments on the issue. But the head of this Administration wriggled and wiggled around and tried to read what he calls a "principle" into his resolution. He finally said to hon. gentlemen: If you do not like this contract, amend it, and we will go to Sir William Petersen and fall at his feet and ask him to accept your will. If you won't have anything to do with it at all, just consign it to a committee and give us something else. In a word, go on, do anything you like, but save our precious lives.

I come back to the contract. In the first place, the covenant of Sir William Petersen that obligations binding on him such as they are, will be carried out, is a covenant which Petersen can set fire to just as soon as this resolution is passed by Parliament. Immediately he forms his company he has the Government bound to accept that company instead of himself. If it is a mere watered-stock concern, if it is a mere cipher without financial responsibility, it does not matter. The Government then has no other security, and no lawyer of Mr. Lafleur's standing ever signed, or would sign, his name to an opinion that Petersen has not power to release himself from every covenant by the formation of a company and the substitution of that company for himself.

I do not need to dwell on all these introductory paragraphs. They are plainly an intellectual harvest of the Government, rather than of Mr. Lafleur. I have seen many documents drawn by eminent counsel, but have never seen any other preceded by a din of political fanfare such as constitutes the larger portion of this contract.

Covenants on the part of Sir William Petersen are as follows: He covenants that he shall (either by himself or by his company):

(a) Build, equip, provide, establish and during this contract, continue and in the manner hereinafter mentioned, operate a regular shipping service between such ports in Great Britain or Ireland or the continent of Europe, and Canadian ports as may be designated by the Minister of Trade and Commerce for Canada or his representatives from time to time.

(b) Establish and continue and maintain and operate as hereinafter set out the shipping service hereinbefore referred to free from the control of and independent of the Atlantic shipping combine or conference or any other combine or conference now in existence or which may be operated or established upon the Atlantic ocean at any time in the future without the sanction of the government of Canada.

First, he must build, equip and operate a regular shipping service, and the government can name the ports; second, he must keep out of the Atlantic Steamship Conference.

The next is:

(c) That such service shall be put in effect and maintained with ten ships as hereinbefore referred to and these shall be built and placed in operation with all possible despatch and shall be fully completed and put in service within eighteen months from the date of this agreement (at least two of the same to be placed in service by August 1, 1925) and pending completion of the same, other ships of modern construction properly equipped and of approximately the same tonnage—

Mark that.

—shall be substituted and operated in the said service until the fleet in question is completely constructed and in operation, the said service to commence with at least six ships not later than June 15, 1925.

That is to say, Sir William Petersen in execution of his covenant shall have in operation by June 15th, six ships of about the same tonnage as those described at the close of the agreement, and he shall have two not later than August 1, 1925. It will be observed that the ships which he may substitute do not need to be of the speed or of any other characteristic of those later to be built, but only of about the same tonnage. The next covenant is:

(d) That the control and regulation of the rates to be charged by the contractor shall rest with the government of Canada and that the government shall fix such transportation rates on·all commodities from time to time.

Let me consider this paragraph for a moment—and I do so with an open invitation to any member of the House who disagrees to say so. What is the alpha and omega, the beginning and end, of this covenant? It gives the Government of Canada a right to fix rates on any and all "commodities." Of that there is no question. But what is its meaning? The Government, in respect of any commodity—and "commodity" has a distinct connotation—can say to Sir William Petersen: The rate shall be so much on your vessels. This the Government can do, and no more. Under this covenant or any other the Government cannot compel Petersen to carry the commodity at the rate fixed. He may fill his ship with other goods whose rates are more to his liking. The Minister of National Defence (Mr. Macdonald, Pictou) takes refuge in a smile. I invite him to dispute that position.

MR. MACDONALD: I will dispute it when you get through; it is ridiculous.

MR. MEIGHEN: That will be safer than to dispute it now. It is quite true that if Sir William Petersen carries a named commodity, he cannot charge any higher rate than the Government may fix. So much is certain. Now, the Prime Minister says, "We will fix rates only on Canadian goods." Of course, if rates are fixed on American goods, American shippers will get the benefit of our subsidies; we should then have been generous enough to bonus our competitors. When the Prime Minister was faced with that dilemma, he escaped by declaring that the Government would fix rates only on Canadian commodities. Evidently what he has in mind is that Canadian wheat is one commodity and American wheat another. But I ask hon. gentlemen to my left,[1] is that true? Is not wheat a single commodity? Is not barley a single commodity? Is not oats a single commodity? Is Ontario wheat one commodity and Quebec or Manitoba wheat another? And can the Government fix one rate for Ontario wheat and another for the Manitoba product? It cannot. It names the commodity and fixes the rate, and that done, the Government's power is exhausted. I should like to know whether the Prime Minister or the Minister of National Defence disputes my contention. They cannot.

The Prime Minister says that the Government will fix rates only on Canadian goods. Let me for the sake of argument accept that position; suppose he is right. What then? The horn of the dilemma which he is on now is worse than the other. To illustrate. The Prime Minister says to Sir William Petersen: "The rate on Canadian wheat shall be 6 cents." We will assume that the general rate on American wheat is 9 cents. Will anyone suggest that Sir William cannot take American wheat? If the Prime Minister attempts to reduce the rate on American wheat to the Canadian level, Sir William, of course, would be as well paid if he took the Canadian wheat. But the Prime Minister rightly says he will not do such a thing. Well, if the rate is fixed only on the Canadian product, Sir William is free to accept in its place American wheat.

MR. MACKENZIE KING: I hope my right hon. friend will not feel that, because I am silent while he makes these overtures, I agree with what he says. I want him to have the fullest latitude to make his case as strong as he can, and that is my only reason for not replying to these absurd views.

MR. McMASTER: Silence does not necessarily imply consent.

MR. MEIGHEN: But silence in the case of the Prime Minister,

[1] The Progressives.

who is never slow in interrupting, does imply that he has great difficulty in answering.

MR. MACKENZIE KING: Well, let me make it clear that such is not the case, for I differ utterly from my right hon. friend in regard to the representations he is making, which are inaccurate and absurd.

MR. MEIGHEN: That is often the answer of a controversialist who cannot give any reason for his position. I say that Sir William Petersen certainly must carry out every covenant of his contract. But what are those covenants? The covenants are these—that he will build, equip and operate a regular service—if he does not do so he cannot sue the Government for a single dollar; that he shall not get into the North Atlantic combine; and, as well, that he must have in operation certain ships at certain dates. These are his covenants and these alone, and when he fulfils them he can demand his money. Now, I am speaking in the presence of at least sixty or seventy lawyers, no one of whom has been overgifted with shyness in the past. I want to know whether any lawyer in the House will contest that position.

MR. McMASTER: I think the Leader of the Opposition must have overlooked sub-section (e):

> Make proper provision for the carriage of perishable and partly perishable produce by means of cold storage facilities.

If Sir William Petersen is to fit his ship in such a way as to carry that sort of produce, how can he fill the vessel with American goods?

MR. MEIGHEN: I am fair in assuming that the best lawyer in the House has made the best reply he can. Certainly Sir William Petersen must fit his ship to carry perishable or semi-perishable produce. But I want to ask the hon member for Brome (Mr. McMaster): Is not Sir William absolutely free, if he desires, to operate this portion empty, or, if he does not like that, to fill it with American goods?

MR. McMASTER: Not if he expects the subsidy.

MR. MEIGHEN: What binds him in the contract to distinguish between American and Canadian goods? What binds him to carry Canadian goods at all? There is not a syllable in the contract which compels him to do so. In other words, he has the whole thing under his hands. I venture to suggest that the Minister of National Defence cannot bring us the written opinion of Mr. Lafleur, or of any other reputable lawyer, that Petersen is prevented or estopped under this contract from carrying American goods as freely as he likes and as freely as he may carry Canadian produce. The rate on wheat to American shippers is, say, 9 cents. He may say to the American, "I will carry your produce for 8 cents." And he carries American wheat at a rate one cent below the ruling level. What does that mean? It means that American wheat is carried lower on the strength of a subsidy paid from the treasury of Canada.

It has been already argued in this debate that Petersen does not bind himself to establish any fixed number of sailings. Frequency of sailings is left with himself. They must be "regular." Such is his covenant and no more. Once his vessels start they must proceed with despatch. They would do so anyway, because there is no money in loitering. He can establish, so far as his contract goes, two or ten sailings a year and then he has fulfilled the contract. Let us assume that this Government fixes rates which are low, say ten dollars a head on cattle, and Petersen provides a sailing or two or three, or perhaps a dozen sailings a year—the less the number of sailings, the less will be his loss—Petersen will get $1,300,000 a year from the Government and be entitled to every dollar. The interest charge on six million dollars is only about three hundred thousand dollars a year, and therefore he will have around a million to the good, and as long as he cannot be forced to operate services enough to bring his losses over a million, he will be entitled to all he can save.

Mr. Jacobs: Would that be the spirit of the contract?

Mr. Meighen: That is distinctly the spirit of the contract. When the hon. member for George-Etienne-Cartier (Mr. Jacobs) draws a contract he does not leave it to the other fellow to fix its terms and thus breathe into it a spirit to suit himself.

Mr. Jacobs: I have forgotten how to draw a contract since I have been in Parliament.

Mr. Meighen: So has the Government. This contract cannot be attributed to Mr. Lafleur. The business of a lawyer is to draft what his client desires. The Government's duty was to instruct Mr. Lafleur; it was for him so to draft the contract as to safeguard what his client said should be safeguarded. The hon. member says that my interpretation is not in accord with the spirit; but, I have found in the history of Canadian politics that when a member starts to talk about the spirit as distinguished from the letter he is pretty near the "chart and compass" stage.

MR. MACKENZIE KING: Will my hon. friend accept what Sir William Petersen says as to the spirit and letter of the contract?

MR. MEIGHEN: Not at all. Of course, I will not. That is the hole the Government is in and it should not try to pull me in too. The Government is in the hands of Sir William Petersen. I hope I am able to read English and understand it myself. An hon. member says that the spirit has to be looked to. Quite true, but the spirit grows out of the letter. If there is one who can suggest that any further covenant Petersen entered into impairs in any degree the argument I have advanced, I would feel indebted to him if he would make his suggestion now. These are his covenants and these only, and these he must keep; and when he keeps these, he gives the service he has promised. When he gives this service, the Government must pay.

The Prime Minister devoted considerable time to showing that rates for immigrants have been raised greatly, and so they have. The immigration policy of this Government, whatever may be the last edition of it, is having a terrible time, according to the Prime Minister, because of exorbitant rates charged by steamships to immigrants. Now I make the statement that under this contract there is no provision made for carrying one single immigrant. Sir William Petersen is not bound, and need never be bound, to carry an immigrant in the next ten years—not one. It is true the contract says that Sir William and the Government may later on agree to establish passenger service; but if they may agree, they also may not agree. Sir William, before he agrees, will fix terms to suit him, and, if the Government does not come to those terms, there will be no contract. On this, again, I challenge contradiction. Ships for passenger service may be provided, but if so, Canada will have to pay the price.

There is still another phase. I set out by arguing that the

Government of Canada cannot by controlling rates on a small fleet of ships meet with any real success in bringing about control of rates generally. They cannot in the first place, because, inherently, they have no right to such single control. Other countries cannot be asked to submit. It is true the Government may contribute to rates; they may pay part of them, or part of a small section of them. This, indeed, is just what they are now undertaking—this and nothing more. By means of a large subsidy they control rates on a small number of boats. I ask: Why did they not use for this purpose the ships they already own? We have had various reasons given. During the speech of the hon. member for Vancouver Centre (Mr. Stevens), the Prime Minister said the ships of the Canadian Government Merchant Marine were no good. Indeed, he did not confine himself to answering a question, but repeated the assertion in his own address. He was disturbed in his serenity only by his Minister of Railways (Mr. Graham), who took a directly contrary line, and claimed that the reason they could not use our Merchant Marine was that those ships were rendering too great a service where they are. He said the services they were rendering Canada on various trade routes were such that the Government could not afford to take them off.

The Minister of Agriculture (Mr. Motherwell), whose closely reasoned, profound, statesmanlike address I am sure the House will long remember, has also made some illuminating observations on this subject. He stated, as reported in the Manitoba *Free Press* of August 11th:

> The using of the Canadian mercantile marine boats at cheaper rates is not practicable, because the five boats fitted up for cattle carrying are not big enough for cattle export trade of any volume. In fact the five boats together only equal one good-sized cattle carrier.

Does he contend that he is providing good-sized cattle carriers now? He is providing boats just the size of the mercantile marine.

MR. MOTHERWELL: Larger.

MR. MEIGHEN: Smaller than two of them; slightly larger, but only by a negligible per cent, than twenty-four of them. He said that because of their size our Merchant Marine boats cannot carry cattle successfully. But he also asserted that they had been built too big for the lakes and too small for the ocean, and he came along with this drivel again in a speech in this House. If hon. members will refer to a return brought down by the Minister of Railways and Canals two weeks ago, they will find a schedule of all Merchant Marine vessels. In that schedule twenty-six ships are shown to have a tonnage of 8,300 and over. The corresponding tonnage of Petersen's vessels is 9,000. Two out of these twenty-six are listed as of 10,687 tons and 10,682 tons, and two more as of over 9,000. I ask the House to remember that twenty-six are above 8,300 tons. Of the remainder, thirty are from 3,341 to 5,000 tons odd. Only one is below 3,300 and that is the *Canadian Sapper* whose dead weight is 2,781. These are vessels which the Minister of Agriculture, with what I must describe as flippant fiction, declared were too small for the ocean and too big for the lakes. In my hand is a list of ships which this year have traded into the port of Montreal, traded to European ports, traded even to South African ports, and sixty-seven of them are under 3,100 tons. There are boats as low as 1,149 tons trading to Meandros, Greece; boats as low as 1,966 and 1,290 tons trading to Copenhagen; boats as low as 1,096 tons trading to Antwerp. Our vessels, all but one, or to be exact, fifty-six of them, are over 3,300. Yet the Minister of Agriculture, who wants to decry the property of Canada, who wants to find an excuse for not taking the obvious course of controlling and lowering rates on our own ships—if the Government wants to control by themselves at all— declares to the people of Canada, on his responsibility as a minister, that boats of 8,300 tons and up are too small for ocean traffic!

What is the nature of these vessels which the Prime Minister says are no good, not fit for North Atlantic trade? In 1923, according to a report of the Mercantile Marine presented by this Government, twelve of them plied the North Atlantic all year between Canada and European ports. In 1922, eleven of them did the same thing and at least eleven of them did so last year. These boats which hon. gentlemen tell us are no good, which the Minister of Agriculture says are too small for the ocean, which we are told are not fit for North Atlantic traffic, are doing service on the North Atlantic year in and year out. Indeed, such good service are they performing that the Minister of Railways and Canals is impelled to declare in the public interest that he cannot take them off. There have been repeated attempts on the part of hon. gentlemen opposite—and from this I must absolve the Minister of Railways, as I never heard him uttering such nonsense—to decry the character, type, design and construction of our ships. I hold in my hand some certificates from men who should qualify as authorities. First there is one from Mr. Isles, a superintendent stevedore of Montreal, one of the most competent and respected in the whole service. Mr. Isles' statement is the most moderate; I read from it first:

> After going over the specifications covering the ships which are to be built under the Petersen contract, I find these ships are about the same type of ship as the SS. *Glentworth*, which loaded here last fall.
>
> Comparing the larger ships of the Canadian Government Merchant Marine such as the *Canadian Constructor* and the *Canadian Cruiser*, 4,413 net registered tons each, they are about the same size as the Petersen ships.
>
> The *Canadian Seigneur*, the *Canadian Pioneer* and the *Canadian Ranger* are smaller boats, but as they would probably be easier to stow and as they carry their cargo both in lower holds and 'tweendecks they are more adapted for the Montreal trade.
>
> Their speed is slightly better than that of the Petersen ships.

I draw this to the attention of the hon. member for Lunenburg (Mr. Duff), who has found endless fault with the speed of our Canadian Merchant Marine.

> They will do their work better, as from personal experience in loading the *Canadian Mariner*, *Canadian Seigneur*, *Canadian Ranger*, and *Canadian Challenger*, it is found that these ships were easily worked and just as suitable as any ships that I have handled, their cargo gear being up-to-date, with hatches of suitable size for economical working. The proposed corrugation or "blister" on the side of the Petersen boats will, I think, cause trouble in docking and undocking, as it will be liable to hit the quay wall causing leaky rivets, which will be a menace and source of danger to the cargo.

This class of steamer is still in the experimental stage, and why should we subsidize experiments?

Yours truly,
DAVID ISLES,
Superintendent Stevedore.

In a subsequent note he says:

The specifications on page 28 of the proposed Petersen steamers are, in our opinion, those of the cheapest class of cargo steamer, which would not compare with either *Cairnross*, *Cairnmona*, *Cairnvalona*, *Cairntorr*, *Cairnavon*, *Cairngowan*, or *Cairndhu*.

All of these ships have powerful fan extractors in every hold, have an average sea speed of 12 knots, and are now being fitted with refrigerator chambers; have powerful wireless installation, direction finders, and every aid to navigation.

Then further (referring to Petersen ships):

We find nothing in the specifications to provide safe carriage for perishable and partly perishable cargoes. In fact shippers today, who demand, and have got by the steamship companies, fan ventilation and refrigerated chambers, would not ship on a steamer built to these specifications.

Emigrant traffic. Neither accommodation nor provision for it. If it is not provided for at building it would never be satisfactory, and would cost ten times as much to add it.

Speed about 11 knots is useless on the Atlantic for this traffic.

The next communication is from Mr. Capper, marine superintendent of the Cunard line:

I am of the opinion that these vessels of the Canadian Government Merchant Marine are a very good type, and equal to any other good cargo vessel on the service at present. As regards the running and working of the vessels, the records of the past two years show they are well manned and handled.

MR. MACDONALD (Pictou): What particular vessels does that refer to?

MR. MEIGHEN: To Canadian Government Merchant Marine Vessels in general.

MR. MacDONALD (Pictou): Oh, no.

MR. MEIGHEN: It refers to all those going in and out of Montreal, because Mr. Capper is a marine superintendent there and knows what he is talking about. The Canadian Government Merchant Marine boats run in and out of Montreal not only across the Atlantic, but to Newfoundland and the West Indies. It would refer certainly to all vessels of the 8,300-ton type, and I presume to many others of the 5,000 and 3,500-ton type.

Another letter is from Mr. Welch. He built a number of the Canadian Merchant Marine boats, and is a practical marine engineer:

> I have examined the abbreviated specifications of the proposed vessels for William Petersen and knowing the Canadian Government Merchant Marine boats of similar tonnage, I have no hesitation in saying that the latter boats have everything in their favour, both as regards cargo capacity and speed.
>
> Yours truly,
> A. WELCH,
> M.I.N.A. London, etc., etc.

Another letter has come to me from Mr. P. L. Miller, naval architect, and a member of the Institute of Naval Architects, England, and of the Society of Naval Architects of the United States. Writing under date of March 4th, he says:

> I have been reading with interest the reports from day to day in the press regarding suggested subsidy to Sir William Petersen to provide and operate ten cargo steamers on the north Atlantic trade under subsidy from the Dominion government, and I have had an opportunity of reading the contract and specifications attached thereto.
>
> My object in writing to you is to repudiate what is implied, namely, that the cargo vessels constructed during the past few years at the expense of the Dominion government are inadequate to meet the conditions indicated by Mr. Preston. It is true that as the science of naval architecture and engineering develops, cheaper methods of propulsion will be found and are being experimented on today. Is there any justification for ignoring a whole fleet of first-class vessels in order to replace them by ten new vessels of very similar specifications?

On a study of the specifications I see corrugated sides mentioned. These are not by any means accepted universally as
fundamentally sound. Furthermore, I think it will be
generally acknowledged that ship owners would expect to
operate a new ship for not less than ten years.

All the vessels of the Canadian Government Merchant
Marine, Limited, have been built since the year 1917. They
have been built under the same rigid inspection of Lloyd's
Register of British Corporation as have been vessels in the
Old Country, which is the same specification called for in Sir
William Petersen's contract, and on the average are equal
to any of the vessels turned out in the same period in Great
Britain.

One must also remember that many of the existing vessels of
the Canadian Government Merchant Marine, Limited, are
already fitted with refrigerated holds; also, practically all are
well fitted for the conveyance of grain, so it is difficult to see
what advantage will accrue in the substitution of the Petersen
ships for the trade required.

He might have added, "except for Sir William Petersen."

How anyone can admit or justify ignoring such a fleet in
order to have a new fleet constructed is beyond the comprehension of any ordinary citizen, let alone one who knows the
details of the business.

I sincerely trust that you will in some way be able to stop
the exploitation in Canada of additional expenditure on a
fleet of cargo vessels which, in my opinion, is not required.

Also there is a letter of very similar effect by the head of
Robert Reford Company, which company writes business for
lines competing with our Government Merchant Marine.

These communications I submit as reply to the uncor-
roborated assertions of hon. members of this Government that
our Merchant Marine boats are not fit for Atlantic trade. Every
one of these letters indicates they are equal, and most of them
state positively that they are superior, to the proposed Petersen
ships. They are undoubtedly faster. "Now," says the Minister
of Railways, "all we want to proclaim by this attempt is the
principle of control. We are ready to pay $13,000,000 just to
establish the principle of control." Well, why does he not estab-

lish the principle over our own ships, the Canadian Government
Merchant Marine? Does the Minister argue that our Merchant
Marine is under management of somebody else, and that the
government cannot possibly recover its control? If our Merchant
Marine under management of the Board which is operating it
today, a Board appointed by this Government, is tied hand and
foot and compelled to charge exorbitant rates, why does not the
Government take it from under that management? They can do
so by Order in Council. Over those eleven or twelve ships which
are running now across the North Atlantic, they can in an hour's
time recover their authority and fix rates for every one of them;
and what is more, can bind captains and all concerned to carry
goods at rates so fixed. Control as a "principle" is already established and only waits to be exercised if and when the Government wishes. Why pay $13,000,000 to attain recognition of a
principle which already is firmly and definitely in our hands—
that is if control can be called a principle? It is really no principle
at all. It is merely an objective, and that objective the Minister
can reach in sixty minutes by passing an Order in Council. Does
he say that to run ships out-and-out and fix charges thereon does
not establish the principle of control, but that if we pay
$13,000,000 to another man's company to do so, we have reached
the perfection of achievement? Surely not. Why then does he
ask us to vote this money to compel recognition of a principle
which he knows is already in being, and which he can give effect
to by Order in Council without a dollar of cost? So I say: If the
Minister wants to reduce rates, if he believes these allegations
that rates are extortionate; that they are set by a heartless Conference, a combine which is strangling Canadian industries, let
him take immediate and permanent control of our own ships
and reduce rates on fifty-seven instead of ten, thereby getting five
times the results which he can possibly get by this expenditure?

This Government which pretends to pay deference to Mr.
McMaster's committee took two years to follow its main recommendation, which was to take our ships out of the combine.
The Prime Minister says now—this I had almost forgotten—that
just a few days ago they took them out and the reason that they
did not do so sooner was they were afraid the combine would

crush them; the combine would boycott the Merchant Marine vessels and thus add to their loss on operation. Well, I do not say this by way of disputing the Prime Minister's statement, but I venture the assertion that our ships are following combine rates to this very hour. And why did the Government take two years to decide upon this step?—if, indeed, it is any real step at all. Why? The Prime Minister says, because we were afraid the combine would crush us. But, he tells us, Sir William Petersen is made of sterner stuff. Sir William is not afraid of the combine; has he not a dock, or two docks, or some more docks, over in England; has he not business interests there? Well, I suppose he has. I know he has four ships of about 4,000 tons which he runs somewhere down the African coast. But the Government of Canada has some business interests too. This country has some influence abroad which I think ought to compare with the influence and power of Sir William. The Government of Canada operates 24,000 miles of railway. Our ships are under, or were under, command of the same directorate as our railways. The Government of Canada has vastly more influence in respect of traffic abroad than Sir William can possibly have. The flag of this country floats in every bay and every ocean of the world, carried by steamships of Canadian registry. This Dominion has infinitely more pressure at its command than Sir William Petersen or five hundred Sir William Petersens can ever hope to possess. But hon. ministers say: We are afraid of the combine; it would come upon us with its big guns and would crush us, and that is why we could not take the Merchant Marine from its clutches. We could not stand the battle; but Sir William—he is ready to fight it out and he has a good chance of victory, because, forsooth, he has some docks and four ships running down the coast of Africa!

I address hon. gentlemen to my left: Was one question propounded by any of them answered by the Prime Minister? Not one. An hon. member rose and asked him: If these rates are so exorbitant why is it that the Merchant Marine which charges them is losing money? What was the answer? His answer was that he supposed it was on account of a differential against Canada; also that rates were so high they were stifling business and our boats could not get traffic. So the reason our Merchant Marine could not make money at high combine rates was because it was charging higher traffic tolls into our ports than were being charged into American ports. The Prime Minister stands here and confesses that for three years he kept our Merchant Marine under a directorate which held rates so high that our trade was being strangled, that our manufacturers were being stifled, that our western cattle trade was being smothered. The same Merchant Marine was also, he says, killing itself because its rates were so high, especially into Canadian ports. Is that not a magnificent way to manage the ships of this country? It is precisely what the Prime Minister has proclaimed.

Special reference has been made to the cattle business. We have been told that our own ships are not fit for carrying cattle. Twenty-six of them can be fitted for cattle just the same as any other ships. As a matter of fact, the directorate have already equipped not less than five; at least four are running, carrying cattle at $20 a head. The Government say, "Oh, this charge is doing harm to Canada, we cannot stand such a rate." The Government go to Sir William Petersen and I see in fancy the spectacle presented. Is it drawing a picture one whit out of line with reality when I describe it thus: The Minister of Trade and Commerce says to Sir William: "There are our ships, we are charging $20 a head on cattle. We and our fellow-pirates are strangling the western cattle trade; we are throttling the Ontario cattle trade. A member of Parliament got up and said we were blood-suckers. The Lethbridge Board of Trade is up in arms. We will give you, Sir William, $13,000,000 if you will come into business and force us to reduce these extortionate rates on cattle." Will even the member for Brome suggest that that is not precisely the bargain which the Minister of Trade and Commerce now submits to Parliament for ratification?

Have we had an answer to this question: Who is to be the arbiter who decides which of our cattle shippers, which of our grain shippers, which of our dairy shippers, which of our clothes-pin shippers—which of all these are going to get special favours at the expense of taxpayers? This argument, admittedly, would apply to Merchant Marine management on a low-rate basis just the same as to Petersen's ships—and, indeed, it indicates precisely why we did not run the Merchant Marine on a scale of charges differing from that of other vessels in and out of Atlantic ports. Had we done so, we would have had to select special shippers in Canada and give them special favours at public expense. But that is just what this Government proposes to do, and besides, for every dollar it gives a favoured shipper, it may be giving Sir William Petersen two. Who is to stand on the dock in Montreal and say to a shipper from one elevator: "We give you our special low rate on wheat today" and say to the shipper from another: "You have to use one of those other boats in the combine"? Has this country any right to discriminate as between its citizens? We cannot possibly operate the Petersen plan without doing so. Either this Government or Sir William Petersen himself will be a bestower of favours. Is the Government prepared to hand over to a man not even a citizen of Canada a right to select pets and give them special rates across the Atlantic? This whole proposition is built on a mad dream; it is unsound from its first word to the last, and I cannot help but think that the Government's only hope is to find for it a secluded cemetery at the hands of a committee.

Those of us who have been in the House for some time can remember vividly a chief article of faith of hon. gentlemen opposite. Canada's money, they were wont to say, should be spent in Canada; no money voted by Parliament should go to help ship-construction in another land. When the Government of the day in 1912-13 proposed construction of three ships of war of highest scientific type ever known, by way of assistance to Britain under shadow of the German menace, hon. gentlemen opposite fought us for days and weeks and months, and the burden of their opposition was that our $30,000,000 was going to be spent in ship-yards overseas. The Government then felt that as we had never built anything of this type before, and as in our belief the menace was near, and as we could not establish necessary docks and other facilities in time, the only defensible policy was to get those three warships built as fast as, and where, we could. But hon. gentlemen opposite were willing to risk everything just to get them built in Canada. When later, in 1918, we came to a programme of constructing merchant ships—a much simpler design—we took care that every one of them was constructed in Canadian yards.

These boats Sir William Petersen is going to build are of a kind we have already very often produced at home. They can be constructed nearly as expeditiously in this country as in any other, perhaps not quite so cheaply, but, better pay something more to give work to our unemployed than send our money somewhere else. The Prime Minister says: Oh, this money is not going into ship construction at all; Sir William Petersen is to provide funds for that. Yes, in a way that is true, but Sir William will procure his funds on the security of these subsidies. The money of this country in effect is to be spent in shipyards of the Old Land or some other land, and, according to the Minister of Agriculture, contracts are already let. This is being done at a time when we have hundreds of thousands of unemployed.

On every count there has been failure to review, failure to consider facts past and present protruding from every side. There has been nothing but a hasty, ill-digested, reckless plunge; and the Government hope, apparently, that because of their mere recklessness and the spectacular character of this legislation they are going to attract attention to the problem and finally drift to a solution. Just let us take this plunge into the Petersen contract, says the Prime Minister; just let us get beside Mr. Preston with his pebble and help him throw it into the Atlantic: In that way we will stir the dry bones of New Zealand; we will arouse Australia, and bring England to her senses; they will all come and gather round us, and we will find some sort of Board or Commission which will control rates on water. Does the Prime Minister really believe that? Do we get any further in the solution of a question by starting with a false step? If hon. members think we do, they ought to vote for this contract.

I go back to 1903. Did we improve our railway situation by hastily plunging into the madness of the Transcontinental? Did we? Did we not rather intensify its magnitude and difficulty for a period of half a century?

Did we, in 1923, help to remedy high freight rates on the Great Lakes by Hon. Mr. Low's legislation of that day? Will hon. gentlemen suggest for one minute that we did? We put through a Statute—and on that occasion also Mr. Preston was a moving spirit, the same man who has wound his malodorous trail through our politics for a quarter of a century—we plunged into a piece of legislation which resulted only in this, an extra cost of at least $3,800,000 in freight rates to our western farmers over what their American competitors were paying who used American boats. No, this was not the only result. Another was that we forced this Dominion later to bend its knee to American boat owners and beg them to come back into our trade and violate our law. We got nothing in the wake of that hasty legislation, save a loss of millions to our farmers and a bitter humiliation to our country.

What position are we in today as respects the Great Lakes problem? Are we as far ahead as we were in 1923? We have a Board which is forced to sham because it is supposed to be controlling charges when everyone knows it has not dictated a single rate. That Board in actual practice has no more to do with control of rates on our lakes than have the wardens of a Confucian temple in Shanghai. The Government may have expected when they took their bewildering step in 1923 they would bring the American Government to attention, and that Uncle Sam would join them in some system of control. But instead, the American Government stood by and laughed, and now, after the whole farce is known, the North American continent laughs as well.

But still hon. ministers call out: Take this step; plunge right in, and if you cannot say anything else for us, please say that we are courageous. The Minister of Railways himself admits they are courageous. Well, if courage consists in ill-considered and precipitate legislation, then the Government undoubtedly is deserving of that meed of praise. Or if courage consists in prodigality with other people's money, then the members of this Administration will leave a memory which will outlive the name of Joan of Arc. Courage! to dip into the treasury in a wild dissipation of $13,000,000 to do something we can do any time we want to without money and without price! As an exhibition of this species of courage, the Petersen contract is to be blessed by Parliament! I appeal to hon. members to make their real will known and to say that this proposal is fundamentally wrong, ill-advised, costly and futile, and deserves no further consideration at our hands.

THOMAS D'ARCY McGEE

Delivered on April 13, 1925, *in the Chateau Laurier, Ottawa, Canada, on the occasion of a Dinner to mark the One Hundredth Anniversary of the birth of D'Arcy McGee.*

THE STORY OF A NATION'S HEROES is the fountain from which it draws the wine of its later life. There is no inspiration that quickens the ambition of youth, stimulates public service and deepens love of country like the memory of great men who have gone. England has erected her Empire of today around the names of Cromwell, of Bacon, of Newton, of Shakespeare, of Pitt, and Burke, and Wellington, and Canning, and a hundred other luminous figures who have adorned her past. The flames of Italian patriotism have been fed for generations at the shrine of Cavour, of Garibaldi, and of Mazzini, and in France there is not a home that has not resounded with the praises of Charlemagne, of Colbert, of Richelieu, and of Napoleon; while in the United States, the perfection of modern democracy, tens of millions of citizens do homage to the memory of Washington, of Franklin, of Marshall, of Lincoln, and of Grant.

Canada has now reached a time when the lives at least of her founders have receded out of politics into history. There are no controversies of today which date back to the era of Confederation—nothing left now to distort the perspective with which we can view the men of that time and measure their powers, their motives, and their achievements. There are some of those giants who have stood every test, who have grown in stature through half a century of criticism and whose place in our annals is now forever secure. One of these is Thomas D'Arcy McGee.

With unreserved enthusiasm I congratulate the authors of to-night's event—and particularly Hon. Charles Murphy to whom we owe its inception and to whose driving power we certainly owe its success. It will be a good thing for the national spirit of Canada, it will help develop a real national personality when we can all join in veneration of the great deeds of the fathers of our country. It will help marvellously the cause of unity in this Dominion when all of us can realize that we as well as other nations have our patriarchs, men and women who have lived great lives, given to their country the last full measure of devotion and left an inheritance of fame which is to every province a common treasure and a common pride. Here we are gathered in hundreds three score years after the death of D'Arcy McGee and we are going to see to it, if we can, that this great Irishman, this great missionary of Ireland, this far greater Canadian and missionary of Empire, comes at last into his own.

D'Arcy McGee was Irish in lineage and nativity, but in every element of his character, in every vein of his being, in every bud and blossom of his personality he was more Irish still; all that the world admires in that race he possessed, a fine generous nature, a delicate sensibility, a passion for the beautiful in everything, in language, in landscape, in literature, in the deeds and thoughts of men. His imaginative gifts added the sheen of beauty to his writings and his speeches; but they did more than that; their spell upon him was so great that they commanded his course in public affairs. Wherever McGee the statesman went, McGee the orator was there, and McGee the poet was not far away.

His boyhood mind was nourished in the most revolutionary of Irish schools. As a talented young man he was drawn into the company of a set of brilliant intellectuals, a group of daring spirits who planned by a combination of oratory and shotguns to overthrow British power. He trained his eloquence by matching flights with Thomas Francis Meagher, who with the possible exception of Emmett, was the most vivid and spectacular of anti-British platform warriors in the last century. With this beginning he set out for America, carried his shining sword into journalism and determined to establish himself in the new world as the special guardian and tribune of his race. But the mind of D'Arcy McGee, while brilliant and imaginative, was fundamentally intelligent, receptive to reason and responsive to experience. He served his people devotedly every hour of his sojourn in the United States, but he soon came to the conclusion that human frailty was not confined to old England, that a republican government had no monopoly of liberty, and that the grievances which had racked his soul under British rule had their counterpart in other lands and were after all not such as should be removed by revolt and revolution, but by the far more certain process of constitutional reform. In this feeling he turned his footsteps to the British flag again, took up his abode in Montreal, and gave to this country the last and best decade of his life.

For the task which was awaiting him in Canada, D'Arcy McGee was wonderfully equipped. The young colony had been torn by feuds and schisms, the bickerings of rival races. Cliques into which men were divided and sub-divided had brought the Act of Union of 1841 into a condition of unworkable futility. The Atlantic colonies were isolated and unhappy, and were seeking access to our larger western populations. People generally were weary of the crudities and bitternesses of political strife. Into all this the fresh, buoyant spirit of McGee came like sunshine after a night of storm. Free from the antipathies of either faction, but with an intelligent sympathy for both, he set himself to preach the evangel of unity, and through all the changing phases of our pre-confederation struggles he pressed cheerfully and dauntlessly on. A relentless militant in other lands, he became a tireless peacemaker in ours.

He caught at once the vision of a great confederation—the union of our provinces in a federal system; this ideal seized his intellect and took possession of his heart; he saw in it the one plan and the only plan of salvation, and to bring about such a union he consecrated all the resources with which he was endowed.

With Upper and Lower Canada struggling to work together, but jealously gathering into rival camps divided by speech and creed, it was a tremendous event to have a man arrive who was a peerless master of the language of the one and a devoted disciple of the religion of the other. At a time when our maritime East and maritime West were further apart than the antipodes are today, it was a wonderful thing that a man should appear whose faith in British institutions had been tried in the furnace of experience and who believed with the ardour of a crusader that the genius of those institutions could weld these sundered colonies into one. The picture of a United Canada which filled the mind of D'Arcy McGee captivated his whole being. He could see nothing but the grandeur of a great young nation towering over the asperities of sectional strife, divisions obliterated, hostilities quieted, distance annihilated, the mountains of the Pacific offering shelter to the harbours of the Atlantic. He could see under union a national culture developed, a national literature nourished; he could see the exposed and straggling limbs of British dominion on this continent gathered into one living frame as guarantee against American absorption. Standing before an enchanted legislature in 1860 he said:

> I look to the future of my adopted country with hope, though not without anxiety; I see in the not remote distance, one great nationality bound, like the shield of Achilles, by the blue rim of ocean—I see it quartered into many communities—each disposing of its internal affairs—but all bound together by free institutions, free intercourse, and free commerce; I see within the round of that shield, the peaks of the western mountains and the crests of the eastern waves—the winding Assiniboine, the five-fold lakes, the St. Lawrence, the Ottawa, the Saguenay, the St. John, and the Basin of Minas—by all these flowing waters, in all the valleys they fertilize, in all the cities they visit in their courses, I see a generation of industrious, contented, moral men, free in name and in fact—men capable of maintaining, in peace and in war, a constitution worthy of such a country.

His voice rang through the whole inhabited area of Canada. An eloquence which had thrilled audiences in Ireland before he was twenty, which had defied British power in the hectic halls of Dublin, which had challenged and conquered hostile parties in the great republic, was turned in the full glow of its maturity into a mighty summons athwart British America to give birth to a British nation. The fiery insurrectionist of Carlingford had become the incomparable evangelist of Empire.

To Sir John Macdonald and Sir George Etienne Cartier it was

given to stand at the front of those men who are known now, and justly known, as fathers of our country. Close around them were George Brown, Tilley and Tupper. It was these men whose skill in the management of parties, whose experience as men of affairs, whose understanding of the unquenchable aspirations of minorities, whose patience through years of adversity and unbending determination to succeed enabled, at last, the lines of our constitution to be settled and the foundations of this Dominion to be laid. To them all honour is due and to them throughout our history increasing honour will be done. But if Macdonald and Cartier were the architects of Confederation, D'Arcy McGee was its prophet. He it was who in its grandest form caught the vision splendid; he it was who spread everywhere the fervour with which he was himself consumed; he it was whose restless pen and matchless platform power carried right into the hearts of the masses his message of tolerance and good will. It was D'Arcy McGee who was the triumphant missionary of union.

The full harvest of what our fathers sowed has been slow to ripen. Still it is true, and only the voice of unthinking ingratitude can deny, that in these fifty years we have garnered much. The obstacles encountered have been greater than we had believed, but they have been as nothing when compared with the obstacles and dangers which by our union we surmounted. And if in these later days we feel again the pains of sectional dissension and there are searchings of heart about our future, let us put on the armour of men of old who fought the same dragons in far more perilous array; let us look back across the span of two generations and watch the bold, brave figures of the captains of that time; let us learn from their patience and emulate their courage and highly resolve to enrich by our devotion the noble heritage they have handed down. And when distrust moves among us to estrange race from race, or class from class, or to whisper in our ear that we are not our brother's keeper, let us listen over the hills to the reverberating eloquence, the lofty patriotism, the warm-hearted toleration, the wholesome wisdom of Thomas D'Arcy McGee.

THE CONSTITUTIONAL CRISIS, 1926

From a speech delivered at Cobourg, Monday evening, September 13, 1926. *The events giving rise to and constituting this crisis are set out below and need not be recounted. The General Election of that year took place the following day.*

IT IS NECESSARY TONIGHT, as at every meeting, to refer to another subject—a most unusual and unfortunate subject to be injected into a campaign.

Mr. King, throughout, has determined to avoid to the utmost the record of his Government, and particularly the Customs scandal, and to dwell upon an alleged unfairness and breach of Constitutional practice which he says was dealt out to him by His Excellency, the Governor-General of Canada. Never before in the Dominion has such a subject been made an election issue, and certainly, not for very many generations has the head of any party in Britain sought to divide the people of that country over conduct of the occupant of the Throne. The undesirability of such a schism is just as great in Canada as in Britain. For purposes of his own, Mr. King has made himself author and parent of the controversy. This responsibility, I make bold to say at the beginning, he has taken with a very plain object but without any justification whatever.

The best approach toward making the issue and its merits clear will be a recital of facts. In such recital I promise you the utmost care and good faith, and by that care and good faith will ask to be judged.

Before prorogation of the Parliament which ended last year, Mr. King's party, then in power, had a total of 118 Members in the House of Commons. The Conservative party led by myself had 49; the Progressive party had 68.[1] On September 5th, Mr.

[1] Including 3 Labour who almost always voted with the Progressives, and 1 Independent.

165

King secured, as was his right, a dissolution. On that date, in announcing dissolution, he proclaimed to this country at Richmond Hill, Ontario, that he was doing so because he had not an adequate majority to enable his party to cope satisfactorily with great problems confronting the nation, and that these problems could not be solved in such a Parliament as had been elected in 1921, where the Government did not command a substantial majority in the House of Commons. It is quite true his Government did not command a substantial majority, or any majority. It was, through most of its term, in a minority of one, but was maintained in power steadily and without difficulty by votes of the Progressive party.

After the election of October 29th, things were vastly worse for Mr. King, instead of better. He, himself, and eight of his Ministers had been defeated. The Conservatives had strengthened from 49 to 116 members; the Liberals had been reduced from 118 to 101; and the Progressives had gone down from 68 to 28.[1] This was, I think, the biggest change in any election in Canadian history.

Mr. King announced, a week later, that he could take any one of three courses: (1) Resign; (2) Call for another dissolution; or (3) Meet the House and see how the Progressives would vote. The second alternative was preposterous; he had no shadow of right to another dissolution, and no person to my knowledge, except himself, has ever suggested that he had. He had, however, a right—if he did not wish to resign—to meet the House and carry on as long as he could. This is the course he chose, and Parliament was called to meet on January 7th last. His majorities were very narrow; twice he had only one; the largest he ever had was 15; the average close to 8.

During the Session a Motion was placed on the Order Paper by Hon. H. H. Stevens, alleging maladministration of a serious character against the Department of Customs, and demanding investigation by a Parliamentary Committee. On February 2nd, while this Motion was still waiting to be called, the Minister of Justice, Hon. Ernest Lapointe, moved that some days later the House should adjourn until March 15th in order to give Mr.

---

[1] Including 2 Labour and 2 Independent

King a chance to get a seat. Mr. Stevens moved in amendment that there be no adjournment until a committee of seven members had been appointed to investigate the alleged scandals in the Department of Customs. Owing to Mr. Stevens' insistence, a committee was appointed and on June 18th brought its report to Parliament. Conservative members were definitely not satisfied with the majority report, and when its adoption was moved, Mr. Stevens proposed an amendment. This amendment declared that in respect of subjects investigated the conduct of the Government and of the Prime Minister himself had been "wholly indefensible," and the conduct of the Minister of Customs "utterly unjustifiable."

While this amendment was being debated, Mr. Woodsworth moved a sub-amendment, striking out from Mr. Stevens' Motion those words which censured the Prime Minister, the Minister of Customs and the Government, and substituting certain words criticizing other unnamed persons and recommending dismissal of the Deputy Minister of Customs. This sub-amendment, you will be careful to note, deleted all censure of the Government and any member thereof. It received the endorsement of the Prime Minister and the entire Administration. The Conservative party vigorously and indignantly opposed it, and when a vote was taken on the night of Friday, June 25th, this sub-amendment was defeated by a majority of two, which meant that the stand taken by the Government demanding that it be relieved of censure was voted down in Parliament. Soon after, one of the Progressives, Mr. Fansher, moved another sub-amendment, leaving untouched the words of censure still standing in Mr. Stevens' Motion and including censure of the other persons covered in Mr. Woodsworth's defeated sub-amendment. To this the Conservative party agreed, but the Speaker ruled it out of order. I thought the Speaker was in error and appealed to the House against his decision. This appeal was carried against the Government by a majority of two. A Motion to adjourn, on the part of the Government, was then made. They had had a very bad night. This Motion to adjourn was defeated by a majority of one. After further debate on Mr. Fansher's amendment, it was agreed to by the Government and unanimously passed. Finally, at 5:15 Saturday morning, a Government Motion to adjourn was carried by a majority of one. Mr. Stevens' Motion of censure was still under debate, and, of course, a vote on it had to come.

That week-end Mr. King put through an Order in Council dissolving Parliament and submitted it, as was necessary, to the Governor-General for his approval. The Governor-General refused.

When the House met again on Monday afternoon, Mr. King announced that there was no Government; that he had asked His Excellency, the Governor-General, for a dissolution of Parliament and had been unconstitutionally refused; and that he had thereupon resigned, and that Canada was without any Government whatever. On the floor of Parliament he criticized the stand taken by the Governor-General. At this point the utmost accuracy is required, and I quote from Hansard Mr. King's words in justification:

> For a hundred years in Great Britain there is not a single instance of a Prime Minister having asked for a dissolution and having been refused it. Since this Dominion was formed there is not a single instance where a Prime Minister has advised a dissolution and been refused it.

Thus, without warning, the Prime Minister of Canada proclaimed to the nation and to the world that an injustice had been done him by the Representative of the Throne in Canada, and to establish such injustice he uttered two very serious sentences, spreading them through the press of our country. I have just read those two sentences, and, knowing thoroughly the meaning of my words, now declare to you that both are misleading, and the implications of both are false. This will be dealt with later.

Thereupon the tub-thumping started. We had not been accustomed to Constitutional problems of this kind. Very few knew much, or anything, about them. A cry went forth that "Downing Street" was interfering in our affairs and striving to injure the Canadian Prime Minister. There are parts of Canada where such cry is effective, and it would, indeed, be effective anywhere if people thought it was true. But it wasn't true; it had not a shadow of truth. The Governor-General was right and Mr. Mackenzie King was wrong. This will be established at the bar of history without a question, and I will establish it in your hearing tonight, as clearly and as briefly as possible; but for the present will adhere to my promise to complete first a recital of the events which constitute the crisis and which brought on this election.

The news of Mr. King's request, of the Governor-General's refusal, and of the Government's resignation, reached me just a few minutes before entering the Commons that Monday afternoon. Before the news broke immediately after lunch, I had never even imagined that Mr. King would ask for dissolution. We all knew the Session was nearly finished, but it was the first Session of that Parliament. Realizing that there were quite a number of Private Bills awaiting final disposition by one House or the other, and a few Public Bills either awaiting such final disposition or still to be approved by His Excellency, I rose immediately Mr. King sat down and invited the Prime Minister to meet with me at once so that we could try to work out together some way of finishing the Session's business. This would save these incompleted measures, much time and travel of members, and a lot of expense. Mr. King curtly refused, and informed the House there was no Prime Minister and no Government. The Commons then adjourned. At this point I add only the fact that never before in the history of this country, of Britain, or of any part of the British Empire had a Ministry behaved in this fashion, and, of its own will, left its country without any Government at all.

A little later the same afternoon I was invited by His Excellency to form a new Administration. It became at once my duty to decide whether there was a reasonable prospect that I could carry on in the House of Commons as it then stood. In my previous Parliamentary life I had necessarily studied with some care Constitutional rules in respect of dissolution, and, on first meeting His Excellency that afternoon, was persuaded that Mr. King's course had been quite wrong. I had also held, during the latter part of the Session, informal conversations with a number of members of the Progressive party and was confident that these members would give me independent support, if I should be called upon to form an Administration. There was no question but that I could form a Government—and a strong Government—from supporters in the House. Nevertheless, I requested time to consider the matter further, and promised to see His Excellency that evening. When we next met, I expressed belief that my chances of being able to carry on were good, and accepted the invitation to try.

At this point it must be remembered that under our law, for reasons which never appeared to me sufficient, any member of Parliament who was not a minister when elected and becomes one after, with a portfolio carrying salary, loses his seat automatically and must be re-elected. This is because a minister drawing salary has accepted what is described in the Statute as an "office of emolument" under the Crown. A member who becomes merely a Minister without Portfolio, even though he is then or afterwards named Acting Minister of one or more Departments, draws no salary and consequently does not vacate his seat. I was advised, however, by the Justice Department that if I accepted the post of Prime Minister I could not accept it merely as an Acting Prime Minister, and, therefore, could not avoid the salary attached to the office; and, consequently, that my seat would be vacated. The immediate situation was not easy. If the usual number of ministers were to be chosen and assigned portfolios with salaries attached, it would mean that these ministers could not sit in the House of Commons and that we would be short approximately seventeen seats—including my own—of our strength. Mr. King has insisted from the beginning that this is what I should have done, indeed, was compellable to do. He said he had known when he resigned that this is what I would have to do, if I undertook to form an Administration. If he is right, just think what it means. It means that once a Session has started no Government can be supplanted by another unless that other can command at least seventeen supporters more than its opponents can command. If this is true, then any Government leader whose party has been clearly defeated, though not heavily defeated, at the polls, can by merely adopting Mr. King's opinions be tolerably sure of lasting through the entire term of another Parliament. One's indignation at such nonsense is better unexpressed. Had the Session been over, the usual procedure would obviously have been followed, but as there was a small portion of its work still to complete, and, as all members—especially the Progressives who came almost entirely from the rural West—were anxious to get the business done and not be delayed six or seven weeks awaiting ministerial by-elections, another plan was adopted.

What I frankly described as a temporary Government was formed. It consisted of seven ministers—all members of the House of Commons—and of myself as Prime Minister. My colleagues were, however, not appointed Ministers of Departments, but were merely named Acting Ministers of Departments. Acceptance of such duties carries the same responsibility in every way, and the same powers in the House of Commons, as ministers appointed with portfolios, but those accepting draw no salary, and, therefore, do not vacate their seats, and, of course, need not be re-elected. In my own case, as just explained, this was not possible, and my seat was vacated. Such a necessity fixed a definite handicap upon me and upon the Government as a whole—though not enough handicap to satisfy Mr. King— because a leader outside instead of inside has difficulty, especially in a House of three parties, in mustering his utmost strength in each debate and in the vote which follows. I was, however, quite sure from Mr. King's attitude in the House that Monday that he would agree to no adjournment—indeed, he spurned my suggestion that I discuss such a subject with him—and his subsequent conduct and language in the House the ensuing week clearly showed that under no condition would he have agreed to adjournment for the purpose of having ministers appeal for re-election. Besides, as stated before, this procedure would have been very disappointing to, and resented by, many members, especially the Progressives. Consequently, it seemed to me that by far the more appropriate course was to form a temporary Government for the purpose only of finishing the Session, and immediately thereafter to put the Administration on a permanent basis for the future.

Shortly after announcing this plan, I learned with pleasure

that the Progressive party had, through their leader, advised His Excellency of their general attitude, this general attitude being that they would be fair to my Government and assist it in finishing the Session's work. Beyond expressions of encouragement and confidence which previously I had had from a number of them, there was no other specific intimation as to what, after the Session's work was finished, would be that party's conduct in future Sessions, but I was confident—and for good reason—that with sound and sane administration there would be sufficient support from them to enable us adequately and successfully to carry on. Very few Progressive votes were necessary for this purpose.

The new Government met Parliament on Tuesday afternoon, the day after Mr. King's resignation. All oaths of office required by law, and all oaths of office not required by law but which had customarily been taken, were on this occasion taken with scrupulous care. These consisted of the necessary oaths of each minister, taken then or previously, as Privy Councillor, and of a special oath of office by myself as Prime Minister, Secretary of State for External Affairs and President of the Privy Council. No member of the Government except myself was made minister of a Department, but all were named acting ministers. There had been acting ministers on many occasions throughout the whole history of Canada, and none of them had ever taken an oath of office, and no oath of office for them was provided by law. The permanent head of the Privy Council Department—that is, the Clerk of the Privy Council—certified in writing that all appointments had been made in exactly the same way as had been the custom in such cases for years past, and the permanent head of the Justice Department also gave a written opinion that all Orders in Council appointing these ministers were validly passed and were as effective as if made on the recommendation of any Committee of Council. These opinions were later read in full to Parliament.[1]

So we had a temporary ministry of eight Privy Councillors—one the Prime Minister with Portfolio; the others acting ministers. What a terrible thing! Jugglery, someone called it. "Illegal,"

[1] See Appendix

screamed Mr. King; and one effervescent gentleman from England said it was unprecedented in the annals of the Empire. Well, I can give him a list of precedents as long as his arm, and some of them in Canada, and not less than a dozen of them of Governments where there was not a single Minister with Portfolio.

On that Tuesday afternoon, the first important business was resumption of the debate on Mr. Stevens' Motion of censure as amended by the Fansher Motion. It contained then and always a declaration that the Prime Minister's conduct and the conduct of his Government in respect of Administration of the Customs Department had been "wholly indefensible" and that the conduct of the Minister of Customs in respect of the Moses Aziz case had been "utterly unjustifiable." Mr. Rinfret, a supporter of Mr. King, moved a sub-amendment striking out all words of censure in the Stevens' amendment. Objection was taken by Mr. Geary, Conservative, to the validity of this sub-amendment; the Speaker's ruling approving its form was appealed from, and the Speaker was sustained by a majority of one. After considerable debate, the Rinfret sub-amendment deleting censure came to a vote and was defeated 119-107—a majority for the new Government of 12. Shortly afterwards, on the same evening, the Stevens' amendment (as amended by Fansher's Motion) definitely censuring the late Administration, came to a vote and was carried by a majority of 10. Following upon this the original resolution to adopt the Committee's report as amended by Mr. Stevens' Motion of Censure also came to a vote and was carried by a majority of 10. Thus ended the first day of the Meighen Government, and three of the most important Parliamentary divisions in Canadian history. One could not think of a subject which would more definitely test the general attitude of the House of Commons as between the old Government and the new than that decided in those three divisions.

The following day—Wednesday—Mr. King tried another tack—a Want of Confidence Motion. He thought if he put the tariff question up to the Progressives, he would force them to vote against us; so he moved a Resolution declaring that the House was opposed to the new Government's tariff policy. After long discussion, this came to a vote in the evening and again the Government was sustained, 108-101—a majority of 7. Here for the fourth time, and this one on an issue of major policy chosen specially by Mr. King because of his belief that on this article of policy, if on any, he could compel the Progressives one and all to oppose us, we had a result quite the contrary—an expression of confidence by a majority of 7. I do not claim that those Progressives who voted with us meant thereby that they agreed with our policy. Very probably the correct interpretation is that they had at least as much confidence in us on tariff matters as in the previous Government, and that any differences they might have with us on that subject were not sufficient to justify them in withdrawing their general support. So up to this point the score stood thus:—on matters of administration, a definite censure of the previous Government emphasized by three decisive divisions; on matters of policy, refusal to withdraw confidence in the new Government even on the most critical issue.

During this same day, Mr. King, seeking to stop progress in voting Supply, moved that the Chairman of Committee of the Whole House leave the Chair. This was defeated by a majority of 21.

One would think that already Parliament had given ample evidence to vindicate the measure of confidence I had expressed to His Excellency, which measure of confidence was that I had a reasonably good prospect of being able to carry on.

On the afternoon of July 1st—Dominion Day—a new line of attack was tried. Mr. King and his followers seemed determined that no business of the Session would be gone on with, and that the House of Commons should be used only as a prize ring for their own purposes. They fixed up and moved a fantastic fabric of legal phraseology, the end and effect of which was to declare that the Government as constituted was not legally a Government at all.

Ordinary, sensible persons would surely think that such a serious, indeed astounding, pronouncement of Constitutional Law should, if its authors were sincere, be passed upon, not by laymen and politicians of whatever party, but by legal and constitutional authorities. They had in fact already been passed upon by those very authorities—the permanent officers of the Privy Council and of the Department of Justice. Their opinions were read to the House and were definitely, firmly, and unreservedly in our favour. If those men were not considered sufficiently competent, then the only higher and appropriate tribunal would be a Court of Law. Repeatedly, by public appeal, I and others have challenged Mr. King or any of his party to take their question in a manly way to the Courts, the same as the Hon. George Brown had taken a similar question in days gone by; but this challenge they declined. Very manifestly they had come to the conclusion that here was a subject on which it should not be difficult to mislead and confuse the lay mind. It was Progressive votes they were after. I would not for a moment say that the Progressive members were not men of intelligence, and comparable in that respect with those of other parties, but I do say, first, that this was not a subject on which it was possible to test the confidence of the House of Commons in either a Government's policy, its administration or its personnel, and second, it did not raise a question appropriate for determination by either a Parliamentary vote or an election, but by a Court alone. It was seized upon only because it was peculiarly susceptible to all kinds of misrepresentation and confusion. One has only to read the speeches made upon it to be certain that that is exactly what took place. When a vote was reached on Thursday night, a Progressive member, Mr. Bird of Nelson, who was against the Government, had been paired with Mr. Kennedy of Peace River, who intended to support the Government but who was ill. That means, each of them had promised not to vote. Mr. Bird broke his pair—the first time I remember seeing it done in the House of Commons. He stood up and voted, and the result was a majority of one against the Government. Mr. Bird had quite a period in which to retract while the vote was being counted and before the Speaker declared the result, but left it until a verdict had been announced, when it was too late to retract. He then expressed regret. This, however, was by no means the only trouble over pairs in those three disorderly days.

It is now time to discuss this last Resolution. It declared that Ministers of my temporary Government had been guilty of breach of Parliamentary privileges because, to quote:—

(1) They have no right to sit in this House and should have vacated their seats therein if they legally hold office as Administrators of the various Departments assigned to them by Orders in Council;

(2) If they do not hold such office legally, they have no right to control the business of Government in this House and ask for Supply for the Departments of which they state they are Acting Ministers.

You will wonder just what those words mean. If Mr. King had wanted to make them simple, plain and understandable, it could have been done, but he did not do so. Take that first assertion! "The ministers should have vacated their seats if they legally held office as Administrators of the various Departments." This resorts to an old device; it assumes something as true which is not true. Ministers without Portfolio do not hold office at all, except as members of the Government. They act as ministers of Departments and do the work, but they have no portfolio, hold no office and draw no salary, and, therefore, do not vacate their seats. These men administer Departments but they do not hold office as Administrators. You can see how easy it was to confuse men unaccustomed to such matters. The assumption in the first statement was false and that made the whole assertion false. The second is of the same type exactly—this one based on three untruthful assumptions inserted just to make it plausible. "If they do not hold office legally, they have no right to control the business of Government in this House and ask for Supply for Departments." It assumes that Ministers without Portfolio hold departmental office as ministers. They do not. They simply do the work but do not hold the office. It assumes that ministers control Government business in the House. They do not. The House itself controls all its proceedings. Third, it assumes that ministers need to hold an office to ask for Supply. They do not. A Minister without Portfolio can ask for Supply with just as much authority as a Minister with Portfolio, and has done so in our history many, many times. In Mr. King's own Government which got such a rebuke in 1925, Hon. E. M. Macdonald was for quite a length of time Acting Minister of National Defence. Further, he was acting minister when there was no minister holding the office. He acted in the House exactly as the minister would have acted had there been one and had he been there. He asked for Supply and got Supply. I could give other instances in this country or any British country. Talk about asking for Supply! One does not need to be a minister at all, with Portfolio or without Portfolio, to be competent to ask for Supply. All one needs, even if he is only a private member, as has been shown by precedent time and again, is authority from the Government in power. Surely this is enough to make clear to you the subtle dishonesty of the Resolution upon which Mr. King and his cohorts thundered to Parliament for almost a day, and with which they succeeded in bewildering and misleading honest members of that House.

The air was filled with charges about the new Government and its ministers not being "responsible." Why weren't they? A minister does not become responsible just because he draws a salary; he does not become responsible merely because he has an office in a Department; he becomes responsible because he is a minister sworn of the Privy Council. That is the foundation of his responsibility. If the present Leader of the Liberal party would look up the history of his predecessor, Edward Blake, he would find what I have just said, expressed by him with definiteness and force, and he would find his own empty contention on this point treated with scorn.[1] The temporary Government of those days was, in Parliament and out of Parliament, and, as long as it existed, under the fullest possible responsibility, the same as any Government that ever was formed, and this the ex-Prime Minister knows just as well as I do.

Mr. Garland, one of the Progressives who supported us consistently until the last vote, made a public statement two or three days later saying that the intimation which the Progressive party had given the Governor-General of their intention to be fair to the new Government and to assist it in finishing the Session's work was based on an assumption that the new ministry would

[1] Ontario Parliamentary Debates, 1871: p. 31.

be "legally constituted" and, therefore, "capable of functioning." Mr. Garland was quite justified in this public statement. Such an assumption is only fair and right. But surely he should have added that the proper tribunal to determine whether a Government is legal or not, and, being legal, is capable of functioning, was not the House of Commons but a Court of Law. As he, himself, realized and stated, it was a naked question of law. Mr. King chose the House instead of the Court, and for a very obvious reason. He would have cut a sorry figure before a Bench of Judges. Again I invite him to have some courage and try. The performance of Mr. King and his confederates on Dominion Day 1926 will, in calmer days to come, stain the pages of our history. The Motion by which enough Progressives were taken into camp on a subject of Constitutional law was a work of guile; it was a plant; it was a piece of verbal chicanery; it was a wily, sinister artifice to take advantage of men untrained in legal reasoning; it was in plain language, a fraud.

Later on, Mr. King raised a hue and cry through the country about my arrogance; declared that for two weeks I was sole adviser of the Governor-General; that there was no one else in the Government constitutionally competent to advise; that other ministers were impostors illegally appointed, and that all contracts made by them were invalid and worthless. No one can imagine claptrap more preposterous! Besides myself, seven ministers were qualified and competent to advise the Governor General in the same way precisely as other ministers had been qualified so to advise ever since Canada was a country. A minister becomes qualified so to advise by being sworn of the Privy Council, and in no other way. "No man," he said, "in England or in Canada ever dared to be the only adviser even for a day." Well, I did not, but Sir Wilfrid Laurier did, for two days in 1896, and he acted perfectly properly. I, myself, remember that just a few years ago Mr. Balfour, to meet a temporary emergency, suggested that either Lord Rosebery or he himself, or both, be the sole Government of Britain for the period of an election campaign! To expose any further the torrent of nonsense talked on this subject those days and since would be a waste of time. Apparently there was determination to part company with truth, and to get back in power by any means whatever.

That one-vote majority against us meant that in the opinion of the House of Commons, thus obtained, our Administration was not legally and constitutionally a Government, and, therefore, not qualified to act as such. This result taken in conjunction with the defeat of the King Government the previous week forced us to the conclusion that neither one side nor the other could carry on in the then Parliament. We, therefore, recommended dissolution to His Excellency. This request was granted, and rightly granted, as will presently be shown.

Let us now revert to the initial question in issue.

Was the Governor-General right or wrong in refusing dissolution to Mr. King on June 28th?

In announcing his resignation, Mr. King declared His Excellency was wrong. For the first two days the tocsins rang throughout Canada that this right and duty of the King in England and of the Governor-General in Dominions to refuse dissolution had gone into the discard and was dead. The idea was to get an impression spread round that "Downing Street" was interfering, that we were being thrown back to what they called "Colonial" days. This simply was not true. The Representative of the Throne in Canada has discretion and duties in these matters, and, if he does not exercise them, a Prime Minister and Government can play fast and loose with the Constitution of our country, just the same as a Prime Minister and Government in England, if all checks and balances were gone, could play fast and loose with the British Constitution. True, over there they would be less likely to do so.

As read to you near my opening, Mr. King's first assertion was that for one hundred years no Prime Minister in Britain had asked for a dissolution and been refused. His next was that since Confederation no Prime Minister in Canada had asked for dissolution and been refused. First, the question is not whether there has been an instance either in England or in the Dominion. There would presumably be no instance unless there was a wrongful request; and, consequently, it would be very rare that there would be a refusal, especially in Britain. There they have high, and very high, regard for correct procedure and Constitutional rights. They do not welcome—indeed, they avoid to the utmost—anything in the nature of a party division over the conduct of their King. But in Britain, none the less, there is not a shadow of question that the power and duty of the Throne in this regard is still intact and is essential to preservation of the rights both of Parliament and people. I venture to assert that there has not been a Prime Minister of that country, in this century or the last, who has ever disputed either that power and duty or the necessity of its continuance. Both, on the contrary, have been propounded in the plainest and strongest terms by leading figures of the United Kingdom, right up to the present time—by Edmund Burke, by Peel, by Gladstone, by Disraeli, by Lord John Russell, by Sir John Simon, by Asquith, by Lloyd George—nearly all great names in the Liberal hierarchy of Britain. Parenthetically the corresponding vice-regal right and duty has been proclaimed in this country by Alexander Mackenzie, by Edward Blake, and by Sir Richard Cartwright—all stout and honoured Liberals—and only because they knew it was real and that its maintenance was essential to our Constitutional system. Less than three years ago Mr. Asquith denied most emphatically that a request for dissolution could not be constitutionally refused. He further denied that the Crown can permit any Ministry to put its subjects to the tumult and turmoil of a General Election merely because it finds itself unable to command a majority in the House of Commons.

No public man in Britain, to my knowledge, has ever sought to dispute or even to modify a famous pronouncement of Edmund Burke that a Ministry must yield to Parliament and not contrive that Parliament be new-modelled until it is fitted to their purposes. If the authority of Parliament, he said, is to be upheld as long as it coincides in opinion with His Majesty's advisers, but to be set at nought the moment it differs from them, then the House of Commons will shrink into a mere appendage of administration and entirely lose its independent and effective character.[1] Surely great figures in public life like Burke, and Russell, and Gladstone, and Blake, Sir John Simon and Asquith, men of preëminent capacity and lifetime training in Consti-

[1] Burke, *Works*, (Little, Brown, 1901) vol. II pp. 553-5.

tutional law and practice—surely these are the authorities we should look to on this question. And these men are not discordant; they are in agreement.

Nothing less than universal has been the common sense doctrine that no Government can be in a position to hold the sword of dissolution over Parliament to be used at its own unrestrained will if members don't vote to its satisfaction. Such a condition of affairs would destroy the independence and usefulness of a House of Commons.

Mr. King said, as quoted a moment ago, that no Prime Minister had been refused dissolution in the past hundred years. Mr. Asquith himself, the man who stoutly upholds the doctrine, asked for dissolution in 1910, not, be it noted, because he was without a majority or was having trouble with the House of Commons, but because he had introduced a great new measure affecting the Constitution, on which the Commons had supported him, but on which he felt the electors should be consulted. Nevertheless, he was seeking to dissolve only a year following a previous dissolution obtained by himself, and his request was not granted—at least it was not granted at once. Subsequently, four days afterwards, he renewed his appeal. The King imposed a condition. Next day Mr. Asquith agreed to the condition, and dissolution was then conceded. If there is a right to delay and, having delayed, to impose a condition, there must be a right to refuse. This I think is the only instance in England in the hundred years, but in the British Dominions and in British Provinces and Colonies, where the same principles apply, there have been thirty or forty refusals in a much shorter period of time, and I venture to say not one of the requests which preceded them was as deserving of refusal as Mr. King's.

In Canada there has been no recorded instance since Confederation of refusal to a Federal Government, though no one in public life has ever questioned the right. But there have been three rejections to Provincial Governments—notably in Quebec and New Brunswick—and the same principles apply in both spheres. The reason there has not been one in the Federal arena is that no Prime Minister before Mr. King has been known to make an improper request.

In other Dominions, however, there have been several refusals. They are more likely to occur in countries where there are three substantial parties. There was one in Australia in 1904, another in 1905 and a third in 1909; the first being to a Labour Government, the second to a Free Trade Government and the third to a Protectionist Government. Again, as recently as 1913, in the Commonwealth of Australia, a doubtful case arose. The Governor General asked for counsel from the Chief Justice of the Commonwealth and was advised that he had full power to grant or to refuse, and was supplied with principles upon which he should make his decision. In New Zealand also there have been repeated instances. Without question an improper request should be declined. Otherwise, as made very clear by *The New Statesman*—a prominent Labour newspaper in England—when discussing this Canadian case, a Prime Minister can by mere persistence prevent his own expulsion from office. I read:

> When he finds he cannot control Parliament, he appeals to the electorate. The electorate rejects his appeal, and back he goes to Parliament and furbishes up a temporary majority. Parliament becomes tired of him and is ready to condemn him, and he asks the Governor General to allow him a second appeal to the voters. Presumably, if Lord Byng had acceded to his demands and he had not improved his position at the election, he would again have claimed the right to meet Parliament and made another attempt to conjure up another majority, which would probably have been available until members earned another sessional indemnity. Then the majority would have crumbled away, and by his doctrine he could have demanded a third dissolution.

This is what I described a few moments ago as playing fast and loose with the Constitution.

What then is a wrongful request? It would be very easy to quote a string of authorities and precedents. This case does not require any lengthy list. To be brief, I will go straight into the camp of the enemy and read you principles, and sound principles, as defined by the most effusive champion, and almost the only champion, Mr. King has at the present time. By the way, you have been hearing a lot about Downing Street domination—

about interference from overseas. Downing Street—that is, British ministers or officials—has not lifted a finger or uttered a word. Over there they have more common sense and know their proper place.[1] The only interjection from across the water has been from a Mr. Berriedale Keith, who for a long time has professed himself—and with some acceptance—as an authority on this question. He has been shooting his edicts across the Atlantic quite vigorously, and in justice to him I venture to believe that when he first took his stand on this Canadian case, there were a lot of facts which he had not been told. Since then he has been driven into inconsistencies and contradictions, so much so that no ordinary mind can tell where he stands from day to day. He is not a clear-thinking man, but one very much in need of what Macaulay described as "purification of the intellectual eye." Anyway, he is the authority Mr. King depends on, so I am going to speak from his writings before he knew of this case. In a book published only two years before, he gave the following rule, and please note that in propounding it he was dealing with Constitutional practice in England where he seems to think the King's discretion is narrower than a Governor General's discretion in a Dominion:

> It is for instance, obvious, that the Crown could not constitutionally grant a Prime Minister, who had obtained one dissolution and had been defeated, a second dissolution of Parliament if any other means of carrying on the Government could be found.[2]

Now, let us apply this rule prescribed by Keith himself: First, Mr. King's Government had one dissolution. Second: In the first six months of its first Session thereafter, it was defeated on a most important Motion—a Motion in amendment washing out censure from a previous Motion—a Motion in amendment which

[1] Subsequently, it transpired that Mr. King had himself taken what is considered a most unconstitutional course of urging His Excellency to consult the British Government, i.e., Downing Street, on the question. The Governor-General refused to do so, no doubt for the unanswerable reason that this responsibility was his and his alone. Mr. King did not make known his extraordinary conduct until after the election.

[2] *Constitution, Administration and Laws of the Empire* 1924: pp. xiii-xiv.

it had vigorously and tenaciously supported. Its defeat is what prompted its appeal for dissolution. Third: An alternative Government could be found, and was found; and further, the alternative Government was successful in four decisive votes, all going to questions of policy and administration. It was then defeated by one false vote on a legal question which it was monstrous to submit to Parliament, and which, in any event, did not go to any question of policy, of administration or of confidence. It would be impossible to find any case more clearly and indisputably within the four corners of Mr. Keith's own rule than this case in Canada.

Again, Mr. Keith used this language:

> The normal form of the refusal to accept ministerial advice is when a Ministry beaten in Parliament, or which is losing its hold on Parliament, asks for a dissolution in order that it may strengthen its hand in the country.[1]

You will observe this is declared to be not an exceptional but a "normal" case for refusal. In the Canadian situation, Mr. King's ministry was defeated in Parliament. In the Canadian situation, that ministry was losing its hold on Parliament. Either one of these conditions, according to Keith, was sufficient; and both were present. Also in the Canadian case the ministry was asking for dissolution in order that it might strengthen its hand in the country. Mr. Keith has been very busy lately berating our Governor General because he followed Mr. Keith's advice. Indeed, everything this man ever pronounced on the subject before June of this year told in favour of the Governor-General's course.

But the precedents and principles I have recited, though conclusive, are not necessary at all. Mr. King did something which no Prime Minister of Canada, of a Province of Canada, no Prime Minister of Britain, of a British Dominion or a British Colony, at any time or any place, ever did before. In the middle of a debate on a Motion censuring his Government and censuring himself, he went to the Representative of the Throne and presented an Order in Council dissolving Parliament. It was a step not only unprecedented anywhere, but incredible. Acquies-

---

[1] *Responsible Government in the Dominions*, 1912, p. 180; repeated in 1928 edition, p. 154.

cence on the part of the Governor-General would have been an utter abdication of duty, and equally incredible. If the House of Commons has one function more sacred than another, it is to hold an Administration to practices of honour and efficiency. Charges of maladministration had been made against the Government. These charges had been investigated, and arising out of that investigation a Motion of censure was before the House. Already two divisions resulting from that Motion had definitely indicated an impending Government defeat when the original Motion should come up for decision. The Commons of Canada was sitting there trying the case. The House—to use the language of Edward Blake uttered in a similar though far less flagrant instance, in 1873—"had within its cognizance a great cause pending between Ministers and their accusers." At this point Mr. King went to Rideau Hall, demanded that the jury be dismissed, demanded that the Parliament trying him should no longer live. Never, never, I say, has there been such conduct in the long history of Parliamentary Government.

You ask: "What is Mr. King's answer?" Here is his answer. First, he says it was not a Motion of censure. Not a Motion of censure? To say that a Motion describing his own conduct and the Government's conduct as "wholly indefensible" is not censure, is grotesque; it is an affront to common sense. When he was pleading in the House for his followers to vote against it, he himself declared time and again that it was a Motion of censure. His Minister of Customs—another who was specially accused—told the House it was a Motion of censure. His Minister of Agriculture, Mr. Motherwell, also pleaded with members to vote against it because it was a Motion of censure. Mr. Motherwell went so far as to quote the celebrated speech of Iago—quite forgetting its original purpose—and apply it to the King Government:—

> Good name, in man or woman, dear my lord;
> Is the immediate jewel of their souls.

On this point, even Mr. King's champion or apologist—whatever you like to call him—Mr. Keith, certainly has not agreed with him. You are wondering how Keith gets over this mountain in his attempt to justify Mr. King. I will tell you. He just refuses to discuss the subject. He persists day after day and week after week in forgetting all about it. What else could he do? I have never heard or read of anyone who, having recognized that dissolution meant avoiding a vote on a censure Motion, still said there was a right to dissolution.

The other explanation Mr. King gives is no better. He says: Granted dissolution was asked for in the midst of a debate on a Motion of censure, I was then in no weaker position than I would have been if defeated on the Motion, and, even if defeated, I would have had a right to dissolution. He would not. Even had he stood his ground for a vote, the fact that he had obtained the previous dissolution less than nine months before made it absolutely necessary, especially so soon after the election, that every reasonable effort should first be made to find a Government which had a fair prospect of continuing with the existing Parliament. On this, British and Canadian statesmen have agreed, and their academic apostles have also agreed, until Keith, a few weeks ago, went back on all his published principles. But it is true that Mr. King's position would have been much better after defeat on censure than it was when he tried to get dissolution to avoid defeat. There are circumstances in which an accused person or a litigant is permitted to appeal from a lower Court to a higher, but no one ever heard of an accused person or a litigant, in the middle of his trial and before a verdict, demanding that the Court be dissolved, that the jury be dismissed in order that he may appeal. This is precisely the preposterous conduct of which Mr. King was guilty.

This conduct puts him out of Court on every count, and out of Court he will remain through all time at the bar of history.

A democracy has an absolute right to the judgment of Parliament on the behaviour or misbehaviour of its Administration. Think of the importance of that right in this very instance. A committee of Parliament had investigated charges and Parliament was moving, by discussion, to its judgment on that committee's report. In the thrust and parry of debate across the floor, where each speaker meets his foe in combat, light and reason are thrown on the issues and truth is encouraged to emerge. To this, and to the verdict finally reached, the public was entitled, and all this Mr. King determined to keep from the nation.

From every angle of approach the Governor-General was right and Mr. King was wrong. For His Excellency to have yielded would have been to make himself an accomplice in an unheard of assault on the prerogatives both of Parliament and people.

A right decision cannot be converted into a wrong decision by any subsequent event. Besides, when it was made there was at least a reasonable prospect—and nothing more is necessary—that another Government would be acceptable to Parliament as it stood. This prospect was indeed afterwards proved by repeated majorities on every test of a political issue—notwithstanding that the succeeding Prime Minister was debarred from his seat by an outdated law. We lost finally by a spurious vote on a spurious legalistic fabrication—no subject for Parliament at all.

Of the necessity for dissolution then, and of our right to be granted dissolution, there can be no doubt. By that last vote Parliament had demonstrated that it would not consistently support any Government. It had not so demonstrated when Mr. King applied on June 28th. We had not asked to dissolve while a Motion of censure was under debate. Mr. King had. Our Administration had not been censured by the House of Commons. Mr. King's Administration had been. We were clearly in a stronger position than was the Ramsay MacDonald Government when it asked for dissolution less than two years ago and Ramsay MacDonald's request was granted.

Just one last word. Nobody claims, least of all the present Governor-General of Canada, any right on the part of the King's Representative to choose as between parties the stamp or colour of Government. That is for Parliament alone. The King's Representative, in the limited sphere as guardian of the Constitution still reserved for him, can only make sure that Parliament is not denied that right. It makes no difference to a free people, said Edward Blake, whether their rights, as reposed in their Parliament, are invaded by the Crown or by the Cabinet. What is important, he said, is to secure that their rights shall not be invaded at all. Blake, at the time, was denouncing an Order of Prorogation which postponed for three months the moving of a vote of censure, and he urged with great power preservation to the utmost of the form and principles of the Constitution and the rights of a House of Commons which our ancestors had handed down.[1]

In fidelity to this teaching, in simple performance of the duty it imposes, guided and directed as well by other great figures over a wider range in our present and our past, the Governor-General of Canada, in silence and in dignity, has done his part. His part being done, it has been my humble but proud privilege to stand at his side.

The Lord Byng of Vimy is not on trial in this contest. His Court is the Court of Conscience and of History. The immediate fortunes of two political leaders and two political parties are before the tribunal of their masters. But more than they, and far more important than they, the people of Canada themselves are on trial. Not by showy strategy—to use a most flattering term—not by empty dexterities of politics can popular institutions either flourish or survive, but only by all ranks seeking steadily the truth and toiling in its light, preserving from the past what has proven good, and thus building on foundations which are solid and abiding. Yes, the people of Canada are on trial. On the integrity of their thinking, as reflected in the verdict of tomorrow, will depend in no small measure the standard of our public life for years to come.

[1] House of Commons (Canada) Debates, as reported in Toronto *Globe*, Nov. 6, 1873, and Toronto *Mail* of same date.

RESPONSIBLE GOVERNMENT

DEFENCE OF THE HAMILTON SPEECH

This address was delivered on October 10, 1927, at the opening of the Winnipeg Conservative Convention. Its background and the circumstances attending its delivery are disclosed in the speech itself.

THE SPECTACLE WHICH GREETS ONE from this platform is indeed magnificent. I am looking into the faces of many thousands of Canadians from every corner of this vast country, men and women who believe that the Conservative party is a party of principle and a great agency for good. When one addresses you he can rightly assume that you adhere in sincerity to its faith, and are determined to forge and consolidate that party into the mighty power it ought to be. Such an event as this is doubly gratifying to one who has been long associated with your councils and has taken some part in your battles.

It does not seem to me fitting that I should have anything to say, especially at this stage, upon the subject of policies or tactics looking to the future. These things will be left to the proper time and to appropriate committees. My words this afternoon will relate entirely to history, but to very recent history. They will relate, indeed, solely to one event which took place in the latter part of my six and a half years of leadership. I intend to have something to say now with regard to a speech I made at Hamilton in November, 1925.

It is my intention to deal in the frankest and plainest language with this subject. The time has come at last when I can do so before the right tribunal, the tribunal to which I was and am responsible, and do so without involving the party as a whole, or any organization, or any others except myself. For the first twelve months after delivering that speech I refrained

189

from defending my position, not by any means because of personal desire, but because, being still head of our party, I was persuaded, rightly or wrongly, that its unity would be better served by silence. For the past twelve months I have been a private citizen; I am a private citizen today, and a private citizen I intend to remain, and as such speak in defence of a proposal made as Leader, and made in good faith because I believed in its merits. It is only truth to say that the pronouncement was not accepted by a substantial section of the Conservative party at the time, and with my retirement from Leadership, the Conservative party became entirely free from its commitment. I do not speak today with the object of re-establishing that speech as binding upon the party now. No such concern is in my mind. What I shall say will be in my own behalf alone. The right to speak in my own behalf now is something which no man can dispute. It is not dependent upon privilege or courtesy, and is a right I propose to exercise to the full.

It is far from my wish to appear before this Convention as one harbouring a grievance or a complaint. Of the rank and file of the Conservative party I have never had cause for grievance, and for them have feelings only of loyalty and gratitude. No Leader whom this party ever had received more devoted support or more generous treatment at the hands of his followers in the House of Commons. But as for the Hamilton speech, it surely is true that I have suffered from a grievous misunderstanding both as to its meaning and its scope. To this misunderstanding my own absence from Canada for a considerable time after the speech was made contributed not a little, and throughout these two years a section of the Press of the country, and especially the Liberal Press, has contributed a great deal more.

It becomes necessary now that you be given in exact language the entire text of the Hamilton speech insofar as it relates to the point at issue. The text from which I read was handed to the Press before the speech was made, exactly in the language now read from this platform, and was delivered in that language at the banquet in Hamilton. It is my earnest hope that every man and woman in this audience will follow carefully these words.

The great object of the Conservative party in the late campaign was to obtain from the people of Canada in every province a decisive verdict on the fiscal issue. To this end we concentrated our efforts. I am glad to say that in a large measure we succeeded. Canada has suffered, and suffered severely, from the uncertainty and haphazard downward revision of the last four years. These dire consequences had come to every province. In most provinces of the Dominion we found the Government and Government speakers striving desperately to confuse this issue and to divert the public mind from the results which had flowed from their own drift and folly. In Ontario they failed, in British Columbia they failed, in the Maritime Provinces they failed; only in the Province of Quebec did they succeed. I do not speak the language of resentment or of bitterness, I speak only the language of truth when I say that never in the history of elections in this Dominion has a great party stooped to methods at once so dishonest and so dangerous as did the Liberal party in the late campaign in the Province of Quebec. While the Prime Minister was talking unity in English-speaking Canada and was presenting himself as its only true guardian and apostle, his lieutenants were adopting every means known to the platform speaker or the pamphleteer to stir up all the old war animosities and to conjure new fears and new hostilities in the minds of the good people of Quebec. There is nothing in what I say which is open to dispute. There was indeed much concealed, but sufficient was spoken from the housetops and thundered in the press to make clear for all time the character of the campaign. I will quote only the utterance of one man, and he a very eminent man, the Prime Minister of Quebec. Speaking on the Island of Orleans on the 26th October, the Hon. Mr. Taschereau used the following words as quoted in *Le Canada*, a Liberal paper edited by a Liberal Member of Parliament, in its issue of the following day:

"In the present contest you have to choose between two men, Mr. King and Mr. Meighen. I do not wish to be lacking in Christian charity, but I believe I am guilty of no wrong when I say that Mr. Meighen is the man of conscription, that it was he who sent our men to fight in Flanders fields. It is he who by his conscription has filled the cemeteries of Flanders with 60,000 Canadians. Has he grown better since? Has he reformed? Has he had perfect contrition? No."[1]

I do not mention the utterances of obscure individuals or of pamphleteers. Those in high authority in the Liberal party harped on the tragedies of war and ascribed all that Canada had suffered to the Conservatives of to-day. Illustrated sheets were distributed in thousands, depicting your humble servant as a tyrant and a man-eater driving the sons of Canada with a whip to be slaughtered in foreign lands. New wars were prophesied and were declared to be part of the programme of the Conservative party. A war with Turkey, indeed, was to come right away if the Conservative party were returned. Do not conclude from all this that the people of Quebec are at fault, do not conclude that the people of Quebec are arrayed in sentiment against the rest of Canada, do not even conclude that there is any lack of fidelity there to British connection because these things were done. These were only plays, these were only phantasies conjured up by political leaders in order to mislead the people and gain an election verdict. If the rest of Canada had thought that the Conservative party favoured war or was looking for war, the rest of Canada would have voted against us just as decisively as did Quebec. It was not against our policy, or against our principles that the people of the Province of Quebec voted on the 29th October, it was against a gross misrepresentation of both our principles and our policy. Your humble servant was depicted, for example, as ready to despatch the sons of Canada to wars all over the world, even without the authority of Parliament. How men can find it in their hearts to utter such words passes my comprehension. The Conservative party believes in British connection and believes in the British Empire; so does the whole of Canada, so does the Province of Quebec. The Conservative party believes in exerting the whole influence of Canada within the Empire to make sure and ever surer the lasting peace of the world. The Conservative party believes that within the Empire the security of this Dominion can best be sought, and the Conservative party believes that the whole of Canada is ready at all times to take every honourable step to make our security certain. This and no more is

---

[1] Hon. Mr. Taschereau has since denied the correctness of *Le Canada's* report, but has failed to furnish a text of the language he did use on the occasion in queston.

what we have always said and what we have always done;
this and no more is what we will ever do.

In the late war, as in every war, the Government had to
decide its course and submit that course to Parliament. Never
did we think of sending troops from Canada until Parliament
had approved our decision. Parliament met on the first day
it could be called and gave its unanimous support to participation by this country. Never would any Government so
much as dream of sending troops beyond our shores unless
the authority of Parliament was first obtained. Indeed, I
would go farther. I do not anticipate that we of this
generation will ever be called upon to take part in war again,
and I earnestly hope that our children and our children's
children may be free from the curse of war, but if ever the
time should come when the spectre of 1914 should again
appear I believe it would be best, not only that Parliament
should be called, but that the decision of the Government,
which, of course, would have to be given promptly, should be
submitted to the judgment of the people at a general election
before troops should leave our shores. This would contribute
to the unity of our country in the months to come and would
enable us best to do our duty. It would not mean delay.
Under the stress of war delay might be fatal. Let me make
clear what I mean. The Government would have to decide
and decide quickly what was best in the interest of Canada.
The Government would have to act on its judgment, but
before there was anything in the way of participation involving the despatch of troops the will of the people of Canada
should first be obtained. I have myself not the slightest fear
but that if danger threatened the Empire, and therefore,
threatened Canada again, this country would respond as it
responded in 1914, but I believe in future it will be best for
all that before a Government takes a step so momentous as
the despatch of troops the will of the people should be known.

For the moment there should be emphasized only two things
with regard to that pronouncement. First: the proposal does
not deal with or affect in the least degree the question of the
proper relation of Canada to the Mother Country, or as to what
Canada should do in the event of another war. It does not
modify in the faintest manner the historic fidelity of the Conservative party to British connection. It does, on the contrary,

most clearly embody an affirmation of unalterable and unswerv-
ing devotion not only to British connection but to all that British
connection honourably involves. In the next place—and this is a
feature which is new, and a feature affecting procedure alone—
it declares that the Conservative party would undertake, in the
event of finding it its duty to participate overseas in another war,
first of all to carry the country on its programme and to stake its
Governmental life on its success. This and this alone is the
commitment to which the Conservative party under my leadership was bound and from which it is now free.

The best way to apply intelligence to a problem is first of all
to get the facts. Let me recite in simple language a few outstanding conclusions of history. I do so in a belief that the
facts now to be recalled are the only important ones bearing on
this question, and that in the light of them an intelligent opinion
can be formed.

First. It is not and never has been a part of Canadian policy
to maintain in this Dominion a military organization capable
of immediate participation in the event of an outbreak of war
abroad. The best we have ever done has been to maintain the
nucleus of an organization out of which and by which an army
can, in the course of some weeks, be trained and welded and
made a fighting force. At the present time it is exceedingly
doubtful if we have even that. This much, however, we ought to
possess, and this much the Conservative party has always
demanded; but so far as I know the Conservative party has never
committed itself to a policy involving the large outlay required
for maintenance of an army immediately ready for war. Situate
as Canada is on this Continent, public opinion, rightly or
wrongly, has not favoured such a policy, and I do not believe
public opinion favours such a policy today. At the present time
I am not discussing whether we ought to launch on a more extended programme. I am merely stating the fact that we are not
doing so, and also that, so far as I know, we don't propose to do
so. Further, from present indications it is not the intention of
the Conservative party at this Convention to put itself on record as
prepared to advance beyond the responsibility which I have defined, a responsibility which we ourselves assumed when in office

and by which we were limited. This postulate is put before you because it is a big and a very important truth. It is a truth in the presence of which, and in the light of which, the proposal at Hamilton was made. If it is the intention of the Conservative party to go further and commit itself to the maintenance of an army in this country immediately ready for war, then this Convention should manfully take responsibility and come out frankly and declare for such a policy. With the humility which befits one who is now of the rank and file, I venture a prediction that the Conservative party will do no such thing. Therefore, I ask you to remember that by virtue of policies, of long history firmly established and recognized, this country cannot send troops to participate abroad except after many long weeks of training and organization. In the last war close to six months were required before we had troops ready to take part. Five or six weeks are ample for a General Election.

Second. Because a Government makes an appeal to the people, it does not mean any delay or weakening of executive action, of preparation or of training. The experience of 1917 demonstrated clearly that not only preparations for the conflict, but, indeed, the conflict itself, may be carried on with relentless vigour while the judgment of the electors is being secured. It is the duty of Government to make its decision. This was emphasized at Hamilton. It is the duty of Government to follow up that decision logically and thoroughly and to lose not a day nor an hour in the execution of its task. This, too, was emphasized at Hamilton. A Government which permits delay, and, therefore, adds to peril when it believes its country is in danger, is a criminal at the bar of history. Unless convinced that no delay was necessitated in the procedure advocated at Hamilton, I would not believe that such procedure could be defended.

Third. There exists in this country an apprehension, altogether unwarranted we all know, and most unjust, that if a Parliament is elected whose majority is Conservative, that Parliament is likely to plunge the country into war. This fiction has been dinned into the minds of vast numbers of our people, especially in the great Province of Quebec, by Liberal leaders and by the Liberal Press. A slander more malicious has never before stained the pages of our political history, but this very poisoning of the wells has been the chief occupation of Liberal leaders in that province for years, and their conduct has had its effect. It has had its effect especially on large sections of the women of our country. Such an apprehension in the minds of our people, whether French-Canadian or English-Canadian, is not only unjust to the Conservative party, but it is bad for Canada and it is bad for the Empire. Here, far away in Winnipeg, it may not be easy to realize how deeply seated this impression, this apprehension, has become, but there is not one man who knows this Dominion and has moved among all its people, who will not agree that I have understated rather than overstated the truth.

A fourth fact must be recited. After the outbreak of war in 1914, the Conservative Government of that day came to its decision; manfully and promptly it proceeded to execute that decision, and, not long after, very seriously contemplated the submission of its course for ratification to the people of Canada. It is not divulging any secret to say that the Conservative Government of that time never were closer to any step which was not taken than a decision to get the vote of the people approving of its course, and their mandate to carry on. In a long journey through the vicissitudes of the next four years there were many hundreds, if not thousands, of Conservatives who told us that it would have been better for Canada if that appeal had been made and if the people had spoken in the early days of the war. Recriminations bitter and blighting which became rampant during the struggle would in that way have been silenced by the most authoritative voice with which a democracy can speak.

From this onward I am going to make some attempt to reason on those facts. At the moment I ask you, my fellow-Conservatives, this question—

If the Government of Sir Robert Borden in the fall of 1914 or early in 1915, had gone to the country and said to the electorate, as it would have said: "We believe this war is a righteous and a necessary war; we believe the very destiny of Canada is in the balance; we believe the life of the Empire is at stake; we have pledged this country to the combat and we want you to ratify our conduct; we want you to proclaim to the world that Canada will do her duty; we want you to add to the strength of our cause the sanction of the Canadian nation";—if the Conservative Government had taken that course, who is there who would have said "It is not British"? Who is there who would have declared it was a threat of separation or a hauling down of the flag?

Yet this is the language which has been applied to me because I advocated that in future this very course be taken.

I hope I may assume that there is no one here who disputes my statements up to this point. Those are four great truths. I do not think they can be denied and do not believe they will be controverted. The Hamilton speech was predicated upon them. Suffice to add that for my part I consider those facts incontestable.

Referring again to the first, the traditional, the actual policy of Canada in the matter of military organization—to maintain only the nucleus of an armed force—there may be some who say that while such is and has been Canadian policy this should not always be so. Possibly they are right. I am not arguing the point at present. What I say is that this is the actual condition and the prospective condition. We have no military force ready to take the field in a distant war, or within many weeks of being ready. We have no honest intention of having such a force, and we may as well be frank and say so. There is no reasonable prospect now of that policy being changed. Assuming these conditions, it follows that so far at least as time is concerned we shall certainly have abundant opportunity to make an appeal to the nation. And let me repeat, these are not merely temporary conditions; they are historic; they are conditions beyond which today we cannot see and in the midst of which we must abide.

Coming now to the concrete proposal, what are the objects to be served? Surely it is worth while of itself to demonstrate to the electors of a British country that their constitutional control of that country is real and not merely a sham. There may be nations where an autocracy is possible, but never a nation of British people. I know that no one suggests autocracy in Canada, but it is to my mind tremendously important that the voters of Canada do not harbour the idea that their control is nominal and farcical or applies only to matters of minor concern. There is nothing so certain to breed discontent as a belief down in the hearts of a people that they are not being trusted in the matter of great public policies; that they are victims of a pretense; that the very principle of democratic control is flouted at will by those in authority; and that while the masses are allowed to speak on matters of trivial consequence, they are really given no voice and are even warned in advance that they will have no voice when it comes to a question of great and momentous import. It is this very feeling which is the prolific breeder of suspicion and discontent and has been many times the mother of disturbance. So I say it is abundantly worth while in this country that there go forth an assurance to the great masses of our people, men and women, that democratic control in Canada is not a farce and that their immediate responsibility is real and vital. I speak these words after many years of close contact with our affairs, and I believe the principle I am now trying to expound is not a mere lifeless platitude, not the empty heraldry of a demagogue, but a great and living truth.

Still further let me say that, in this Dominion, with its varied racial composition and in presence of the consequences of many years of propaganda designed to create in the minds especially of one of our two great parent races distrust of a Conservative majority in respect of this very issue, it surely is doubly important that the whole people be given renewed assurance that they will not be ignored. Speaking with a confidence born of some practical experience, a confidence which it is just possible a few years of trial will generate in others, I say it is worth while to quiet apprehensions honestly held by large and estimable sections of our country; that it tends to unity, harmony and goodwill to have all assured that these apprehensions are the product of nothing but mischievous party propaganda, and that in fact as well as in name the people are the real rulers of Canada.

No one would suggest, or ever did suggest, that a Parliament elected with a mandate on a question of this kind should be dissolved and a new Parliament secured. What has been stated is that where a Parliament has no such mandate and was elected on other issues altogether, then so long as the will of the people can be obtained without involving either added danger or delay, the people must be given opportunity to express their will. You can justify refusing that right by showing that there would be an impairment of preparatory effort; that there would be an imperilling by delay of the national defence; but to show this is, in my judgment, after the experience of the last war, an utter impossibility. It cannot be shown, because it is not true.

This brings me to the necessity of answering objections which have been raised against the proposal. I have taken pains to gather these from every possible source, and shall give you all of a rational kind which have been urged. Permit me to state in the most emphatic language that almost everything which has reached me in the way of protest has been based upon a misunderstanding, usually a misstatement, of what was said. The public was given an impression at the very first that I had uttered something of a general nature antagonistic to participation in wars of the Empire; that I had expressed a sort of frigid and indifferent disdain of Empire responsibility; that the corner stone of Conservative faith had been shattered and the flag itself besmirched. The public also got an idea—and this was the main misconception—that what I had proposed was a submission of the whole question to a plebiscite, the intimation being that a Conservative Government would be satisfied no matter what the result. At this point it might be well to read again an extract from the exact text of what was said at Hamilton.

> I believe it would be best, not only that Parliament should be called, but that the decision of the Government, which, of course, would have to be given promptly, should be submitted to the judgment of the people at a general election before troops should leave our shores. This would contribute to the unity of our country in the months to come and would enable us best to do our duty. It would not mean delay. Under the stress of war delay might be fatal. Let me make clear what I mean. The Government would have to decide and decide quickly what was best in the interest of Canada. The Government would have to act on its judgment, but before there was anything in the way of participation involving the despatch of troops, the will of the people of Canada should first be obtained. I have myself not the slightest fear but that if danger threatened the Empire, and, therefore, threatened Canada again, this country would respond as it responded in 1914, but I believe in future it will be best for

all that, before a Government takes a step so momentous as the despatch of troops, the will of the people should be known.

You are asked to note first that, insofar as those words touch on the question of Canadian responsibility, I took precisely the same stand that the Conservative party has always taken, and I trust will always take. Most clearly it was stated that while control of our conduct is in Canada, our responsibility as a member of the Empire would not be shirked. No, there has not been one article of our tenets doubted or denied; our flag has not one shred of it been furled. And I ask you to note secondly, that what was proposed was not a plebiscite in any sense whatever, but an appeal to the people in the British way, by a Canadian Government in a General Election, to ratify its course in lending a hand to the Empire, and to return it to power. I call attention to these features because for me there has been nothing so hard to endure as the flippant taunt that I did not propose to risk anything ever again, or to have the Conservative party risk anything again; that my feelings had become anti-British, or, in the language of some, that I would fain haul down the flag.

It has been declared over and over again that what was said at Hamilton was an invitation to separation; that it was proposed in the event of war to give Canada an opportunity to separate. I did not need to give such opportunity. No man and no party could give it, because Canada has now the opportunity to separate, and has had it for a quarter of a century. Adherence of this country to the British Empire has been throughout this generation a matter of our own free will, and because it has been a matter of our own free will, British connection is just as secure today as in the days of Macdonald. Let the people of Canada think, though, that it is not a matter of their own free will, and do you believe Canadians will be as proud of their Imperial position as they are today? What was said at Hamilton was not that any Conservative Government would invite Canada to separate, but that as soon as we felt it our duty to participate we would invite Canada—the whole of Canada—not to separate but to seal the bonds again with blood for the sake of our own security and the life of the Empire itself. What was said at

Hamilton was that if the forces of separation were to succeed, they could only do so by defeating the massed strength, the last phalanx, of the Conservative party; that if the forces of separation were to succeed, they could only do so over its prostrate form. And this is the declaration for which I have been arraigned by ribald newspapers as guilty of disloyalty and treason! This is the declaration on account of which I have had to listen to the gibes of a Lapointe and the silly claquery of a Motherwell! If a plebiscite had been proposed with a Conservative Government looking indifferently on, such an idea would be repugnant to the Conservative faith, and I would justly have been condemned. No such thing was suggested. What was pronounced was this—that a Conservative Government would stake its life on a contract to carry the country on its programme.

Does any Canadian in his senses suggest that if a Government was not certain of success in such an election, they would dare commit this nation to a conflict? In the last half century of British history I do not believe there has ever been a war in which Britain was engaged, where, at the commencement at least, overwhelming masses of the people were not in its support. So far as Canada is concerned this has certainly been true; and, indeed, if there was not a majority and a very large majority of our population in favour of the conflict when the conflict commenced, there would be no possibility of making the conduct of that war on our part a success. The terrible disasters which some people rashly conjured up would prove in the practical event an absurd delusion.

Others have advanced an argument that the very submission of such a question to the people contemplates that a Government's decision to participate might be reversed, and this, they say, would be very serious. Well, I suppose theoretically it does, but in an exactly similar sense a submission of the same question by a Government to Parliament contemplates as well that the Government's decision may be reversed by Parliament. Now, is there a Canadian today who would suggest that a Government should, without authority of Parliament, engage in war and despatch troops of Canada to war abroad? There is not one.

How is it then that to contemplate an adverse decision by Parliament is righteous and constitutional, but to contemplate an adverse decision by the people of Canada means an end of the British Empire? I don't believe these objections signify anything to those who have a practical knowledge of our country and are acquainted with its history. The party of Macdonald was not afraid in other days to trust the people and I would be sorry to think that in the confession of faith of the Conservative party now to trust the people is an act of heresy. Canadians have never failed in the past in these matters and they will not fail again. But even if they might, what I say is this: if a country under the leadership and impetus of a great party cannot be brought to see the need of war, then it cannot be bludgeoned into a course which it resents, and I tremble for the Government that would try.

It has been said as well that a General Election would divide our people and that this would be harmful to the unity so necessary in war. Here is a contention which is worth examination. My first argument is that a General Election does not make division, it only records it. It may indeed accentuate division, but there is this great truth to remember—that, after all, a minority which has been denied a right to express its opinion is a far more dangerous minority than one which has been permitted to exert the full limit of its strength and has been shown that the mass of people are against it. It is the very spirit and genius of British institutions that a minority knows how to submit to the will of a majority, provided it has had a chance first to show its full strength at the poll. In the actual event of war, which I think very unlikely in our time, what would almost certainly happen would be this—that an Opposition would be compelled to join hands at once and unite with the Government at the penalty of political extinction. In the presence of that overwhelming demand which must exist before a war commitment can be made, an Opposition, knowing that the Prime Minister of the time, after pledging his country to the conflict, is bound by his word to submit his Government to the people—an Opposition under such circumstances would find it the part not only of duty but of wisdom to join hands at once and we would have an end of politics for the whole war, and not for part alone.

There are those who cry out against a war-time election as the worst of all evils. That it has objectionable features no one will dispute; but those who refuse to contrast those features with the consequences of any other course are submitting themselves to the influence of emotionalism rather than to the light of reason and experience. No one to my knowledge has ever argued that the war-time election of 1917 could have been avoided. The consequences of any alternative were so manifest and so appalling that every voice against an electoral contest was silenced. We got to the pass where there had to be a mandate, and that mandate we set about to obtain. If, then, there was no way of getting through the last war without an appeal to the people, will someone please tell me what is the ground for hope that we can avoid such an appeal in the next? Humanity today stands in no fear of any minor conflict; the only dread—if dread there be—is of a great world-devastating war—one which if we enter will command the last limit of our strength. Again I ask what is the ground for hope that our experience will be happier, and harmony will be more persistent, than in the last? Is it not better, then, to get the authority of the nation first, and authority to do all that may be necessary to see the struggle through and save the nation's life? If in 1914 an appeal to the people had been inevitable because of an antecedent binding engagement of the Prime Minister, I have not the least shadow of doubt that each of the two great parties would have been compelled right then to have formed a Union. The temper of the country would have tolerated no contest on mere partisan lines. There would have been an immediate Union, an overwhelming verdict, and the election of 1917 would never have taken place.

Another objection is advanced, and with this one it is not easy to be patient. We are told, "The people would not know the facts and could not intelligently judge." "A Government or a Parliament," we are assured, "has inside and vital information and would know best what to do." This was not the case in the last war and I do not believe should ever be the case. The whole truth went out to the nation; there was no reason for reservations and there never should be reservations. The time has gone by when the people of a British country can be asked to accept conclusions, to be denied the facts and to put their sons in uniform.

Some have written me and said, "Oh, we would be quite prepared to get the verdict of the people in an election before anybody is sent except volunteers, but we object to getting a verdict for the sending of volunteers." Carefully analyzed, does not that mean simply this—that the Government of this country, without a mandate from the nation, may carry on war in any part of the world, provided only that military service is governed by caprice and chance? Put another way does it not mean this— that a Government may, merely on the authority of Parliament, commit a country to war on a limited liability scheme, but if it is going whole-heartedly and thoroughly to its task, it must have public approval? How can anyone, after serious thought, argue such a proposition as that? For myself I cannot comprehend any such thing as a limited liability war. If we are ever forced into war again, which Heaven forbid, let us go at it man fashion from the start, and I submit we can do so best after we have shown that the people are on our side.

If a country takes the responsibility of despatching troops to far-off theatres, it must right then take the responsibility of supporting those troops, when they get there, with reinforcements and everything else. There is no logic in saying that a Government may, without a mandate, send its volunteers abroad and compel others to pay, but that it must get a mandate before it can support them there and compel others to go. The responsibility to support troops sent abroad is incurred the moment those troops are despatched. It does not arise some time later. How then can it be argued that no mandate is necessary before a responsibility is incurred, but a mandate is imperative before the same responsibility can be discharged?

My object was not and never has been, to throw a shadow of indifference or doubt over the fidelity of this country to its rightful obligations as a member of the British Empire. My object was, first of all, to remove an apprehension which was doing injury to Canada; to quiet fears which were utterly unfounded; to assure the whole people that this is a real British democracy and that whenever they can be consulted in the British way on a great public issue they will not be ignored. My object was not to sow dissatisfaction in the heart of a single Canadian, but, on the contrary, to plant the seeds of contentment; to give assurance to the whole people that their just rights would be respected, and thereby to establish on a firmer and a more lasting foundation British institutions and British fidelity.

For the time you have given me and for the patience with which you have followed me, I am deeply grateful. This defence has been brief, but I do not want to go beyond my rights. For almost two years I have been silent, but must now make plain to this Convention that if what I have said this afternoon is made the subject of attack, I claim the right to reply and intend from this platform to exercise that right.

To conclude, I will venture a word of some personal significance. It is spoken under the influence, perhaps under the handicap, of deep feeling. It has never been my custom, nor have I the needed gift, to kindle fires of sentiment or of passion. Whatever resources I may have were intended for another kind of appeal. But extraordinary occasions bring products meet for themselves, and this is a great and extraordinary occasion, moving in its retrospect, moving in the wonder of its outlook to none perhaps so much as to myself.

This great party is being born anew. Dark years of strife and cloud and pain lie behind it as they lie behind our country, behind the Empire, behind the scarred and suffering world. Among such years my lot of service and of leadership, and the task of my colleagues were cast. It was ours to cope with the subtle and sinister forces of the post-war interval, amid which all men, all parties, all nations were staggering to their feet. It is probable, far more than probable, that errors may have marked my course. But now that I stand apart, after nearly two decades, from public office and heavy responsibility, there is this conviction within me which means a great deal; I can look in the face of the Conservative party, of the whole Canadian people, and all the world who care to listen, and say there was no falsity or faltering, no act, no deed, no episode over which the pen of history need be shaded, no period or place into which the keenest enquirer may not go. There was no matter over which now I want to make petition. The book can be closed and I am content.

Looking again to the future, and bringing up the past only to shed its light, let me say: There will be more danger on the side of the party itself than on the side of the leader you will choose. Even here at this Convention the supreme consideration is not: who shall be the leader of this party? The supreme consideration is: what manner of party shall he have to lead? The chords of memory unite us with the past, and this is the time and this the place when all of us, and the millions we represent, should catch the spirit and hear the voice of the noble founders of our political faith—those men whose children to the second and third generation adorn our gathering now. If those men could speak, they would call on us to keep ever in front the vision which inspired our fathers, and, in order that this party may be strong to achieve that vision, they would plead that we be loyal to each other and to those who serve for us. They would urge us to be conscious of our mighty heritage, proud of the Imperial Fountain of our freedom and of the flag that floats above us, worthy of those ideals of British liberty and justice which have sent their light forth and their truth among all races of men. To our history, our principles, our traditions let us be faithful to the end.

BEAUHARNOIS—AND IMPLICATED SENATORS

In the House of Commons Session of 1931, a Special Committee was appointed, at the instance of Mr. Gardiner, leader of the Progressive party, to inquire into the Beauharnois Power project. The unanimous Report of this Committee to the House of Commons contained startling revelations, and, as well, reflected seriously on the conduct of three Senators. When this was transmitted to the Upper Chamber shortly before prorogation, it was decided by resolution that, at its next session, consideration should be given thereto. Pursuant to this decision, and with approval of all members, a committee was appointed at the following session to take under review this Commons Committee Report. After careful and extensive inquiry, it submitted its report to the Senate, finding grave misconduct on the part of Senators McDougald and Haydon. On April 27, 1932, a debate ensued on a Motion for its adoption proposed by Senator Tanner. The following speech was made on April 28th, in reply to Rt. Hon. George P. Graham who had spoken in opposition to the Committee's finding. Senator Tanner's motion was finally passed by a considerable majority. Before the vote was taken, Senator McDougald had resigned his seat. Senator Haydon, who for some time had been ill, died shortly after.

HONOURABLE SENATORS, THIS IS THE FIRST TIME in six and a half decades of our national history that a duty has devolved upon the Senate of reviewing the conduct of its members and making decision thereon. We all hope it will be the last.

It behooves us in our deliberations to observe the utmost fairness and a sternly judicial attitude towards our fellow-members. So far as those senators especially associated with myself are concerned, I have been anxious, and am still, that no pressure of any kind be brought to bear. My desire has been that they should examine the facts in a spirit not only of fairness but of sympathy for all affected, and come to their conclusions under the compulsion of conscience and of nothing else. There never was a case where anything in the nature of party prejudice or party ambition had less right to intervene. Those feelings should be foreign—and we must try to keep them foreign—to the problem. I hope by my own remarks to-day to convince honourable members that I have endeavoured to view the subject wholly apart from influences of that kind.

There can be no complaint, on this score, of the speech just delivered by the right honourable senator from Eganville (Right Hon. Mr. Graham). From the standpoint of the debater, it was fair. I fear he disclosed himself as so devoted and enthusiastic a friend of at least one of those concerned that he is disqualified as a juror in the case. My principal objection, though, to his speech is this, that it dealt not in the essence of the question. It cannot be said that in every feature he avoided fundamentals, but in far the greater part of his address he was speaking of the mere trappings, the trivial externals, taking note just of fleas and insects around the corpus of this great matter, and not of the substance of the problem which we confront.

May I make clear one or two matters of principle before entering on the argument? I would not for a moment say that because a senator makes a statement not in accord with facts, he should be expressly censured. If he makes such a statement inadvertently, it is only a subject for correction; if he makes it with intent in the ordinary course of debate, it becomes a subject for rebuke. But there is a realm in which the statement of a senator assumes a wholly different aspect. When he is talking in that realm, a responsibility far heavier falls upon him. The class of subject to which I refer is that of his personal interest as related to his public duties. When he is in that sphere the utmost scrupulousness is demanded of him, not only in the care of his utterances, but in absolute fidelity to and full disclosure of facts. Over the history of British Parliaments and all Parliaments on the British model there has been demanded, on the heaviest penalties, not only candour but as well a rigid adherence to truth in every utterance on that class of subject. The reason for such uncompromising insistence is very evident to all. Without such a responsibility resting inexorably upon a member, our institutions would fail of their purpose; fail because the public would not have confidence in them.

Another thought. I do not think a man coming to trial should have a prejudice against him simply because he has been a custodian of party funds. First, it cannot be designated an offence, or unworthy conduct, for a man to act as such custodian. I go even further: That fact alone is rather a certificate of character; it evidences on the part of those who knew him best a confidence in his personal integrity. Having said so much, I hope no one will accuse me of approaching this question in a spirit of self-righteousness or of prejudice against those whose conduct is under challenge. I can say, and am confident senators concerned will believe it to be true, that I have no prejudice at all, unless it be a prejudice in their favour.

It is my duty now to place in perspective the history of this case, and, in as little time as will do the subject justice, to outline the connection therewith of senators affected.

To recite the connection of Senator McDougald with the Beauharnois affair is to give an historical summary of the whole drama. He enters at the beginning and he stays till the close. On May 7, 1924, he was appointed a member of the National Advisory Board to inquire into a proposed canalization and power development of the St. Lawrence River. That Board continued until January 11, 1928, when it made its report. Possibly this is the place to refer parenthetically to that section of the speech we have just heard which was designed to convince honourable members that a grave injustice had been done this Advisory body, and that such injustice in some unspecified way affected the guilt or innocence of those accused. I had never heard that the report of the Commons committee contained any sneer on this National Advisory Board. On the whole, I think, it was composed of very good men. There does appear in the Commons report a reference to the establishment of that body, giving names of only two members—Right Hon. Senator Graham and Sir Clifford Sifton—and the way in which they are referred to is this: It is said that the Board "included" those two men and other men "interested in hydro-electric development." That is the sneer. . . . so it is described.

RIGHT HON. MR. GRAHAM: It was not true.

RIGHT HON. MR. MEIGHEN: It was true.

RIGHT HON. MR. GRAHAM: No.

RIGHT HON. MR. MEIGHEN: Of course it was true. The Board included those two men; that is true?

RIGHT HON. MR. GRAHAM: Yes.

RIGHT HON. MR. MEIGHEN: It included other men interested in hydro-electric development. Who were they? When I repeat their names it is not to insinuate that they were not good men. Sir Clifford Sifton, Mr. McDougald, and Mr. Ahearn were other members. Certainly, therefore, the statement was true. It may not have been worth while to point out the fact, but that is the only criticism one could make. Even these few words are too many to devote to what is just an external.

On that Board Senator McDougald sat until it made its report nearly four years after, on January 11, 1928. In the meantime he had become a senator, called in June, 1926, taking his seat and being sworn in December of that year. In the Spring of 1928, on April 20th, he took his place on a special committee of this House whose purpose was to inquire into and report upon the development of the St. Lawrence River for purposes of navigation and power. That committee made its report on June 7th of the same year.

During this period, and from early in 1922, Senator Mc-Dougald had been, except for a very short interval in 1926, chairman of the Harbour Commission of Montreal.

Now I go back again to review, historically only, other things with which he was occupied, so far as they affect the cause in issue. On July 5, 1924, or about two months after he took his place on the National Advisory Board, Mr. McDougald had incorporated a company known as the Sterling Industrial Corporation. He stated—honestly, I do not doubt—that the five shares which he held represented this property and that he intended to divide them in some way with Mr. R. A. C. Henry. The stated purpose of this corporation was to interest itself in hydro-electric development. On July 5th, the day of its incorporation, it filed an application with the Railway Department for power to divert 30,000 cubic second feet of the river St. Lawrence on the south shore at Soulanges for power production. Two days later it filed a similar application with the Department of Public Works. Its formation was due to an understanding between Mr. McDougald—not then senator—and Mr. R. A. C. Henry, who by this time had become head of the Department of Economics of the Canadian National Railways, by which understanding some plans of Henry were to be investigated and, if they proved good, to be adopted with the object of making money. Mr. McDougald undertook to finance Henry in this investigation to the extent of $10,000, and actually did finance him through his Sterling Company to the extent of not more than $3,500.

Commencing in 1902, there had grown up a corporation known as Beauharnois Light, Heat and Power Company, whose mission was to secure the old Robert rights relating to St. Lawrence power development in this same district and on the same south side—just as was the plan and purpose of Sterling. This Beauharnois Light, Heat and Power Company in 1927 became the property of Mr. R. O. Sweezey under an option, and thereafter he proceeded, step by step, to secure for it development franchises of an extensive character, making application therefor to the Government of Canada, and making and pursuing an application to the Government of Quebec. In due course, on April 27, 1928, it obtained from the Government of Quebec authority for execution of a lease of 40,000 cubic second feet of water, and the lease was completed the following month. At this point the company reached a first milestone of its progress.

We have come to the establishment of the Beauharnois Light, Heat and Power Company and the conferring upon it of necessary franchises and concessions by the Province of Quebec. This company's principal owner and moving spirit, Sweezey, knew that even if it were conceded that jurisdiction in respect of water powers in the Province of Quebec belonged solely to that province—a question which is not yet decided finally—it was still necessary, because of the Navigable Waters Protection Act, to obtain approval by the Dominion Government of all plans for production of power and canalization of the river.

The Beauharnois Company, through Mr. Sweezey, set about obtaining this approval. In January, 1928, it filed its application

with the Department at Ottawa. But approval of this application was long delayed. Many exigencies intervened. Many,
indeed, were the methods employed to expedite its progress. At
last, on March 8, 1929, favourable decision was given by the
Government, with conditions attached thereto. A second milestone had been passed and the company was well on its way.

At this point it is essential to recall that after Sweezey got his
option on the shares of Beauharnois Light, Heat and Power
Company in 1927, he went about financing his purchase by
organizing a syndicate known as the Beauharnois Power Syndicate, which became owner of the option and subsequently
owner of the stock. Mr. Sweezey was principal holder of units
in this syndicate. Some other men became holders. The number
was comparatively few, totalling on April 4, 1928, about eighteen
or twenty.

The amounts paid for these units—which cannot technically
be called shares—varied. Some persons got their units at $37.50
each, others at $40 odd, but the general run-of-mine subscribers
paid $100. This syndicate was converted on April 4, 1929, into
another—the second—commonly called the Beauharnois Syndicate. All who had units in the first got for them, by conversion,
twice as many units in the second as they previously had in the
first. There is nothing wrong with that. They were given also
a right to subscribe for as many more units in the second as they
had already received by converting their units in the first. That
is to say, if a man had 800 units in the first, those were converted
into 1,600 in the second, and at the time of conversion he was
given a right to subscribe for 1,600 more in the second at $100
each. All subscribers took advantage of that option. This meant
the issue of four times as many units of the second as there had
been of the first. There were 5,000 of the first, 20,000 of the
second. Additional units of the second were disposed of in one
way or the other, chiefly, be it noted, by way of purchase of
Sterling Industrial Corporation, until, all together, 25,000 units
were outstanding in the second syndicate.

Shortly after approval by the Government of Canada had
been given to Beauharnois Light, Heat and Power Company's
application and to the concession from Quebec for development

at Soulanges, the second syndicate formed Beauharnois Power Corporation, a mere holding company, for the purpose of taking over the assets of that syndicate, which assets consisted of the stock of Beauharnois Light, Heat and Power Company and a trifling amount of cash. An arrangement was made on October 31, 1929, at a meeting of the provisional board of directors of Beauharnois Power Corporation, the holding company, under which it would take over the shares of Beauharnois Light, Heat and Power Company now held by the second syndicate. The arrangement was that it should pay $4,750,000 for these shares, and that former holders of units of the second syndicate would receive as well a right to subscribe for a million shares of the stock of Beauharnois Power at $1.00 a share. That would mean $1,000,000 for a million shares, or the great majority of the stock of Beauharnois Power. So net receipts of members of the syndicate would be $3,750,000, and they would also receive, free, the million shares of Beauharnois Power. Hon. Senators who have followed carefully the story of this glittering promotional adventure driving resolutely for a great public franchise will realize now how gigantic were the stakes which the chief actors, their friends and beneficiaries could see awaiting them not far ahead at the journey's end.

To resume—such was the destiny of the syndicates, and from this time on, Beauharnois Power Corporation has been owner of the stock of Beauharnois Light, Heat and Power, and has proceeded to finance thereon. At this same meeting of October 31, 1929, at which, for these large sums, purchase was made of the assets of the syndicate, it was further decided to sell to Dominion Securities Corporation and Newman, Sweezey and Company $30,000,000 of bonds of Beauharnois Power Corporation, secured on the assets of that corporation, which assets consisted of the stock of Beauharnois Light, Heat and Power. These two vast transactions were put through at the meeting on October 31, 1929. The right hon. senator from Eganville appealed to us all to agree that it is quite the thing for provisional directors, who usually are clerks or stenographers, to stay there until the company is organized. So it is. But in this case, though it is of no great importance, because the real owners directed every step anyway, the provisional directors stayed much longer. They stayed so long that the actual bosses never came on the scene and took responsibility until these provisional directors had sold $30,000,000 of bonds and taken over everything the syndicate owned.

The bonds were secured only by stock of Beauharnois Light, Heat and Power Company—all the assets the Corporation had—and out of proceeds of these bonds was provided money to pay the syndicate a net sum of $3,750,000.

This is a proper place to call to attention that, in the process, there was a trade here and there of units of these syndicates, and Senator Raymond made money by a sale to Jones, and someone made money by a sale to Simard, and someone else made money by a sale to someone else. All these profits which were being secured had to be paid for ultimately out of proceeds of bonds to which the public subscribed. The public paid the money—not the public in a political sense, but business men, widows and orphans, and hard-handed peasants, who bought the $30,000,000 of bonds.

I think this account is now practically complete save to refer to the programme for securing concessions. I make no reference to those obtained from Quebec; they are not our business. The important concession was approval of plans by the Government of Canada, which plans contained an express right to divert 40,000 second feet. In securing that concession, the efforts of Sweezey and his associates are what constitute the main part of this drama. Many persons were engaged, many methods were resorted to, in order to overcome obstacles, legal, and political. All sorts of people—mostly lawyers—were employed, who declared in evidence that their duty was to "create an atmosphere." Apparently they were not lawyers, but perfumers. Efforts were made to get into the vortex of these syndicates men who were believed to stand well with the Government. It is all too common a habit on the part of some people to think that if they can include such men they can get anything. This is the way Sweezey went about his task, and one cannot blame Sweezey, who was after his objective. As long as he did not break the law, one cannot find fault. But the point is: Did he or did he not induce others to take money for what could be nothing but their political influence?

It is not necessary to carry this survey further. I go back to treat those affected, one by one, and shall endeavour, if I err at all, to err on the side of fairness, if not generosity.

RIGHT HON. MR. GRAHAM: Would the right honourable gentleman like to call it six o'clock?

RIGHT HON. MR. MEIGHEN: I should like to refer to one man first—I can complete what I have to say in this regard before six o'clock—the name last mentioned in the speech of the right honourable gentleman from Eganville.

I find myself more in accord with the remarks of the right honourable gentleman on this point than in any other portion of his address. There is no question that the conduct of Senator Raymond, as defined and reported by our committee, is in every way distinguishable from the conduct of other senators. The committee makes no express censure of Senator Raymond. It does say, evidently more by way of guidance for the future than for any other reason—and of this the right hon. gentleman from Eganville makes no complaint—that it disapproves of the action of senators in becoming largely interested in companies which are dependent upon government concessions, favours or franchises, and it also disapproves of senators afterwards becoming intermediaries for collection of campaign funds from such companies.

Now, as this committee is charged, impliedly, with unfairness, I ask honourable members: Could any committee of this House even allow an implication that senators have a right to engage in such undertakings? Would any hon. member care to go before an audience in Canada and say, "I have a right, as a senator, to put my money into a company whose very breath of life is a concession from the Government which presides over the nation of which I am a senator, and whose actions I am called upon to review day by day in the course of my duty?" Could the committee have taken any stand less critical and attempt to justify itself before the people? I think not.

No one was more pleased than I that the committee felt able to report as it did with regard to Senator Raymond. His standing in this House and in this country has been high. I am not intimating that the committee was unduly generous to him. Its criticism is fair and right.

The next portion of the report which I wish to discuss refers to Senator Haydon. I shall not do more before six o'clock than speak of my knowledge of him. It has been very slight. I cannot call my acquaintance with him by the name of friendship, but such as it was, it disposed me in his favour.

The committee accepted the statement of Senator Haydon that he is ill and has been ill for many months—severely, perhaps seriously, ill—and in disposing of this unpleasant duty we are justified in keeping his condition in mind. It sought to treat him not only fairly, but with kindly consideration. But it had to decide, "Shall we or shall we not investigate the relationship of Senator Haydon to this Commons report?" If a suggestion had been made to postpone action—I do not think it was made— I should have found no fault with the committee for acceding. The right honourable senator from Eganville nods his head, confirming the fact that no such suggestion was made. The committee felt that the Senate, knowing of his condition—it had been well known for some time—had resolved that this subject should be investigated, and investigated now. How could it have done otherwise than pursue the mandate on which it rested, and seek to discharge that mandate to the best of its ability?

At 6 o'clock the Senate took recess and resumed at 8 p.m.

RIGHT HON. MR. MEIGHEN: Honourable senators, before coming to a discussion of the connection of Senator Haydon with these matters, I want to make mention of some other circumstances alleged in general extenuation or defence of the three senators, by the right hon. gentleman from Eganville. He argues that this subject has not been treated properly, that an indignity has been done the Senate of Canada, because a committee of this House in rendering its report chose to make quotations from findings of the House of Commons committee referring illegitimately, it is alleged, to senators, and to add its confirmation thereto. I should like to think that this Chamber will never suffer any greater indignity than that. What are the circumstances? The Senate last session professed to be "gravely disturbed" by findings of a House of Commons' committee as they affected three of our members, and unanimously resolved that a committee should be appointed this session to examine into those findings. In pursuance of that decision we unanimously agreed this session to refer the Commons report to a committee of this House for examination and report. Well, if there is any illegitimacy—and I do not know why that term should be applied—to the Commons' report, surely we should not have referred it to our committee. But we unanimously made such reference. It was done with the approval of the senator from Eganville. Consequently this House adopted the illegitimacy then, if there was any, and it was done with the right honourable gentleman's own vote. But what illegitimacy is there? I should have liked the right honourable gentleman to have expanded on his argument; and if he had expanded on it I should like to have seen him make a greater success of his effort than that made by counsel for Senator McDougald in urging the same argument before our committee. Counsel for Senator McDougald merely gave two quotations in an endeavour to show that a Commons committee commits some breach of decorum or of constitutional practice in making reference to senators in any report to its own House. I have before me the two citations which counsel used. The first is from Bourinot:

> Each house, however, exercises and vindicates its own privileges independently of the other. . . . Each House declares for itself what cases are breaches of privilege, but the grounds for their action are based upon the same principles and precedents.

How can anyone read into that dictum an opinion that if a committee of one House is investigating a subject and finds members of the other House to be involved, it must be silent as to those members? No human mind could extract such a conclusion from those words. They merely say that each House is independent in the exercise of its own privileges.

The second quotation is from May's *Constitutional History:*

> Both Houses of Parliament "must act within the limits of their jurisdiction, and in strict conformity with the laws. An

abuse of privilege is even more dangerous than an abuse of prerogative. In the one case the wrong is done by an irresponsible body; in the other, the ministers who advised it are open to censure and punishment. The judgment of offences especially should be guided by the severest principles of law."

I ask honourable senators opposite if they think that quotation has the slightest bearing on a contention that a committee of one House is debarred from bringing into its verdict any reference to or reflection upon a member of the other House. It is not there. Both quotations are wholly irrelevant to such a contention. When three able counsel, after searching authorities and examining constitutional jurisprudence, can bring forth only these quotations, surely it is quite a stretch in the way of a personal appeal for the right honourable senator from Eganville to ask us to find that what the Commons committee did was illegitimate, and that our committee is offering an indignity to this Senate in daring to say that it found the verdict of a Commons committee to be true.

The right honourable gentleman says the committee searched for means of holding Senator Haydon up to contempt or misrepresentation. It even reports, he tells us for the purpose of emphasizing responsibility, that the law firm of McGiverin and Haydon was "Senator Haydon's firm." The right honourable gentleman says that the head of that firm, until he died, was Mr. McGiverin, and that at the time of the occurrences with which we are concerned Senator Haydon was only a junior partner; therefore, it is doing him a gross injustice to refer to the firm as his firm. While he was on the subject I took a minute and a half—no more—in turning up evidence and found that in no less than three places Senator Haydon, in his own evidence, and speaking of that very time, had called it "his firm." Do I need to quote? Look at the foot of page 193. Senator Haydon was asked:

> What were your relationships with him? Business relationships?

That is, with Senator McDougald. Senator Haydon replied:

> My firm and myself had business relationships with him, yes.

Senator Haydon added:

> I want to say further that any retainer my firm had was a
> retainer that any lawyer might accept. . . .

This was part of a prepared statement; it was written out
and read. And on the next page he said, "My firm" incorporated
the company. What heinous offence was it for a Senate committee to adopt Senator Haydon's own language in reference to
his own firm?

But the right honourable gentleman from Eganville was at
least occupying our time better when he sought to argue that it
is a mistake, in any event, to investigate the conduct of a member
of either House unless some other member takes responsibility
for making a charge. I have a great deal of sympathy with that
general view. Indeed, I think that principle has been too
frequently violated. But what are the circumstances here? Why
does he urge this as a reason for not adopting this report? Why
does he urge it even by way of suggesting that there was anything unfair in the proceedings? No one on this side of the
House, at any time or in any place, entered into pursuit of these
three senators, or evinced the slightest interest in making trouble
for them in any way whatever. The situation we are in has been
forced upon us, though not by anyone who had other than the
public interest at heart; nevertheless, so far as our position goes,
it is an involuntary position. The other House, on the motion
of a member who certainly is no friend of the party to which I
belong, appointed a committee to investigate a definite transaction. In the course of inquiry certain things developed, which
convinced the committee that if it was to report facts and not
ignore them it had to make certain statements with regard to
three senators. The committee felt it should present its report to
this House so that we might have opportunity to exercise our
independent judgment thereon and thus, faithful to that duty
expressed a moment ago in language quoted by the two lawyers
for Senator McDougald, vindicate the Senate's proper place in
the Parliament of Canada. This House never for a moment
doubted that such procedure was right, and it unanimously voted
a year ago that as soon as our next session opened we should take

that report into consideration. We appointed a committee, and the committee, taking as instructed a report from the Commons under review, felt it its duty to frame its verdict thereon. If there could be a more logical sequence of events, my mind is not able to comprehend or suggest what it would be.

I am not going to compete with the right honourable senator from Eganville in the eulogy he gives Senator Haydon. I am not qualified from any point of view. He has placed around the Senator's head a halo of arresting colours. Whether true or not, that question is not the issue before this House. The honourable gentleman seeks to impress upon us that if we find any fact adverse to the three senators, we are refusing to accept their own sworn testimony. He says their own sworn testimony is that they did no wrong. Is not Senator Haydon, he asks, on record as saying that he took only a retainer he had a right to take? Is not Senator McDougald on record as saying that he did not make a dollar except what he could have made if he had not been a senator? It is our duty, he pleads, to protect our fellow senators, and not find such a verdict as may lay them open to a charge of having sworn falsely.

I venture to submit that if a court were to accept sworn opinion of men accused of wrong-doing in any particular transaction, there rarely would be an adverse finding. All tribunals, this tribunal included, must go down beneath opinions, especially those of the accused. They must get at underlying facts and try to find out where truth really is, and where guilt really attaches.

Now, I proceed to make that inquiry in the case of Senator Haydon. Surely there is no room left for an idea that there is anything unfair in the development of the whole case; in the conduct either of lawyers, or of the committee, in relation to any of these men. Throughout the entire report hon. members will find repeated tributes, on the part of counsel for the three senators concerned, to the fair way in which the entire proceeding was conducted, and especially to the fairness of counsel for the committee in their attitude towards and treatment of those affected.

To put the accusation against him briefly, Senator Haydon has to answer for two courses of conduct. One is that his firm, including himself, with his knowledge and approbation, accepted from Sweezey a retainer contingent upon approval of Sweezey's application to the Governor in Council for ratification of his St. Lawrence plans. I ask hon. gentlemen opposite, who are concerned equally with us for the good name of this Senate, for its place in our constitutional structure, for its future as an instrument of government—I ask them, will it be contended that a member of this House who is a lawyer has a right to take a fee, however large or small, conditional on success of an appeal to the Administration for a concession? Will anyone within hearing suggest such a thing?

HON. MR. FORKE: I do not think it was ever put as baldly as that.

RIGHT HON. MR. MEIGHEN: No, but it should be.

HON. MR. FORKE: That he would not be paid unless they got the Order in Council put through.

RIGHT HON. MR. MEIGHEN: On Mr. Sweezey's examination the following questions and answers appear:

> Q. Yes? A. Then when I saw him again he had— apparently the other retainer had worked its time out and he was free to act for us, and then I entered into a discussion upon the terms upon which he would represent us, and he asked a retainer that I thought was much too much, particularly as we were not sure of our ground up to that time. He asked a retainer of so much a year, which, as I remember it, was in excess of $30,000.
>
> Q. A year? A. Yes. So I thought it was too much; but after quite a lot of discussion, I said that if our efforts were successful and the company were launched and going, it would not be so bad to pay that much, but if we did not succeed and I had to take it out of the pockets of a few members of the syndicate, it was difficult. However, by a compromise I agreed that if the thing got through I would much prefer to pay on that basis; if it went through I would pay him $50,000, and a retainer for three years at $15,000. To me it looked much easier to do so in the event of success than to do it regardless of the time and conditions we then faced.
>
> Q. It always makes the lawyers work harder?
>
> A. It is human nature to work harder at a price.

Further:

> Q. And when you employed Senator Haydon and agreed to
> pay him $50,000 that fee was contingent on the Order in
> Council passing?
> A. Yes.

HON. MR. FORKE: That was Sweezey's statement?

RIGHT HON. MR. MEIGHEN: Whose did the honourable
gentleman think it would be? It was not Haydon's anyway.
I would suggest to the honourable gentleman that he should
have at least a remote acquantance with the evidence.

HON MR. FORKE: I have read it several times.

RIGHT HON. MR. MEIGHEN: Certainly Haydon has never suggested that it was a contingent fee. We have never said he did.
Sweezey is the man who made the bargain, chiefly with Mr.
McGiverin, of McGiverin, Haydon and Ebbs. He (Haydon)
knew of the bargain, and that is what we propose to discuss.
The fee, according to Sweezey, was contingent. Had Sweezey
any object in telling that story? Senator Haydon had an object
in giving his version, very grave and vital to him. To him it
was a matter of honour or dishonour. With Sweezey it was
nothing of the kind; it was just as good, though not as credible,
a story for Sweezey to say, "I agreed to pay him $50,000 in a lump
sum, and $15,000 a year for three years, for legal services he was
to render." That would have served Sweezey's purposes just as
well. But he did not make such an assertion. The story he told
is in every way comprehensible and rational. He knew what he
was after—he never sought to conceal it—it was to get that
Order through, and he was ready to pay men of influence
because they would work harder at a price. I doubt that Sweezey
would have been believed if he had said anything else. Who
would have believed that he or any other man, in October of
1928, some months before approval was obtained from Ottawa,
when all he had was an emphyteutic lease from the Province of
Quebec, would make an agreement with Mr. McGiverin under
which, whether the Order went through or not, he was to pay
$15,000 a year for three years and $50,000 besides, for legal
services, and to pay disbursements on top of that, and for Ebbs'

time as a manager on top of all? We have to get at facts, and we have to apply common sense.

What was the work done? Senator Haydon says it was a clean-up of the past, and also of what was to come in the way of incorporating a clean-up company to take the whole thing over; that is, the Beauharnois Power Company. A clean-up of the past? There was no past. Up to that hour there had not been a charge to Beauharnois Corporation or the Beauharnois Syndicate. As for a clean-up of the future, if the Order in Council did not go through, what would there be to clean up? Absolutely nothing. There would be no future. There would be no object in forming Beauharnois Corporation. What would be its value? It could do nothing. The clean-up of the past was a clean-up of nothing; the clean-up of the future would be a clean-up of nothing or next to nothing, for all that would amount to anything would be Beauharnois Corporation—its constitution and its charter— and it would never exist if the approval did not go through.

Exhibit No. 152, which is sworn to by Ebbs (Haydon's partner), illustrates the work done. It was chiefly agency work. Counsel for the committee were generous in suggesting that $5,000, instead of $95,000, would have been ample. One can understand high fees for important legal services such as Mr. Geoffrion performed in this matter; but this kind of work is of the cheapest variety. For anybody to talk of agreeing to pay $50,000 in a lump sum and $15,000 a year for three years for this kind of humdrum work is an affront to the common sense and intelligence of Parliament. If Mr. Sweezey had never given evidence, if Mr. Ebbs had never given evidence, if Senator Haydon had never given evidence, none of us would think of any business man making a bargain of that sort. The work which was to be done would never have had to be done if the approving Order in Council had not passed. The inherent facts tell against such a proposition, and they are more powerful than an interpretation given by any witness. The basic, outstanding, protruding facts, which one cannot lose sight of if one tries, just scream against Senator Haydon. I should like to appeal to the honourable senator from North York (Hon. Sir Allen Aylesworth), if he were here, and ask him if in all his experience he ever knew of a bargain for legal fees such as Senator Haydon suggests. Why, it never was made! There was no reason whatever for this bargain, save to secure the passing of the Order in Council.

Furthermore, the work, when it came to be done, arose out of the Order in Council, and the evidence shows that all work which amounted to anything even then was done by a firm in Montreal and a firm in Toronto. The position of this firm (Haydon's) was that of an intermediary, largely that of an agent. Does any one believe that these fees were to be paid whether Order in Council No. 422 passed or not?

Then, if we have admitted—and I hope everybody in his heart has admitted—that no member of this House, no man acting in a legislative capacity and sitting in review on Government policies and administration, has a right to take money contingent on a Government concession going through, how can we stand before the people and tell them that Senator Haydon is an honourable man, and that, therefore, we will not find that he did wrong? No man of any experience in courts of law will read the senator's testimony without coming to the conclusion that Senator Haydon, when he was telling his story, knew he had done wrong. He would not have given testimony of that character if he had felt that his conduct had been above reproach.

I do not read into his evidence something which he said and which the reporter did not take down. I read within the four corners of his evidence taken upon two occasions when he was a witness, and I say that he was evasive—not only was he evasive, but he was flippantly evasive and defiant. Every time he got a chance he swung off the track into a byway, a political or a legal discussion. This is notoriously a method followed to get away from facts—to get into some other sphere.

The right hon. senator from Eganville tells us that it was only when Senator Haydon was pestered, when they drove and drove at him to find out if he had had any conversation with Sweezey, that he made his most unfortunate statement. I ask the right hon. senator to read the evidence again.

RIGHT HON. MR. GRAHAM: I heard it.

RIGHT HON. MR. MEIGHEN: Well, he will not find it there. Senator Haydon is asked something two or three times, and then Mr. Mann, Counsel for the committee, says, "Wouldn't it be well if we were to adjourn now and take a rest?" Is that pestering? Long before those questions were asked, similar tactics on Senator Haydon's part were adopted. Senator Haydon is an intelligent man; he knew that he had a reputation to protect and never would have assumed the attitude which he took towards counsel and the committee had he been sure that the path he had trodden had been right.

I come to campaign funds. I said in opening that the mere fact of being a trustee was no ground of prejudice against any man; that, on the contrary, it was insignia of confidence. But what about their source? I do not think the right hon. senator from Eganville could have been—one does not like to use the word "sincere"—I do not think he could have thought the subject out, or he would not have sought to convey to this country an idea that it did not matter a fig where campaign funds came from or how they were obtained. He said any suggested impropriety was like a newspaper taking advertisements from people making whiskey.

RIGHT HON. MR. GRAHAM: No.

RIGHT HON. MR. MEIGHEN: That people did not look to find where money came from. I hope I am not assuming any attitude of self-righteousness—I have been through three campaigns as leader of a party and know that funds are necessary, and very difficult to collect—but I ask you, hon. gentlemen, if you really want to subscribe to that doctrine which the senator advanced. Remember, there is a line beyond which you dare not step, beyond which, if you tread, you are doing what is inherently and eternally wrong.

Suppose a company is formed for the purpose of getting luscious Government contracts; that it gets them to secure funds, and that those funds are used to help the party that gave it the contracts. Would the honourable senator say, "That is only like money coming from makers of whiskey; we do not care where it comes from"? The fact is that, by a rather circuitous route, the money comes out of the treasury of Canada. I do not need to say that this case is or is not in that class, but give the illustration to show that the wide doctrine which the honourable senator opposite sought to preach cannot stand intelligent examination.

Here is a company from which the committee finds, and I submit rightly, that Senator Haydon received a very large sum of money. It was a company whose success, whose existence, was contingent upon getting powers from Dominion authorities; a company to which concessions, first from the Quebec Government, and then from this Government, were absolutely vital, as its very breath of life, and which without them had nothing whatever. I ask whether a senator or any other person is justified in accepting a subscription to a campaign fund for any party from a company occupying such a position. I do not think he is, and I do not think that a senator of Canada, knowing the facts as Senator Haydon knew them, can ever justify acceptance from such a company of huge sums of money for any campaign fund. He knows that what he is doing is, in effect, extracting assets of Canada for the uses of a party. This is the reasoning which had to do with the committee's finding, and I venture to submit that we ought not to stand before our people and say that we have, in such a Company, a source from which, especially through the hands of a senator, such contributions can be legitimately secured. If we cannot say that, how can we do otherwise than adopt this report?

Let us pass now to Senator McDougald. In the early part of my remarks I reviewed his association with the long train of events which commenced early in 1924 and ended with the investigation in 1931. As in the case of Senator Haydon, in recalling these events, I want to ask honourable gentlemen to link together transactions on about four particular occasions. I first call to attention the position that Senator McDougald occupies, in the light of the evidence, with respect to a statement he made to the Senate of Canada on April 19th, 1928. On that occasion he read some extracts from an attack made upon him and others in an article of the Toronto *Globe,* and extracts of a similar nature which appeared in the *Mail and Empire.* The *Globe's* words to which he objected were as follows:

> Hon. Senator McDougald is reputed to be connected with the Beauharnois Power Company, which recently obtained a charter from the Quebec Legislature for a gigantic development in the Quebec section of the St. Lawrence.

He gave to that, in unequivocal terms, an absolute denial not only of its words but of its implications.

Then he passed to the *Mail and Empire,* and I ask that these words be carefully observed.

HON. MR. DANDURAND: The answer to that *Globe* despatch would be correct.

RIGHT HON. MR. MEIGHEN: I will refer to that in a moment. Here is the *Mail and Empire* despatch:

> That the report was written by Senator McDougald, Sir Clifford Sifton and Thomas Ahearn is believed, and the other members of the committee played unimportant parts and did not influence the decision.

What the papers were principally finding fault with was a decision that the national section should be developed by private enterprise.

> These three capitalists are either known or suspected of being interested in power schemes, and the proposal to develop the national section first at the expense of private interests who would have the power, is credited to them. . . . The criticisms so far advanced are many and pertinent . . . that the proposal endorsed by the Government was prepared by power interests represented by Sir Clifford Sifton, Thomas Ahearn and Senator McDougald.

Honourable gentlemen will notice that neither Beauharnois nor the Beauharnois Company is mentioned.

Now I recall to the minds of honourable members the emphasis which, earlier, I sought to lay upon the imperative duty—imperative to a degree it is hard to overstress—of every member of any legislative body being absolutely frank and accurate in any statement on a subject as to which there might be conflict between his own personal interests and his public duty. He must choose his steps with the greatest care; he must tread the path warily. If he does not, and if the public does not insist that he tread warily, our institutions might as well be gone.

The honourable senator opposite (Hon. Mr. Dandurand) suggests that the denial of the first statement was right. At the moment I do not take issue with him. Later on I shall. For the moment I deal with the denial of the *Mail and Empire* claim. It was said that three members of the National Advisory Board were interested in power schemes and their private development, and that such interest affected their verdict. One sentence is merely a charge that they were interested. Were they not? Can Senator McDougald stand up today in the face of the evidence and say he was not? When those words were uttered he was in absolute control of the Sterling Industrial Corporation, which had applications filed for power schemes at the very point in question, applications in respect of which he and his associate afterwards reaped $300,000 in cash, and stock which at the time was worth close to a million. No implication that is correct in the *Mail and Empire* article? The whole implication was correct.

What was his answer? He said, "I was not thinking about Sterling." Well, he should have been. He said, "I had given it up. I had forgotten about it." Why? "Because," he said, "the National Advisory Board, of which I was a member also, on January 11, 1928, reported in favour of development on the north side of the Soulanges canal, and inasmuch as Sterling's application was for development on the south side, I forgot about Sterling."

Let me make one or two remarks on that. If the fact—if it was a fact—that the report by recommending development on the north side shut out all thought of the south side, why did Senator McDougald take an interest in Beauharnois? If he thought the report settled the matter, why did he take an interest in Beauharnois? It too was concerned with the south side. His interest in Beauharnois shows that his explanation falls to the ground.

But did the report recommend development on the north side? Throughout these proceedings it has been assumed that it did. The right honourable senator from Eganville assumed that it did. In the brief read by Senator McDougald, and no doubt prepared by counsel—for its language is almost copied in an argument of counsel at the close of the inquiry—it is asserted that the Joint Engineering Board recommended a north side development and that the National Advisory Board adopted this recommendation, and, therefore, recommended to the Government a north side development. All through the proceedings this contention seems to have been accepted by everyone. The attempt to make a disinterested public man of Senator Mc-Dougald rests on this contention altogether. His supporters say: "Talk about this man being influenced by his private interests! He sat on the National Advisory Board, and though his Sterling Industrial Corporation wanted development on the south side, he was party to a majority report which recommended the undertaking should be on the north side." Therefore, they say, he acted against his own interests. That statement has been repeated over and over again. Even if it were correct, it would not affect the facts. Why? He may have used his influence the other way in the Board, but decided, when he found a majority against him, to join the majority. Or he may have thought it did not make any difference what they recommended, because he would go ahead and get what he wanted, anyway. And in so thinking he would have been right.

But will honourable gentlemen be astounded to learn that the committee never made any such recommendation at all, and that this virtue which has been so strongly stressed as appertaining to Senator McDougald is nothing but moonshine. I have read the report—I have it here; I have submitted it to honourable gentlemen opposite, and I defy anyone to find a recommendation of the National Advisory Board in favour of the north side or of any side. Its finding makes reference to a report of the Joint Engineering Board, which apparently was composed of three engineers from Canada and three from the United States, and it adopts that reports—"concurs," is the word used—to the extent of its conclusion that a canalization scheme of the whole St. Lawrence is feasible. Beyond that one article of concurrence it does not adopt a word of the report. Indeed, in two instances it declares that there will have to be further investigation before the document can be said to be of value. I repeat that in the report of the National Advisory Board, which Senator Mc-

Dougald signed, there is not a word adopting, or concurring directly or indirectly in, the north side or any side.

One can comprehend how hard put these counsel were to try to find a single incident in this long procession of events to place to the credit of Senator McDougald, when they laid stress on the importance of something which had no being. No one for a moment can argue that it had. Therefore, Senator McDougald in this regard never acted against his own interests.

The National Advisory Board recommended mainly that nothing should be done for some time. The principal recommendation was that development should be by private interests in the national section, and that power should be used to pay for canalization. Was Senator McDougald interested in that? He was the man who owned Sterling Industrial Corporation, which had very early got in its applications and established its nuisance position out of which hundreds of thousands of dollars were afterwards extracted. Was he then acting as a public man should act? Had he a right to capitalize a nuisance for the extraction of money which ultimately had to come from the people of our country?

The honourable gentleman opposite (Hon. Mr. Dandurand) says that Senator McDougald was right on April 19th, 1928, when he denied that he had any interest in Beauharnois. The committee does not find specifically that Senator McDougald had any interest in Beauharnois until the 18th day of May, 1928. The committee says, though, that Senator McDougald, because of certain circumstances disclosed, is open to the gravest suspicion of having owned his Beauharnois shares from the very time that Winfield Sifton got them. If such suspicion be justified, he owned them on April 19, 1928, when he made his speech in this House.

I put myself in the judgment of every man before me in undertaking to recite abundant evidence to sustain the statements I am now about to make. The committee was exceedingly generous to Senator McDougald when it failed to find that he owned those shares all along. Members of the committee were not guilty of prejudice against him. If there was any doubt, they certainly gave him the benefit: but there was no room for doubt.

Let me relate some facts in support of my allegation. The first syndicate, which Sweezey formed in order to get money to push forward his enterprise, owned the stock of Beauharnois Light, Heat and Power Company, Limited. That syndicate had what was called a management committee, and Sweezey sat in a position of virtual control of the disposition of its units. Very frankly in his evidence before both committees he said, in effect, "I wanted them to go where they would do good, where they would help me along in this enterprise." If he had not said that, would it not clearly be true anyway? He had some units, Mr. Jones had some, and a number of good citizens had some. Sweezey testified that Winfield Sifton—who had been acting as his guide, counsellor and friend in relation to matters legal as well as political, whom he had known at college, and whom he employed in order, if possible, to ascertain what was holding back approval of his plans at Ottawa—had said to him many times that he ought to bring Senator McDougald into his Beauharnois family. Sweezey added that late in the winter of 1927 or early in the spring of 1928 Mr. Sifton went to see Senator McDougald with a view to getting him in. At this time Mr. Sifton did not have a share allotted to himself, in any way. According to Sweezey, he brought back a report that Senator McDougald declined, on the ground of being on some committee; but Sifton then added, "Put 800 of those units in the name of Clare Moyer of Ottawa, and I shall be satisfied."

In order that nothing relevant may be omitted, it has to be said that at the time those words were uttered Senator McDougald was not on any committee. I think it probable that he said he had been on a committee. Anyway, Senator McDougald did not come in—at least not openly. But 800 units were put in the name of Mr. Moyer. Why? Moyer swears that within forty-eight hours after he got them he left for New York—and he was there on March 31st, so he must have left by the night of the 30th. Sifton had come to his office at Ottawa and told him he wanted to invest some money, stating in what, and that he desired Mr. Moyer to be trustee and to hold the certificates. He also said that Sifton wanted to go down to New York and put the initial steps through there. Moyer and Sifton went to New York and were there on March 31st. Moyer swears that Winfield Sifton gave him that day fifteen $1,000 bills—$15,000.

Be it noted that the price at which these shares were allotted to Moyer, or to his name, was $30,000 for 800 units; that is $37.50 per unit. The sum of $15,000 was then paid and put to Moyer's credit at the Bank of Nova Scotia on Wall Street. Moyer came back and on April 4th, four or five days afterwards, he issued his cheque in Montreal for $15,000 in part payment of those units, against that $15,000 in New York.

I ask honourable members to note the secrecy which shrouded this whole transaction—a trip to New York in order to pay $15,000, and payment in bills and not by cheque.

On April 4th the cheque was issued and it was cashed on the 6th. Half of the $30,000 was then paid. On May 17th the trail was again followed down to New York, where Sifton gave Moyer another $15,000, this time in the form of a draft, with nothing to indicate who provided the draft. Moyer says he does not know. I have no reason whatever to dispute the good faith of Moyer's testimony, and I ask honourable members to note what he says. In effect he states, "In looking back on it now, I think the only reason Sifton wanted me to go to New York was in order that there would be no way of finding out where the money came from." Remember he says only "I think." But that shows what is in his mind.

Payment of $30,000 had then been completed. What happened next? Senator McDougald says that on May 18th, serious negotiations having been carried on for a week previously, he decided to buy those units which Sifton had. In a space of twenty minutes $46,000 in bonds was handed over to Winfield Sifton. Again the blinds were down. Of that sum $30,000 was to cover what had already been paid for the 800 units at $37.50 per unit, and $16,000 was to apply on a subscription already made by Sifton for 1,600 more units in the second syndicate.

I ask honourable members to pay closest attention here, because to my mind there is something which has not been fully appreciated, even by the committee. These units cost Sifton $37.50 each, but on April 4th each unit became two in the second syndicate. So he had 1,600 units for the $30,000. Then he had also the right to buy 1,600 more of the second syndicate at $100 each and made his application for same.

Winfield Sifton on the 10th day of May elected to buy 1,600 units at $100 each, which was equivalent to $200 each for units of the first syndicate. On May 18th he sold the same units— that is, mark you, first syndicate units—to Senator McDougald for $37.50 each. Is that explainable? Winfield Sifton, who on May 10th regarded it a privilege to subscribe for units at $200 each—keeping in mind what I said about each unit of the first syndicate being equivalent to two of the second—was ready to sell and did sell them to Senator McDougald for $37.50 each on May 18th.

If what Senator McDougald swore to is correct, then only one conclusion is possible. It follows that Winfield Sifton must have been a simpleton. And he was not. Winfield Sifton was one of the brightest young men of his time. He knew business. He had run the gamut of speculation. He knew that nothing on earth occurred between the 10th and 18th, or for months, on either side, to diminish the value of those units. On the contrary, on April 27th, four weeks after he had bought the stock in Moyer's name, the Order in Council had gone through at Quebec, this being a first milestone in the long transit of this company. Are we to believe that he who decided on the 10th that a first syndicate unit was worth $200 was ready on the 18th to sell the same units for $37.50 apiece? Such things are irrational. I venture to suggest to honourable members of this House that if that fact stood naked and alone, no man could possibly reconcile the words of Senator McDougald with candour and with truth.

But here is a further reflection: If Sifton had owned the units, would there not be some record of their receipt or of their sale? If he paid with his own money the $15,000 on March 31st, and another $15,000 on May 17th, would there not be some cheques against his account? Would there not be some deductions somewhere by which those payments would be revealed?

Winfield Sifton died on June 13th. His executor took the

witness box and in the frankest possible way swore that they had searched his records, had examined his bank account, and could not find in his whole estate the receipt of a single bond at all, not for months back, nor record of a cheque of anything like this size, and could find no entry of money the proceeds of bonds. It may be, says some one, that he held for another; possibly for his father, who was then alive. His father was a very able man of business. If his father or any other human being with an ounce of brains was the real owner, does any person suggest that what he elected was worth $200 on May 10th he would sell for $37.50 on the 18th?

It does not matter if he did hold for somebody else. If he held for anybody independent of Senator McDougald, then it is impossible to conceive of what the Senator alleges as a fact really having taken place. But if the units were Senator McDougald's from the beginning, then, especially if Senator McDougald wanted to keep his name out and felt it vital to do so, he would have pursued just the course he did pursue; and, if Sifton was helping him, he too would have pursued just the course he did. Facts never collide; in their long procession there is always harmony from the first movement to the last. On the theory that these units were Senator McDougald's from the beginning, all known facts fit together. On any other theory there is collision, confusion, irrationality.

Why keep the curtains drawn all through the piece? Why are the lights out? Why is all this darkness deliberately sought and loved? Why is everything so beclouded? Senator McDougald says, "I did not want others to follow my example; I was ready myself to gamble." And he calls it a "political gamble," honourable gentlemen: that shows what was in his head, a gamble as to what would be done politically. He says, "I was ready to gamble with my own money,"—and this is raised in his defence by his counsel—"but I did not want my friends to be following me." Senator Raymond gave a similar reason for his conduct in putting shares into the Crédit Général du Canada. That is a sensible, a customary way, a method many a man adopts. He takes his private shares and a trust company or a private company holds them, and there is no blazoning to the world. But why go to New York? Why pay, in $1,000 bills, through a deputy? Why have the deputy of his deputy go to New York and furtively put through his three-times-removed transaction?

Moyer is to hold units for Sifton and he in turn for Mc-Dougald, and Sifton and Moyer have to go to New York, get money in some wholly inscrutable way, and deposit it there, and then a cheque is issued against it in Montreal; and these precautions are taken for fear some poor, straying innocent Montrealer would buy some units in this scheme, following the example of Senator McDougald! But nobody could, for those units were not on the market; those units were not open to public subscription; they were under the jealous eye of Sweezey, who wanted in his enterprise only people who could do something to help him. Sweezey did not know for whom Sifton held units from the beginning, but he said, "I never imagined that Sifton owned those units; he would not tell me for whom he held them, whose they really were." Sweezey knew, however, that Sifton had said to Moyer, "In case of my death I want you to take your instructions from Senator McDougald."

Here is Moyer, who had not the least thought that those shares belonged to Sifton; here is Sweezey, who says on his oath that he too had not the least thought; here is Sifton, going to New York to keep those transactions buried. Here is all this ingeniously constructed mystery, and here is the estate of Sifton, where there is not an entry, a mark, a cheque or a memorandum, or proceeds of any sale.

Yet because Senator McDougald stood in the box and swore that he had not made a dollar which he could not have made if he had not been a senator, we are asked to conclude from those imperious, those immovable, unchallengeable facts—every one of them—that he bought his interest only on May 18th. The senator stood in this House on April 19th to deny his interest, and I say the evidence is insurmountable that he was the owner then of those Beauharnois units, and in addition, and admittedly, he was owner then of the Sterling shares.

RIGHT HON. MR. GRAHAM: On the 19th of April?

RIGHT HON. MR. MEIGHEN: Yes! Sifton's buying job had

been done in March. If he was owner of one or the other, he flagrantly misled this House in a matter concerning his own private interests and their relation to his public duty, and, on the evidence, he was beyond all question owner of both.

On May 20th, 1931, he rose for the purpose of reaffirming what he had said in 1928. It was a prepared statement which he read to this House, and he knew it affected something vital to his own honour. He said he did not own a Beauharnois share when his 1928 speech was made; but he did not go on to declare that he did not own stock in any company which had power developments in sight, as he had stated before. He said, "It is true I did not own them (the Beauharnois shares), and I did not own them for six months afterwards." He said, "I was not interested on April 19th, 1928; I did not become interested for six months, until October." Then he comes to our committee and says, "It is true the initial step was taken, the initial transaction was made, on May 18th." Why such assertions or perversions? The whole transaction was, as I have shown, entered into on or before March 30th, and, if we accept his own account of it, was completed on May 18th. The stock was bought and paid for. Moyer from that hour became his trustee. In October the trusteeship was changed to Ebbs. As between him and Sifton the transaction for the 800 shares—or 1600 in terms of the second syndicate—was completed on the 18th of May; the whole thing was over, and his statement of the bona fides of his declaration in this House is impossible to entertain. There was no reason why Senator McDougald should have forgotten the early steps, for they are part of the whole transaction which ended in payment on the 18th of May. And it is unpardonable that in his evidence, over and over again, he should keep on saying: "I did not make any mistake; what I said was correct." When he is shown it is incorrect, he says: "I say it was not incorrect; it may have been ambiguous." The word "ambiguous" has no more relationship to these facts than any word in the dictionary of Demerara or China. His statement was absolutely incorrect and wrong.

It is said, "Oh, but anybody may make a mistake in dates." Yes, he may, but it is not very likely that a mistake would be made of that magnitude, of that importance, aside from a further consideration into which we now must enter.

Was there an interest? It is argued that it did not make a particle of difference whether the date was May or October; that he had no object at all in fixing it in October, instead of May 1928, when he spoke here in May of last year. There was nothing to be gained by it, we are told by his counsel; therefore, it was not deliberate. Was there nothing to be gained? I think there was very much to be gained, and will tell you what it was. Senator McDougald knew that he had been on a committee of this House dealing with this very matter, from April 20th, 1928, to June 7th, and he knew that he would rather not be brought to the surface as owner of a large interest in Beauharnois during the time he was sitting on that committee.

Did honourable gentlemen hear the rule on this subject read by the senator from Pictou (Hon. Mr. Tanner)? Senator McDougald had absolutely no right to sit on that committee. I will assume for the moment that he did not know the rule; but he knew thoroughly well that this matter of navigation and power development had actively engaged the committee. It had been treating of a subject in which he was himself definitely and very practically interested, but he had never revealed that fact to his colleagues. He knew that he had called his own associate, Henry, before them. He prepared questions which he put to this man, having seen to it that Henry had deliberated about them beforehand, questions such as, "Do you think this private development should be gone on with at once, and if so, why?" Henry had answered that it ought to be gone on with at once. If Senator McDougald had so conducted himself while he was a holder of Beauharnois stock, is it human nature that he would want that fact to be known? True, he was the owner of Sterling shares as well, but Sterling, he says, was not much to the fore. He did not want it to come out that he also owned Beauharnois units. He was advancing Beauharnois' interest by stimulating the Senate to the necessity of something being done quickly, and this as a member of the committee, himself.

Therefore, in those two particulars he is answerable solemnly to this House for a breach of its privileges. But more: In his account of his proceedings given here on May 20th, 1931, he said, "I paid the very same for my shares as every other member of the syndicate, and when it was closed up I got just the same as the others for what I had in." The latter part of this statement is true, that he got just the same as others; but the main part was that he had paid the same as all his co-owners. I noticed that this was not mentioned by the senator from Eganville (Right Hon. Mr. Graham). After reading his evidence, there is not a mortal in the shape of man who could assert that he paid the same as others, for he did not pay the same at all. How many shares did he hold? He says he held only in the second syndicate. Well, technically that is true. He held 5,200 shares—the 800 of the Sifton units had become 1,600, and 1,600 more that Sifton bought made 3,200, and he had meantime secured 2,000 shares more for that precious asset the Sterling Industrial Corporation. This made 5,200 in all. In this House he said he paid the same for them as anybody else in the syndicate. When it was put to him that for 1,600 units of the new syndicate—1,600 of the 5,200—he paid only one-half of $37.50— that is, $18.75—while the great majority of other holders paid $100, he said, "Oh, I was just in the second syndicate." What an answer! His shares derived from ownership of Sterling cost him what he put into that company; that is, 2,000 shares received for Sterling cost him $3,500 all told; $1.75 apiece. Units in the first syndicate were converted into shares in the second and cost him only a fraction of what most purchasers paid. His answer is just equivocation, just a quibble. What did those original 1,600 shares cost? If they cost him anything, they cost him exactly the money paid for the units which were converted into them. For those he did not pay anything like what others paid. He paid the same as Frank Jones, the same as Hon. W. G. Mitchell, the same as Senator Raymond; but not the same as others.

Do not take from my words that I am criticizing him merely because he bought more cheaply than his fellows. That is not the point at all. The point is that his assurances to Parliament, when in a sphere of solemn responsibility, were not true. He did not pay the same as others; he paid the same as only two or three, even for the first 1,600 units. As for the second 1,600, subscribed for initially by Winfield Sifton, they were taken over by him, and for them he paid the same as others paid. Then there are the 2,000 units he got for Sterling. He did not pay the same for them as every other, or any other, member paid for his syndicate units. All they ever cost was $3,500—nearly nothing. Yet he stood in this House and said he paid the same for his shares as every other member of the syndicate.

When he was reminded in the box about Sterling shares, he said: "Oh, I was not thinking of Sterling shares. Neither was the public." Why, certainly the public was not; the public never had heard of the Sterling Company. But should not he have thought of what was handed him for Sterling when he spoke of his shares? They, too, were his. He had become owner of 5,200 Beauharnois shares; most of them—a lot more than two-thirds of them—he got for a fraction of what others paid; yet on this subject where the utmost fidelity and frankness were demanded he dared to stand up and say that he paid the same price as his fellow holders, because, forsooth, he was not thinking about 2,000 of them at all, and because 1,600 had been first bought in the form of units in a syndicate!

May I ask: Does the right honourable senator from Eganville think that Senator McDougald's answers were honest answers? It was just a quibble for him to assert that he received no favours in any shape or form. When he made such an assertion, his conduct was not in harmony with either candour or truth.

Again I come to his connection with Sterling Industrial Corporation, whose shares were "merged," to use the language of the right honourable senator from Eganville, in the Beauharnois Company. I do not care what you call it—a merger, an amalgamation, a sale. Like a rose, by any other name it will smell as sweet. I am concerned with the facts and history of Sterling Industrial Corporation in relation to the conduct of Senator McDougald. On July 5, 1924, that Company put in its application to the Department of Railways, and on July 7th, to the Department of Public Works. From that time on it left those applications dormant, because it was not ready to proceed. Some investigations were made through an engineer, for which not more than $3,500 was paid.

There was, perhaps, a financial situation to be considered, and the possibility of getting money for this work. At all stages Senator McDougald is kept in view. Senator Haydon went to New York for his Sterling Company in December of 1925. In April, 1925, he had had a conference with Senator McDougald about it, and he had another conference about it in December, 1926. The evidence is literally strewn with conferences with Senator McDougald about this company.

RIGHT HON. MR. GRAHAM: Does my right honourable friend say that Mr. Haydon, or Mr. Henry, went to New York?

RIGHT HON. MR. MEIGHEN: Mr. Haydon. Does the right hon. gentleman want the reference?

RIGHT HON. MR. GRAHAM: Oh, no.

RIGHT HON. MR. MEIGHEN: He took an active interest in the concern all through. Then, in 1928, Mr. Sweezey, finding that there is an obstacle, or believing that there is some obstacle in the way of his success at Ottawa, searches around to find out where it is. He is mystified, and does not know what to do to get his Beauharnois application through. He employs Colonel Thompson, Mr. Ainslie Green, Mr. Pugsley, Mr. McLaughlin; he keeps these men busy "creating atmosphere" in his struggle to get this approval through the Governor in Council. But still he cannot succeed.

Then he finds out about this Sterling Industrial Corporation. What does he learn about it? He learns that it has nothing, no assets, not a pen nib. He also finds that it is owned by Senator McDougald, or at all events that Senator McDougald owns it for himself and another. He talks with Senator McDougald about it, with Mr. Henry, and also with Senator Haydon who states what I have no reason to doubt—that he is merely its solicitor. Senator Haydon's firm had taken out its charter, presided legally over its birth, and charged an account to it for some time. After his talks with Senator Haydon and Senator McDougald, Mr. Sweezey comes to the conclusion that there is someone else interested. He has not given even a hint, or a word from which anybody could get a hint, who that was, but he tells us he got the impression from Senators Haydon and McDougald that there was someone else, and that he or they had better be taken in and not overlooked.

The right hon. senator from Eganville says that Sweezey made a deal for Sterling with Henry because he was anxious to get Henry. I wonder what the right hon. senator will think when I read him evidence given before the committee, which shows that he did not make a deal with Henry at all, but made it with Senator McDougald. It is Senator McDougald's evidence which I shall read. It shows that he is the man who did the job, as of course he is. At page 160, hon. members will find the following:

> Q. There is no doubt about this, that irrespective of documents, the payment of 2,000 part interests for the five shares of Sterling was the result of discussion between you and Sweezey? A. Yes.

That was a question put to Senator McDougald. Right through the evidence it is shown that he is the man who made the deal, and the reason given by Sweezey—a reason which appeals to everybody, and which, indeed, is not contradicted—is that he felt there was an influence against him somewhere, he did not know where, and that he began to think Sterling was his stumbling block, and wanted it removed. He says Sterling had a prior application. Yes, it had a prior application. But, he adds, it had nothing of any intrinsic value. Two other companies had prior applications, but, he says, "I didn't bother with them. The reason I bothered here was that these were responsible men. They might give me trouble; they might even get money and seriously go on." Then he says, "The great reason was that I wanted to get rid of the nuisance." He told the committee that the only value it had was a nuisance value, and Senator McDougald said the same thing; and, what is more, he said before the Commons committee that that was all the value it had. The evidence given by Senator McDougald before the committee, at page 165, shows that he could not tell the committee of any value on earth which this concern had, except as a nuisance. He controlled it and owned it. He was under some indefinite and unenforceable understanding, as the report words it, to divide with Henry; but he was in absolute control. He, a senator of Canada, made use of his "nuisance" to enrich himself at the expense of a public utility company in process of securing its basic assets from Canada.

I ask: Has a senator of Canada a right to capitalize on a nuisance as against a company absolutely dependent on concessions from Governments, including the Government of Canada? If he does so, can he keep his place in the Senate as an honourable public man?

Before our committee the senator said that the great thing this Beauharnois Company got when it bought the Sterling Industrial Corporation—and he cannot tell of anything else it got—was Mr. Henry. Mr. Henry, he says, was a fine engineer, and they secured him by buying the Sterling Industrial Corporation. In a word, in order to get Mr. Henry they had to buy a nuisance from Mr. Henry and Senator McDougald, at a price ultimately of $300,000 and 80,000 shares. They had to pay $300,000 plus 2,000 units, or about one-ninth of the issued capital of their whole enterprise, in order that by the purchase of a nuisance they might get an engineer. They paid Mr. Henry $40,000 a year, which was more than twice what Henry had ever earned in his life before, and he was handed a huge block of shares besides, and they did not take him until some time after the nuisance had evaporated.

I do not see how anyone who takes his fellow-man to be intelligent can dare to say that Sweezey had to buy Sterling Industrial Corporation before he could get Henry as an engineer. It is absurd, grotesque, an affront to common sense. Sterling Industrial Corporation was bought, according to the evidence of Sweezey, because he thought by buying it he could better advance his interests in getting his Beauharnois application approved at Ottawa. That is why he bought it. Senator McDougald and Senator Haydon persuaded him to buy it with that object in mind, and this is established by the evidence without the slightest possibility of contradiction.

All these gigantic profits were accumulated along the road, and every dollar of them was taken care of out of money subscribed by the public, money upon which the same public had to pay interest in the form of rates. It may be that a private citizen has a right to do some of these things. It is at times difficult to decide just when a man is within the circle of honour and just when he is without; but in the case of Senator McDougald, a public servant and member of this House, there is no question that he was away outside its circumference. What is more, his whole conduct shows that he knew it; otherwise, why all the concealment?

Nobody has ever given even a sensible answer to the question: Why was all this kept under a smudge? Why these trips to the ends of the continent, these drafts and thousand-dollar-bills, these agents and sub-agents and sub-trustees? Such things were totally unnecessary even if the senator was anxious only that others should not follow his example. There was not a possibility of others following his example, even though Sifton had given his cheque and he himself had paid by cheque instead of by bonds. These reasons are afterthoughts; they are useful only as showing the state of mind of a man holding high office in his country, who knew that his conduct was inconsistent with his position and did not want it revealed.

I ask honourable senators, while being scrupulously careful not to do injustice to one of their fellow-members, to be at least equally careful not to do injustice to those who are our first concern, the people whom we are here to serve. Let us, I beg of you, not be contemptuous of the long-established, fundamental rights of those people in respect of their legislators. This country is passing through trying times. These are testing hours. Few are the homes not now struggling in the ruthless grip of economic forces. Questionings are abroad everywhere as to whether the system under which we live will endure. Even while we speak, the institutions of democracy are being held up to interrogation, and there are those who wonder whether they will survive the storm. The public mind is today more sensitive than ever, perhaps, within memory of those now living. At this time, if ever in history, we must stand faithful to our trust. But whether the public mind is uncommonly sensitive or not, assuming that we act as we would in normal days, can we face the people of our country and proclaim to them, and before the world, that the conduct of two of our number has been such as to be within the right of every senator?

If we vote down this motion and say that their conduct is not censurable and unbecoming, what are the people of Canada going to think of the Senate? Yea, more, what are they going to think of our institutions, one and all? If confidence in parliamentary government is still further reduced, if it is affected detrimentally by our verdict, it will be the responsibility of every member who votes "Nay," and a very painful and lasting responsibility.

I should lament a party verdict. I should not like to see hon. members on this side vote their approval of misconduct so plainly revealed, but I would rather see a divided conception of duty behind me than that honourable senators opposite, to a man, should vote against this motion. A party verdict on this matter would be a very serious outcome. We do not want it. Honourable senators should vote as impelled by their consciences, and I cannot believe that any man, on any side, will be driven by his conscience to vote against this motion—the verdict of a unanimously chosen committee of this House and the unanimous verdict of a committee of the other.

IN MEMORIAM

Address of Sympathy in the Senate of Canada, January 30, 1934 on the death of Senator F. L. Béique and of Senator Gideon Robertson.

IT WOULD BE DIFFICULT INDEED to compress within the boundaries of a brief speech the long record of achievement which stands to the credit of our late colleague, Senator Béique. He was for more than sixty-five years at the Bar of Quebec; three decades in this House; all those years, or nearly all, a member of the governing bodies of very large industries in our Dominion, active in educational work, prominent in at least half a dozen other spheres—president of a university, president of a bank, member of the executive committee of the Canadian Pacific; and throughout, perhaps the most indefatigable advocate at the Bar that the Province of Quebec has seen. All of us will agree that he was one of the best informed and most practically useful members of either House of Parliament.

HON. MR. CASGRAIN: Hear, hear.

RIGHT HON. MR. MEIGHEN: Some who knew him best would use the single superlative; probably my brief experience in this Chamber warrants adoption of the more cautious phrase. One could not work with him or talk with him without realizing that he was possessed of a mind of ample scope, of comprehensive grasp, of keen analytical power, all dominated by that spirit of fairness and determination for service, which forms the base and the background of worthwhile public work. He has gone now, having reached by reason of strength far beyond the three score years and ten, with the unanimous acclaim of all lovers of true citizenship, and followed by the benedictions of his people.

We all had observed for a period of many months that failing health had wrought something approaching collapse in the

245

splendid physique and fine intellectual endowment of Senator Robertson. I well remember, nearly seventeen years ago, when for the first time I was introduced to him. He on that day entered the Cabinet of which I had been for some time a member. As he had never occupied a seat in the House of Commons, nor taken any part in political warfare, he was to his future colleagues comparatively unknown. His admission to high public office had been attained, certainly not because of service to any party, for such service he never had rendered, not because of advocacy of any special policy or theory on the hustings, but because of marked capacity shown in the realm of organized labour, to which he had given his life. Starting as a telegrapher at the age of eighteen, he became, in course of a decade and a half, chairman of the union of telegraphers of this country. This gave him scope for his splendid, indeed unexampled talents, as a mediator—and a born mediator he was. To the order of which he was the head, and to organized labour in general, his heart was attached, his energies were dedicated; around these things all his interests revolved and for them he lived. He was not in those early times, nor indeed was he ever, a partisan in the sense in which we usually understand the term. As a member of a party government he necessarily had affiliations, and to those affiliations he was loyal, but beyond the allegiance by which as a colleague he was bound to his associates and leader, he knew not the meaning of the term partisan at all. His interests were elsewhere, his whole mission and purpose in life was foreign to any such activity. I know that his closest associate—certainly an associate closer to him than was any member of the Government to which he belonged—was the honourable senator from Parkdale (Hon. Mr. Murdock). He can in a personal way speak of him better than can any of the rest of us. Mediator in some of the fiercest and most dangerous disputes which ever shook the social fabric of our country, Senator Robertson conducted himself with credit in all, and with almost universal success; and the volume of service he rendered this Dominion by that success is hard for us at this time to measure. But as years advanced, intense concentration, unselfish toil began to levy inexorable toll. The resources of his mortal frame, strong and rugged though we know them to have been, could not longer endure the heavy chains of his exacting office; the pitiless demands of democracy in this trying time brought upon him a burden heavier than human nature could sustain; he broke and fell under the load. Let us hope that in those last days of weakness and of parting he felt some warm breath of assurance that he had not lived in vain. Let us hope that in the silence of the receding world he listened in happy premonition to the first accents of a gratitude too seldom heard in life.

To those who mourn these our colleagues, I know it is the wish of every member of this House that you, Mr. Speaker, should convey, on behalf of the Senate of Canada, our humble tribute of esteem and regard for the loved and lost, and of deep and earnest sympathy for all whom they left bereaved.

WHITHER ARE WE DRIFTING?

*Delivered at Toronto, Monday, November 4, 1935, before a joint
meeting of the Board of Trade Club, the Young Men's Section of the
Board of Trade, and the General Membership of the Board of Trade.*

You, MR. PRESIDENT, in a very kindly introduction, have informed
this gathering, among other things, that I have been practising
law since coming to Toronto in 1926. Well, I have never yet had
a client. My obscurity obviously is all that could be desired.

Please keep in mind that I am not a public lecturer or
itinerant speaker or Chautauqua orator; I am alleged to be and
definitely trying to be a man of business like yourselves, wrestling day by day with the embarrassments and irritations of
company affairs, struggling against taxes and red ink. The time
one can give under such circumstances to ordering one's thoughts
or even generating them for the purpose of a public address is
limited indeed. You will understand, therefore, my anxiety and
the reason for my earnest hope that you have all enjoyed your
dinner and have measured its value advantageously against the
admission price.

A suggestion was made just a few moments ago that there
would be entertainment in this speech. Whatever else there may
be, there will be no entertainment, and it is just as certain that
my words tonight will bring me no accession of popularity, much
as I may need that very thing.

My purpose is to make some comments on the character of
thinking in matters of public concern, which seems to be per-
vasive of our whole country, if not of democracies generally, at
this time, and to make some inquiry as to whether or not the
people in mass who now under universal suffrage determine the
fate of many nations are really cognizant of their responsibility

as well as their power. You will apprehend already that I am somewhat doubtful myself.

Universal suffrage is relatively new in this land and in modern civilization. Manhood suffrage prevailed here until about eighteeen years ago. We now have womanhood suffrage as well—and that makes it universal. There was a writer quoted with approval by Dean Inge and other thoughtful men, who stated that universal suffrage had always heralded the end of popular Government. We are not first in trying the experiment. It behooves us to enquire just where it is leading. Because I make inquiry, it does not mean introduction of a doctrine that we have to make a change. I do not believe change is possible; the Anglo-Saxon spirit is to cling to democracy in this its most extreme manifestation. Therefore, we must make the best of it; seek to inform it, but above all we must understand how seriously it is taking its duties and what we must guard against in the way of perils, present and potential.

As an illustration of the kind of thinking which finds expression in public speeches in our day—no better, in my judgment, but worse than in years gone by extending back over a generation—I am going to refer to something spoken since the late election contest by a man of learning—a member indeed of the ministerial profession. I read in the press of Toronto this pronouncement by him:—That now we had been driven to a condition where one per cent of our population own eighty-five per cent of our wealth, and that such is the oppression of the masses under this state of affairs that at a time during this depression when dividends of companies were increasing wages of workers went down.

I select those two statements because of their illustrative value. They tend in a direction which seems almost always to be the bent of public speakers under universal suffrage, a resolve to inflame great masses against the few, and thereby endanger the very fabric of the state and the peace of society.

It is difficult to estimate in exact figures just where the wealth of a country lies. I have gone to our Statistical Bureau at Ottawa, which under Dr. R. H. Coats is recognized as perhaps the best and as certainly unsurpassed among Governmental Statistical

Bureaux of the world, and I asked them to make investigation and give me such facts as they could present bearing on both assertions. I found from their data this:—that in farm wealth alone, we had a net total of four billions four hundred and fifty millions; that the total wealth of Canada estimated in the same year, 1931, was something slightly over twenty-two billions of money. Four billion four hundred and fifty million was a total after taking away a mortgage farm indebtedness of eight hundred million from a grand total farm value of five billion two hundred and fifty million. I ask you to remember only the above figures—twenty-two billions of total wealth for our country in 1931; four billion four hundred and fifty million of net farm wealth after debt, distributed among all farmers of our country. That alone is twenty per cent of our total wealth.

Then there was presented to me the value of our homes and our urban buildings and properties—a total value of eight billion two hundred and fifty million, against which its total mortgage indebtedness was seven hundred and fifty millions of dollars. This mortgage indebtedness in the case of urban property as in the case of farm property is not necessarily nor indeed substantially owned by very wealthy men. It is held by individuals throughout our country; by insurance and loan companies whose securities are held by vast thousands of our people. But assuming it is held by the wealthy alone, it leaves a net asset of seven billion and a half held by the general public in our urban property. There again is thirty-four per cent of our total wealth. These two together make fifty-six per cent into which this one per cent of wealthy people do not invade to any important extent. But in addition, of all the grand total wealth of our country, six billion eight hundred million is held by British and foreign investors. Our one per cent of rich folk have no part in that sum. There is twenty-one per cent more and a total of seventy-five per cent of the wealth of Canada in which the very wealthy have little or no part at all, for landlordism is a negligible factor in this Dominion; and the process of addition has much farther yet to go.

I ask you to stand those facts furnished me by the Statistics Department at Ottawa against a statement of a man who said to

the people of our city that one per cent owned eighty-five per
cent of our Canadian wealth. This is the kind of material which
constitutes the loose and lazy demagogic utterances of men who
seek to attract to themselves the focussed rays of public attention
or who determine to pander to the masses because it is the masses
who have votes and power.

They lightly interchange "control" and "ownership." Even
if the word "control" as meaning management were intended,
the figures are grossly and preposterously wrong, but control or
management is wholly different from ownership. If one per cent
did manage the main business of our country, it would mean
that such management was distributed among ten thousand
people, and this is a considerable total. But managership means
trusteeship, which means service. It is as distinct from ownership as anything in the world can be. One who studies management or control for a time will wonder if a betterment is to be
attained by a mere multiplication of numbers. He will wonder
if things would be improved, if it would be any better manifestation of our responsibility to democracy if our Boards of
Directors were composed of five hundred instead of five, if, say,
the Dominion Bank, of which Mr. Carlisle, sitting on my right,
is President, had a Board of Directors of a thousand instead of
ten. Would that be more democratic? Would that be more in the
interests of hundreds of thousands of shareholders and depositors?

I have gone far enough to illustrate how shockingly and, I fear,
dangerously wrong is the demagogism spread abroad at election
time and for election purposes, for the offender in the present case
no doubt absorbed his information from a political platform.

Then, as to his statement about wages going down while
dividends were going up, I have figures here in exact and
dependable form. Taking the average real wage of wage earners
as 100 in the year 1917, when wages were not low compared to
what they had been, taking that as the index figure and having
reference not only to amount of wages but to relationship of
wages to cost of living and, therefore, to their real value, our
Statistical Department shows against a 100 index in 1917, 113.6
as the real value of wages in Canada in 1930. The last year I can
get is 1933. The real value of wages that year was 113.8 or prac-

tically the same as in 1930, a very slight and negligible increase. As opposed to those figures we take the returns from company investments—dividends paid. In 1930, $420,700,000.00; in 1933, $270,247,000.00 So the statistical fact is that while company returns by dividends were reduced in the depression by about 36% from 1930, to 1933, wages of labour stood untouched in respect of their real value as governed by the cost of living.

I now pass to something else, and in doing so ask you to believe that my indictment tonight is not against any Government. I have no Government in mind. My indictment is against the way the public have of thinking little, and quickly coming to conclusions, and against exploitation of the public by dishonest men and charlatans. It has not reference to any particular election result. I do not think the result in the late election was in any important degree attributable to merits or demerits of the Administration. In fact, it is only frankness to say that the merits of any Government do not contribute as they should at all to make certain its subsequent return. I am not analyzing now what does so contribute, but am examining where we are drifting under universal suffrage, and urging that while admittedly we ought to retain that principle, we certainly must inform our average voter better than we have been doing in the past.

There is something which over the centuries has been deemed vital to the very fabric of society and progress of humanity, and that is a sacred regard for the validity and enforceability of contracts. I was talking within the last week to a leading citizen of Western Canada. No man is better known in our entire West than is this man, and no man knows Western Canada better than he. He said to me, and not in any spirit of criticism: "Well, in our country now there is no general feeling that onerous contracts ought to be enforced; there is no general sense of obligation to carry out a contract if it is painful or difficult to do so. Public opinion now is not in favour of that principle." I do not challenge his statement; I can hope it is not true; but I wonder if public opinion is considering where such a state of mind is going to lead this great organization known as the civilized world. Upon what does the fabric of law and order rest, if it does not rest upon the enforceability to the extent of the contractor's capacity of all terms of his contract? When you and I were young, we did not hear talk along the lines and on the level we hear today. We were brought up in an atmosphere where if a man failed to pay his debt, or if that proved impossible, failed to divide proportionately among all he owed, he was considered a fraud and an enemy of society. He was considered an example to sun. Is he today? Can he be so considered again in our time? If there is not to be strict accountability for contracts—in the absence, of course, of fraud or misrepresentation—isn't there going to ensue a light and loose, a free and easy habit of entering into contracts from this time on? Isn't that care, caution and prudence which ordered society has heretofore sought to instil into people and which we have been seeking to teach our children throughout our lives likely to go by the board? Into what future are we about to drift if we lead people to think that agreements are made to be lived up to when they pay, and made to be repudiated when they do not? It is not long since some of us here heard a doctrine impliedly if not specifically preached, that repudiation if it can be shown to pay is not repudiation any longer; that its paying feature gives a different colour and aspect to the whole matter. Now I ask you:—Were our fathers right in their teaching or were they wrong? Isn't it well to pause and enquire just what the doctrine of the future is going to be? We used to believe that it was not only morally right to take this time-honoured attitude, but that honesty was the best policy, that in the long run it paid—best for us and best for the world. Were we wrong in that belief? Apparently a newer school has evolved something else. For myself, I do not believe the thinking of today is nearly as careful or as well-informed or as thoroughly guided by moral principle as the thinking of forty years ago. We frequently read in the press:—"Oh, people are beginning to think for themselves." My conclusion is quite the contrary. They are ceasing to think for themselves. A myriad of diversions and preoccupations are stifling the processes of real thought. Those who represent the public have to forge ahead of their public in these matters. We have to get away from the idea that if some gilded and dishonest proposals show signs of popularity, the only thing to do is to get behind and cheer. Believe me, democracy cannot long survive that standard of service. If we do not get away from such habit of mind, we will deserve the consequences, and those consequences will be such that there has been nothing in our past to which they can be compared. We can expect a veritable inundation of chaos, if anything like general contempt for law and order overtakes us. Ulysses was thinking of this when he said:

> The bounded waters
> Should lift their bosoms higher than the shores
> And make a sop of all this solid globe.

Now I come to another phase, and this is the last. It is of value to inquire into some very complacent and satisfactory hypotheses—self-satisfactory—upon which we have been resting our consciences in relation to Canada's duty toward the rest of the world in matters of, say, Peace and War. In this connection I am speaking of the general, average, everyday sentiment of Canadians and not of present public policy as reflecting that sentiment at all.

I wonder if our modern-day disposition toward Canada's responsibility is a reasonably fair and honourable one. There is still a League of Nations. It is not what we hoped it would be; it is a League outside of which three or four very powerful nations stand, but it is composed of some fifty other countries, many of them very great, led by Britain and by France. The Dominion of Canada is an independent member of that League. We find the League in difficulty today, facing one of the gravest crises of its existence. We find it struggling, by means of a threatened application of sanctions, to prevent, or at least to mitigate a heinous and senseless war.[1] What is Canada's attitude? When one is criticizing countries, he had better, if facts justify, criticize his own. There are others, it is true, in the same category as we. I wonder if the people of Canada feel that we are playing a fine, a proud or a very honourable role at this time. We have agreed to be parties to sanctions. That is, we have agreed that we will cease exporting to Italy or purchasing from Italy goods barred. This is well, this is right. We have in effect, though,

---

[1] The invasion of Ethiopia by Mussolini.

notified the League of Nations that beyond this contribution we will not step—at least we have insisted that it is not to be assumed we shall step, and I personally have no doubt that if the general sentiment of our people were to do the expressing, it would go this limit and say:—"Beyond we shall not move." Our contribution, therefore, to the maintenance of peace is a self-denial of a measure of trade, and a measure of trade so inconsiderable that it would not amount to a shilling a head spread over the population of our country. To say the least, our profit therefrom would not be much to sacrifice. When we sit down and think, we must conclude that if sanctions are to be effective they must bring a real responsibility upon those who apply those sanctions, and put them under necessity of making sure of enforcement should there be resistance. Are we today telling those who may have to strike the blow that we will stand behind them? Are we not saying to our own mother country:—We believe in your going to it; we want you to hold back the aggressor, show your might, but if there is any blood to be shed do not look to us; if there is any danger to be encountered, just forget that we are here; we are at the peace end of this controversy and nowhere else. Isn't that the stand we have taken ever since there was a League of Nations, and are we quite right and reasonable in assuming that this is all we ought to do? Can there be an effective League of Nations if such is the spirit of its component parts? Are we quite justified in hoping that there will ever be a League ready to enforce its demands and to vindicate the just claims of mankind, if nations go no farther in support than we as a nation are prepared to go?

The United States sees its Kellogg Pact torn to ribbons and stands complacently by. This is the job of European powers, say our cousins to the south.

Let us examine now just what this situation means to us—just what we have at stake. Have we ever reflected why it is that Italy is invading Ethiopia instead of Canada? Ours is vastly a better country, vastly more desirable from the standpoint of climate, of soil and of resources. We have no more people here to defend ourselves than they have—far less; our navy is no stronger. Does anybody open his eyes to see why Italy is looking south instead of west? Most of us, if we scan the horizon, will descry that there is a British fleet in between us and Italy; many of us will be comforted also by the reflection that there is a Monroe doctrine on this Continent, and we do love that Monroe doctrine. But have we ever inquired where it would be or where we would be if things were put to the test?

Next, why are these dire and distressing events disturbing, if not overturning, the peace of mankind at this hour? What are the deep-down fundamental truths and facts out of which these disturbances grow? We have an interest in those facts. Whatever front is put on, whatever argument may be advanced as justifying the invasion of Ethiopia, everyone knows it is just the ambition of Mussolini and his Italian nation to extend their territory and have more resources for their people. Do not think I am excusing that country. I believe its conduct is a breach of its covenant, a breach of its pledges to the League, and I fear it is even worse; it is an attack on an almost defenceless people. But the far-down driving power which impels Italians so to act is an anxiety to enlarge the volume and value of their property, their resources, and make better the future of their race.

What are the facts about these resources? Italy is rather barren. Japan is another nation in similar position. To be brief, I confine my references in respect of resources to those two countries. Do you know that we in Canada have over seventy thousand tons of known coal for each single individual of our country; that Italy has just six, or enough to last them about a year? Do you know that Canada has for every single one of her population four hundred and fifty-eight tons of raw iron ore which she does not use because she can buy better, but which doubtless will be used and which doubtless Italy could use? Italy has exactly one-fifth of a single ton. Of these coal resources, while we have seventy thousand tons apiece, Japan has one hundred and twenty-six tons; of these iron ore resources, Japan has one and two-fifths per head; more than Italy which has only one-fifth of one. Italy is without iron, without coal, without oil, without copper, without steel, without cotton, without wool, without nickel, without mica, without lead, without rubber and without tin. Italy has attempted to provide a living for her people by producing silk and rayon and by manufacturing raw cotton brought from other lands. Italy finds herself in this position. She has made her way through these times by dependence upon three sources of income: First, income from her people who went out to other lands, earned money and sent it home. Her income from this source averaged about one hundred and twelve millions a year. These other lands have put up barriers and shut Italians out and we ourselves have done just the same as others; so has Australia; so has the United States; so have all countries which enjoy a plethora of great possessions. The Italian cannot go abroad, and now he sends home less than one-half of what he sent a few years ago. Their population is forty-three million, increasing four hundred thousand a year. That pressure of population was relieved for years by six hundred and twenty thousand emigrating annually and settling in other lands. That six hundred and twenty thousand is now reduced to fifty-five thousand—less than one-tenth of what it was.

She had a further income from tourists. Tourist income has gone down from about one hundred and ten millions of dollars to around fifty million. The rest of her income, its main part, was from sale of manufactured goods. Because of depreciated currencies and tariffs, those sales have been cut to forty per cent of what they were, and the result is that from those three sources she cannot get foreign currency with which to buy raw materials to keep her people at work. Japan is in an analogous position, and Italy and Japan are only illustrations of what a large portion of the world suffers from today.

We in Canada have perhaps per population the largest area and volume of vital assets of any land on earth. Australia comes closely next. A few other countries are like us. Great Britain, on the other hand, has a population of eight hundred to the square mile; Italy has three hundred and sixty, but there are far less resources and far less cultivatable land in Italy than in England. What of others? The United States has thirty-eight; Argentine Republic has eight; Canada has three and Australia has two. Such is the division of inhabitable area of this world among the world's people. Canada is in enjoyment of a tremendous heritage relative to other less fortunate countries. These people look upon us and they say:—"What is your title?" to which we reply:—"We are here." Can we even claim that we won this country by force? I do not think we can. If any nation won this country by force it was Great Britain and the taxpayers of Great Britain; it was not we. But we are here. That is the best title we can plead. It may be necessary and right that we plead such title and refuse to contemplate its qualification, but if we do, aren't we obligated to sustain it?

I have lifted the curtain far enough to let you see that there are deep and terrific forces pressing against the League of Nations, threatening its authority and even now invading world peace. We quietly and complacently sit back and think that all we have to do is to deny ourselves for a short time our small share of trade with Italy. The obligations implicit in this terrible situation are surely not foreign to us. They challenge us more than they do Great Britain herself.

The British people do not stand in the midst of a wealth of happy possessions the way we do in Canada. Of territory they have the least of any—only one square mile for eight hundred souls. As a consequence of pressure of population against their economic maximum the British birth rate has gone down. When in 1881 their numbers were twenty-six million, their birth rate was nine hundred thousand, but now with a population of over forty million, their birth rate is down to six hundred and thirty thousand. The annual increase in Great Britain is now only one-half of one per cent, or five per thousand; in Italy it is twelve, or about two and a half times the rate in Great Britain; in Poland it is seventeen and in Russia twenty-four. Britain has sought to adjust herself, to bring her population within the compass of her resources. Possibly she has a right to say to Italy:—"You must do the same." Canada has not equal right. The obligation upon Canada to meet this ever-growing crisis is more direct and impressive than the obligation upon Britain.

Italy under the preachments of Fascism is just now bursting with a new vitality. Her standard of living, though her birth rate has gone down, is only two-thirds the standard in France, one-half the standard in Germany and one-quarter the standard in England. "Italy," says Mussolini, "must expand or she will explode."

We sit here in comfortable occupation of our vast and various possessions—six acres per human being against four-fifths of one acre which they have over there. We learnedly discuss what has to be done: done by us?—No! by England and the League of Nations! We shut our doors to emigrants from Italy; we shut our doors to emigrants from Japan; we wall our country round against England herself. We admit only those who conform to all our specifications. To others we stand on our shores in proud proclamation of our plenary autonomy and cry, "You shall not come!"

Maybe it is right that the *status quo* shall stand, maybe it is right that those who have shall hold, maybe it is right that people who are fruitful and multiply shall not inherit the earth, or shall not because of that fact alone inherit the earth. But there is a huge body of opinion the other way. There are vast cosmic forces working the other way. It is probably true that the *status quo* is better even for the crowded poor than driving this world to war. But it may be that economic concessions ought to be made. It may be a solution along that line can be found. What I am trying to make plain is this—that of all populations on this planet there are none to whom a solution is of more direct and imperative concern than to Canada and the United States.

Right now in the throes of a first great effort to cope with a crisis brought on by this pressure, and to still the thunders of a war, we announce that we are ready to contribute profits on a share of our trade—profits which would hardly buy us peanuts for a ball game.

I read very lately a book on this subject by Dr. Warren S. Thompson, Professor of Social Science—whatever that is—in an American University. He portrayed in livid colours and with fidelity to truth these facts with which I have now dealt, but strange to say he saw in them no problem for the United States. It was all a baby on the doorstep of England. It was for England, he said, to share her resources, she could not any longer retain her wide possessions, her best day was over. It was for England to find some means of alleviation for the struggling, pressing multitudes who inhabit bereft and crowded lands. Dr. Thompson, like many others over there, regards Canada as in the gift of England—Australia too and all her other Dominions. But we in this country know better. Canada is ours; it is in the disposition of this people and not in the disposition of England, and the same is true all round. Even Britain's colonies, especially those which others would want to possess, enjoy a large measure of autonomy. But if Canada is ours, then in the name of reason I demand to know, is not this problem ours?

Really, seriously, is there nothing here for the consideration and co-operation of the United States? Is there nothing at all on the doorstep of that Republic? Their possessions are far richer than our own. They could support a population, not of thirty-eight per square mile, but of several times that number. In the Philippines there are ten million people where fifty million could be provided with a living. In the whole mighty structure of world stability and world repose the United States has an interest as vital as has Britain herself.

Not just at the door of England, of France, or of Germany does this problem lie. They have not the most at stake in its ultimate solution or its ultimate catastrophic consummation. These great new countries with resources and territory wholly out of proportion to their use and present needs—it is at the door of these countries that the problem really lies, and one of these countries is Canada.

I have exhausted my time, but have gone no farther than intended. I for one am pretty weary of the attitude of a complacent people looking upon external troubles and fears as something for England to remove for our benefit. When we take upon ourselves the rank and stature and rights of nationhood we take upon ourselves all the dangers and duties which nationhood implies. If we persist in blindness to an imperious obligation, we court an awful penalty, and that penalty will one day overtake us.

I have sought in these few words to call attention to our curious indifference amid these world responsibilities, and, as well, to some of our domestic failings, some of the loose thinking, some of the loose talking of our day and generation. I have endeavoured to persuade you to look at, understand and accept a number of necessary and inescapable obligations, and have made bold to ask you, by way of appeal against practices which are growing upon us, to lay hold again at this time upon principles which have developed over a long past, which have stood the test of centuries and which, though they have not, and in any final sense will not, rid the world of error and injustice, of cruelty and wrong, have certainly brought our own country from poverty to tolerable comfort, and have brought great masses of mankind over a long journey from chaos to order, from tyranny to freedom and from darkness into a measure of light.

ISOLATIONIST NEUTRALITY

*Spoken before the Canadian Society of New York on February 8, 1936.
Speaking also at this function was Senator Alben W. Barkley of
Kentucky, later Vice-President of the United States. At his request
this address was subsequently dictated for printing in the Congressional
Record.*

I HASTEN IN THESE OPENING WORDS to tell you on behalf of the
Dominion from which I come how much we have been touched
in recent weeks by the high courtesy of your people as evidenced in many manifestations of sympathy which they have
exhibited following the death of our late beloved King. From
one end to the other of this tremendous country public bodies
of all kinds—legislatures and even business institutions—have
seen fit to mark in one form or other their appreciation of a
great and good man and a righteous King, though of another
land, and have tendered to us British people tokens of sympa-
thetic regard which have impressed us much and which we will
long remember. King George V was a wise counsellor, a man
of world-wide interests, and held in his heart nothing but sincere
good will for all nations. He concerned himself actively and
earnestly with the well-being of all classes of his people, and
especially of the unfortunate and afflicted. His character was as
noble as his rank, and he was universally beloved. Nothing you
could have done would have evoked from us in Canada a response
so spontaneous and wholehearted and a sense of gratitude so
lively and abiding.

It is with some anxiety that I now venture to address you.
We in Canada feel so close and friendly to the people of the
United States that we are apt sometimes to forget when over here
that we are in another country, and the restraints which that

fact imposes. I want to say something on a subject which is, to my mind, common to us both. It touches on your relations and our relations with the world outside and has to do with what might be described as the policy of isolationist neutrality now in effect in this Republic. I am sincerely and keenly anxious to keep within bounds of courtesy and good taste and will, indeed, be a victim of remorse if in this respect, under the ardour of earnest conviction, I should fail.

No matter what may be the forms of expression used, it must be understood once and for all that I am speaking only for myself. I am now a member of no government and leader of no party. I may undertake to give at times the generally accepted view of the Canadian people, but whether I give it correctly or not is entirely my own responsibility.

We in the Dominion always assume that you know a great deal about us and understand our ways of looking at matters international, and we think we ourselves enjoy similar advantages with respect to the people of the United States. We assume, rightly or wrongly, that you will listen to us more charitably and more generously than you will to others who are farther away.

The neutrality policy now described as isolationist is not the same character of neutrality policy which has usually been followed in this and other lands. Legislation passed by Congress in August 1935, in anticipation of troubles then brewing across the Atlantic, reflected a decision on the part of the United States to retreat at some distance from that stern adherence to neutral rights which has characterized United States neutrality in other years. A firm resolve to keep out of foreign wars has led to a belief that it is better to sacrifice rights and sacrifice interests— individual and national—than to hazard the alternative of being involved in war. Your intention is, therefore, to recede from insistence on rights, privileges, and interests heretofore asserted and usually enjoyed, in the hope that this very receding will take you farther from the scene of conflict and more certainly insure the blessings of peace.

With the object which you have in mind, certainly no one can find fault. The same object is just as precious to us and just as universally desired.

In proceeding to discuss the implications of this policy and how far the goal sought is likely to be attained, I want to lay down at the outset some very simple truths.

First—and this one is so simple as hardly to need stating—everyone must recognize that the decision is entirely your own. You have a right to make it as you may feel in the best interests of your country, and no one can complain.

Second. We all recognize without the least reservation that the United States has nothing in mind but peace and the triumph of peace. Whatever your policy may lead to, we know for certain the objective to which you intend it to lead. We in Canada make no question whatever of the good faith of this American Republic. Your chairman has just referred to our one hundred and twenty-five years of friendly and intimate relationship; to our unfortified border over thousands of miles. That unfortified border has never caused us concern. Indeed, we recognize that the credit for its existence and for the long era of peace and friendship which has reigned between us is much more yours than ours. You have been the powerful nation of these years, and we could never, even if we had a desire to do so, possess adequate means of defence. We cordially grant you full credit for this achievement and have all the reasons that can be furnished by twelve decades of happy neighbourhood for trusting in your good faith.

The question I want to put is this: Is a policy of isolationist neutrality likely in the end to contribute to your well-being and your freedom from war?

Obviously an isolationist attitude is not new. It is a natural state of mind into which nations fall who are tired of the turmoil and follies of competing international ambitions. Over and over again it has appealed to statesmen of different countries as a sane and proper refuge after years of tiresome entanglements and strife, but even in days when the world was bigger and nations were farther apart than they are now, all plans designed on the idea of isolation have one by one been abandoned. At least it can be said that no great nation has been able to pursue that happy course for long.

There must be some reason and some very powerful reason why this has been the case.

An eminent citizen of this country, Mr. Charles Warren, Assistant Attorney General of the United States during the Great War, has lately given the world an analysis of the experiences of his country in that conflict, while it was pursuing with all the steadfastness of which it was capable a policy of neutrality. Mr. Warren's recollections of those years and his long study given the subject brought him to the conclusion that the security of the United States is best promoted by friendly co-operation with other nations on this globe; by seeking tranquillity for itself along the path of world tranquillity; by helping to secure collective decisions and collective action in the maintenance of peace. He has set down no less than twelve conditions which must, in his judgment, be lived up to if any alternative policy of isolationist neutrality is to be pursued. Most of these conditions involve sacrifice of neutral rights. I am not arguing that such a sacrifice is not wholly capable of defence and, indeed, might not be worth while if by that means the larger goal could be reached. Peace is an ideal, noble and worth while. In this age of vast mechanisms and appalling scientific discoveries it is an ideal vital to the world, and is worth a lot of sacrifice. What I call attention to is that the conditions set out in Mr. Warren's catalogue are not likely to get you very far in steering this or any country away from the maelstrom of war. They provide for definite resolutions to be taken by the American Nation; for statutes to be passed forbidding this, that, and the other thing. Submarines are not to be allowed to enter American ports; enemy aircraft must be forbidden to land on American territory or fly over lands or waters under American jurisdiction; ships are not to be allowed to carry implements or provisions of war to vessels of belligerent countries wherever they may be; passengers are not to be protected if travelling on belligerent ships or on any ships equipped even for self-defence. All these things are to be done so that dangerous situations may be avoided.

When the last war was raging great nations were fighting for their lives. They were grasping at every means to crush the enemy and save themselves. They were impinging here and impinging there and more and more on neutral rights, going in every case just as far as they dared to go in order to help themselves survive. None of them wanted to incur the enmity of other lands—least of all the enmity of the United States. None of them were so foolish as to seek to add to the numbers of their foes, but the very necessities of war drove them in one direction today and another direction tomorrow; encroachment followed encroachment; nation after nation was dragged into the fire, and finally your great Republic decided that if the name of honour was to mean anything to the United States this country, too, had to vindicate its honour on the field of battle. Have you any reason to believe that human nature will have changed when the next war begins? Have you any reason to believe that, however far you recede in your abnegation of rights, a belligerent country battling for its existence will not press you back to the very last concession and away back beyond that concession, if it thinks it can save its life by some advantage? You point then to your statute which refuses to submarines an entry into American waters. You point to your prohibitions against belligerent aircraft flying over your territory. You point to your warnings against travelling in dangerous seas, but you wake up and find the submarine has come; you find the aircraft has landed and even refueled on your shores in spite of your prohibitions. What then are you going to do? You learn some morning that a big passenger liner without ammunition and without even a place for a gun has been sunk in the darkness of the night and that American citizens have been torpedoed by thousands into eternity. At such a point what will be the value of your statutes? At such a point people of this great land will reflect that this is only what has occurred time and again in the long history of mankind.

Do you tell me that after such an event you will still be at peace? Do you tell me that after a succession of such events you will be quietly exploring in what direction you can still farther withdraw? Do you tell me that after humiliation follows humiliation your people will still be flocking to the banner of isolationist neutrality? Forgive me if I speak plainly. I know you will be doing nothing of the sort. This country never has behaved in that manner and never will.

Again I ask you: Is there any reason to believe that the spirit of war and the practice of war in this ever-narrowing world is going to be more merciful and more considerate in days to come than it has been in the past? Is it not about as certain as anything can be that the very contrary will be the fact—that ever-expanding and ever-spreading methods of transport, accompanied by ever-widening and intertwining interests of all big countries in the four quarters of this globe will bring every one of them within the compass of a great conflict, no matter where it starts? What the British Empire has had to decide and what this country will have to decide is whether the way to keep out of war is to help peace-loving nations wherever they may be to see that there is no war. With every respect I beg the liberty of suggesting that the true path to tranquillity for this Republic is the path of world tranquillity and that all other paths are vain.

A feeling prevails that all these disputes over which nations seem determined to fight in other parts of the world are really no concern of yours and ours. Even if it be true that they are not, the result, nevertheless, is much the same to us as if they were our concern. The cause of the conflict matters little, but its consequences fall everywhere on the just and the unjust as soon as the conflict begins. But is it really true that we on this continent—either Canada or the United States—have any right to look in scornful mien across the Atlantic or the Pacific and conclude that people who battle over these things which do not seem to concern us are inferior people, people with whom we cannot agree and whom we cannot help to keep out of trouble? Let us look just now at Italy and Ethiopia.

What one has to do if he really seeks an enlightened view of the interest of other nations in that conflict is to penetrate to the actual causes of its outburst and see whether or not other nations have an interest in those causes. Wars may be started by an incident, a mere spark may light the flame, but behind the incident there is always a background which accounts for the aggressor taking upon himself the frightful risk of war.

Italy talks about injustices to her citizens in Africa; she talks about her mission to extend the borders of civilization; but, surely, everyone knows that deep down in the hearts of leaders of the Italian people is a determination to extend Italian territory, to enlarge Italian resources, and to open up opportunities for the crowded masses of Italian subjects. I make no excuses for the conduct of Mussolini. He has not scrupled to flout the honorable engagements of his country. He has broken its bond in the Kellogg-Briand pact. He has violated the covenant of his country with the League of Nations. He has ignored his special agreements with Ethiopia and launched a heartless attack on an almost defenceless people, and he has done all this against the warnings of a well-nigh united world. But what is the lesson to be learned? The lesson is that if there are powerful basic underlying necessities, if there are urgings that grip the very soul of a nation, these things either have to be met and satisfied or compromised or they are going to break out in bloodshed, which only a united world, armed for the purpose, can restrain.

Italy finds herself with a congested population; she finds herself bereft of those vital resources which enable a congested population to exist; she has forty-odd millions of people on a narrow strip of land—most of it unproductive—three hundred and sixty to a square mile. Industry depends upon raw material; commerce depends upon certain definite and all-essential resources, and with these Italy is sparsely endowed. She has six tons of coal per unit of her people against over seventy thousand tons which we have in Canada and against a vastly more impressive total in quality, if not in quantity, which you have in the United States. Of iron ore she has only a pittance, one-fifth of a single ton for each person. We in Canada have fifty-eight, and in the United States you have huge reserves, and of finer grade than ours. Italy is not only without iron and without coal, but without cotton, without oil, without copper, without wool, without nickel, without lead, and without either rubber or tin. There are, of course, those who say these things can be bought. On certain conditions they can, but even then buyers lose the advantage of possession and production. But these people cannot buy without money or without purchase of their own products by us. Italy's revenues from outside sources have been cut in half through exclusion of her emigrants by other countries and by virtual prohibition of her exports in the tariffs of other nations. Her tourist income has gone down. Her population expands, increasing four hundred thousand per year. Her standard of living is only two-thirds the standard of France, one-half the standard of Germany, and one-quarter the standard of England. It just cannot be compared with the standard in either Canada or the United States. About 1,900,000,000 human beings inhabit this planet. Statisticians tell us that on the scale on which the average man lives on this continent there is room only for 1,000,000,000, but that on the lower standard of Europe and Asia there is room for 2,500,000,000. We cannot afford to look down with scorn upon the reflections of great nations who live on these lower standards and who do not think it quite right that conditions which compel them to do so should be regarded as eternal and not subject to alteration either by reason or by force.

I do not for a moment believe that thinking people in this country can feel themselves without any concern in these formidable and elemental causes of world unrest. You are happy here in the possession of a domain of hemispheric dimensions. Your numbers, though great, amount to only thirty-eight people per square mile. You have a geological heritage enormously rich in essential metals, both precious and base. Your soil for the most part is fertile. You have everything, or nearly everything, that Nature can contribute to industry and the fruits of industry. We in Canada are similarly endowed, and our population is sparse. How can it be said that we have no interest or that you have no interest in those gigantic facts and forces which throw out of balance the scales of racial and national advantage, and as a result threaten from time to time the peace of nations?

There are scores of millions of mankind, virile, valiant men, some of them congregated in the Orient, others crowded together on the northern shores of the Mediterranean, all of them denied by geography and the innate selfishness of men an outlet for their energy and their enterprise, an access to those unused and abundant stores with which Nature has blessed the fortunate inhabitants of newer lands. I said a moment ago that these powerful and restless countries cannot be despised because they are not content that this state of affairs should be considered as crystallized forevermore. They are not to be despised because they look for a solution of their troubles around the council table of reason or on the battlefield of force.

I am not contending that in all respects Italy has reason on her side or that Japan has reason on her side. Mussolini discourages emigration and extols the virtues of war. What I am contending is that there are forces fundamental and tremendous disturbing the minds of these peoples, and bound to disturb their minds through the years which are ahead of us, and that in these forces we in Canada and you in the United States have a vital and even a predominant interest; that in the ultimate we have the most to lose; and that whether we like it or not we have to address ourselves to the task of meeting the situation by contact, conference, and compromise, or by resistance in arms.

Do I hear someone say, "These things are not the real causes and motives which bring on war"? What actually happens, it is said, is that ruthless, bold men in positions of power are moved by thirst for glory; they want to secure for their country and for themselves a place in the sun; they dare everything to attain that end. Suppose we grant that this is the truth—and without doubt sometimes it is—is not the consequence just the same? Is not the necessity for prevention just the same; and is there any means of prevention in this tough old world except by bringing to bear a collective will and showing in united phalanx a collective power, of which alone these glory seekers are afraid?

Whichever path we choose, we ought surely to move together and move collectively rather than separately and in conflict. We cannot assume any role of exalted unconcern. We cannot be content in the complacent assumption that others will solve these matters for us and that all we have to do is look on. If we like the path of reason and not the path of force, we ought then to sit down and reason together with other powers in other parts of the globe and try with them to find a way out. If we cannot, then we ought to stand together with other powers in other parts of the globe and prepare to resist the upsurgence of bereft and discontented or reckless nations with whom we cannot agree.

This is the message which I dare to bring. There was a time when the six score millions of this Republic were more favourable to the thought I have tried to expound than they are today. There was a time right in the wake of the Great War when, if overwhelming evidence is to be believed, these forty-eight united states felt much as we do now. This was on the morning after the war. Since then memories have faded and old habits of mind have returned. I venture to ask you to reflect that fading memories do not alter facts, and habits of mind must be made to conform with the world as it is today.

There seems to be an idea prevalent in this Republic that Great Britain has immense territories which can be used for purposes of adjustment and allocation, and that it is Great Britain who should open her gates to the thronging overflow populations of other lands, and thus restore something like a balance of possessions. This idea has been taken up in certain academic circles of this country, and books have gone out driving the suggestion home. It seems impossible to get other nations to realize that British Dominions are masters in their own households; that Canada is not the possession of Great Britain but the possession of the Canadian people; that similar statements apply to Australia, New Zealand, and South Africa, and in all essential features to India; and that the very might and glory of the British Empire arises from this very truth. If there is to be any compromise affecting Canadian soil, we are the people who have to be dealt with. The problem is ours; it is not the problem of England. The same is true of every dominion; and, indeed, it is true of every colony whose lands any others would want. We have to get over the habit of assuming that responsibility mainly lies on the shoulders of old England, where eight hundred people are gathered already on every square mile, and who already assumes a share of the white man's burden unequalled in the family of nations.

Canada is a peace-loving country. Why wouldn't it be? The United States is a peace-loving country. Why wouldn't it be? But don't let us think that we have a monopoly of this aspiration.

Don't let us think that in our interests, in our hopes, in our common sense we are all alone in this world. The Frenchman can think as well as we can. He is just as good a man as the Anglo-Saxon and no better. Do you imagine the Frenchman doesn't know that all he needs is to be left alone? We accord you, the people of Britain accord you, with unreserved sincerity, a genuine dependable purpose of peace, a determination ever to live in amity with all countries. The British people do not look with envy on your strength; they rejoice in your strength. They do not want at any time curtailment of your arms except insofar as curtailment can be made to contribute to world disarmament. No article of British policy, no shilling of British expenditure has any relation to the God-forbidden idea that there could ever again be war between these nations. Does anyone doubt the sincerity of Great Britain in her herculean efforts to hold the world steady at this time? If so, I am sorry for such a man; there are fantasies too irrational to be worth discussion. And Britain, France, the United States, British Dominions, even all these are not alone on the side of peace. There are others—many others—over the planet, just as earnest in this cause as we are.

I am not even remotely in the councils of any government, but I know there is a floodtime in the affairs of men which it is perilous to neglect. Look around, I beg of you; look around! Can there be any questions in the minds of serious people that that very floodtime is now? At this hour when the sky is dark, at this hour when already in two sectors of our globe there is heard the thunder of alien arms, at this hour when there gleams before the shuddering gaze of distraught and wasted humanity nothing plain but the way of blood, surely this is the time when all who love peace, not part only, but all, should do something to bring it about. Surely, this is the time when the resourcefulness of every nation should be summoned and the united action of every nation invoked to find a way of life.

There is not an intelligent reflecting mind anywhere which is not even now overwhelmed with distress. Are we going to have to wait until another terrible price is paid, another more ghastly, more crushing, more ruinous than the last? Are we going to have to wait until the young manhood of another generation has been ground out under the guns, until the ghoulish devices of destruction and pestilence have spread fire and death through home and nursery, field, and factory, and bleached the face of the earth? No. We cannot dare to give up hope. It is hope we cling to, hope for a getting together of hearts and brains and unselfish might, to the end that sanity may yet prevail, hope that the chords of confidence, coöperation, and good will may soon be struck and another chance given mankind. For this, I fear, we cannot much longer delay.

IN MEMORIAM

Address of Symypathy in the Senate of Canada, February 12, 1936, on the death of Senator Charles Murphy. Senator Murphy spent most of his life in Parliament. He was for many years a Minister in Sir Wilfrid Laurier's Cabinet and subsequently was a member of more than one of Mr. King's Cabinets before his elevation to the Senate.

NONE WHO HAVE BEEN SO LONG in either House of Parliament as I have, and therefore so long associated with that very distinguished man, the late Senator Charles Murphy, can ever forget the sense of shock and dismay with which we heard of his death. How often since has the picture of him returned to our minds, with all that his personality meant to us throughout the years!

When one thinks of Senator Murphy, one thinks of him first as a typical Irish intellectual gladiator, as a man who embodied all that has made the Irish people great, who loved everything associated with that race, and was perhaps its greatest pride on this continent.

I have sometimes wondered what would have been the destiny of Charles Murphy had his parents not emigrated to this hemisphere. Had he been born, as they were, on the Emerald Isle, there is no question that he would have taken his place in the front ranks of the Nationalist Party of that country, that he would have ornamented the halls of Westminster, and might have gone down to posterity as hero of the achievement of Home Rule. Some of those who took an eminent place in that battle, I have had the privilege of knowing, a few fairly well, others from afar; all their orations I have read. But I know of none who was capable of such passionate and eloquent advocacy of the cause of Ireland as was Charles Murphy himself.

We think of him, however, not only in that relationship, but also as an eminent Canadian public man, a party man of the Canadian type, a strong fighter in the ranks, a favourite of his chief, a lover of his leader, a man who could deliver perhaps the most telling blows of any who sat opposite to us in the House of Commons in the old days. He "drank delight of battle with his peers," and well was he equipped both to battle and to conquer. But I have to add to that reflection this: however severe were the assaults he directed, however relentless was the war he conducted, I never in the whole course of my public life heard from any member of the party to which I belonged, and which was opposed to his, one word in the way of resentment or personal bitterness against him.

The reason was that he demeaned himself as a man at all times. He never behaved as a ruffian; much less did he ever behave as a bandit. He struck above the belt, and all knew that behind the masculine and virile brain and person of Charles Murphy was a kindly and generous heart. His friends he knew and, their adoption tried, he grappled them to his soul with hoops of steel. Those who were not his friends in the warfare of politics he possibly knew how to crush, but very, very rarely was he able to hate.

We think of him, though, not just as a public man, but as a lover of literature and especially as a student of history. The honourable leader on the other side (Hon. Mr. Dandurand) has told us how our friend now departed had linked himself with men of his own race and cause in the United States, in England, in Ireland and on the Continent, and how he conducted voluminous correspondence with these men to the end of his days. He liked them because they were giants of achievement. In whatever sphere they might have wrought, he was interested. But he was interested most if they had truly at heart the common cause so dear to him, the cause of Ireland. He wanted to experience in his own life all the highest and best thrills of living, and he got this experience from these personal associations.

How he loved to tell of incidents and conversations with men of note, especially those of the land to the south and those of the last generation across the Atlantic. No man ever excelled him as a raconteur. No man ever excelled him in presenting the interesting and the gripping side of a conversation in which he had taken part, or of a stirring event through which he had passed.

Naturally he had his heroes in our own country. I do not know that anyone in this Dominion quite filled his ideal of political capability and personal charm, except one, Sir Wilfrid Laurier. He did love Sir Wilfrid! But he whom he most revered in the past records of Canada was D'Arcy McGee. No one contributed so much to the immortality of that great figure in Canadian history as did Charles Murphy. He was a student of McGee for the same reason that he was a student of many other noted men. He himself had the same love of learning, the same poetic temperament, the same ardent patriotism. In the story of this Dominion there will perhaps be none who will be found to have shared in more bountiful degree that statesman's legacy of literary fire, of practical political wisdom and of ardent love of country.

Not only was he possessed of peculiarly Irish traits, but he was also a man of real business capacity. When an administrative task was given to him, he discharged it with consummate ability. His organizing power became a legend. There was nothing he undertook to organize of which he did not make a real and striking success.

Very deeply we lament the death of our colleague. It will be a long while, I think, before one passes from our midst whom we shall miss as we miss him. And because we can realize how they feel, we all join in sympathy with his brothers who remain and with the members of their families of the next generation. We sorrow with those who survive in the home where he lived, that home to which he was endeared and which he had so long enlivened and adorned.

THE GREATEST ENGLISHMAN OF HISTORY

Address delivered before the Canadian Club, Toronto, February 24, 1936.

IF ONE CAN FIND in the speeches of D'Arcy McGee a portrayal of any great figure, it is certain to be striking and impresssive. Seventy-two years ago, on the occasion of the three hundredth anniversary of Shakespeare's birth, this great Canadian said:

> I come as a debtor to acknowledge his accounts to his creditor, as a pupil to pay homage to his master, as a poor relation to celebrate the birthday of the founder of his house, as a good citizen to confess his indebtedness to a great public benefactor, as an heir-at-law to repay, in ever so imperfect a manner, his obligations to a wealthy testator who has left him riches he could never hope to acquire by any labour or exertions of his own.

In such a spirit does every student of Shakespeare approach his shrine. Students he has had, and many, all through this long stretch of time and in every land on earth, but to the rank of student in its proper sense I do not dare to aspire. For half a century I have read his works with the ardour of a devotee, and it is the testimony of a lover rather than the learning of a critic which I desire to bring you today.

My life, like that of most of you here, has been spent in the busy battlefield of affairs. In literature I am only a layman and it is to laymen alone that I have a right to speak. But for years I wanted, and opportunity finally came, to satisfy what seemed a sense of obligation; to reach back among giants of long ago and put my hand in gratitude on the man, who, more than any other of all the bounteous past, had contributed to make my own life worth while to myself, to bring light and warmth and joy to

277

those pilgrimages of the mind which fill one's quiet hours. What I seek to do is to pay tribute in my own way to him who appears to me to have quaffed most deeply and passed around most generously the very wine of life and to have left to us of later times the richest legacy of all the dead.

This is an age of cinemas and sport. Those diversions on which our fathers thrived are not at all in general acceptance now. It is well to remember that there is no law of inevitable betterment applicable to our race. It should be our constant endeavour to get the most out of our time, for the road downward is easier than the road upward. After all accumulations of wealth and harvests of science, good literature is still our finest possession, and reading it vastly the most profitable occupation of our leisure. My hope is to do something, be it ever so little, to re-awaken interest in the very best of its treasures, the writings of William Shakespeare.

It may as well be said quite frankly now that I am not going to moderate my language below the level of unparalleled veneration which I feel for the memory of this man. There are those who say that enthusiasts of Shakespeare are always searching for superlatives and leave their senses by the wayside. Maybe so! Ben Jonson, who lived with him, said that he loved him to the very borders of idolatry. I join with hosts of others, who know him only from his works, in the same paean of affection.

Admittedly there are imperfections in his writings; sometimes he was hasty or careless, inartistic in his puns and quibbles, even once in a while inconsistent. But these things are only spots on the sun; they are merely incident to the glorious freedom with which he traversed our world of fact and fancy. He swung through his work with a joyous strength and did not always stop to complete the finishing and polishing.

Let us look first at the biggest fact of all about him. By common consent of leading critics of many nations, by an acclaim which can now be said to approach the universal, Shakespeare stands as the greatest intellect of whom we have record in the literature of the world. That, I know, is an assertion sweeping and challenging, but in support of it one can call an array of witnesses more formidable than was ever gathered to endorse any other verdict given on this earth as to the comparative achievements of men—Carlyle, Macaulay, Emerson, Browning, Dumas, Goethe, Ruskin, Oliver Wendell Holmes—and behind these the chorus of an unnumbered throng of lovers of literature in every land. No one is loved, though, just because he is a genius, and we do not read men long unless we like them. We have to look at the elements and attributes of his genius, and, through both, to the man himself.

When we speak of great intellect, we at once enquire—Well, what doctrine did he preach? What were his views on religion, or the principles of Government? What light was he able to throw on the overwhelming mystery of existence? I have read and revelled in everything Shakespeare wrote, and I have not found any doctrine that he preached or tried to preach. No man ever known was farther from bondage to theory or dogma or slogan. He had a definite mission. What he lived for was to reveal human life as it is, ourselves, our friends, the high, the low, the great, the little, on fortune's tide, in sorrow's plight, conduct, character, and their changes under the buffetings of fate; and this he did with an understanding so luminous, so powerful that it passes the mortal frontiers of admiration, and with a sympathy as boundless as the globe. What makes it of value to us, besides the rich enjoyment we get from it, is this:—We find our interest in our fellow beings quickened; we find it growing broader and deeper and more wholesome. Out of it all we emerge, without any particular explanations advanced or special ideas established, but we do feel surer than we ever did that it is worth while to live, that there is always at hand an eternal common sense ready for the using, which will see us through, and that everywhere there is a right and a wrong, a good and a bad, and that the good is to be loved and the bad to be avoided and deplored.

I do not appeal to busy folks to study Shakespeare. I just say to you—Read him and enjoy him; read his works over; read the best of them, or those you like the best, and then read them over again, and keep on. You will discover that each time you like them better; that each time you get more out of them. There is nourishment for mind and soul rich and various all along his shores. You will find yourself gaining possession of a storehouse which is adding light and charm to your every day existence. You will find yourself thinking more of your species, more of your friends and more of your enemies. You will realize that this man understood all of them; that he saw to the very depths of all of them; that he did not hate them but loved them, and that he loved them, if for no other reason, just because they were part of the great panorama and that every one of them added something to the astounding spectacle of creation. There never has been anything in all history more engaging than the fathomless sympathy of Shakespeare.

If he does not come to you with a solution of the riddle of existence, you will never conclude that he has not explored and wrestled with this problem, as, of course, everyone has. No mind ever travelled farther than his into the darkness. He sailed all the seas of human thought and encountered all the storms, and saw the great miracle more closely than did any man of whom we have record. So truly splendid and majestic is his vision that he seems at times to be expressing an inner and infinite harmony appertaining to the very Universe. But whatever his subject, whatever stage he mounts, he is immediately master of the scene. As soon as he enters an arena his mind sets everything in order, and it is not the order of the trim garden or the carefully elaborated show; it is the order of Nature herself.

What I want earnestly to impress is this: that in Shakespeare sheer intellect is the essence but only the essence of his genius. It is adorned by a generosity of character, by a magnanimity which makes his mind a very heaven of hospitality. You like to go with him on his excursions; you know that you will have lots of joy and lots of tears, and, though you may come back a mystic, you certainly will not come back a cynic.

The rest of what I have to say will be less general and less analytical. Its purpose will be to have you enjoy some of the more obvious values of this man's productions, some things nearer the surface and to be found on any one of hundreds out of the thousands of his pages.

It is a wonderful thing just to watch in operation his powers of expression. In doing so never forget that, while language is the vehicle of thought, it is a great deal more. It is part of the texture; it is inseparable from thought itself. Nobody says things in the Shakespearean way because nobody thinks in quite the Shakespearean way. Similes come trooping to his pen because his mind sees myriads of objects in their relations and in their unity.

All of us have felt at times the sting of ingratitude, a sense of despair over love's labours lost. But who ever expressed such a feeling in terms so arresting and with an appeal so memorable as did Cardinal Wolsey in his famous monologue in "Henry VIII." The Cardinal, after long years of service, had been abandoned by his King:

> Farewell! a long farewell, to all my greatness!
> This is the state of man: today he puts forth
> The tender leaves of hope; tomorrow blossoms,
> And bears his blushing honours thick upon him:
> The third day comes a frost, a killing frost;
> .   .   .   .   .
> I have ventur'd,
> Like little wanton boys that swim on bladders,
> This many summers in a sea of glory;
> But far beyond my depth: my high blown pride
> At length broke under me; and now has left me
> Weary and old with service, to the mercy
> Of a rude stream, that must forever hide me.
> Vain pomp and glory of this world, I hate ye:
> .   .   .   .   .
> O, how wretched
> Is that poor man that hangs on princes' favours!
> .   .   .   .   .   .
> And when he falls, he falls like Lucifer,
> Never to hope again.

Some people question the authorship of parts of "King Henry VIII." I cannot believe that anyone but Shakespeare ever wrote those lines. Think of that comparison to a boy swimming on a bladder. One of the things which has always amazed me is his power to take a commonplace incident like that and weave it into the fabric of the finest poetry.

You and I have mused a hundred times on a tendency of the

masses to turn on their heroes; to cheer for the latest victor just
because he is a victor. There is no better told story anywhere to
illustrate this frailty than one given in "Julius Caesar." Pompey,
a popular idol, has been crushed, and Caesar returns to Rome a
conqueror to receive what they called a triumph. This is how a
tribune addressed those Roman crowds:

> O you hard hearts; you cruel men of Rome,
> Knew you not Pompey? Many a time and oft
> Have you climb'd up to walls and battlements,
> To towers and windows, yea, to chimney-tops,
> Your infants in your arms, and there have sat
> The livelong day, with patient expectation,
> To see great Pompey pass the streets of Rome:
> And when you saw his chariot but appear,
> Have you not made an universal shout
> That Tiber trembled underneath her banks,
> To hear the replication of your sounds,
> Made in her concave shores?
> And do you now put on your best attire?
> And do you now cull out a holiday?
> And do you now strew flowers in his way,
> That comes in triumph over Pompey's blood?

A poet's great gifts, of course, must be creative. Shakespeare
created by delineation, until his dramas seemed to reproduce
every possible experience. This was his incomparable power,
but in the execution of his task what a master he was of the
choice of words! There are some so precious just where they
are placed that they are simply unforgettable. Macbeth, conscience stricken, after a murder, sees the blood of Duncan on
his hands:

> Will all great Neptune's ocean wash this blood
> Clean from my hand? No; this my hand will rather
> The multitudinous seas incarnadine,
> Making the green one red.

One of the best speakers who ever addressed this Club
described that word "incarnadine" as nothing less than a
triumph. The adjective "multitudinous" as applied to the ocean
is even more conspicuously right.

Some years ago I found it impossible, for weeks, to recall in exact terms a sentence of Cleopatra, which had struck me on reading as peculiarly perfect and worth remembering. The Egyptian Queen had put into a terse phrase her determination to be constant, unshakable of purpose, and said the moon was no model for her because it moved and was not a fixed star. I tried, off and on for days, to express her idea, the substance of which I remembered perfectly, but all my efforts produced only a puny second best. At last the Shakespearean original returned, and this is it:

> —from head to foot
> I am marble-constant; now the fleeting moon
> No planet is of mine.

Speaking of Cleopatra, will anyone ever again dash off an apostrophe to a conqueror like the one she spoke over the dead body of Anthony?

> His legs bestrid the ocean; his rear'd arm
> Crested the world; his voice was propertied
> As all the tunéd spheres.

Even this did not mean as much to Shakespeare as the tribute he had Anthony lay on the tomb of Brutus. In it Brutus was proclaimed a gentleman, the highest praise an Englishman can bestow:

> His life was gentle; and the elements
> So mix'd in him that Nature might stand up
> And say to all the world—"This was a man!"

Simple and beautiful! It has been on the lips of orators since the days of Addison. Where it should be is engraved on the tomb of the poet himself.

There was no aspiration of the human spirit that he did not understand and share. He knew the longing of every natural man, especially of every stricken man, to be kindly remembered after death. This is from the last dying words of Hamlet spoken to his friend Horatio:

> If thou didst ever hold me in thy heart,
> Absent thee from felicity awhile,
> And in this harsh world draw thy breath in pain,
> To tell my story.

There is a glorious abundance in his powers of definition and description. Analogies roll into his mind from everywhere like rivers into an ocean. He may come to the same subject over and over again but his treatment will always be fresh and different. It will be the same topic, but gleaming and glowing in a new attire. We all remember his encomium of sleep:

> Sleep that knits up the ravell'd sleave of care
> The death of each day's life, sore labour's bath,
> Balm of hurt minds, great nature's second course,
> Chief nourisher in life's feast.

What a princely procession of similes!

At another place King Henry V complains that the poorest slave gets more of this blessing than he does:

>   —thou proud dream
> That plays so subtly with a king's repose:
> I am a king that find thee; and I know
> 'Tis not the balm, the sceptre, and the ball,
> The sword, the mace, the crown imperial,
> The intertissued robe of gold and pearl,
> The farcéd title running 'fore the king.
> The throne he sits on, nor the tide of pomp
> That beats upon the high shore of this world,—
> No, not all these, thrice-gorgeous ceremony,
> Not all these, laid in bed majestical,
> Can sleep so soundly as the wretched slave.

On still another occasion King Henry IV finds himself in the same predicament. He discovers that a sailor boy even outside in a thunderstorm sleeps perfectly well while he, a king, wanders around torn with care. We marvel at the versatility with which the dramatist swings off into another sector and drives home the same truth again. The quotation I give you now has always impressed me as one of the noblest flights of poetry:

> How many thousand of my poorest subjects
> Are at this hour asleep!—O, sleep, O gentle sleep,
> Nature's soft nurse, how have I frighted thee,
> That thou no more wilt weigh mine eyelids down,
> And steep my senses in forgetfulness?
> Why rather, sleep, liest thou in smoky cribs,
> Upon uneasy pallets stretching thee,

And hush'd with buzzing night-flies to thy slumber,
Than in the perfumed chambers of the great,
Under the canopies of costly state,
And lulled with sounds of sweetest melody?

.   .   .   .   .   .

Wilt thou upon the high and giddy mast
Seal up the ship-boy's eyes, and rock his brain
In cradle of the rude imperious surge,
And in the visitation of the winds,

.   .   .   .   .   .

Canst thou, O partial sleep, give thy repose
To the wet sea-boy in an hour so rude;
And in the calmest and most stillest night

.   .   .   .   .   .

Deny it to a king?   Then, happy low, lie down!
Uneasy lies the head that wears a crown.

A famous American has made this fine observation:—After finishing a play, he says, one would think all subjects, cogitations, by-paths of mortal interest had been exhausted, but the next play opens like the dewy gates of another day.

The rapturous strength of the man imparts to his readers an exhilaration. There is no straining, no tiring. In method he is always distinctive, invigorating, resourceful.

Owen Glendower was boasting that earthquakes and other prodigies accompanied his birth; the front of heaven, he said, was filled with fiery shapes, and argued from this that he was a person extraordinary—not in the roll of common men. Hotspur sets out to explain that earthquakes are natural events—and this is how he does it:

Diseaséd Nature oftentimes breaks forth
In strange eruptions; oft the teeming earth
Is with a kind of colic pincht and vext
By the imprisoning of unruly wind
Within her womb; which, for enlargement striving,
Shakes the old beldam earth, and topples down
Steeples and moss-grown towers. At your birth
Our grandam earth, having this distemperature,
In passion shook.

If ever there was a passage definitely Shakespearean, it is that.

With him Comedy and Tragedy walk hand in hand just as they do in life, and of both he is a consummate master. He has created as much human interest in Falstaff as in Caesar—Falstaff, a corpulent, sunny-souled mountebank who trifles with truth, who exudes wit as he drips with perspiration and "lards the lean earth as he walks along."

His characters are faithfully men and women, not caricatures; so their views and moralizings change under pressure of events. Richard II was quite emphatic about the divine right of kings as long as he was a king:

> Not all the waters in the rough rude sea
> Can wash the balm from an anointed king;
> The breath of worldly men cannot depose
> The deputy elected by the Lord.

But when Bolingbroke defeated him his philosophy took another colour:

> —of comfort no man speak:
> Let's talk of graves, of worms, and epitaphs;

for

> —nothing can we call our own but death.

The poor dejected King then comes to that superb soliloquy which most of you, I fancy, are anticipating right now. I will give it in a moment. Abraham Lincoln used to read these plays in bed at night. Once he got up, wandered through the White House corridors in his long nightdress, book in hand, woke up his secretary, John Hay, and read him these lines:

> —let us sit upon the ground,
> And tell sad stories of the death of kings:—
> How some have been depos'd; some slain in war;
> Some haunted by the ghosts they have depos'd;
> Some poison'd by their wives; some sleeping kill'd,
> All murder'd:—for within the hollow crown
> That rounds the mortal temples of a king
> Keeps Death his court; and there the antic sits,
> Scoffing his state, and grinning at his pomp;
> Allowing him a breath, a little scene,
> To monarchize, be fear'd, and kill with looks;

> Infusing him with self and vain conceit,
> As if this flesh, which walls about our life,
> Were brass impregnable; and humour'd thus,
> Comes at the last, and with a little pin
> Bores through his castle wall, and—farewell king!

An American critic has expressed the opinion that there is more meaning wrapt up in the short proverb I shall give you now than in any other single sentence in our language:

> Love is not love
> Which alters when it alteration finds.

and yet how simple!

There is another so pregnant and inspiring that we should keep it ringing in our ears for life:

> Yield not thy neck
> To fortune's yoke, but let the dauntless mind
> Still ride in triumph over all mischance.

In "Measure for Measure," Claudio is being put to the test as to whether he will give up his life to save the honour of his sister. Skilful arguments are advanced to persuade him. Claudio is impressed, but ventures to put forward a view against embracing death. At this point Shakespeare comes right to the verge of the unknown and looks down into its darkness: he does not know what is there, and his mind plays in fancy's field with an exuberance which is all his own:

> Ay, but to die, and go we know not where;
> To lie in cold obstruction, and to rot;
> This sensible warm motion to become
> A kneaded clod; and the delighted spirit
> To bathe in fiery floods, or to reside
> In thrilling region of thick-ribbed ice;
> To be imprison'd in the viewless winds,
> And blown with restless violence round about
> The pendent world;
> .   .   .   .   .   'Tis too horrible!
> The weariest and most loathed worldly life
> That age, ache, penury and imprisonment
> Can lay on nature, is a paradise
> To what we fear of death.

No one should close an appreciation of Shakespeare without giving his hearers those truly magnificent outbursts of poetic fervour—two of them in number—in which this great Elizabethan seer has reached, by unanimous acclaim, the very loftiest heights. The first is from "The Merchant of Venice," where Lorenzo is interpreting to Jessica the oneness of our life on earth with the eternal scheme of things, the universal concord of creation:

> How sweet the moonlight sleeps upon this bank!
> Here will we sit, and let the sounds of music
> Creep in our ears: soft stillness and the night
> Become the touches of sweet harmony.
> Sit, Jessica.   Look, how the floor of heaven
> Is thick inlaid with patines of bright gold:
> There's not the smallest orb which thou behold'st
> But in his motion like an angel sings,
> Still quiring of the young-eyed cherubins,—
> Such harmony is in immortal souls
> But whilst this muddy vesture of decay
> Doth grossly close it in, we cannot hear it.

Poetry sublime!

The other is from almost the last and perhaps the most perfect of his plays "The Tempest."   What I shall quote you now was never intended as a scientific hypothesis but is strangely in accord with beliefs of scholars in this twentieth century.   Its closing lines clung to the rugged intellect of Carlyle, and were many times repeated by him in the last years of his life.   I found them about a year ago, inscribed on a plaster scroll, held by the hand of Shakespeare in a statue of the poet at Melbourne.

> The cloud capp'd towers, the gorgeous palaces,
> The solemn temples, the great globe itself,
> Yea, all which it inherit, shall dissolve,
> And, like this insubstantial pageant faded,
> Leave not a rack behind.   We are such stuff
> As dreams are made on; and our little life
> Is rounded with a sleep.

Twice I have mentioned Carlyle.   The nineteenth century produced no mind more searching or realistic.   His life was devoted to study. Once, when past the three score years and ten, a Miss Bacon was visiting at his home—probably a far down relative of the great Sir Francis. She intimated in conversation that perhaps, after all, Bacon had written these Shakespearean plays. "It would have been just as easy," said Carlyle, "for Francis Bacon to have created this planet as to have written 'Hamlet'." Later on, the old sage of Chelsea said something more:—"This man Shakespeare," he said, "knew more about animals, plants and all the visible world a hundred times over than I do. How—how did he learn it?" When Carlyle said that, he was seventy-seven. Shakespeare died at fifty-two.

Who was this man?—this man acknowledged now by two hundred million people as the architect of their language, who at any rate shares that honour with the translators of the Bible; this man who became, says De Quincey, the glory of the human intellect; this man on whose forehead, says Elizabeth Barrett Browning, there climbed the crowns of all the world; this man, who, in the concept of D'Arcy McGee, planted his compasses in his own age and with them swept the circumference of time: Who was this man? He was the son of a Warwickshire peasant. He has told us much of others but very little of himself. He kept no diary, did not live for his biography, did not even think it worth while to record the date of his birth. Born of old England's middle class, he took his place in youth among the myriads of her children, no favourite of fortune except in his brain and gladsome heart. Back from the ancestors of his father and of his mother of the lovely name—Mary Arden—there came, there must have come to him, the richest strains of English blood, for never was man born in that Island more truly an Englishman than he. Confident he was of fame, as shown by his sonnets, and zealous to deserve it; but unbelievably careless in making certain that the foundations of that fame were preserved. He took no pains to publish his writings, did not even collect them, was content with a misprinted "Hamlet" and an interpolated "Othello," but strained every effort to secure for his family a coat of arms, that he might enjoy in law, as he merited in nature, the coveted title of gentleman. Years after his death, two others, under no obligation, took upon themselves to gather together the scattered and deserted children of his brain, and thus saved for the healing of the nations the finest flower and fruit of the human mind. After having earned, by long years of toil, a place on the highest mountain of remembrance, he neglected to confirm his seat and muddled through to immortality.

Tolerant to a fault of others, an admirer of other nations—and in these respects again exhibiting qualities characteristic of his people—he was none the less splendidly English in his patriotism, and never did his verse ring with a deeper sincerity than when he sang of

> The land of such dear souls, this dear, dear land,
> This precious stone set in a silver sea.

or of her soldiers

> Whose arms were moulded in their mother's womb

and

> —whose limbs were made in England.

True to the genius of his race, Shakespeare was a chivalrous and consistent champion of the Reign of Law. Read the oration of Ulysses on this subject in "Troilus and Cressida." Opinions, of course, imparted to his characters cannot be attributed to himself, but nevertheless there are times when his own principles shine through. He believed in respect for authority, and a just seniority of station, as essential to the whole plan of civilized society.

Like his people also, he knew no vindictiveness; his soul was aglow with a happy perennial humour, and he faithfully portrayed his countrymen as fortified with this unconquerable grace against all vicissitudes and saved by it even in their blunders.

He was English, too, in the reverence of his reaction to the profundities and mysteries of life, and in the attraction these subjects had for his mind. And, just as surely, he was English in his practical commonsense views on the day to day problems of living, in his distrust of theories and the exactions of logic, in his conviction that it was actions and not axioms that counted and in his enthronement of conduct as above all else, above ideas and above beliefs.

Then again, he had no freak habits, no eccentricities such as are usually attributed to genius. He was jovial, even convivial, joyous in company, contemplative even to sadness in solitude, and would have liked himself to be described as he described another—a plain blunt man who loved his friend. He paid his way, depended on no one but himself, insisted on his legal rights, made money because he produced best sellers, provided well for his family and retired in comparative wealth to his country home at Stratford to spend the evening of his days. In all this there is something that smacks of England. Yes, English were the traits he possessed, and he possessed them in super-quality and superabundance. True enough, as is so often said, Shakespeare belongs to the world, but it was England who gave him to the world and it was no exotic that she gave; it was an English product through and through. This is not to say that geography has special significance. He is the pride, in just right, of the entire Celtic Anglo-Saxon race. But if it be true, and it is, that what really makes a nation is a heritage of common memories, common exploits, common sufferings, then surely he is the peculiar and immortal pride of that great country, of whose children he is the all-expressive voice, in the book and volume of whose memories, achievements, traditions, he takes the noblest and the sovereign role.

His name is honoured now in every quarter of the globe. It is written first on the scroll of fame in country after country, which, for years after his time, had never heard his name; in nations, which, in his day, were still unborn, and in continents which were then unknown. Pilgrims in tens of thousands journey yearly to his tomb.

It is said that as a young fellow on the streets of London, to earn an honest shilling it was his custom to hold horses outside a theatre for patrons who were listening to plays. Many a grateful admirer, in the generations who since then have come and gone, has tried to look back across the centuries to that figure in the dark, lonely lane, to picture the well-knit form, the kindly face eloquent with intelligence, and behind, the brain rejoicing in the morning of its promise, and then to think that there was the lad whose name and fame would one day be more precious to England than all her other possessions. Is there a privilege in the realm of fancy which any of us would more dearly prize than to be allowed to transpose himself on time's dial plate back to those distant and now hallowed years, to take his place on a London thoroughfare and watch the approach of this man of destiny, or at a by-path on the Thames where he sometimes tramped to attend a play called "Hamlet," to see him walking by, buoyant, reflective, benign, the pointed beard, the classic brow, showing equal courtesy to high and low, and to realize that there was passing there the intellectual monarch of his era, the King of England's Kings?

These delights cannot, unfortunately, be ours, save in a land of dreams—but into that land how many have wandered just to indulge such visions. With a reality, though, with a fulness of reality which commands a gratitude more than we can utter, Shakespeare is with us still. The bounty of his overflowing mind is open to us all. It has spread to the alcoves of every library and reposes, let us hope, on the mantel-piece of every home. "God forbid," said Coleridge, "that these plays will ever fall dead on human hearts," and may the time never come, especially to us his heirs in direct descent, when lighter preoccupations and alluring diversions of fleeting value will lead us into habits of neglect unworthy the priceless treasure which this, the greatest of Englishmen, has bequeathed to the sons of men.

TRIBUTE TO SIR JOHN ABBOTT

Delivered at the old Anglican Church at St. Andrew's East, County of Argenteuil, P. Q., on October 3, 1936, on the occasion of the unveiling and dedication of a memorial tablet to Sir John Abbott.

I HAVE SPENT THE FORENOON wandering around this beautiful village which nestles on the banks of a typical Canadian river winding through a fertile and picturesque countryside to join the Ottawa. To my mind there came impressions of the good fortune which fell to young John Abbott, in that his childhood was assigned to so charming a locality. How richly blessed is the youth who is able to spend his early carefree days in quiet and lovely surroundings such as these hills and streams provide! He can carry on his reflections and build his castles undisturbed by the artificial contrivances of cities. He has the measureless advantage of solitude, and, without solitude in one's younger life, a habit of real thinking is less likely to be cultivated.

It is indeed interesting to witness this ceremony today. More than forty years have passed since Sir John Abbott died, and now, in a church founded by his father, and amid scenes where he roamed as a boy, this tablet to his memory is erected by friends and descendants of friends who knew him most intimately in life. His Excellency, the Governor General, has well said that such a tribute would be vastly more appreciated by him than would any monument in a public place in our Capital. Sir John Abbott, as we all know, was a man of modest, retiring disposition whose enjoyments were among his friends and in private life. He really had no taste for the storm and bustle of politics.

As one reviews his career, one is struck by the fidelity with which his characteristics as a man are reflected in his performances as a statesman. Sir John Abbott was essentially a lawyer.

The great energies of his life were given to law. Solid and logical attributes of his mind equipped him for success in law. In that profession he reached the highest posts of distinction— certainly the highest in the realm of commercial jurisprudence. In Parliament his principal achievements were along very similar lines. It was he who evolved and drafted the first bankruptcy law for Canada. This measure he took charge of and piloted through Parliament, and so well was his work done that the framework of our insolvency legislation even now is very much the Statute of which he was author. He had what we call a legal mind, but he had at the same time an exceedingly practical mind. He knew the requirements of business and what the administration of big enterprises meant.

It was Sir John Abbott who worked out and finally established as law our jury system of today, or rather the scheme of administration of our jury system of today. He it was also who planned and finally had enacted notable reforms in our revenue laws. As a result of those reforms the stamp system came into actual use, and out of the enactment of that time has grown the very extensive practice of collection of our revenue by stamps. It is noteworthy that in all these endeavours he laid his foundations well. On the ground-work put in place by Sir John Abbott the legislation on these subjects today has been with much fidelity constructed. These are services such as one would expect from a man of his type, predisposition and training. They illustrate a truth that what one does in the sphere of public performance is pretty much a reflection of what one is in his private activity as a citizen.

Your very distinguished guest, the Governor General, spoke of certain points of similarity between His Excellency's own experiences and those of the man whose memory we are honouring. As between myself and Sir John Abbott I can think of only one comparison. There was a similarity in our tenure of high office; both were exceedingly brief. His was brief because of the visitation of ill-health, and mine because of other impediments which have since become somewhat epidemic.

This is a day long to be remembered by the people of these parts. It is a day long to be treasured by the Abbott family, not a few of whom have, in their own time, done honour to their distinguished kinsman. Those of us who have come among you to take part in tribute to one whose illustrious and useful life this county made available for Canada join in a hope that over long years to come the inspiration of this event will not easily be forgotten among you but will return and still again return with all its happy memories.

IN MEMORIAM

Address of sympathy in the Senate of Canada, February 24, 1937 on the death of Senator Patrick Burns and of Senator Horatio Hocken.

A MORE FAITHFUL COMPENDIUM of the career of Senator Burns than that which we have just heard from the Government leader would be difficult indeed to compose.

The senator's passing was not wholly unexpected. For many months he stood bravely on the edge of the grave, and his last long struggle for life was witnessed in tender sympathy by thousands upon thousands of those, particularly in the West of Canada, who had learned to love and to follow him.

One's mind goes back to the little school near Kirkfield, just a few miles north of Toronto, which as a country boy Patrick Burns for but a short period attended. Curiously enough, another great Canadian, Sir William Mackenzie, was a pupil there at the same time. Often have I heard Senator Burns tell of his difficulties as a lad being settled by the master mind of the school, the then Billy Mackenzie. Interesting it is that as their lives unfolded, both in a big and masterful way, they were still associated. When Senator Burns launched his tremendous business in Western Canada, his loyal second was Sir William Mackenzie, whose share in that enterprise continued to the day of his death.

It is now about fifty years since Patrick Burns left Ontario and took up a homestead near Minnedosa, where, with nothing but oxen for his power, he carved out a shelter for himself and started his career. To the very last there was nothing nearer his heart than the experiences of that time. He loved to tell about his meagre belongings, the simplicity of his life, how he was befriended, the goodness of his neighbours and the honesty of everyone.

Very soon he started travelling through the country buying cattle, driving them through the concessions and selling them where he could; and it was his proud boast that he could sell without taking a note or any other evidence of debt, and always be paid. That he could do this was, unconsciously to him, a tribute to his own remarkable character. His neighbours trusted him and could never bear to lose his respect. Of education as generally understood he scarcely had any. To others this would have been a handicap almost insurmountable; to him, I sometimes thought, it was not a handicap at all. He seemed to have the instinct of business and the instinct of friendship developed equally.

His judgment on matters large and small was almost errorless; his judgment of men rarely, if ever, failed.

He passed from the little homestead into small outside ventures, and one by one being successful, they accumulated and finally flowered out in the great Burns packing business of Western Canada. With this were joined his ranching interests and his farming enterprises, all on a scale the vastness of which had never been paralleled in that country. He seemed to direct the destiny of these ventures with a sure, steady, firm hand, and to direct them easily; and the marvel of it is that though throughout his career he gathered much and became a man of great influence, a pillar of the West, and rich, he nevertheless wholly escaped the envy, so marked in recent years, that others in like position have had to endure. From the time I went to Manitoba, now nearly forty years ago—all through these decades, right up to this day, I have never heard an individual, rich or poor, humble or proud, say a single unkind word of Pat Burns.

His name is a queer compound of Irish and Scotch. His surname does not designate his origin. I think there was some change in late generations. Anyway, Mr. Burns was Irish in every line and lineament. He had all the fine qualities of the Irish race. He was the soul of honour in all things, and never did he leave his fellow-man after a bargain made or after a promise given and learn later of resentment or a lingering sense of injustice.

Pat Burns became an institution in the West. He had no

peer; he was the leader in that country for certainly four decades. He took an interest in public affairs merely because he felt that a citizen should. If he had party leanings at all, he was a Liberal. Certainly he was more liberal, in a wider sense, than any other man I have known. He had nothing ungenerous to say about anybody or any party. It was not because of his activity in public affairs, or because he was a politician or had any political ambition, that he was appointed to this Chamber. I had nothing to do with his appointment, but am safe in saying that he was made a senator from Alberta only because he had been for decades the first citizen of that province. He lived domestically, for the most part, alone. It is some years now since his wife died, and his only son unhappily passed away about a year ago. None of the family now remain, but there stands as his monument the multiplied evidence of tremendous achievement scattered throughout a veritable empire, and a memory as lovely and wholesome as perhaps any Canadian ever left behind.

Senator Hocken was a man whose career was wholly different from that of Senator Burns. They were about the same age, having reached approximately four score years. From very humble beginnings as a printer young Horatio Hocken, by dint of energy, hard work and sound principles, continued his rise until he became a publisher. It was as publisher and journalist that he really performed his finest work in Canada.

I listened very sympathetically to the words of the leader of the Government as he commented upon the man he discerned after he got to know our late colleague. Senator Hocken, particularly in earlier years, was looked upon by many excellent Canadians as a man of not only strong convictions, but strong prejudices. Often, I lament to have to say, I heard him described as a bigot. I have not known anyone much farther from that category. During all of his life he was a strong churchman, and through most of it a church worker, in an active and enthusiastic way. He had in his heart no enmity to any church; it was full of generosity and sympathy for all religious effort. But he had a very determined view, a clear and definite opinion, as to the line of demarcation between the legitimate activities of church and of state, and in laying out that line and driving home among the people what he felt to be the correctness of his view thereon, so zealous was his advocacy that it unhappily and without warrant gave rise to an impression that he was narrow.

Senator Hocken was beloved by those who knew him. His best public work, of course, was done before he reached this House, and that work was mainly municipal. He was a good alderman, a good mayor, a man who left a fine reputation after the discharge of every public responsibility, a member of Parliament never defeated, as acceptable at the close of his career as he was welcome at the beginning.

One does not, however, reach a faithful estimate of the character and work of Senator Hocken without taking into account the place his wife occupied in his life. She was the source of his comfort and his happiness, the fountain of his ambition, the inspiration of his career, the companion through all vicissitudes and along every step of his journey. For fifty-seven years they walked hand in hand and, at the last, even the stern Messenger of Death was powerless to divide them. Stricken within the walls of this building not many days ago, he was carried soon after to his home. Gallantly he struggled, as would any true man, for return to the bright day. But lying not far from him, his wife also was passing through the valley, and when tidings reached his mind that she had resigned this anxious life, he gave up the battle, wrapped the draperies of his couch about him and lay down to quiet sleep. Under bright winter skies surrounded by sorrowing friends, the two were buried last Saturday in the same grave. I am sure our sympathies go out to the remaining son— one died on the fields of France—and to the two daughters who have lost so much.

THE STATE OF THE WORLD

*Delivered at a Luncheon at Cleveland, Ohio, on November 13, 1937.
Quite unexpectedly this address was broadcast.*

You HAVE GIVEN ME—all through this day—an exceedingly warm
and delightful welcome. In real earnestness I thank you.

Under the rigidities of timing for radio purposes, the attain-
ing of balance and a rounded argument is difficult. One has to
be in position to stop at a pre-directed moment.

Within the circumference of twenty-one minutes I am going
to try—probably to the disappointment of many—to say something about the state of the world. That subject may not be
very relevant to the design of this meeting, and I fear you
neighbours of ours will be concluding that Canadians can think
of nothing else. This conclusion is, indeed, not very far from
truth. All of us would like very much to forget the terrible
events of today and turn our eyes from a forbidding future, but
in all seriousness I say we must not and we dare not. Speaking
definitely about the people of my own country, I assert that we
ought to be much closer to realities than we are.

I shall be content to lay down two or three postulates, which
I respectfully submit are true, and which also I respectfully submit are of incomparable importance to us all. I shall not leave
out of mind that this country decides its own course. We in
Canada decide our course. We are not in the same boat, but we
are pretty much in the same waters, and it will not hurt us as
neighbours to discuss these things among ourselves.

My first is this:—The peace of the world is precarious. There
is no peace in Asia; its two mightiest nations are at war. China
at this hour is in the agonies of a merciless and murderous invasion; China is being done to death.

Great nations of Europe are in battle with each other even now. They do battle under other banners than their own and on the soil of Spain. There can be nothing more obvious than that the averting of a major struggle, which, if it comes, will have consequences no man can imagine, is a task calling for the united efforts of all peace-seeking Powers—Powers bound together by mutual purposes and mutual trust. I do not think any of us can remember a time of peace when the future was overcast by clouds so dark and so persistent.

A great newspaper of your city says today that these conflicts are inspired by ideas foreign to American soil. That is true: but these conflicts are none the less real facts, and from their consequences I fear we cannot escape.

Why have we all this trouble?

Many people say it is because of drastic provisions of the Treaty of Versailles and a consequent psychosis of rancour in the hearts of the vanquished of the last great war. We have to admit, though, that this cannot account for the aggression of Italy; it cannot account for the aggression of Japan. Both these countries were victors in the Great War. Indeed, no sooner had Mussolini declared that, after conquest of Ethiopia, Italy could take rank among the satisfied powers, than he proceeded on his still more dangerous project of intervention in Spain. The last war was not brought about by any impositions of preceding Treaties. Germany was living in a Europe which resulted from another Treaty of Versailles imposed by herself. Even if we attribute the cause of that War to others, we cannot say that it was brought about by any injustices deriving from previous Treaties forced upon the Powers.

It is said the League of Nations has failed. All we have today is a half League of Nations. With the United States, Germany, Japan and Brazil out, and with Italy in defiance, there is nothing left but a shattered remnant. We are compelled to admit that as an instrument of collective security the League of Nations which we have, or did have, has not proved equal to its task. Any League which recognizes the unrestricted national sovereignty of each of its component elements can never be an instrument of collective security. In my own judgment the present League could not have become such, even if every country in the world had been a member.

My second postulate, therefore, is that if one big truth has been learned from the last fateful decade, it is that collective security can only be attained when founded on collective force. Collective force can never be commanded while the sovereignty of individual nations remains unimpaired.

This Republic of the United States, the United Kingdom, the Republic of France, the Soviet Republic of Russia—these countries are all prepared to draw the sword in defence of their own territories and their own vital interests; but as yet they are not prepared—and in this respect the attitude of the peoples of all of them is the same—as yet they are not prepared to go to war on behalf of a covenant—a covenant, say, against aggression— unless those vital interests are challenged. Until the obligations of a covenant become as sacred and as certain of enforcement as the vital interests of an individual nation, there never can be a possibility of that collective force upon which alone collective security can rest.

Some place their trust in economic sanctions—and in threat of non-recognition of territories taken by aggression. Look back over these last two years: it is hard to find inspiration for the hope that these methods alone can succeed. Sanctions carry in their bosom the danger of armed resistance, and nations not prepared to fight hold back from their application. A practical unanimity is necessary and this proves impossible. An agreement not to recognize new conquests will of itself never deter. More than one country in the past has managed very well without recognition. In a word, we have been compelled to learn the heart-breaking lesson that a nation determined on expansion, and burning with nationalistic fervour, will not stay its hand unless it sees another Power or a union of Powers stronger than itself reaching for the sword.

Others say the situation might be cured by a concession of colonies to over-populated powers. Germany at this very time demands return of colonies taken from her in the Great War. Peace cannot be secured without concessions, and peace is worth many concessions; but I want to examine the sincerity of this demand and the value of the concession, if made.

German colonies, almost wholly in Africa, were conquered in the Great War—conquered mainly, in fact, by military forces of the Union of South Africa. By the terms of Versailles, these colonies were handed over to the principal allied and associated Powers. Please note, they were handed over to the greater Powers who won the War, and not to the League of Nations. They, however, accepted the colonies, dividing them among themselves in the apportionments in which they were conquered, all accompanied by a declaration made to the League of Nations that each one would so administer its territory as to take no advantage to itself, but wholly for the good of the colonies and the general good of the world. This declaration was asked for by President Wilson of the United States, and readily complied with by all nations concerned. In fact, an examination will show that in the same spirit and on the same principles Britain has administered her own colonies for many decades.

German colonies of pre-war times, administered now under the mandates I have described, are, for purposes of trade, not a whit more of advantage to Britain than they are to Germany. All British colonies in Africa, including mandated colonies, are forbidden by the mandate or by Treaties to give preferences in trade to Great Britain, and indeed, the great bulk of their trade is with countries other than Great Britain. One-sixth of the whole exports of British West Africa goes to Germany herself. Even before the war, Germany could not, by reason of Treaties, take any advantage in trade out of her South African possessions. Her trade there was almost negligible. She had only twenty thousand people in all her colonies, as contrasted with her own population of sixty-six millions. Her sales to her colonies were 1/180th of her total sales and her purchases 1/200th of her total imports. Whatever position she was in when the colonies were hers, she is in just the same position today as regards the procuring of raw material and the benefits of trade. A nation can only become of special commercial benefit to another major power if

that nation is exploited by such other major power. Germany
claims that all would be different if she could purchase raw
materials in her old colonies with her own currency. Raw
materials, like any materials, can only in reality be purchased
by the creation of credits due to exports. No colony can continue
to take mere paper for its goods.

There is a feature of this problem which it is very important
to understand. Great Britain benefitted out of the late war in
no way whatever materially. In fact, no country benefitted.
What Great Britain did obtain was greater security. That greater
security she throws away if Germany is to be permitted to establish armed strength across the line joining the old British
Dominions in Africa. The advantages, and the only advantages,
which Germany can obtain from recovery of her colonies are
advantages from a military standpoint. You can realize the
feelings of people of the British Dominion of South Africa.
What they want is security, and they see in a return of these
colonies the imperilling of their country.

I quite agree that if surrender of those mandated territories
to Germany would contribute in truth to stabilization of world
peace, those territories should be at once returned. Leading
papers of England are prepared to discuss their return. For
myself, I despair of finding in this method the slightest alleviation of that tension under which the world is straining today.

On the other hand, there are some alterations of viewpoint
which I think all of us must make. We have to realize the
necessity of equalizing trade conditions over the whole range of
nations. We cannot expect over-crowded and aspiring people to
be contented if their trade is selfishly throttled.

Another change of viewpoint I think also must be made. The
barriers of immigration must be lowered. This applies more to
our country than to yours. We people in possession of the world's
richest and widest territories, with comparatively thin populations, can hardly expect mankind to remain at peace if we stand
on our shores and forbid all others to come. There is something
to be said from our own immediate standpoint for this policy,
but I do not believe it can be continued compatibly with our
expectations of peace.

Another speaker remarked a few moments ago that we are living in swiftly moving times. Yes, the pace of the world grows faster, the pressure becomes heavier as complexities of civilization multiply. Distances are closing up, events crowd upon events and thunder past us with terrifying speed. Perils and perturbations everywhere shoot their repercussions swiftly around the brief compass of our globe. Anything in the nature of a world confederation is yet far, far away, and even when it comes, a readiness and willingness to do battle in the last resort for the covenants of that confederation will be an inescapable price of peace.

I have only a moment left, and in it shall give you one article of my own confession of faith.

Because of her geography, because of her tradition, Britain carries a mighty responsibility. That responsibility she is discharging with unquestioned fidelity not only to her own people but equally to humanity at large. That responsibility she is discharging with an intelligence, not, of course, beyond challenge, but entitled to very great respect. I believe that Great Britain is the stoutest, the most patient and the most determined of all forces on the side of peace. The potency of her voice depends upon her power and the co-operation of her friends. Canada is doing something to re-enforce that power; she ought to do more. I believe that if war must come again, Great Britain is our first line of defence, yours and ours—perhaps our only external line— and I say "amen" to those writers of this Republic who proclaim that the problem of defence for this entire Continent will be changed, and changed vastly for the worse, if that line of defence should fall.

THE DEFENCE OF CANADA

Delivered before the Conservative Convention at Ottawa
on July 5, 1938.

I AM, OF COURSE, HUMAN ENOUGH to feel very deeply the cordial demonstration with which you have greeted my name, but hardly capable, under the circumstances of the moment, of expressing my thoughts.

Honoured by your committee with an invitation to speak to this assembly, I had intended merely to outline my views on domestic policies, well-known though they are to you all; and indeed such a course would be much more my own desire than that which I shall pursue. But yesterday I agreed to undertake the task, with the approval of your distinguished leader, of reviewing with you a subject which, if we look openly and squarely at it, towers above all others in its consequences today—the subject of our external relations and our duties in respect of defence at the present time.

In approaching this matter, I realize, more fully perhaps than any of those present, that I must keep in mind, in every word as I am compelled to improvise them now, the significance of this great gathering, called from the far-flung limits of this broad continent and derived from varying origins and from varying traditions; and I must observe with scrupulous care that spirit of tolerance and openness of mind which always must characterize discussion of such an issue.

I yield to none in my devotion to peace; I yield to none in regret that the time has come again when peace-loving countries of the world can no longer confine their meditations to local and domestic affairs.

The time, unhappily, is here when we are compelled to turn

our eyes, temporarily at all events, from that hoped for insurance against war, which we called collective security, and to admit that we no longer can look to that creation, great in its conception —the League of Nations—for the protection which, until very recent years, we thought it would afford.

Nor do I yield to anyone in my appreciation of the enduring importance of Canadian constitutional rights and autonomous powers.

I would be the last to consent to the surrender of any of those attributes of nationhood which over our history we have reached, though I deplore and have often deplored the constant disposition of some to be forever fighting over again the battle of autonomy, which was won and conceded long decades ago.

I ask all of you present to look abroad, to look around and canvass in your hearts the situation which meets your eyes. Can anyone do so and sit with complacency at his fireside and think that from the single standpoint of Canada no duty devolves upon us?

Can anyone commune with his own thoughts and for a moment contemplate that there flashes in the sky no peril to this our home?

A division of international sentiment into new camps has taken place. In the main, those peoples of the world who love the institutions of democracy are feeling as one, seeking to act as one, in recognition of a common heritage. And against these— one should not yet say against, but contrasted with these—are those who appear to have revived that worship of the kingdom of Might, that love even of the horrors and devastations of war which not so long ago broke forth and almost crushed our civilization, and which, with deep lamentations, we are now compelled to acknowledge as threatening us all again.

In the midst and throughout the history of this development we have been proud to witness Great Britain, standing in line by the side of France, exerting her every effort, her every ingenuity to hold fast the fabric of world peace, and to prevent a conflagration which too often has seemed impending. We have seen that noble Lion enduring humiliations never before endured, bringing to his aid a patience which has been the consternation of humanity in a resolve to prevent resort to arms—hopeful still, struggling still, while his Government is goaded by the great Labour Party and the Liberal Party to put into effect without delay retaliatory measures which might hurl mankind into an inferno of war.

We see the world getting steadily smaller—distance is no longer a defence.

In that situation it is difficult indeed to convince ourselves that we have no concern. My first proposition is this: While acknowledging and sharing the conviction that our primary duty is the protection of the security and happiness of this Dominion, I address this simple question to the minds of all those within my sight; is there such a thing as the separate and independent defence of Canada? Is such an idea more than a fantasy and a delusion? Is it within the compass of possibility or even within the contemplation of common sense?

Look the world over. Can you see a single nation which can confidently say that its own defence is entirely within its single power? And, looking over great nations whose heritages do not compare with ours, can you believe for a moment that this country, with its vast domain and its small population, can in its hours of sanity ever come to the conclusion that the defence of Canada is something within our single capacity?

Surely you must agree there is no such thing as the separate and independent defence of this Dominion. Then I ask, where do we look? Where, from the selfish standpoint of Canada, is it wisest first to look? Where have we looked through the long history of this country? And when we have looked there, have we ever looked in vain? The answer is in the mind of every one of you.

I have endeavoured to speak to you, all of you, the language of reason and not the language of passion, because if ever the hour struck when reason alone should dominate our thinking and determine our convictions, that very hour is now.

I do not claim that we of the Conservative party are the only citizens of this country who realize that the strength and loyal fidelity upon which through these years we have leaned, and upon which still we can rely, is that great Mother land, the senior partner in this Empire.

I question if there is a single responsible leader of the party in power today who, if he were asked, would not admit the truth of every sentence I have uttered up to this moment.

In my hand is the Hansard report of a speech delivered on March 24th last by him who is mainly responsible for defence policy in our country, the Hon. Ian Mackenzie. I ask any of you who think that I have drawn an exaggerated picture of world peril, any of you who think I have described in exaggerated terms the relationship of this country to that peril, to listen to these words of the present Minister of National Defence, with every line of which I am in complete accord:

> We are confronted with very grave international problems which at any moment may explode against the ordered progress of our national life in the Dominion of Canada.

Those are pregnant words. Where does the Minister of National Defence look for the strong arm which we may call to our aid, the nation with whose hands we may join our own to insure our common defence?

Now, note again his words:

> In regard to the exact position of Canada it is only fair to say that today the main deterrent against a major attack upon this country by an European power is the existence of the British fleet in the North Atlantic.

The main deterrent against a hostile force, the arm which surrounds and has ever surrounded our country is the arm of that fleet!

What is our defence, says our Minister of National Defence, when we turn to the westward and look toward the Pacific? He admits that the best that Canada can expect to do by herself is to provide against sporadic, occasional attack, but that in respect of a major assault this country depends in the Atlantic on the fleet of Britain, and in the Pacific on the presence there of some other friendly Power.

It is assumed that the friendly Power which he had latterly in mind is the Republic to the south.

No one will go further than I to live in amity, in co-operation, and alliance in time of peril, with that great nation; but I say this, in the presence of everyone:

Note, if you note nothing more, that the first line of defence of that Republic, as the first line of defence of this Dominion of Canada, is the same British Fleet—the same Fleet which stands today between our peaceful homes and the thunderings and flashes of a storm-ridden world.

I ask you seriously to consider and to answer: is our problem of defence now in association with Britain while Britain still is strong—is the problem of defence for us Canadians not an easier undertaking, not an undertaking more clearly within the compass of our strength than would be, if the British Empire falls, our problem of defence in association with the United States of America?

Those who can seriously consider depending alone upon such an association—as I cannot—ought to be able to imagine what this stupendous question of defence would mean to us if we relied upon that association after the Empire of Britain falls. This Dominion, as does democratic civilization, hangs upon the maintenance of the power which has all along centred in that great Empire, the shield of the world today.

I am not uttering words with which only adherents of the Conservative party can agree. Again let me quote from the language of our Minister of Defence in the present Government. On last March 24th he laid down these principles:

First: Each self-governing portion of the Empire is primarily responsible for its own local security.

Second: *The security of the Empire is a matter of concern to all its Governments.*

He said also, quoting with approval a report of the Imperial Defence Committee, "each of the self-governing dominions is responsible for protecting its territory and coastal trade against aggression *until support comes from outside.*"

A VOICE: Go on.

Certainly I will go on. I have not finished. I am not accustomed to quit any task in the middle, but have gone far enough to show that the independent, separate defence of Canada is an idle dream and that we can better take care of ourselves in our present relationship with Britain than under the best possible conditions were England to fall.

What is the pertinent question at this moment? Within the course of a few days, in fact on Friday last, it was disclosed in the Parliament of Canada that approaches had been made to our Government by the Government of Great Britain, not, it is pretentiously urged, in the form of official requests, because Britain never would make a formal request of this Dominion until she was certain that such request would meet with an affirmative reply, but, to use the language of the Prime Minister of Canada, in the form of "confidential, informal and exploratory conversations."

The specific nature of that approach he has not had the candour to disclose. But he goes on in his address of Friday last to say that if a formal request is made to this Dominion that the British Government be permitted to establish in Canada, at the expense of British taxpayers and for the training of citizens of Britain, a flying school and flying facilities, such request will be met by the Government of Canada with a naked negative, in the name of Canadian autonomy.

I yield to none in maintaining the principle of control of Canada over the forces of Canada, civil or military; in maintaining trusteeship of the Canadian Government over the citizens of Canada and the arms of Canada wherever they may be; and in maintaining that such control be exercised even in time of war, though our forces then may be under a form of unified command.

But I want to know when the principle ever developed in this Dominion that if Britain wants to train, not our men, but her own, with only such of ours as choose to join and by consent of our Government may join—to train her own men for her defence, the defence of her liberty within which comes our liberty, for the defence of her shores and our shores, she cannot control the training of these men on the soil of Canada; that she cannot herself conduct that training as she alone knows how to conduct it; that those who are to use the men after they are trained, and who are manifestly the best-equipped to do the training, shall not be freely granted such right.

These trainees, remember, are to be airmen of Britain, unless Canadians wish to join with Government approval, for only in that way can Canadians join the Royal Air Force at this hour.

These are to be her own people, to be made ready for her purposes and ours. The whole thought is that they may develop their training, modified maybe from month to month as necessitated by ever-growing scientific developments, modified from month to month as disclosed to be essential for proper coordination of air defence with naval defence, for proper development of the protection of the heart of the Empire and, simultaneously, of the shores and homes of Canada.

I ask you: Have we come to the pass in this country that Canada locks the gate on Britain when the Old Land asks for permission to establish at her own expense, and train in her own way, her own citizens for their defence and ours?

This subject is fit for this Convention's concern. This subject this Convention cannot ignore. This subject today arrests the attention of the Canadian people and must continue to arrest it until the decision of the nation is known and rings throughout this Empire and goes to the ears of the Government of Britain.

Is it the spirit, is it in the heart of the people of Canada now when opportunity comes, in which we really can co-operate and do something of value, that, instead of stretching out the arm, we assume a posture of tremulous apprehension, apparently afraid that Great Britain may conquer Canada; that we become absorbed in an anxious analysis of constitutional niceties instead of trying to make our partnership worth while?

To compress into a last sentence the conclusion of this whole matter; if we call ourselves partners in this Commonwealth—and many prefer that title to member nations of a Commonwealth—let us behave the way partners behave when they have a common purpose and when they know that purpose is right.

Let us at least be ready to help others to help themselves and thereby to be of advantage to us all. Let us act in these matters of mutual defence in a spirit of common interest and not in a spirit of distant and suspicious deliberation.

Let us open our eyes to the truth that a building up of our defence is a thousand times more important to us than punctilious constitutional technique. Let us live and work on the assumption that this partnership in the British Commonwealth is a partnership we desire to endure, a partnership we aim to deserve, a partnership we are proud to own.

I want this country to stay, and not only to stay but to be worthy and fitted by its conduct to stay, within the compass of the British shield.

I want that first, because I believe that thereby we provide in the best, the safest, the sanest and surest manner for our own defence; and, second—and here I speak for myself—because within that shield I have lived to this hour and my forebears have lived for centuries, and there we love to be.

But if there are those who are not stirred by the same feelings, those who, perhaps naturally, cannot be expected to be so stirred, those who declare their only interest and only affection to be Canada, to them I address no words of criticism or hostility, but I do in the deepest sincerity present to them this thought: Keeping your eyes focussed on this land we call our own, looking to its future with clear vision and undivided devotion, is it not true that when we take the course we have taken in the past, when we do as we ought to do now, when we rise to the high calling of free associates for a worthy end, we do the best we know how, to save the soil of Canadians, to save the liberties of Canadians, to save the lives of Canadians, to preserve the name of our people as a people of good faith, a people of self-respect, a people of honour, among partners who themselves are staunchly loyal, and in the presence of all nations of earth?

FAREWELL TRIBUTE TO MR. BENNETT

Spoken on the occasion of a Dinner in honour of Rt. Hon. R. B. Bennett, K.C., P.C., LL.D., at Royal York Hotel, Toronto, Jan. 16th, 1939.

THIS DINNER IS BY WAY OF TRIBUTE to Mr. Bennett—a demonstration of esteem to a very eminent Canadian who has already done a life's work and is leaving to reside abroad.

If one should attempt at the present time, and in a gathering such as this, to make an appraisal of the service our guest of tonight has rendered this country, he could not expect his estimate to be accepted either by Canadians as a whole or by those assembled here. We are too close to the events, too near the controversies which lately divided our people and which raged around his head. But what is one to do? It is impossible—for me at any rate it is impossible—even to merit a hearing, if one confines himself to the eulogies which are commanded by custom when one speeds a departing guest. Mr. Bennett may forgive me, and he may not—there are some things for which he has never forgiven me—but platitudes of affection do not appertain to him. He is not, as Laurier was, so spontaneously affable, a personality so universally gracious and engaging that one likes him, sometimes follows him, though he believes him wrong. He is not, as Macdonald was, so intensely human and companionable as to be loved even for his faults. He is, as everyone knows, a different stamp of man altogether. He is a product of this generation rather than of the last. He is a man of affairs, a man who has been in contact with realities, and hard realities, from his earliest years to this very hour. On the rough, ruthless battlefields of life he has triumphed, and he depends, and does not fear to depend, upon his achievements for his following and

314

his fame. It seems to me best, therefore, to give a very brief review of what Mr. Bennett has accomplished in public life. I give it from the standpoint of one who believed in the important elements of his policies—though I know there are many here who did not. What I shall say will be candid and certainly without offence, and all are at liberty to differ and still be welcome at this banquet.

We can pass over the far-away years at the turn of the last century when the young, slender Calgary lawyer was scintillating in territorial politics in Western Canada, also his later period as a private Member at Ottawa. At these times, politics was only a secondary feature of his life. His real work was in other spheres, and that work he was performing with the same boundless energy which he afterwards devoted to public affairs. When at last in 1930 he found himself at the head of the Government of Canada, he faced for the first time a task which challenged all his powers.

This is an age of business, and to a degree unknown in older times, Government is a great business organization. Legislation and administration nowadays touch business at every point, and it is of cardinal consequence that those who forge the weapons of legislation know something of the principles upon which alone our commercial and industrial activities can live; that they know thoroughly well from hard experience the competitive relations of this country in the world of affairs.

In 1930, even before Mr. Bennett came to office, our Dominion, in common with all other lands was headed down the slope into a depression of unprecedented intensity. I for one believe it was fortunate for Canada that we had as Prime Minister a man who understood the meaning of it all, a man who had a firm grasp of practical affairs, who turned away from mere slogans and nostrums and went about getting something done which would stimulate production and revive our trade. It was well we had a man who knew that this was the only way we could fortify our national finances and re-employ our people.

You may differ if you like, but the Ottawa Agreements of the Spring of 1932 were a really big achievement, a landmark in the history of this country. Wrapped in the body of those Agreements was a revolution in the fiscal policy of Britain. What happened? Right from the fisheries of the Pacific to the farms of the Maritimes, from the forests of British Columbia to the apple orchards of Nova Scotia, they gave new hope and new life to our people. They steadied and strengthened the financial structure of Canada. For the first time in the history of North American depressions this Dominion led the United States up the hill. These Agreements we owe in very great degree to the business vision and iron resolution of the guest of tonight. Let us assume—and critics of Mr. Bennett will certainly contend— that the recent modified arrangement in which the United States is included is wise and for the public weal. On that point I will say this:—that, aside from the balance of commercial advantage or disadvantage, there is a great deal to be said for Canada entering into an arrangement which makes possible at this time a Trade Agreement between England and the United States. Granted then, for the moment, the wisdom of this modified plan, there is no disputing the fact that this plan could not have been consummated but for the effect of what was accomplished in 1932. The man whose will-power literally blasted a way to those Agreements should not be an unhonoured prophet in his own home.

Another fine piece of work should be mentioned now. It is the St. Lawrence Treaty. Only those who have some comprehension of the complications of our Federal system, of Provincial water rights and power requirements, of Federal responsibilities in respect of navigation, of United States' counter-requirements in navigation and in power, and of the inevitable difficulties of making an agreement on any subject of great consequence with the American Republic—only those can realize what it meant that, after months of labour and a long succession of disappointments, a Treaty was finally reached between representatives of these two North American countries for the development of the River St. Lawrence. It is true this Agreement failed to gain approval in the American Senate. The same fate has awaited almost every Treaty of moment we have ever effected with the United States, but, nevertheless, a Herculean task was done. At last the ground is laid, indeed the structure is in being, which should make consummation of that task a relatively simple thing when the two countries are ready again. It certainly is not too much to say that the Dominion of Canada was fortunate in having those negotiations conducted on her part by a man who had a broad, thorough and practical grasp of all interests involved.

These two achievements alone would have been sufficient to mark Mr. Bennett's tenure of office as a period distinguished by important performance.

In that period also, Canada for the first time laid the foundations of her law of Shipping. Until this was done we had been able to get along under the British Shipping Act, but, because of the Statute of Westminster, we needed a code of our own. That code was enacted after two Sessions of work, and I can say that in difficulty of draughtsmanship and in multiplicity and complexity of detail, it was one of the most onerous pieces of legislation ever constructed. Though almost a volume in itself, it is a public service excellently done. Four years of operation have demonstrated the practical efficiency of all its provisions.

I can no more than mention the re-constitution of our Patent Act and our several Insurance Statutes, and there were many other useful measures which had been long delayed.

Let me come, without further recital, to better-known legislation which marked the last Session of Mr. Bennett's regime.

There are many excellent citizens who have still something of a horror of what is called the New Deal programme of 1935. I am a long way from being a visionary radical, but I know something about that legislation, and make the statement that in all its important features it was sound and timely. Our guest will not be offended when I say that what a lot of people have still in their minds like a nightmare is not the legislation, which was enlightened, but the speeches, which frightened. The Statutes, indeed, received almost unanimous approval from both Houses of Parliament. This is not the time to impeach the wisdom of their being submitted, as they were, to the Privy Council on a question of constitutional jurisdiction. Personally I do not think they should have been so submitted, and personally I think that in respect particularly of those Statutes which implemented

Treaties already made by this country, such as the Hours of
Labour Act and the Day of Rest Act, the Chief Justice of Canada
was right, and the negative verdict of the Privy Council was
wrong. I not only think, but know, that that verdict has precipitated our Dominion into a constitutional chaos from which we
cannot emerge for years. Far from ranging myself with those
who seek to sever this Dominion from the Motherland in the
matter of Constitutional Appeal, I, nevertheless, lament a decision
which maims and paralyzes our country's powers as a nation, and
condemns us to perpetual incapacity in the making of proper and
necessary arrangements with other countries on subjects which
are usefully dealt with by Treaties, and Treaties alone. Anyway,
this legislation of 1935 is a credit to the Prime Minister of that
time and will be a beacon light to guide our footsteps in years to
come after we emerge, if we ever emerge, into that state of
constitutional regeneration which we are groping for today.

There is something more I want to say and it is not intended—nor is anything else intended—as a reflection on any
other public man. For five Sessions I was leader of the Senate,
and for three later Sessions, leader of one section of that House—
the section favourable in a general way to Mr. Bennett's party.
Throughout that entire period, and it was a long one, the leader
of the Conservative party recognized, without limitation, the
distinct and independent status of that branch of Parliament.
The Senate, during his term of Premiership, altered Government
measures hundreds of times, altered them in important features,
even defeated policies submitted with his recommendation, but
never did Mr. Bennett interfere or seek to interfere with the
duties of the Second Chamber—never at any time did he go so
far as to complain, or even to make suggestion that we should
take another course. He has a right understanding of how the
constitution of Canada should work.

We sometimes hear it said: "Oh, Mr. Bennett was defeated.
His party was crushed. Its members in the House of Commons
are few. He failed as a leader of Canada."

This reasoning I dispute.

What I am about to say certainly will not add to my popularity, probably it would be better to say, will not rescue me

from unpopularity, but the opinion is mine and it is going to be expressed.

I think R. B. Bennett did a splendid job as Prime Minister, and I do not think it argues in the least to the contrary that he met defeat at the hands of the voters of Canada. I go further and say this: that in our Dominion where sections abound, a Dominion of races, of classes and of creeds, of many languages and many origins, there are times when no Prime Minister can be true to his trust to the nation he has sworn to serve, save at the temporary sacrifice of the party he is appointed to lead. Without a question there never was a Prime Minister who could have done so in the years when Mr. Bennett was in office. I believe in the British system of democracy, and would submit to almost anything before surrendering those liberties which we as British subjects enjoy, but if anyone tells me that fidelity to party and fidelity to country are always compatible, or that the wisdom of mere numbers is the wisdom of heaven, then I tell him that he loves applause far more than he loves truth. Loyalty to the ballot box is not necessarily loyalty to the nation; it is not even loyalty to the multitude. Democracy has failed and fallen in many lands, and political captains in Canada must have courage to lead rather than servility to follow, if our institutions are going to survive. There must be something better than an ambition to be re-elected, or democracy will fall, even in this Dominion.

The guest of tonight must not leave our shores with any consciousness in his heart of failure as directing head of this country. There was no failure in that capacity. He certainly cannot now leave our shores without knowing that he has the admiration of many, the gratitude of some, and the respect of all; and after tonight he must know that his friends can be numbered in legions, and to number his friends in legions such as he sees before him now must be some gratification, because, of the whole succession of leaders we have had in our country, he, most of all, never feared to make a foe.

Mr. Bennett, in a few short days you will be a citizen of Canada no longer; but your rank will still be high. You will take your place as one of a great people with a noble history. You will be a citizen of the first of nations, and no prouder title did a free man ever share. We know the part which that nation played in our own time—in dark days of the world's travail. We see her now twenty years after, holding the light of reason before threatening Powers, striving to find a way of peace, striving again and striving still again, suffering disappointments, it is true—cruel disappointments—suffering perhaps passing humiliation, if only the reign of common sense can be restored, a convulsion averted, and mankind saved from an ocean of blood. Surely this is an object worth striving for—even by the bravest of our species. Chronic critics may snipe and flippant ingrates may scoff, but in the beclouded hearts of humanity at this hour, Britain is the world's chief hope. The masses of human beings in two hemispheres, longing for wise guidance and a chance to live—the masses of our race amid the threatening thunders of our time—look to her for leadership and help. And, as they look, they know that if all should fail, and the dread hour should strike, the stoutest heart in the long whole range of nations will beat from those islands—the last to abandon the struggle for peace, the last to leave the field of war. To her the worried world looks today, to her we look, and by her we stand, that the light of the individual soul shall not be quenched and that human liberty shall not perish from the earth.

Oh, you critics of this continent and especially of this country, just look in upon yourselves! What are you doing to strengthen the defences of democracy? What is your country doing? How far are you trying to persuade and to help your country to act?

For critics of the British Government in those islands where they are bound by consequences of alternative policies—for them we must have respect. But for you critics here, who refuse to be bound by anything, but who always find fault; for you who never define any course, but who always find Britain wrong as soon as Britain acts; for you who roar and scream for peace and then complain about the price; for you how can we have respect?

Great Britain's past is the pledge of her fidelity. The best we can ever hope for is this: that our standard of loyalty to duty will measure up to the standard of Old England.

There are those who seem to think that we on this continent

need have no concern for the fate of Britain or of France; who are building up with insidious industry distrust of Britain's policy, indifference to Britain's life—professors, neutrality experts, continentalists, provincialists, wise-crack correspondents—men who want to save us by new constitutions and resolutions, brave men who I suppose are going to jump into some kind of North American resistance after the front-line has gone. These men say that the time to start defending democracy is not now but will arrive after three-quarters of its fortifications have been swept away. They tell us in Canada that our turn to look around will arrive, and they themselves will fight like demons, when guns are booming against these Eastern cities and war planes of the enemy are roaring over the Rockies!

When the call for decision comes, these theorists will count for nothing.

Right now we depend, and depend as never before, on the common sense and vision of our public men, and on what Disraeli called the primitive and enduring virtues of our race.

And you, Mr. Bennett—I envy you. You are leaving us for a stage which has summoned men of spirit and of brain for centuries past. You are not going over there to loll around in idle comfort in some sequestered vale, however well you may have earned your rest. That is not the way you are built. The gleam of your eye tells me that there are years, many years, of glorious living still ahead, before that frame falters and the glimmering landscape fades. You are going over there to put your hand to work, to any and every work, big or humble, which you can find to do; to add the weight and wealth of character and training that is yours to Britain's will, to Britain's brain, to Britain's might, to Britain as she is seen now, leading Europe's crusade for peace, and bending herself under the most appalling load that ever bore down upon a nation. Over there, there is work for you.

Such is the mission beckoning you—of that I am sure. Canada will follow you with pride; Britain will welcome you with pride; but what do these things matter? It will be a worth while close to a life of toil, a fitting climax to a fine career.

UNIFIED MANAGEMENT OF RAILWAYS

Early in 1938 *a Special Committee was appointed by the Senate, pursuant to a Resolution unanimously passed by that Chamber in the following terms:*

> That a committee of the Senate be appointed to inquire into and report upon the best means of relieving the country from its extremely serious railway condition, and financial burden consequent thereto.

This Committee sat throughout the entire Session and resumed its work in the succeeding Session of 1939. *In all, fifty-four meetings were held, at which forty-five witnesses were under examination—principally officers of the two railway systems and special economists in railway matters.*

On May 11, 1939, *a majority report was presented to the House. This recommended continuance of co-operative efforts between the Canadian National Railways and the Canadian Pacific Railway Company, as provided for in the Canadian National-Canadian Pacific Act of* 1933.

A minority report was also presented, signed by nine members of the Committee. This expressed, first, a conclusion that nothing of substantial value in the way of economies was being, or could be, obtained by co-operation between competitors with different objectives, and then recommended that a plan of management of the two systems by a united Board should be worked out, in which plan each railway company would be equally represented.

The following speech was made on May 25, 1939, *in reply to the leader of the Government in the Senate (Hon. Raoul Dandurand) and in support of the minority report.*

Next day the House divided and this latter report was adopted by a vote of 25-21.

WHILE I VALUE SINCERELY the addresses, or most of them, which have been delivered in this debate, I cannot say that I rise with any sensations of pleasure to add to the discussion. I feel, rather, a very real and distressing sense of futility, because, to my mind, the usefulness of this House is under serious reproach and the function intended for us in the scheme of Confederation is being reduced to atrophy. I had long ago resolved to rid myself of every constraint which would impede me in the exercise of my soundest judgment as to how best to treat this great business problem; but I am sorry to find this Session in the conduct of the honourable leader (Hon. Mr. Dandurand) an intervention of other than business considerations and a regard for matters for which we were never intended to have regard. He appears to have almost a unanimous following in support of the position taken by his party. Possibly I should have no ground for such complaint were it not that the past conduct of himself and of those who agree with him shows they have not reasoned about this subject in other days as they now do; that impulsions which bind them today did not bind them but a very short time ago.

Fourteen years have passed since a committee of this Chamber, long before I was a member, unanimously declared itself in favour of unified management of the Canadian National and the Canadian Pacific railways. It is true that the financial terms then recommended would not now be considered by us, but the Senate favoured the principle of unified operation. And it is only six years since the basis of the Senate's resolution of 1925 was again unreservedly approved by the honourable gentleman who now leads the House.

Hon. Mr. Dandurand: And repudiated by my right honourable friend.

Right Hon. Mr. Meighen: It is only seven years since he said that while in his judgment some good might result from the measure then under consideration, he apprehended we should have to return to the principle of unified management at no distant date. At that time he read a list of advantages which would accrue if we did return to, and enforce, that principle. All this he repudiates now. He says to me, across the floor, that six years ago I did not favour unification, but supported the bill then before us. That is true. The whole railway question had been inquired into by a commission in which, in common with the whole country, I had entire confidence.[1] That commission had made specific and clear recommendations. Manifestly in such circumstances the best that could be done was to give those recommendations a fair opportunity to produce relief. However one might have felt about the prospect—and I myself had hopes that much more would be attained than has been—it is certain that in face of the commission's report there was nothing further we could do than what we did. I remember observing then that in the case of great utilities between which there had been severest competition beneficial effects had been obtained from co-operation, and I expressed my belief that in the railway field there was a sphere within which it could be made to produce desirable results, even while competition continued.

Well, we have had six years of this kind of co-operation, but results achieved would not fill the hollow of our hand. Both railways have explained why more co-operative measures have not been put into effect. The honourable leader of the House refuses to accept their explanation, or to be guided by the result. He tells us he is now against unified management on principle, and he calls upon his followers to vote it down.

HON. MR. DANDURAND: My right honourable friend is wrong. I do not ask anyone to follow me, and I have called no caucus.

RIGHT HON. MR. MEIGHEN: It is not hard for any of us to hear the call, even though it is not addressed to us. Results speak for themselves. The honourable leader of the Government has veered at a right angle from the course he took just a few years ago, and has professed principles directly contrary to those which he twice commended to this House. His party followers have done the same.

Another reason why participation in this debate gives me no pleasure is this:—I find myself in direct and definite conflict with the avowed platform of the party with which I have been associated through life, and with the leader of that party, a man whose gifts I admire and for whose person I have affection. Performance of my duty in these circumstances, with no organized body of public opinion in support, certainly cannot carry with it any gratification. I had hoped that others on both sides

[1] The Duff-Flavelle Commission.

of the House could consider this matter from its business and national aspects alone, and thus enable the Senate to show the country that we are seeking to serve rather than to please.

Hon. Mr. Gordon: Hear, hear.

Right Hon. Mr. Meighen: It would be waste of time to go far into history in order to portray a background of today's condition. This I have done on previous occasions. There are persons who have flung at me a charge of pessimism, of failure to see the bright side of this country's destiny. The whole source and essence of the problem which we now face, and which has been described as the most obdurate and dangerous confronting Canada, has been false optimism. Who does not remember the optimism that swept our Government off its feet in the early days of this century, an optimism out of which grew thousands of miles of railway which today constitute the deadweight and wreckage under which we struggle? Who does not remember the intoxication of the twenties, led by that prince of all optimists, Sir Henry Thornton, under whose gay and garish leadership this enterprise, the Canadian National Railways, was sunk beneath $900,000,000 of added debt in nine years? To those two frenzied cycles we owe the railway troubles of our time.

Ah! we are told, troubles of railways are universal; the United States has them, the Argentine has them, France has them, Britain has them. There is not one of those countries which has the situation we have. Not one of those countries had these burdens at the early time we had them. We were in trouble before the era of railways was ever invaded by truck, bus or any other new form of competition. The ordinary worries which beset industry overtaken by new competition beset railways everywhere, but there are more than those things to be overcome in Canada. This Dominion is bound by guarantees, by advances in scores and hundreds of millions of dollars, guarantees and advances into which we tied ourselves because of the primary errors of those earlier years, and because of that delirious swirl in the twenties of this century. These are special maladies of Canada, and it is these which now we must attack.

We listened to the senator from Moncton and the senator from Montreal telling us that things truly are not so bad. They got the cue from the senator who leads the House, who said that everything was just fine up to the end of the twenties. We were getting along so well, he thought, up to the depression and, he added, if we just had 15,000,000 instead of 11,000,000 population we should be in a sort of railway paradise—our troubles would be over.

I regard our situation as serious to a dark and portentous degree, and do not consider it any offset that we are able to borrow money cheaply to pay our deficits year by year. I look around in this country at governmental units which not so long ago could do just the same, whose very facility of borrowing spelled the miseries in which now they are engulfed—units even in the dimensions of a province. Borrow, borrow—it was easy, and so they continued to borrow until now they are encompassed with the ignominies of repudiation and the shadows of shame. Their numbers would be far greater even counted in provinces if they had not had the credit reservoirs of this Dominion on which to rely—if there were not still a period within which we can borrow for them.

We poured $54,000,000 into the Canadian National last year. "But," we are told, "it is not much. Why, look at the taxes it pays—$15,000,000 or $20,000,000, taxes from the salaries of its officials! This thing really is not a deficit! Look at the service we get, and the Canadian National pays taxes to our towns." I heard some time ago that debt was not a liability at all, and am hearing much the same tonight.

But $54,000,000 really is not the figure. That is the sum after a writing down programme in which we have been engaged during previous sessions. They tell us, "Oh, don't regard the Canadian National the way you would regard a commercial road, the Canadian Pacific or the New York Central. Much of this road was built to unite Canada and for colonization purposes." That assertion is true. But it is only two or three sessions since we wrote off what was attributable to colonization, and what was contributed to unite Canada. We wrote off the whole interest on it as well. We added this write-off to the debt of Canada, and lifted it from the debt of our railway, and we lifted a lot more into a vague account called "proprietors' equity."

Why, the total was about $2,000,000,000. We did all this under assurance that it would reduce capital liabilities until we could look upon the Canadian National as a commercial enterprise. Now after we have done so we are told: "Do not look on us as a commercial institution. Look at the pioneering we are doing around Noranda mines, look at the pioneering we are doing around the once-expected metropolis of Prince Rupert; look at all these things." We, like every other country, are getting these services from our ordinary roads. But in Canada we have to extract this huge sum as well out of our taxpayers' pockets year by year, taking out more than all individual income taxes of the entire Dominion. Still we have honourable members of this House telling us that we really have no great worry, that we are just marching with the rest of the world through difficulties of railways! Why, honourable members, figure out the amount in cash which this Dominion has advanced to the Canadian National; never mind the building of the Transcontinental nor the Intercolonial; never mind these pioneer political roads at all; just think of cash advanced and count the interest we pay today out of taxpayers' pockets on cash borrowed, and you have to add $50,000,000 more every year as cost to this country of the Canadian National Railways!

When I see that situation, five and a half years after we passed the Canadian National-Canadian Pacific Act, I ask myself, "Are we able to conclude we have solved the problem?" Can we honestly look the taxpayer in the face and say, "These troubles are behind us, the legislation is there, and all we need do now is to give a little advice to Mr. Canadian Pacific President and Mr. Canadian National President"?[1] Is there a man who sat through the committee for two sessions who in the bottom of his heart has any belief whatever in the problem being even on the way to solution if we do nothing more? He may find difficulties in the way of a new proposal, but to say we have the job done seems to me to be blind to as plain a truth as ever challenged the human mind.

Hon. Mr. Dandurand: Every country is trying to find a solution.

[1] A suggestion of Hon. Sen. Dandurand.

RIGHT HON. MR. MEIGHEN: I am talking about Canada. I got rid of other countries some time ago. Our problem differs from the problem of every other country on earth, and the reason it differs dates to the false optimism of this Dominion long ago led by many public men, including my honourable friend.

I intend now to inquire as to whether there is hope of improvement if we depend upon the majority report of this committee, sponsored by the leader of this House. We were a committee commissioned unanimously by the Senate to find a remedy for the "extremely serious" railway problem of Canada. "Extremely serious": so described by every member of this House, and so described with a fidelity to fact which no mind could possibly call in question. Such was our committee's assignment. What is its majority report? What solution does it offer? I say to everyone here, defying contradiction: there is no solution offered. The country groans under $54,000,000 a year in direct outlay; $50,000,000 more in respect of interest paid on advances actually borrowed for the road; the country, I say, groans under this weight, and hundreds of thousands of people stand on our doorsteps out of work because, in part, of consequent stricture of enterprise in Canada; and this committee tells us, "We have nothing to suggest but stay just as we are." In effect, the committee says to the taxpayers of our country, "Stand and deliver; smile and swallow; grin and bear it." Such is the report which this House is asked to approve.

We are told that we have obtained something out of voluntary co-operation. Yes, last year we had reached a total of $1,135,000; precisely that and no more. And last year was the fifth year of co-operation. If everything is granted and completed which has been agreed to up to this hour, we shall have a total of $1,771,000 at the end of six years. At this rate of progress, to reach even the utterly inadequate aggregate savings set by Canadian National officials will take us sixty years.

But that is not the worst. The situation disclosed by evidence is that we shall never move more than a hair's breadth farther; hardly far enough even to calculate. Did witnesses hold out any hope? They did not last Session. They tried hard this Session, but they did not succeed. I heard no words of hope. Some reason then had to be found by my hon. friend for predicting a flicker of light for the future. What reason did he find? "There is that Canadian Pacific and its propaganda for unification. It did not want co-operation to succeed, so it balked co-operation. If we will just put our foot down on unification, then all will be fine, the Canadian Pacific will go ahead and co-operate, and we shall make our savings." Faith sublime! Did we not put our foot down on unification six years ago? We did. That was the ultimatum of Parliament; that was the declaration of leaders of both Houses. We turned into the field of co-operation. Did we get anywhere? Did the idea of unified management die?

Is it a fact that the Canadian Pacific balked co-operation? The report as drafted first by the leader of the House said it was; but when it was called to his attention that there was not a sentence, not a breath of evidence to support such a contention, his report was changed and this allegation was erased. There was no suggestion from Canadian National witnesses of any failure on the part of the Canadian Pacific. Neither was there a suggestion from the Canadian Pacific that there was failure on the part of the Canadian National.

There was, in fact, read to the committee, out of the annual reports of the Canadian National Railway Company for 1934 and 1935, a statements of its president, that failure to proceed farther was not the fault of anyone, but was inherent in the very situation. Still honourable members will say to this House, "Just tell the Canadian Pacific to stop flirting with unification and we will have fine co-operation." Until you can fix on the Canadian Pacific responsibility for delay, you have no right to make such a claim—and you have not fixed it, and you cannot.

It is said that the railways could have enforced co-operation and did not do so. That is true. And the reason is just the same as the reason why they got nowhere on a voluntary basis. This reason was agreed to by every witness. Every time we nailed a witness down to particulars he said—whether he was from one road or from the other—"We have different objectives; our interests are distinct. We, on our part, want the problem solved one way because it will best help our road when we get beyond the area of co-operation. We do not want to bear the big end of the burden; we do not want to get the light end of the reward. Our interests are diverse. We are competing, fighting each other for business, therefore we have this balancing of burden and advantage." Is not that answer clear? Until we get rid of diversity of objectives, we will never get rid of the impediment to progress.

Let me repeat. The reason was exposed by witnesses from both sides as inherent in a competitive situation, and they did not hold out hope that important progress can ever be made. "If we can only keep on," they said, "we think we might get so many million." They did not venture to mention over ten million; they never even expressed a belief that they would get to ten million. But still we are told that by co-operation we can hope to solve the railway problem of Canada.

Now I come to a more masculine report presented so ably by the honourable senator from Montarville (Hon. Mr. Beaubien). We who agreed with him felt that we had no right to be forgiven if we came to Parliament without a recommendation as to the best means of relieving the country of its burden. In order to find such means, surely it is not necessary to show that the whole burden must go, and go quickly, or nothing is accomplished; to show, as one honourable senator put it, that there is some magic remedy which can be applied. In this world of affairs, there is no magic remedy for anything. For the ills we suffer by reason of our own sins there is no remedy but toil and straight thinking. I am in unison with every honourable senator who says that from the whole incubus we have brought upon ourselves we can never escape. Possibly, had this revolution in transportation, this new competition, not come upon us—it has been coming for twenty years—there might have been hope. Now there is none. All we can do is the best we can; all we can do is remove every ounce of deadweight that is within our control. The fact that it cannot all be thrown off is only greater reason for lifting whatever we can, and starting as soon as we can.

I am going to inquire for a few minutes whether the principle advocated by the report embodied in Senator Beaubien's amendment can reasonably be expected to lead to relief, and if so, how far and in what length of time. Later I am going to inquire whether in the attainment of that relief we shall be paying a price in another way which subtracts from or cancels the relief.

On the first point one would not think the onus should be difficult to discharge. It should not be hard to establish that we will get tremendous advantages by unifying two roads in the way of management. Surely no business man needs to be convinced. He may feel, as a citizen, that he does not want monopoly; that point remains to be argued. But the question as to whether we can save money should not need to be argued. The hon. senator opposite me (Hon. Mr. Dandurand) has said time and time again that in that way we will save most and save it most quickly. I cannot explain why he signs a report which says we will do just as well in another way. I am sure he does not think so.

I pause to correct the hon. senator from Moncton (Hon. Mr. Robinson). He said we did not have evidence of possible savings from unified management; that what we had was evidence of possible savings from unification. In some way in his mind this unification is mixed up with property amalgamation. I do not care what he calls our plan—unified management, unification if he likes—it is management by a single board. Such is unified management. It is not amalgamation; amalgamation has different implications altogether. Once we amalgamate the physical properties of two systems, there arises a mutuality of obligation and ownership. It cannot be avoided. But unified management involves no such result at all; it is merely a system of managing two as one.

Hon. Mr. Murdock: Does not the dictionary define them in the same way?

Right Hon. Mr. Meighen: Fortunately, for simple words I do not need a dictionary.

Hon. Mr. Murdock: That is a very smart answer.

Right Hon. Mr. Meighen: It is the right answer.

Hon. Mr. Murdock: The dictionary describes them as the same thing.

Right Hon. Mr. Meighen: Call it what you like, it is unified management we recommend; and I know what it is, and so does the hon. senator from Parkdale. It is not amalgamation of properties.

The reason one starts from a position of advantage in proving that savings flow from unified management is that it has been a matter of experience all through the history of business that when you have single direction you can immediately get rid of duplicate services. While you have competition it is the hardest thing imaginable to do so, because those duplicate services are the very services which compete. Until we get rid of duplicate services, unnecessary services—

HON. MR. DANDURAND: Then unification begins.

RIGHT HON. MR. MEIGHEN: The honourable member wants to get me away from my point. I am coming to his bogeys very soon. I do not take these fears of the honourable gentleman seriously; they were born too recently. In the past and best years of his manhood he never had them at all; they are an outgrowth of certain political nightmares of recent months.

HON. MR. DANDURAND: I beg your pardon.

RIGHT HON. MR. MEIGHEN: I do not take them seriously.

You can have unification of control and operation without amalgamation. I have never seen an instance of unification of management, or, for that matter, of amalgamation of two great enterprises fighting each other in the same field, where tremendous savings were not made. Either one, but particularly the latter, can be objected to on other grounds; for instance, either can conceivably be objected to on public grounds; but to say that it will not save money is simply to ignore the dictates of common sense.

HON. MR. DANDURAND: Nobody says that.

RIGHT HON. MR. MEIGHEN: Of course not. And until my honourable friend brought in his report nobody ever suggested that as much money could be saved in any other way as by unification. Only through that singleness of objective which comes from a common purse can the utmost savings or, indeed, any worthwhile savings be realized.

It was contended by Canadian Pacific witnesses that aggregate economies of $75,300,000 per annum are practicable under unified control if business returns to the scale of 1930, which they thought was an average year. I am disposed to think 1930 must be regarded as above an average year, but cannot agree that Canadian Pacific witnesses failed to substantiate their estimate of economies. In fact, I do not regard arguments of Canadian National officials as meeting the case in any way. The methods adopted by Canadian Pacific witnesses were certainly thorough and impressive. That Company had twenty-one committees dealing with every phase of railway operations over a space of months, checking and re-checking one against another. These committees, composed of officials of high standing, conducted their studies in a serious way, carrying out suggestions made by a commission with whose objects they had the utmost sympathy. And yet figures arrived at by these committees are lightly described to us by some honourable members as "theoretical." I should like to ask what is meant by "theoretical" savings. It is an easy thing to trip an adjective off the tongue, but is it suggested that railway officials of the type of Mr. Neal, and of various other gentlemen who gave evidence, were putting something purely imaginary before the Duff Commission and before ourselves? What would they have had to gain by that? Were they not able to support their estimates? I do not know of any material impairment of their testimony.

Those projected economies were made up of a long array of elements; savings in the amalgamation of head offices, savings in reducing supervisorships from two to one over the whole range of operation, savings in maintenance of way and structures—those alone aggregated about $14,000,000—savings in maintenance of equipment, estimated at another $14,000,000, and these were established dollar by dollar all along the way. Then there were savings in accounting, savings in unification of hotel and steamship operation, and, most of all, under the head of transportation, where advantages of shortest and cheapest routes come into play, advantages which cannot be obtained except under a system of unified management. There were also economies in respect of delivery of empty cars. We were given a picture of empty cars running east on one road, while another stream of empties ran west on the other road. This would be avoided under single control. And there would be economies in re-delivery of empties to American roads, in consolidation of trains, by having cars fully loaded instead of half loaded. All these things are made possible only if the two systems are operated under joint direction. Further savings in seven figures were estimated from unified management of express and telegraph offices.

Estimates were presented under these various headings, and there was no difficulty in understanding them. That vast savings would result was made abundantly clear.

How were these estimates attacked? First, it was said that a lot of reductions in expenses had been made already. Canadian National witnesses—chiefly Mr. Fairweather—protested, "Our expenses are $47,000,000 lower than they were in 1930, and this reduction cannot be made over again." In such statements those witnesses persisted, unless one cornered them very closely. But the fact finally emerged that savings made by a single road are entirely or almost entirely distinct from savings possible under unified management. For instance, there can be no avoidance of duplication by a single road. It was shown that out of the $47,000,000 mentioned by Mr. Fairweather, only about $4,000,000 had been included in estimated savings under unification. And while it was admitted that estimated savings should be reduced by that $4,000,000, it was also established that there was an additional $9,000,000 of practicable economies which had been omitted from figures submitted to the Duff Commission; so original estimates submitted to that Commission and re-submitted to us were left intact and unimpaired.

A second ground for attack upon the estimates was that unit costs of the Canadian Pacific Railway would not apply to Canadian National operations. In this new document which was not put in evidence but was handed to my hon. friend opposite (Hon. Mr. Dandurand) and presented by him to the House, Canadian National officials lightly toss aside $20,000,000 of estimated savings as due to wrong application of unit costs. May I discuss that for a moment? One of the main methods employed by Canadian Pacific officials and accountants was this. They took costs of a unit of railway operation in respect of, say, express trains, or freight, or car repairs, or locomotive maintenance, or right-of-way maintenance, and applied that over the united system, and, comparing their total with existing totals under separate management, thereby showed what reductions could be made in respect of those various items. Canadian National officials said: "It is not fair to apply Canadian Pacific unit costs to the Canadian National, because our density of traffic is less, our conditions are different." The Canadian Pacific made an answer, to which the Canadian National obdurately refused to refer. The answer was this: "We are not applying our unit costs to your road. We are not impugning the efficiency of your management"—and they never did, though they made no admission that it was as good as theirs—"we are only seeking to apply our unit costs to a new system composed of both roads."

Hon. Mr. Dandurand: But covering the Canadian National.

Right Hon. Mr. Meighen: Certainly. But that is far different from saying that the Canadian Pacific were applying their unit costs to operation of the Canadian National as a separate system.

Hon. Mr. Dandurand: And they could not.

Right Hon. Mr. Meighen: They never said they could. What they did was to apply their unit costs to a combined system. If the Canadian National had the same density of traffic as the Canadian Pacific, and there were an equality of other conditions, then unification would result in lower unit costs over the combined system than those now applicable to the Canadian Pacific alone. That is quite apparent, because the more business handled the lower unit costs must be. But the Canadian Pacific said: "Admitting that you have a more expensive road to operate than ours is, we feel that reduction in expense consequent upon unification would result in unit costs for the combined system as low as those presently applicable to our own separate road." I ask hon. members if that is not reasonable. Is there anything there in the way of a boast? At least the reasoning was never afterwards attacked. Yet my hon. friend asks the House to deduct $20,000,000 from estimated savings because Canadian Pacific unit costs are not applicable to the Canadian National.

It is true that in certain very minor particulars the Canadian Pacific's estimate was found to be erroneous. In the aggregate those errors were small. They were atoned for by other economies shown to be practicable, though their exact extent could not be calculated. All these things only went to establish what should have been obvious from the beginning that savings of the largest and most impressive order, larger far than by any other means, could be made by united management of the two systems.

Now the leader of the House says, "Well, we are going to get this by co-operation." I have already discussed the prospects. I do not think that in his own mind he believes they are real—though I do not like so to allege. It is hard to see how anybody could sit through the meetings of our committee and seriously expect such results. To this I shall return.

I digress for a moment; be it remembered that an adroit politician, this same gentleman, Mr. Fairweather—what he is as a railway man I do not know—laid before Sir Henry Thornton in 1931, and subsequently before the Duff Commission, estimates of savings of $59,000,000, on the basis of 1930 traffic, as resulting from unified management. It is true he added a rider. Of all the senseless things I ever read this rider is the worst. He gave an estimate of $59,000,000 of savings and then added a rider saying we could not get those savings. It reminds me of a report made years ago, during the South African war. There was a long, circumstantial account from a distinguished soldier of the capture of 200 Boers by the exercise of outstanding bravery, and then there was a postscript saying, "The Boers escaped." Of just the same nature is this testimony of Mr. Fairweather's. "Oh," he said, "I did estimate for the Duff Commission savings of $59,740,000. I made it up dollar by dollar. I went to terrific trouble. I had eight technical assistants and thirty clerks and we worked at it day and night for months. We had access to Canadian Pacific offices and the benefit of all their organization. We did it for the Duff Commission on instruction of our chief, and we showed detail by detail, $59,740,000. But really we could not save that sum. It was all 'theoretical,' it was all in my imagination, and I put a rider to my report saying that while these figures are an estimate of savings, they are savings we cannot make." Such is Mr. Fairweather. I think that "theoretical" idea was an afterthought when the plans of himself and Sir Henry Thornton had changed.

I will tell you something more. The same Mr. Fairweather before the same commission estimated $35,000,000 as savings from co-operation, and to this he did not attach any qualification. He did not put in a rider saying, "Those figures are 'theoretical,' they are savings that might be made if we had a docile public and a servile staff." He did not say anything of the kind. They were definite economies which he estimated as capable of being achieved by co-operation. Does anybody question my assertion that they were given to that commission without qualification? If so, I want to ask on what evidence the Duff Commission reported in favour of co-operation. They reported in favour of it, I think, mainly on Mr. Fairweather's evidence. If they did not, no one can explain on what they based their report. There he stood committed to that $35,000,000.

Where does he stand today? Before our committee he whittled his figure down to $10,000,000, and then did not express any belief that we could attain even this lowered level. He told us it was only a guess. To the Duff Commission Mr. Fairweather gave a definite, unqualified estimate of $35,000,000 based on his long study and his reputation; to our committee he estimated $10,000,000, and then told us it was only a guess. This is the character of evidence upon which the hon. leader of this House hangs his report to Parliament!

Now—to revert—we will suppose for the sake of argument that you really can achieve $35,000,000, or whatever you want to make it, by co-operation. Think a moment! What were those objections to unified management? Were we not told that men would be thrown out of work? "They will lose their jobs," said the Senator from Moncton. "Fewer supplies will be bought, and therefore there will be less sales tax. There will be disturbance by closing a station in some town and using another, one hundred feet away. All these calamities will befall our country." "Therefore," declared the senator from Moncton and the senator from Montreal, "let us get these things done by co-operation."

I put a question now to the senator from Montreal: If this same thing is done by co-operation will not men lose their jobs? Will there not be less material bought and therefore less sales tax paid? If two stations are merged into one by co-operation, instead of by unified management, are they not afterwards one rather than two?

Proceed along that line. Save your $10,000,000 or $15,000,000 or $20,000,000, and what have you done? Just as far as you go, every man is out of work who would have been out of work if you had gone the same distance by unified management. Every reduction in purchase is made, every line is abandoned under co-operation, just as under unification. All these things which have been pictured as calamities will happen, if they happen at all, just the same by one plan as by the other. Oh, no, I mistake, they will not all happen. We will still have two head offices everywhere, filled with high salaried men. We will still have our Fairweathers and our Hungerfords, and all attendants around them, but others will be gone. "As long as you proceed by the route of co-operation we are satisfied," say Mr. Fairweather and Mr. Hungerford, though the same things precisely result *pro tanto* as result from unified management. "Ah, but you don't hurt us. Go ahead and produce all these economies, which brought about by single management are calamities, bring them all upon our heads, but don't invade the precincts of the supervising officers. Throw Jim out as a wiper, throw Jack out as a checker, but keep your profane hands off our velvet chairs and we shall be happy and satisfied." Those words summarize their case.

Just think of the position we are in! Go, if you can, the whole route under co-operation which you certainly can go under unified control and you will have thousands of persons employed on pool trains, in unified express and telegraph offices and the like, half of them under charge of one set of head office officials and half under another set, and both engaged in the very same work. Can we even contemplate such fantastic folly? Can we picture such a hydra-headed monster in the realm of business? One long body and two heads wherever we look! So I say, if for a moment you hope to get worthwhile results from co-operation— much more, if you hope, as your report says, to get the distance you would reach under unified management, you will have

brought upon the country everything that you have pictured as
dire calamity if done by unified management, but you maintain
a double-headed institution, two chiefs everywhere, two bosses,
two sets of authorities over the same jobs and the same men.

Surely I have gone far enough to establish that we get results
by singleness of direction. I have shown—I did not need to do
so for those who attended the sittings of our committee—that we
will not get anywhere worth reaching in this other way, and that
the likelihood of our even moving may just as well be forgotten.
I have shown further that if by any chance or miracle we do get
any distance along this road of co-operation, we are vulnerable
to all objections and exposed to all disasters that hon. senators in
their imagination have painted as awaiting us under unified
control.

After all, what are these disasters? One would think to hear
hon. gentlemen talk that, under single management, wholesale
dismissals would be the only route to a reduction of aggregate
personnel. A reduction in totals of the two systems will, of
course, be reached but not by a process of dismissals. Every year
thousands pass out of service by retirement, by illness, by death,
by choice of the worker himself. The simple practice of not
taking on unnecessary men in a united system will bring about
reductions without hardship to any. Not a single employee will
be imperilled. Of this the firmest guarantees were given our
committee and could be without difficulty enforced. There are
tremendous undertakings fast becoming absolutely necessary in
this country, which can usefully absorb our labour and not waste
it as we are doing today.

There is the bugbear of abandonment of lines. It is hard to
order one's thoughts consecutively and make at the same time a
reply to speeches immediately preceding. This subject comes
under the same general argument as everything else, but, to listen
to hon. senators who want to get a vote against unified management and the saving of money, one would think that the whole
problem revolved around abandonment of lines. The hon. leader
of the House said, and I was surprised to hear him, that if we did
not abandon lines we had to take $16,000,000 off the Canadian
Pacific estimate of savings. That is not true. The $16,000,000

item includes far more than mere savings from abandonment. Without abandonment at all we make substantial economies by directing the great bulk of traffic over a single line, leaving only local traffic on the other, and, therefore, permitting a reduced standard of maintenance. Only $7,240,000 of that $75,300,000 is attributable to abandonment of lines. We can get all but $4,000,000 if we do not abandon more than the Canadian National officials themselves admitted to be justified. If we do not shut down a single mile, we reduce our savings by less than 10 per cent.

Some persons think of reduction of mileage as something that can happen only under unified management. Unless we use our heads and common sense, abandonment may be a lot closer in this country than hon. members like to believe. They talk of pioneer branch roads being torn up. No one suggests such a thing. We must keep our pioneer roads in operation on the Canadian Pacific as well as on the Canadian National. Maybe they show a loss on the books but they feed trunk lines. Those pioneer roads are needed by people who have settled along them. But if we do not do something to bring rationalized business methods into our railways, we may have to close down those very branches. What is proposed by unified management is not abandonment of lines that serve the farmer, the miner and the fisherman, but abandonment of duplicate mileage, lines which double over each other and are still operated because they belong to competing concerns. The leader of the House says the Canadian National is making money out of one or more of these duplicating roads. So it is. But does that prove they are any good? Suppose we have two lines paralleling one another for five hundred miles, one Canadian Pacific and one Canadian National; it may be that both are making money; they may be each fed by branches which show a loss; we no more need both of those five hundred mile stretches of rail than a coach needs a fifth wheel. If we are not ready to make that saving, if we keep on throwing money down the drain and doing no good to anybody, then we may later have to close lines we really need. We will bring our railways into a position where they cannot afford to operate most useful branches in sparsely settled country.

If we want to save for the pioneer a road which reaches him we must make our saving in more thickly populated areas where duplicate services are crowding on top of each other, where there is unproductive expenditure of energy and capital.

I have not any doubt at all that some day economic law is going to compel efficient management of our railways and discontinuance of waste. When the day will come no one knows, but that it is sure to come there is no question. I hope it arrives at a time when substantial private interest still remains.

These words are not spoken with pride. I have never been partial to government operation, but was convinced years ago, and rightly, that we had come to a point where, as mortgagees of many railways in distress, we had to take them over and try our hand. We had no other course open to us. I must not now be drawn into a long discussion of that dilemma. We were mortgagees and creditors, or we had guaranteed their bonds. We might have wiped these securities out by a receivership, but if we did so we wiped out ourselves as creditors and mortgagees.

I have since seen government operation in several spheres, and my apprehensions have become convictions. There are sometimes advantages of unification even under government operation. We have these in the Hydro Electric System of Ontario. But do not let anyone think the benefits of that great system are due to government operation. They are not. Much duplication of services and consequent capital waste and operational waste are avoided because it is a united system—because of that and nothing else. I have had enough of government operation. My hon. friend from Vancouver (Hon. Mr. McRae) says he has not given up his faith. He says the state can find men capable of managing a business of this magnitude in an efficient manner. I ask the hon. senator if he thinks our business is managed that way now.

Hon. Mr. McRae: No.

Right Hon. Mr. Meighen: No, and the hon. gentleman does not need to look very far back to be sure he is right. He says, "Put these men by legislation where they cannot be interfered with." I would remind him that even so, all that needs to be done is to pass a new Act, repeal the old one, and they are gone.

Another way is to ignore the law. Do not tell us any Board can efficiently operate a railway with ministers of the Crown directing its policies from by-election platforms. Do not tell us that a directorate is running the Canadian National Railways. It is not. "Vote for our candidate," say cabinet ministers from the hustings in Montreal, "and we will climb into that hole on Dorchester street and rear upon it a palace." A few months afterwards the Canadian National Directors meet together and say to themselves, "We have heard our master's voice," and dutifully they pass a resolution. Business operation of railways! Says a minister of the Crown: "Do not bother about the Canadian National-Canadian Pacific Act calling for co-operative terminals, pool trains and the like; do not bother your heads about those things. We need to win this election. Keep us in power and we will borrow millions on public credit and out of holes we will make gigantic and duplicating stations, no matter what that Act may say."

Talk of business operation by government! I could point right at this hour to some things which would very quickly erase such a conception from one's mind. Wipe away, as we have done, all capital contributed in any way except as investment for the purpose of revenue. That done, last year the C.N.R. did not even earn taxes or rent of equipment, though our leader's report says it did. His report says that all it went behind was interest on money invested by the public. That is not so. Outside of such interest altogether, it went behind in seven figures. In addition it earned not a cent on money put in by the public for railway purposes. Do you tell me a road which could not earn a nickel upon that basis in the year 1938 is a well-managed road?

Some seem to think it better to endure all these things than to have monopoly. The bugbear of monopoly surely covers a multitude of sins. I know many people are fearful of it but I do not think it is the duty of hon. senators to endeavour to inject into the public mind something that does not appertain to railway monopoly at all. Surely it is our part to lure on to brighter, saner worlds, and lead the way. Who is afraid of a public utility monopoly controlled—though not operated—by the country? We are told competition will be gone. When the Canadian

National-Canadian Pacific Bill was before us the hon. gentleman (Hon. Mr. Dandurand) was not afraid of the disappearance of competition. What, indeed, have we to fear? Service has to be up to Transportation Commission requirements; fares and rates must be dictated there; every form of service to the people— railway stations, trains, sidings, crossings—is under supervision of the nation through its commission. Monopoly in transportation? We know that vast areas of the country never have had anything else, and they have not suffered. People there get, in general, just as good treatment as people who are situated in the midst of duplication.

But are there not rival services grasping for almost every type of business a railway lives upon? Old competition has been reinforced. New competition has arrived in the form of buses, trucks, motor cars and air lines—a keener competition in many ways than that of olden times. Never fear that any method of transport will be without rivals long. Even water competition is more severe than ever before.

The leader of the Government tells us that everything was fine at the end of 1939, that all we need is more population. "Give us four million more," he says, "and all will be well." Sometimes in his speech he forgot the evidence; once he even forgot his own report now under debate. What will he find if he reads these two productions? He will find that the door of hope which he opened in his speech is closed in his report. He told us there that in 1923, when we had nine million people in Canada, our railways had far more business than in 1937 when we had a population of eleven million. Though our population had gone up by two millions, the business of the railways had gone down 26 per cent. If he will consult statistics for 1938 he will find the population had gone up since 1923 a great deal over two millions, and the business of the railways had gone down 30 per cent. Passenger business had fallen by at least 50 per cent. Now, if an increase of population of over two millions meant a 30 per cent reduction in business, how does he reason that an increase of four millions will mean a 40 per cent increase in business? The hon. leader, as I have said, not only forgot the evidence, but forgot his own report.

Lastly, he says he is afraid of unified management because if it is to be adopted, the next thing we know we shall have amalgamation of the two roads, under Government ownership. I should like to look into that for a moment, just to see the true nature of this bogey and how to dispel it. We have taken over roads before, I admit. We took over the Canadian National, the Grand Trunk, and operation of that precious conception, the Grand Trunk Pacific. Why did we do so? In all cases, because the roads were bankrupt, or nearly bankrupt, without funds to continue, and we had to operate them. Does anyone suggest we took them over for any other reason?

I am not going to predict that the Canadian Pacific will go downhill, but I ask hon. members seriously to pause and reflect. In the past some things have happened which we did not expect would happen. I know the Canadian Pacific is a well-managed system, that its name is almost synonymous throughout the world with the name of Canada, and that it has been the major contributor to our country's greatness. But in this world of men nothing is so well managed that, if compelled to operate on a wholly unsound basis, will not be in danger of insolvency. Just acquiesce in the continuance of policies which mean unnecessary waste to the Canadian Pacific, to the Canadian National and to the whole country, and you help to imperil not only the nation but its institutions large and small. That danger can be avoided by taking sound courses, which reduce costs without curtailing services. Get rid of duplication, stop forever all drains on our resources that can be stopped—and they run to scores of millions year by year—do this and you will strengthen the overall economy of Canada, give new life to her great enterprises and thus ward off the scourge of Government ownership and operation.

There are economic laws which no man or group of men and no country has ever successfully defied. We may impede their operation, if we are foolish enough, but we shall have to pay the price; we may ignore them, if we are stupid enough, but sooner or later they will grind us to powder. It may be politically important for some to watch complacently the tragic spectacle of unconscionable waste and resultant deterioration of public morale, to seek acclaim by echoing moods of the populace, and to forge their own opinions in the light of what they think the public want. But, seriously, that is not the duty of the Senate of Canada! Surely if we have one function it is to point the way and try to advance public thinking toward settlement of business problems on business lines. What we have in front of us is nothing but a business problem. If the Senate is to disregard its duty—and I say with reluctance that this session we have made in that respect a more sorry performance than ever before—then let us retire from these seats of emolument and dignity, and let us go back among the masses of our people, whom we are always ready to load with burdens and always eager to flatter and to cheer, but whom we fail to serve.

DECLARATION OF WAR, 1939

Delivered in the Senate on September 9, 1939, *on Motion for approval of a declaration of war against Germany.*

OPPRESSED AS I FEEL, and as indeed everyone must feel, with emotions which grow out of the gravity of this time, I would very gladly follow the example of the mover of this resolution (Hon. Mr. Lambert) and of the seconder (Hon. Mr. Prévost), and speak with unwonted brevity, thus allowing action more quickly to follow our words. It is my hope, though, and I shall try, to contribute something that may clarify—I do not dare to say inspire—public thought and promote unity among our people. Let me premise a few sentences before entering upon what chiefly I have to say.

No one would for a moment think that any motive can animate me, or for that matter anyone else in this House, except a yearning to assist our country. In whatever I say as to the Government and its head I am going to keep in mind that this Government is the Government of Canada and represents us all, and that the Prime Minister is no longer to be regarded as the head of a political party; he is the head of our Dominion. In him must be typified the honour, the dignity, the sense of duty of our whole nation. It is he who must interpret now our interest and our duty and show us that they are one.

It must not be presumed, because I do not make issue of certain subjects now, that I am not thinking something else might be done which is not being done. There are matters on which many of us would act differently, but we must realize that a united front at the present time, and indeed throughout, if it can be secured, may on balance be of more importance than even the prevailing of a better line of conduct. Therefore, I

346

defer controversy to the utmost and seek that my words shall have the effect only of encouragement, of assistance, and of rallying to our cause the devotion of our people.

There has been confusion in the public mind and in the mind of many of us up to now as to just what this Government purposes, some confusion and wonderment as to whether we really have been at war or not. On the latter phase the statement of the honourable leader of the House (Hon. Mr. Dandurand), and the corresponding statement of the leader of the Government in the other Chamber, have set all our thinking at rest. It has been the commitment of the present Administration, as I have always understood it, that Parliament would determine what should be our participation in any war. Apparently this has now been interpreted in somewhat extended form as meaning that Parliament has to determine whether we are at war or not. I do not think any good has come from this special way of advertising far and wide the status of Parliament. Parliament always decides anything within the competence and function of Canada to decide. No other body and no one else can do so. I have never felt that it has been within the single competence of Canada to decide as one isolated fact whether we are at war. I do not feel so now. Either we are part of the British Empire or we are not; and we know we are a part. We cannot as such be at peace while the head of this Empire is at war. The pronouncement of Laurier[1] on this subject stands, and will ever stand. We could, without physical restraint, refuse to be at war, by moving outside the circumference of the Empire; I say without physical external restraint, for Great Britain would bring none to bear. But Canada as a member of the British Commonwealth cannot refuse.

We may, of course, and must, decide what shall be the measure of our participation. We always have so decided, and always on the recommendation of our Government, exactly as we are doing today. The only difference has been this, that the confusion, which has already done some harm, comes because of the present artificial and circuitous device. Further, this circumnavigation has prevented us taking our stand at a time when the

[1] Hansard, Aug. 9, 1914, (Special Session) p. 9: "When Great Britain is at war we are at war."

decisive taking of a stand might conceivably have been of some value in preventing war itself. It is by no means impossible that if we could have declared ourselves two weeks ago as we knew we ultimately would—subject, if you will, to confirmation by Parliament when it would meet—then, before the final die was cast by the arbiter of Germany, our declaration might have had some effect in holding back his hand from that awful throw. I did what I could to have this Government take such a course several days before Poland was invaded. My efforts failed.

We now have been at war for some time. We are to make a declaration on the passing of this resolution. The Orders in Council laid on our table two days ago proclaimed distinctly, in many places, a state of war. I have perused them. In Order in Council after Order in Council reference is made to the enemy; and provision is made for internment of enemy aliens. Unless we were at war when these Orders were passed, there could have been no enemy, and therefore no enemy aliens. No wonder the public mind has impatiently sought the light!

I close these remarks by saying this: It is unfortunate that Canada stands in the position of having contributed to the prevention of this catastrophe precisely nothing.

Now, what confronts us? On the merits of our case there is, I am confident, no difference of opinion. Let us hope it will not later be said that we have been dragged into this conflict to serve selfish purposes of Britain or of any other country. For myself, I am not a critic of the course the British Government has taken throughout these later months. There are some who are critics. I may be wrong—I have been wrong. This thing I know, that all through these years the door of British councils has been open. Our Canadian Government has been in a position, and probably has been invited, to makes its wishes known, to give its advice. How far, if at all, it has availed itself of that privilege, I know not. It is probable Canada has said nothing. But after communication to us of facts and proposals as they evolved from day to day and month to month, after being given every opportunity to make suggestion or criticism, of which no advantage has been taken, then, even though there be those who think something else might have been done, who criticize a Berchtesgaden conference or a Munich conference, such persons cannot possibly be heard today against united action in our land.

We have witnessed a long struggle for peace, a struggle all could follow, a struggle carrying in its train impatience and internal attacks, involving indeed passing humiliation. We have seen the prestige of governments deteriorate because of exhaustion of every possible effort to restore the reign of common sense and save the world from torture. We have now to admit that all this has failed. At such a pass, surely there are none so perverse that they cannot see the reality and magnitude of the issue. Germany claims that the Treaty of Versailles was severe. Oh, yes, it was. You cannot fight a great war and look forward to a soft or even generous peace. You can look back and wish there had been one. I do not know whether we should have been better off if the Treaty had been more generous. There are those, and they have some vindication today, who, in the light of what has happened since, believe that the Treaty, and still more its aftermath, erred on the side of confidence in Germany, on the side of liberality. But whatever may be said about the Treaty, is there among reasonable people who believe in right, who believe in justice innate and equal between man and man, not just in proportion to individual strength, who value those achievements of civilization which alone make life worth while, is there a single being who can be blind to the issue which faces us now? Germany, or rather the man who stands in sole command of that country, said, "We must have room to live," and in order to have room to live he invaded Poland, where density of population is double what it is in Germany itself. He gave his word, on the honour of his country, first to Austria, then to Czechoslovakia, then to Poland, then to Britain, and at a moment opportune for himself he flung every covenant to the winds and declared for the rule of blood and iron.

If the principles of Hitler are to prevail—and they will prevail unless the Allies win—then the world as we have known it will have passed away. It will mean not just another dynasty in Europe; it will mean another and a cruel dispensation for all humanity. It will mean that there is nothing left us worth living for.

I come to Canada's duty, and to the means by which that duty is to be discharged, as revealed by the Government. There are some things contained in the Speech from the Throne and in what has been said by the Prime Minister, particularly in his remarks of Sunday, the first of September, for which I am grateful. The Prime Minister said, "There is no home in Canada, no family and no individual whose fortunes and whose freedom are not bound up in the present struggle." Those words express no platitude; they are meaningful and true, as true as ever fell from human lips. Learn well those words. Then your own minds will tell you the duty that flows therefrom, what rational beings must do so that this struggle may end in the only way which will mean either liberty or life to us all.

The Prime Minister also said that we take our stand "for effective co-operation by Britain's side." I am grateful for those words. That decision flows from the first premise. Let us remember that declaration, and let us stand as one people to make certain that it is translated into deeds, and translated with no avoidable delay, and that no guilt falls upon Canada in respect of our part in this struggle.

There is one misapprehension—I will call it that—with which I should like to occupy the attention of honourable members for a moment. Many a time and oft we have heard the assertion that our duty is to defend our own land. While it is true that this is our primary duty, I rather regret the prominence that assertion had in the speech delivered elsewhere yesterday, and I refer to it now only to make certain that it is not misunderstood. That our first duty is to do all we can to render our own people and country secure from attack by air, and from internal disturbance, there is no question. What I want to be emphatic about, as I have been many a time before, is this: that when we shall have done everything we can to protect ourselves in that isolated sense, we shall not have provided for the safety of Canada. We shall have carried out only certain local duties which, if we were not here to perform them, would have had to be performed by an expedition to our shores from the strength of Britain. But security as so conceived is merely local and temporary. That we must, in and around our national home, do, and do well, military, naval and air policing, I quite agree, and agree as earnestly as can the most ardent advocate of Canadian defence. But, I ask honourable members, what becomes of that form of protection if on crucial battlefields the arms of the Allies fail? Will Canada then be secure? The few provisions we have already made for our own defence, and any others that we may build up with our own strength, will they mean our survival? No. We shall know nothing but perdition unless this new World War is won.

I read with pleasure an address delivered by the Minister of Justice in the other House on 31st March last. He appreciated rightly the actual state of our defences and the impossibility of providing anything in the way of ultimate protection by efforts of Canadians alone. He said we must look elsewhere for that, as we have ever looked. Against, attack, he said, we can but do our best till help comes. And then he asked: "If we depend on others to help us, how can we refuse to those others, when in need in a common cause, the help of Canada?" We cannot. If there is a mind which can deny the immensity and certainty of that truth, I cannot understand that mind. Are we defending ourselves now? Well, we try, but we are not equipped. The present is not the time to criticize our incapacity. But while we sit in these seats this afternoon, warships of Britain line the shores of our Dominion. The security of our coast cities today rests under the wing of the British Navy.

AN HON. SENATOR: Hear, hear.

RIGHT HON. MR. MEIGHEN: This is pertinent only because the truth is pertinent, and will always be pertinent, that the big, decisive battlefield is not here; it is over there. German submarines along the Atlantic coast may be reduced or destroyed; that does not make Canada secure save for the moment. The fate of our country hangs suspended on the success or defeat of the arms of Britain and France. Keep ever before you those words of the Minister of Justice: "Shame on the land whose people say, 'We accept our defence from you—our survival depends on you—but if you look to us for help in the most critical struggle that ever the world has seen, you look in vain.' "

Are there those who, abandoning all sense of obligation—I had almost said, all sense of decency and honour—would say,

"Even though those nations fall, we can scuttle from under their wing to the wing of another"? One must be very careful in the words one employs on this phase of the present issue. Another nation to the south has its rights, as sacred as our own. It is judge of its own obligations, its honour and its interests. It is a great, friendly and powerful Republic. What its course will be I will not venture to predict, but I will venture this: it is only human nature that the course of that great country will not be uninfluenced by the conduct of this Dominion, its nearest neighbour and friend.

AN HON. SENATOR: Hear, hear.

RIGHT HON. MR. MEIGHEN: But can we look forward, even if we are of a spirit to do so, to such an alternative? Let us get together and seriously think. I have heard it said that the duty of the United States, in fact the duty of this continent, is to keep the war away from us so that we may preserve the treasures of civilization. Yes, I should like the war to be kept away from us; it is very, very important that it should be; but does anyone know any means of keeping the war away from us except to defeat those who, if they are not defeated, will bring the war over here—right to our doors and our homes?

AN HON. SENATOR: Hear, hear.

RIGHT HON. MR. MEIGHEN: There is a way to save the treasures of civilization. So far as my mind can carry me, there is only one way, and that is to defeat the destroyers of civilization.

SOME HON. SENATORS: Hear, hear.

RIGHT HON. MR. MEIGHEN: That is, to see that Britain and France come triumphant through this struggle.

If it is permissible for us to peer into the future, let us inquire just what the situation would be in the event we must provide against, which we abhor even to put in words, and which we definitely do not believe will occur—a defeat of the Allied Powers. I read somewhere just a few days ago an article—I will not permit myself to mention the writer's name, but he is a man of eminence—giving expression to the sentiment that he could contemplate without despair the destruction of Great Britain and of France. The efforts of the dictators, he said, in bringing about such destruction would so exhaust them that this continent would be safe for a quarter of a century. Meditating on that pronouncement, I do not know whether one should express astonishment at its callousness or at its stupidity. Germany, defeated in the last war, beaten to her knees, stripped of her arms, drained in large measure of her life blood, rose from that prostration and in ten years was again a threat to civilization. Will anyone tell us that Germany as she may be tomorrow, with subservient allies standing at her side, Germany triumphant, Germany with the resources of her victims at her feet, able to levy on the most virile and richest people the world has ever known, would not at once be a menace? Can anybody imagine this war ending with her triumph and there remaining a single Atlantic island now in the possession of Britain or France which would not be a German possession? I do not mention Canada. You can judge of the fate of this country just as you like. Leave it aside for the moment. Just picture German occupation of the West Indies, the Cape Verdes—all those Atlantic territories and bases of air warfare. Do you tell me: "We will not permit their occupation by another power?" I know the Republic to the south cannot countenance their occupation by another power: the policy of that country from its birth has been to deny the right of cession of those islands and to regard the taking of them by another power as a hostile act. And that country in such policy has been absolutely right. Therefore—and this is all I ask you to accept—imagine, if you will, a day when the massed might of Germany crushes to the ground the forces of Britain and of France: then, not in twenty-five years, nor in twenty-five days, but in an instant, the battle must be taken up by the arms of this continent. The burden then will be as much on the backs of Canadians as on the backs of citizens of the United States. If we are still a free people when that awful hour strikes, we shall know then, certainly, what a burden is; we shall know what a death struggle is. We could not get within two thousand miles of the homeland of our foe, and he would be at our doors. All I beg of you to believe is this: The tremendous task we stand in front of now is simple in comparison with what would face us if this issue between the forces of Germany and the forces of Britain and France should end in disaster for those who are at once our allies and our kin.

Let us not lull ourselves into false reasoning by any theory that duty in this crisis arises out of sentiment alone. Why, duty today arises out of our will to live. If we have a will to live and to preserve the reasons why we want to live, then we must build everything behind those great powers who have defended for generations the citadel of liberty and have led the world along the path of light. If the dark day comes—I mean the day of final darkness—then everything we have preached and everything we have debated will be forgotten, and the state of our minds and the anguish of our souls will be a thousand times more bitter than what possesses and distresses us now. If we do not win this war on the banks of the Rhine, we shall have to fight it on the banks of the St. Lawrence and the Mississippi. We may far better take advantage of the light we have and learn the lesson which that light reveals. We can then get the meaning of this thing into the minds of all our people, of all who are willing to think.

I say no more. But as we square ourselves for the task ahead, as we stand erect and commence the long journey through troubles, through trials, through tragedies, through blood, let us not forget that others of our lineage for the same great purpose have trodden this path before. Let us remember every hour the two great nations from which we spring, the two great nations who today stand at the side of Poland, the two great nations who have set out together to preserve the treasures of civilization in the only way they can be preserved, to save the altars of liberty, the altars of religion, the altars of democracy, from destruction by pagan force. To the heritage we derive from those heroic peoples let us all be true.

HELP TO FINLAND

After invasion of Poland by Germany, Soviet Russia, which had previously concluded a pact with Hitler, made demands on Finland, and to enforce them, launched an invasion of that tiny country. On January 4, 1940, at a mass meeting in Massey Hall, Toronto, called in furtherance of a programme of aid from Canada to the Finnish people, the following speech was made:

WE HAVE LIVED FOR a quarter of a century in a troubled, anguishing and revolutionizing world. The very weight of events tries and strains the sustaining power of the human will; their swift succession bewilders the mind. Never was tension greater in every quarter of the globe; never was the maze of tremendous problems more baffling than it is right now. Even at such a time there is one spot in this war-torn planet which commands the attention of mankind. That spot is Finland. There everything that appeals to sympathy, everything that appeals to justice, everything that appeals to decency between man and man cries out to all nations and all continents.

Nobody anywhere, no matter where he lives, in this country or any other, can turn his eyes coldly away from the Finnish people and call himself a man.

Let us look facts in the face and get a picture of what is going on.

There is Finland with less than four million people working hard on a narrow stretch of land reaching up to the top of Europe. It is the most northern of civilized countries; and well can we call it civilized. It has a system of government not only thoroughly democratic, but thoroughly efficient. Every man and woman over the age of twenty-five has a vote by secret ballot. Even its President is elected directly by the people. Its

355

Cabinet is responsible to Parliament and must resign if defeated in Parliament. As many as eight hundred thousand of the country's small population are members of one or more of its co-operative societies. These societies run themselves under government supervision, and have proven a success.

Not less than ninety-nine per cent. of the people of Finland can read and write. Where is there another country which can claim that record? Every youth between the ages of seventeen and twenty-one must devote himself for approximately a year to military training. A strong civil guard on a purely voluntary basis has reached large dimensions and stands ready to defend the nation. Indeed, at this very hour, this civil guard is at the front in the brilliant discharge of its duty.

Their hospitals and social services cannot be surpassed by even the most advanced countries. Legislation affecting working men is thoroughgoing in its provisions, fair, sane and effective. There can be no exploitation of labour. The standard of living is good. Highways and railways are modern and well-managed. Railways are owned by the State, and though rates are low, have annual dividends instead of deficits.

One restriction on personal liberty might be mentioned. When in 1917 the Bolshevists of Russia attacked Finland and were defeated, that little country decided it had seen enough of Bolshevism, and, ever since, Communist propaganda has been forbidden. In the eyes of the Finnish people Communism means fealty to another country, and, therefore, means treason. Whatever Communists were in Finland after the defeat of the Bolshevists, emigrated from that country, and some came to this continent. There are none left in Finland, as the present invaders have discovered to their cost. These heroic northerners have taught us that patriots are not made of Communists.

We can now envisage this industrious, intelligent, peace-loving people—farmers, lumbermen, manufacturers, following with credit every available pursuit of commerce and the arts—of unsullied behaviour toward the rest of mankind, guilty, at no time in their long history, of assault, aggression or dishonour against any member of the family of nations.

Never can it be said that the Finns are an inferior, thriftless, lazy race, holding back in barrenness the resources of nature, and, therefore, to be removed on biological excuse to make way for better men. On the contrary, with the most enlightened and progressive forces of civilization they march abreast.

The puny plea of racial affinity to justify assimilation breaks down as well. There is no common origin between Slav and Finn.

If ever native people had a right to the possession of their own land, surely those people are the Finns. Even before they could claim to be a nation, which was about 800 A.D., their ancestors had roamed and toiled for three hundred years through that northern wilderness—lone, scattered tenants of space and night. From 800 on, when they could be said to be a country, they have struggled for independence, prized and cherished that independence when they had it, but have never attacked anyone else except under compulsion of some overlord. They have minded their own business, left others alone, and hungered only for the land of their fathers.

Independence, which meant everything to them, was lost to Sweden over two hundred years ago, and they remained under rule of that country until conquered by Russia in 1808. About a quarter of a million Swedes are still numbered in their population, and no greater tribute can be paid to the fairness of any government than to say, as can be truthfully said, that these two hundred and fifty thousand citizens of alien blood are to this day unswervingly loyal to the Finnish nation. After the first Great War its independence was restored.

Finlanders have an appeal to the Anglo-Saxon. They were Christianized long centuries ago under leadership of English bishops, and the name of one comes down to us as their patron saint—Saint Henry. Something else should be remembered, too: When Finland was torn from Sweden and annexed to Russia in 1808, the thing was done at the instigation of Napoleon, who sought in that way revenge on the Swedes for refusing to join him in an invasion of England.

It is against such a people that a wrong has been done as black as ever was perpetrated, the horror of which shocks the world.

Russia with its one hundred and seventy millions claims to

fear the fangs of imperialism, and calls belligerently for concessions. Just what imperialism is feared no rational mind can
imagine. Intellectual perversity can sink to dismal depths, but
when it tells us that Russia is in danger from Finland, or through
Finland, it is in the sphere of impudent effrontery. What the
Soviet has demanded from the Finns is just the same as if the
United States, with drawn sword, were to demand from Canada
the Province of Nova Scotia, the Western slope of the Rockies,
and an airport on Hudson Bay. Common sense throws their
miserable excuses back in their faces, and brands the Soviet
despots as brutal bullies without courage or conscience. They
swoop down with their one hundred and seventy million on a
nation which has scarcely four million. They bomb women and
children, hospitals, houses and churches. They have added a
ghastly and shameful chapter to the long story of man's in-
humanity to man.

But if the Russian Goliath has brought forth nothing but
universal groans, the Finnish David has earned universal cheers.
His gallant defence electrifies every continent. If ever a nation
by sheer bravery, skill, resource and tenacity can be said to command the admiration and active sympathy of all others, surely
that nation is Finland. Those best worthy of help are those who
help themselves. When the Finnish army defeated the Russian
Bolshevists in 1917, it was under the command of Mannerheim,
and the same man now leads his indomitable soldiers against the
Soviet octopus.

France plants herself again—for a third time in a few short
years—in the path of a conquering Germany. Britain stands at
her side, Britain the mainstay of civilization, her strong arms
reaching into every sea, her far-flung but ever-gathering might in
grips at the throat of the foe. These countries await with calm
courage the most terrible onslaught ever seen in this world. In
solemn reality these two nations are in a struggle of life or death.
But even in that plight, the heart of France and the heart of
Britain beat in warm sympathy with Finland, and their people
do not stop at sympathy. Their hands reach out across the Baltic
and they give all the help they can.

What then must be the duty of others who feel the same way,

and whose burdens are not so great? Can there be now or ever a theatre of action before human eyes where right is more nobly right and wrong more nakedly wrong? Through the snows and ice of that stricken country, through the wreckage of their homes, their churches, their Capital, the manhood of Finland has marched right up to a million guns turned on them by the legions of Russia. Had they marched to defeat it would have been glorious—but, wonder of wonders, they have marched already far toward victory. They have achieved something as nearly a miracle as is recorded in the history of war. We Canadians are proud to join with our fellowmen and women the world over in sending a helping cheer and cheering help to as brave an army as ever took the field, in warming the hearts and healing the wounds of suffering civilians, and in insuring as best we can that, under the guidance of Him who stands within the shadow, their righteous cause may struggle through from the scaffold to the throne.

CANADA'S WAR EFFORT

Delivered in the Senate, Ottawa, May 21, 1940, on the opening of Parliament after the General Election of that year. About this time the war outlook was at its blackest.

THE RESPONSIBILITY WHICH ONE FEELS in discharging his duties as a member of the House, in time of crisis, is very present to my mind now. Honourable members will one and all agree that they have never in the past addressed themselves to their work as parliamentarians with a greater sense of difficulty, with the pall of responsibility hanging over them more heavily, than in these dark and near-tragic hours. But we must all remember that reverse, to the races from which we are so proud to spring, is usually only a starting point at which their tenacity, courage and resiliency so inspiring over the long years, come with new and abounding vigour into play. Never can reverses daunt the British or the French, for the cause in which they are now engaged is a matter of death or victory and these people have never yet bowed to an oppressor.

Here in Canada it is no pleasure to rise for the purpose of calling attention to what I believe to have been grave errors on the part of this Dominion. There are those who will say, "You should get behind and cheer in a critical moment; you should not find fault. But the time has come when we must criticize, when we cannot hope to get what is vital—momentously vital—unless we do.

Reference has been made to the recent election. I do not know of any event in our history less creditable to our country than the late election. When I heard from His Excellency in this House a sentence which dissolved Parliament the moment we met, I could scarcely believe my ears. I had never thought it possible that any Prime Minister would put into the mouth of the Representative of the Throne words carrying such insolence and rudeness to the Parliament of this Dominion. That dissolution was a breach of a solemn pledge given Parliament by the Prime Minister in the session of last fall—the pledge of another session before an election would be held—an open, defiant, callous breach. To tell members of both Houses, immediately they set foot in these halls, that they had been brought here from the ends of Canada only to be sent home was a crude and shocking insult. Very discreetly, no opportunity was allowed for protest or denunciation. The practical effects are worse, if possible, than the character of the deed.

An election on a party basis in war time can be nothing but a catastrophe, no matter how it results. I well recall that when the last war broke out—it was not so near the end of the term of the then Government, but still it was fairly near—the cry went forth throughout Canada that there must be no party election, and the very purple was torn from the clouds by the Liberal press, one and all declaring such an act would be the vilest of our history, because both sides supported the war, and on that one and only issue both sides agreed. The same demand rang forth after the usual term of Parliament was ended, and so long as there was anything like unanimity on the war issue. Only when it became essential in the view of one side and of many on the other that a very drastic and momentous step should be taken, in which all the other side could not concur, was there an election. Even then it was not on a party basis. The party element was removed to the utmost within the power of men to remove it.

What has occurred now? While both sides were one behind the war, while the voice of every man on either side of either House supported the strongest possible prosecution of the war, our Prime Minister, suddenly and with callous affront, dissolved Parliament and called upon the people to defeat supporters of the war because they had not proper party labels on their backs. That action split the war unity of this Dominion down the centre; that action paralyzed and benumbed this country when under shadow of the darkest prospect it had ever known. The

Prime Minister of Canada has had a long and distinguished career, but to the last page of our history that arrogant and utterly needless dissolution will blight and stain his name.

SOME HON. SENATORS: Hear, hear.

RIGHT HON. MR. MEIGHEN: I want to make some very earnest references to the progress of our war effort. If experience is of value, I should know something of the difficulties of conducting an overseas conflict. There are those who think regiments fall from the clouds; there are some who think it takes only ardent desire to get more things done in quicker time; that it matters little whether we are prepared or not; that if we are just eager enough we can do everything in a moment. These miracles cannot be performed. Even with the utmost unanimity in our country it would have been hard indeed to satisfy the nation with a war effort. Unanimity could have been secured. Parliament had lasted nearly five years, and had I been in the place of the Prime Minister I would have reorganized my Government on the widest possible basis at once. I would have had represented in it every considerable element of this Dominion which was behind the conflict, and with that Government I would have gone to the country for a mandate and would have endorsed for re-election every member of the Commons who supported the war.

HON. MR. DANDURAND: We had a unanimous mandate.

RIGHT HON. MR. MEIGHEN: Whatever you had you split the Dominion to get it.

HON. MR. DANDURAND: We did not.

RIGHT HON. MR. MEIGHEN: You proclaimed everywhere that the important thing was the triumph of the Liberal party.

HON. MR. DANDURAND: The country was split in two in 1917 by my right honourable friend.

RIGHT HON. MR. MEIGHEN: I have indicated how the best results could have been obtained. True, even had the best results been obtained, it would have been difficult to satisfy everybody that all possible was being done. If, however, the Government had gone about it in a spirit of goodwill, all of us should have had sympathy with them under criticism.

Let us inquire now into what has been achieved. We have

been nearly nine months at war. True, we have spent vast sums of money, and we contemplate spending millions more. What I have witnessed most until very recent days has been the total or almost total absence of a war spirit in this Dominion. There is no honourable member who has not noted it. Many have noted it with despair. I have already stated one of the main causes for this situation, and I am going to state what is another equally important cause. Unless a war spirit permeates this country, our utmost strength cannot be exerted.

The second important cause is that the onset of the conflict found our people without a proper appreciation of their Empire relationship. They had been taught for years, not that our safety rested on British strength, not that we could best insure our own security by adding to that strength, not that there was such a thing as the common defence of this Empire, but that our defence was something separate and apart, and that our money should be spent for a defence separate and apart. Such teaching was fathered and prosecuted down the years by none more zealously than by the present leaders of both Houses of Parliament. So, when this war began, our country faced the great conflict without any vivid recognition of what in reality it depended upon for its life, and under delusion of a false security or hope of security.

I recall, only a year ago, in the 1939 session, listening to a Speech from the Throne which referred to expenditure for defence of Canada, which asked support of Parliament for that expenditure, but made no reference at all to that cardinal feature of our true defence which overwhelms all other features:—the fact that our security necessarily rests upon the might of Britain and, therefore, upon the basis of our co-operation with Britain and the other Dominions. There was no mention at all of co-operation, and on that ground I took exception to the Address. But I was ridiculed by the honourable leader of this House (Hon. Mr. Dandurand). I was told by him that they could not co-operate with a wobbling British Government, and he referred to a difference of opinion about some option clause in the League of Nations covenant—as if that had anything to do with the subject of co-operation in defence!

In upholding such a view the leader of this House has not been alone. Time and again the leader of the other House (Right Hon. Mr. King) has been a party to persuading Canadians that co-operation in defence with the Empire was not a principal, or any necessary, feature of our policy, and when estimates have been brought down he has been at pains to explain that all monies to be voted were for Canadian defence, not Empire defence—at pains to banish from the minds of our people any thought of such thing as common Empire defence.

Anyone who wishes to do so can examine and check the Prime Minister's statements and explanations on those estimates and their purpose. I should like, with the consent of the House, to read briefly from what were almost his latest words upon this subject. Speaking in the House of Commons on March 30, 1939, after calling attention to the great need in Canada for roads, and to our heavy burden of debt, and so forth, he followed with this language:

> There is no great margin of realizable wealth for this purpose; we must, to a greater or less extent, choose between keeping our own house in order, and trying to save Europe and Asia.

How well designed those words were to indicate where, as we all know now, our defence really lies!

HON. MR. DANDURAND: Not our defence.

RIGHT HON. MR. MEIGHEN: The Prime Minister went on to say:

> The idea that every twenty years this country should automatically and as a matter of course take part in a war overseas for democracy or self-determination of other small nations, that a country which has all it can do to run itself, should feel called upon to save, periodically, a continent that cannot run itself, and to these ends risk the lives of its people, risk bankruptcy and political disunion, seems to many a nightmare and sheer madness.

There is no difficulty in discerning the purpose, certainly no difficulty in ascertaining the effect, of language of that character on the Canadian people. Such language was not designed to bring us to the point where if danger, inescapable danger, loomed in front, we should be ready and able to help in an effective defence. The consequent reaction was inevitably in the other direction. Throughout this country dissemination of such doctrine has been encouraged by this Government for years, and nowhere has it been given greater encouragement than under the aegis of the Canadian Broadcasting Corporation. A public man in Canada could not broadcast loyal, sensible words favouring common defence for us all, unless someone else, probably a semi-pink professor, was subsidized to traduce Great Britain, to tell the people of Canada that Britain was a traitor to democracy, and that the United States would soon be taking over leadership of democracy throughout the world.

Hon. Mr. Dandurand: Where did my right honourable friend get that?

Right Hon. Mr. Meighen: I listened and heard it. One speaker uttered the last sentiments which I just recited and I wrote the Broadcasting Corporation to find out about it, and was told that he had been paid. The rest of what I have indicated was heard from other radio speakers. This kind of thing has been going on unchecked; certainly in no way resisted or rebuked by Government members. Two or three editors of this country have done their noble much to the same end. In consequence we faced this war as an Empire country divided and benumbed, and in no spirit to rise immediately to the common cause. These practices have prevailed for a long time and one of the consequences is that our war effort as yet has not been anything to be proud of. It is only lately, under pressure and impact of terrific events, that the people of Canada have risen to a sight of the reality. Now they are very much dissatisfied, now they are restive, now they are for the most part determined. Had those in authority long ago made plain to them their mortal concern in the British Empire from the standpoint of defence, helped them to develop that spirit, we should have from the very beginning exhibited a unity and alacrity which would have made our contribution more powerful and far more quickly effective.

What is the sum of our war effort? Anyone speaking on this subject is apparently expected to re-utter the words of the Prime Minister; otherwise he may be charged with violating the

Military Secrets Act, or with giving encouragement to the enemy. There is no man in this Dominion who wants to encourage the enemy less than I do. I speak with a depth of feeling born of facts which I am not particularly eager to expose to this House. It is my judgment, none the less, that we have now to realize just where we are, or we shall not get farther very soon.

After nearly nine months we have, I estimate, about 20,000 men in England. They have been there four to five months. We have a second division mobilizing in Canada, but as I am informed, not yet entirely mobilized, not all the units being complete. We now have promise of a third division, and are told that at some time in the future a Canadian corps will be in France. It sounds well, but from the point of view of real, immediate progress toward actual fighting I fear it is not much better than a façade of words and visions.

Our first division had in it twelve infantry units, of whom nine are rifle and three machine-gun units. It also had a complement of cavalry and artillery, and in personnel was complete. This division went over with rifles, with machine guns, with artillery equipment. But when one has said that, one has not told the whole truth. The rifles, I am ready to agree, are such as can be used in the field. Let us hope that concession is not too great. Their machine guns could not be used. Their artillery weapons were not modern, and only under bitter necessity could they be taken to the field at all; they are used today only under the stern compulsion of scarcity.

But had those rifles, those machine guns, those artillery weapons been modern in every way, this division as it went over would have been very far from being equipped. We have to keep in mind that today, relatively speaking, rifles have not great importance; they still are important. Besides, every unit of the whole nine—I take the rifle units first—must have 22 anti-tank guns, 14 infantry mortars and 4 signal pistols, a total of 60, or 540 in all; and of these they had none. The rifles presumably they still have. The machine guns and the artillery weapons are being replaced on the other side by Great Britain. Whether they are all replaced I cannot say; I do hope they are.

In addition, for all these regiments, wheeled vehicles are

essential. Every infantry regiment has to have 66 wheeled vehicles—lorries, trucks, Bren gun carriers—or a total of 594; and they had none at all. To go further, the artillery and cavalry and three machine-gun units, called infantry, must as well have those vital accessories and in large numbers. These thousands of vehicles apparently have to be supplied by the over-strained factories of Britain. They should have been provided in Canada.

We, over here, have learned of late that in addition to all this mechanized infantry and cavalry there must be fighting vehicles for the whole division, consisting of 86 anti-tank guns, 49 scout carrier cars and 38 other armoured cars. Those are big fighting vehicles the division has to have, and they had none of them.

I wonder now whether someone would undertake to question those facts—someone who listened before the election to assurances that the division went over equipped. It is only fair to say that in my opinion, in the state we were in when the war broke out, no Government could have supplied all those vehicles at once; but I do object to dissemination, over the radio and otherwise, of assurances that the division went over equipped. This was heard almost daily. I object to it with all the earnestness and resentment of which I am possessed. It was dishonest.

Now, the young men of this country have special adaptabilities. They showed it in the last war. In the air they were very distinguished. They would be the same in this war. One air squadron has gone over, which would include, I should think, about 40 pilots and a number of ground men. As yet, to the actual fighting front we, as Canada, have contributed nothing. We have air men there who went over and enlisted in the British Air Force, and it is those men we hear of in the honour rolls and casualty lists today.

Besides, this country is specially qualified to provide railway troops, forestry men, tunnellers, tank-drivers, and signallers. We have young men in our agriculture, indeed in all spheres of our outdoor activity, who are accustomed to driving over territory such as in tanks they would have to traverse. Where are we with tanks? We have some light ones at Camp Borden. They are so light and so small in number that they are not even part of the equipment of our second division. They are used for training.

There is no country in the world better equipped to make tanks than we are. We could make them in Hamilton alone in two factories, and one factory there could make 250 in a month, and do so right along. If there is a weapon that is paramount in this mechanized conflict, it is the tank. We could provide tunnellers from our miners, and signallers as well. I make this statement, that in signalling we have not equipment to train our men; we have no modern equipment with which to train them yet.

I mentioned railway troops. A public man in Ontario made the statement some months ago that the British Government had requested railway troops, but that these have never been sent. So far as I have been able to find, that statement has never been denied. I do not know whether the request from Britain took the form of an inquiry as to whether we should like to do so. If it did, this Government would not consider it a request at all. It may have taken any form; I know not what. But personally I believe the statement. When the Prime Minister of Canada tells us that he is in constant consultation with the British Government, I believe him. But if he wants to imply that he is meeting Britain's urgent wishes for this war, then I cannot accept his statement. Admittedly, he himself has never gone so far as to say that; but he has a minister who has, and newspapers who do. One of the latter is in Brockville. They have assured us we are doing all we have been asked to do. It is very well to talk about being in consultation, but it is not fair and it is not right to give the people of Canada the impression that consultation means practical and full co-operation on our part.

It is true that in the last war there were things Britain would have liked us to do, which were at the time beyond our power. Possibly we cannot do now all that is urged of us, but we can do much more than we have done. Everyone knows that we could send railway troops and forestry troops. And, while we are not doing, and perhaps are not able to do, all we are asked, surely it is wrong to lead the people of Canada to think we are. But this very representation has been scattered far and wide.

I make another complaint. Home defence is part of our work, though far from the major part, for we defend ourselves best and most effectively by strengthening in our own appropriate way the arm of Britain and our Allies. If they go, we go. If they stand we stand. There are not very many in this country trying to find other sources of comfort now; there were months ago. Today, speaking for myself, I cannot find any, no matter where I look. We know where the fortress is, behind which, if it stands, we are going to survive—or beneath which, if it falls, we are going to perish. There are some—very many—even across the line, who are not of the opinion today which they held months ago. Today they are not so confident that they, or rather, that they and we, can win after the great democracies of Europe have failed; can win after the might of those totalitarian powers has been multiplied and after they have come closer to our continent by the conquest of Atlantic islands, closer by thousands of miles than we will be to theirs. There are, I know, some of them who so believe, but they are mostly confined to fifth columnists or to petted children of fortune. The United States people are coming to the view of their President, the mightiest and one of the brainiest of their sons, who, from the altitude of his great position and in the light of his luminous mind, sees the situation as it is. Over there in Europe is our defence. Over there is their defence. Let us act on that knowledge. Let us not live in a vacuous paradise which we know is a sham. Let us not invite the day when we shall have to take up a desperate position beside our neighbours and fight the totalitarian world pretty much alone.

Home defence, none the less, is still part, though a small part, of our duty. According to a Government spokesman, we need for our home defence six divisions. Without admitting the wisdom of such a disposition I ask:—Have we those divisions? We know we have not. What have we? I referred to the condition of our men who went overseas. We hope they are equipped with modern weapons of warfare now. I do not know. But I do know this: that, to get them over, our non-permanent units were largely stripped of their military clothing and training equipment. In that plight those units were left.

Further, among the nine infantry battalions that went across, there were our only three permanent-force infantry battalions, the Royal 22nd of Quebec, the R. C. R. and the Princess

Patricias. What has been the purpose of maintaining our permanent force? The true purpose was always stated to be that they should be an administration and instructional force in Canada for the training of our non-permanent militia when the day of trouble should come or be approaching. What has happened since those three battalions have gone, the only three we had? The Second Division is without training personnel; not only the Second Division but also the members of our nonpermanent militia. Perhaps these are not wholly bereft, for there was a percentage of those others left behind, but that percentage has been mostly absorbed in administration duties, and there is now a complete dearth of instructional personnel in this country. Presumably the reason those units were sent overseas was that they were the best trained. It may be they were sent in a belief that war would be over soon; but it is hard to see any justification for stripping the Dominion of a force so vital in its training function, so essential to the prosecution of this conflict.

Such is the condition of our non-permanent units. They were stripped of clothing. Part of this deficiency has now been supplied. I have today a letter from a prominent Montrealer, a supporter of this Government, who tells me there was a parade the day before yesterday of all non-permanent militia forces in his city, not one of which was completely equipped, the web equipment particularly being missing.

Even our oldest units, the Queen's Own Rifles and the Irish Regiment, are still without clothing. They have some, but important parts are still wanting. This may not be of tremendous importance, but surely after nine and a half months there is no excuse in this industrialized country for compelling men to train and march without appropriate dress.

Second Division men are going mainly to Camp Borden, but not all; they are spread all over the place. I should think they would have to train in one area. Otherwise how are higher officers to gain experience of and train men in large formations and in the co-ordination of one branch of the service with another? It cannot be done unless they are together.

The Second Division cannot commence open-air training for a while yet even though it is now past the middle of May. Why?

Last September the Government started building huts for their accommodation, but stopped. They commenced again lately, but it will be the end of this month before open-air training, which should have started on the first of April, can begin. After open-air exercising commences and after the men have equipment which they have not now, they cannot possibly be trained in less time than six months. Two years is usually considered necessary, but under war conditions the aim is to have it done in six months. This means it will be near the end of the year, anyway, before the Second Division is trained. And we are asked to breathe happily because a Third Division is promised! What is going to happen to them? Outside of the training at Aldershot, we have wasted about nine months in preparing our men for the front. This is the condition of affairs, and the people of Canada feel it. They did not realize it nearly as soon as they should have, but they do now under the strain and crash of the ghastliest events this world has ever known.

What is to be done? I have read the programme which is now foreshadowed. Programmes we have had in plenty; it is in realization that we have failed—and we have failed tragically. Our effort is today the scorn of many in Canada, and I am afraid it is becoming the scorn of many outside our country. We have been no example to our friends to the south. Read their press. They are wanting to know why they should come in when we are simply going through the forms. We are no model, and yet there is no country which by example, rather than by precept, can do more than we can to bring our great neighbours to the south into line with us to save democracy on earth. For this purpose a splendid, arresting effort on our part was vital, but that effort has not been in evidence.

We are told an air training scheme is under way and is going to do great things. We hope this is so. There is nothing on which I feel more keenly than on the history of this air training scheme; there is nothing that better reflects the principles of the men at the head of our Government than does the record of this affair. I was told during the session of 1938—not by anyone from the Department of External Affairs, not by any Civil Servant anywhere—that not once, but twice, in 1937 and 1938, there had been approaches from the British Government, with a request to be permitted to train their airmen for a conflict which they feared, and that these approaches were repulsed by the Government of Canada. On June 14th, 1938, I rose on the Orders of the Day and asked this question:

Honourable senators, at this point I should like to ask a question of the honourable leader of the Government. I have not given him notice of the question, and while I should be glad to have an answer today, I shall of course find no fault if it does not come until tomorrow.

I have received information to the effect that within recent months the British Government has made a request to the Government of Canada for permission to establish, wholly at the expense of the British Government, a training school in Canada for flyers. One can understand that on account of the large open spaces such a location might be desirable for the purpose of such training. The request, I am advised, has been made on two occasions and refused by the Government of Canada. I would ask whether the information has any truth in it, and, if so, why the request is refused.

To this the honourable leader of the House replied:

I am quite ready to confess to my right honourable friend that for several reasons I cannot at this moment answer his question. He occupied this position for a number of years and was sometimes unable to attend Council, so much was he engrossed with the work of the Senate and its committees.

RIGHT HON. MR. MEIGHEN: Yes.

HON. MR. DANDURAND: I am in the same position today. So I must ask my right honourable friend to give me twenty-four hours in which to furnish an answer to his question.

Next day, June 15th, there was this:

HON. RAOUL DANDURAND: Honourable senators, yesterday my right honourable friend opposite (Right Hon. Mr. Meighen) asked me whether "the British Government has made a request to the Government of Canada for permission to establish, wholly at the expense of the British Government, a training school in Canada for flyers." And he added:

"The request, I am advised, has been made on two occasions and refused by the Government of Canada. I would ask

whether the information has any truth in it, and, if so, why
the request is refused."

My answer is that no such request has been made to the
Canadian Government.

A blank negative.

I then rose, and these were my words:

> Would the honourable leader of the Government be suf-
> ficiently non-technical with the House to follow up his
> answer with some statement as to just what the facts are in
> this connection? It may be that exactly in the terms in
> which I have asked the question there has not been a request,
> but has there not been one on the same subject-matter and
> not very far unrelated to the very terms which I used? And
> if so, what has been the reply? And what is the policy of the
> Government of the day?

To which the leader of this House (Hon. Mr. Dandurand)
replied:

> I can perhaps enlarge upon the answer I have made. There
> has been no request to the Federal Government either in the
> terms in which my right honourable friend's question of
> yesterday was couched or in those he has just used to obtain
> further information. In a word, there has been no request
> from the British Government to the Canadian Government
> in any shape or form—

I ask the House to remember these words—"in any shape or
form."

> —concerning the matter mentioned in the query of the right
> honourable gentleman.

I then asked:

> Will the honourable leader of the Government say there
> has been no inquiry—

Honourable members will note the word I used there,
"inquiry."

> —of the Canadian Government as to what its attitude would
> be with respect to the subject-matter?

My honourable friend replied:

> That I am unable to answer.

This was on June 15th. He went on to say:

> I asked the department, "Has any request been made by the British Government to the Canadian Government?" The answer was in the negative.

I then added:

> I have put the question in the broadest terms I can, and for the time being I shall have to accept the reply. I find it very difficult to conclude in my own mind that the information given to me is wholly unfounded.

The matter was closed on that day by these words from the honourable leader of the House:

> I am unable to enlarge on the statement I have made to the right honourable gentleman.

It will be noted that I asked whether there had been an inquiry as to what our attitude would be. I was told there had been no request, and on the matter of the inquiry no answer was then, or even later, vouchsafed.

Six days after, on June 21st, I again rose on the Orders of the Day, and spoke as follows:

> Honourable members, last Tuesday, on information I then had, I addressed a question to the Government as to its attitude towards giving permission to the British Government to establish flying school facilities in Canada. On Wednesday I received an answer to the effect that no request had been made by the British Government for such permission. I then took the liberty of following up the question, my only purpose being to have it in such a general form as would enable the Administration to enlighten this House as to what, if any, conversations there had been on the subject. When I put my question in that general form the leader of the Government (Hon. Mr. Dandurand) answered as follows, as reported at page 503 of the Debates of the Senate:
>
> "That I am unable to answer. I asked the Department, 'Has any request been made by the British Government to the Canadian Government?' The answer was in the negative."

Then I went on:

I wish today to renew the question, emphasizing particularly the generality of its form. I earnestly hope the Government will see its way to take the House into its confidence in respect to a matter of such vital and perhaps permanent consequence, not only to Britain, but to this country.

Then there was the following interchange:

Hon. Mr. Dandurand: Of course, I could at the time only give the right honourable gentleman the answer that I had received. Now he is asking whether there have been conversations. Is that the meat of the question?

Right Hon. Mr. Meighen: Yes.

Hon. Mr. Dandurand: I will get an answer for my right honourable friend.

The following day, June 22nd, the subject was discussed for the fourth time in this House, as follows:

Hon. Raoul Dandurand: My right honourable friend yesterday asked me whether I was in the position to answer a certain question. Last week he asked me whether the British Government had made a request to the Government of Canada to establish a training school for flyers here. I answered him that no such request had been made. Yesterday my right honourable friend asked whether any conversations on the subject had taken place.

Requests have been received from the British Government during the past year regarding short-service commissions for Canadians in the United Kingdom Air Force, and the Canadian Government has co-operated in making the arrangements proposed.

That, I suppose, was a kind of red herring. It had nothing to do with the question. My honourable friend went on:

No requests have been received from the British Government for the establishment in Canada of an air school or other agency of the United Kingdom Air Force. Some informal conversations have taken place with persons who did not indicate they had been authorized or instructed by the British Government to make any proposals.

I direct special attention to this statement he then made:

> It is not customary or desirable to refer to inquiries of this description.

It was not "customary or desirable" that they should even be mentioned! In other words, it was none of our business! My honourable friend added:

> Should any such proposals be made by the Government of the United Kingdom, the Canadian Government would of course be prepared to discuss them with that Government, and at the proper time to make its position known to the Canadian people.

I then asked:

> Would the honourable leader of the Government state whether the persons with whom the Government had conversations were Canadians or citizens of the British Isles?

To this my honourable friend replied:

> It seems to me that informal conversations can hardly form the basis of an inquiry in this Chamber or the other when they are not followed by some official action.

That is to say: If the British Government's suggestion is declined, then the matter becomes no business of the Canadian Parliament! My honourable friend added these words to his statement:

> I simply submit that as my own answer to my right honourable friend; not as an answer from the Government.

The subject was pursued that day in the following manner:

> RIGHT HON. MR. MEIGHEN: What I am getting at is this. Informal conversations may be just as important as if all the formalities in the world were attached. It depends on whom they were with. Will the honourable leader of the Government say whether the informal conversations were not with a person who might reasonably have been expected to be feeling out the position of this Government on behalf of the Government of Britain?
>
> HON. MR. DANDURAND: I cannot answer the query of my right honourable friend as to whom they were with. It would strike me as extraordinary that informal conversations should

produce rumours which would reach this Chamber or the other and form the basis for a query as to the action of the Government on such conversations.

RIGHT HON. MR. MEIGHEN: I do not see anything extraordinary about that.

On July 1, 1938, the last day of that year's session, this subject came up again in a debate in the other Chamber, and with the permission of the House I should like to read briefly—but as much as anyone wants—from a statement of the Prime Minister. The subject having come up at the instance of the then leader of the Opposition, the Prime Minister was, as will be seen from the report, incensed that any news of these conversations should have got out. Whether for the purpose of wreaking vengeance on an informant, I know not, but he did his utmost to find out where the news came from, and sought to pour abuse on anyone who would not disclose the source of his information—as if the source were important, and not the information itself. He said this:

> Confidential and informal exploratory conversations with respect to training of British air pilots have taken place, but nothing has developed which it was felt warranted a statement of policy.

I will inquire in a moment whether policy had not already been determined and concealed from the people of Canada and their representatives.

Now I will quote something more. A radio speech was made by the Prime Minister on the eighth day of March this year. I have here the *Globe and Mail*'s report of the next day, which says it was a fifteen-minute speech. The heading is "King denies he delayed air scheme," and the report in part reads:

> In May of 1938, the Prime Minister said, Sir Francis Floud, then British High Commissioner in Canada, told him the British Government "wished to explore the possibility of sending to Canada, for further training in Canada, some British air pilots who had already received training in the United Kingdom."

I hope honourable members have noted the language. The British Government "wished to explore the possibility" of getting done that which they desired done. Then the report goes on:

The British Government had wished to ascertain if there would be any objection to such training in Canada in establishments to be owned, maintained and controlled by Britain.

I did not gather from him—

Oh, this is characteristic:

—that there was so much as a suggestion of any plan for the general training of British pilots in Canada.

What kind of training was it to be? But listen to this sentence:

"Partnership in the Empire was never mentioned," said Mr. King. How amazing! Before he would know, I suppose, that we were partners in the Empire, it would have to be mentioned! Why that was inserted passes my comprehension. But listen further:

I pointed out to the British High Commissioner that, apart from any possible controversy which might arise, for the Government of the United Kingdom to own, maintain, control and direct any air training establishment in Canada would involve certain questions of jurisdiction and administration.

I explained that our position in the British Commonwealth demanded that all military establishments in Canada should be under control of the Canadian Government. With that stand I believe all true Canadians will agree.

Now I proceed to discuss the effect of all that has been quoted. The replies given to me in this Chamber are, I believe, not ultimately attributable to the leader of the Senate. They were given, I doubt not, at the direction of the Prime Minister of Canada. Obviously they should have been so given, because the Prime Minister is head of the Department which has to do with this subject. Further, on July 1, 1938, referring to questions which had been asked here and replies given, he confirmed the accuracy of those replies by saying he did not want to add anything to them. Therefore, he is responsible.

Now, where does this record place him? In May he was approached by the British Minister in Canada and asked what would be our attitude towards a wish of the British Government to establish air training facilities in this Dominion. I ask the honourable leader of the Government who sits in front of me: Does he think the Prime Minister of Canada gave us an honest answer when he told us no request had been made? Does he?

HON. MR. DANDURAND: It was not in the form of a request.

RIGHT HON. MR. MEIGHEN: I made very plain, repeatedly, in my questions that I was not interested in the form. What is the distinction between a formal request and what the British Government did? I will tell you the distinction. In what they did they took care, so far as they possibly could, that no difference would arise between them and this country. That care they always take. Even at the price of flattery and extreme courtesy they will make certain to have no difficulty with Canada. If they had made a formal request and received a negative answer, there would have arisen a difference between them and this country, which might have been harmful to the Empire. No; their request is made in another way. They say they would like to do certain things, and inquire what our attitude would be. We say, "No, you cannot." And the Government of Canada tells Parliament that no request at all was made. I ask: Can we trust the Government of Canada again?

Never was there a more courteous, but nevertheless, a more direct request. Yet, not only was Parliament informed that no request at all had been made, but when I followed the matter up we were told by the honourable leader of this House that it was none of the business of Parliament what the Government's attitude was toward the British inquiry as long as that attitude was negative. I repeat, we were told that policies going to the very root of our right to live can be determined by the Government and concealed from Parliament and that conversations between the High Commissioner for Britain and the Prime Minister of this country, entered into for the purpose of finding out what is Canada's position on a proposal of great consequence, are none of our business. We were told that by the Government which is in office today, the Government which is conducting this war! This is the Government upon which, in the blackest hour we have ever faced, we are asked to depend.

Honourable gentlemen will remember that when I asked

whom those conversations were with, we were answered that the information could not be given. Honourable gentlemen will remember also that later, on June 22nd, we were definitely informed by the Prime Minister, through the leader of this House, that the party with whom conversations took place had not even indicated that he was speaking for the British Government. How does that answer look now alongside the disclosure by the Rt. Hon. Mr. King in his radio speech of March 8th this year, that the conversation he had was with Sir Francis Floud, the High Commissioner for Great Britain, who had told him he was making the inquiry on behalf of the Government he represented? In Germany such contempt for Parliament has been for many years the habit of that nation's master. Is Germany to be our example?

Now, what are the consequences of refusal to give this information? The first consequence is to destroy trust in the Government of this country. No longer can we rely on any information it gives with respect to subjects the most vital to Parliament.

The next consequence is this: two years' delay in the provision of the most essential arm designed to save the Allies and ourselves. In the name of the sovereignty of Canada! "Ah," we are told, "all they wanted were just a few men." I do not know how many they wanted, nor on how large a scale they desired to train, but I know the nature and the reasonableness of the request, and that measuring up to the opportunity, if it had been given, would have been, or would have become, commensurate with the peril. But the gates of Canada were locked to our partner who desired only the better to help defend this country, and the whole Commonwealth, in the air. What a record! Who in this Dominion cares whether British officials or our own trained those men—even if they were ours, which they were not—providing they were properly trained? There is not a soul in Canada who does not realize that we then had not the facilities for training, and that it would have taken many months, if not years, to get those facilities. But peril meant nothing; national sovereignty meant everything. There sits the Government of this Dominion! Ah, when the Allied effort failed in Norway because of deficiency in air defence, the man who should have resigned was not in Great Britain, he was right here in Canada.

HON. MR. HUGESSEN: Rubbish.

RIGHT HON. MR. MEIGHEN: Oh, I thought something like that would come from the honourable member. I have watched him. There never was such a sin committed against our security as the sin committed there. No one knows what air strength might have been achieved had we met our partner in the spirit of partnership, and not in the spirit of contention about the sovereignty of Canada.

HON. MR. DANDURAND: My right honourable friend is totally unfair in his conclusions, as I shall prove to him when I speak.

RIGHT HON. MR. MEIGHEN: I might hope you can, but I know you cannot.

HON. MR. DANDURAND: We shall see.

RIGHT HON. MR. MEIGHEN: We are partners, or we are not. If we cannot trust Britain in matters of our common defence we might as well dissolve this Empire.

HON. MR. DANDURAND: My right honourable friend speaks of 1938?

RIGHT HON. MR. MEIGHEN: Yes, I am aware there have passed only two years yet. I am by no means certain it is only two years we have lost.

HON. MR. DANDURAND: We have not lost three months.

RIGHT HON. MR. MEIGHEN: We are told now we are going to have 169 pilots by November, and we have not lost three months.

HON. MR. DANDURAND: No.

RIGHT HON. MR. MEIGHEN: Well, if that is the best we can do, it is important to depend on others.

HON. MR. DANDURAND: We shall discuss the negotiations of 1938.

RIGHT HON. MR. MEIGHEN: I know what they have done over there in Britain. I know our limitations and I am very doubtful that we are going to get even what is foreshadowed by the Government today. Britain was convinced she had to get an organization in Canada to prepare for our common defence. If we cannot trust her, then the Empire had as well be dissolved; and I would rather see it dissolved by ourselves than by somebody else. I feel strongly on this subject. There is not a doubt in my own mind that the 1938 approach was not the first. How do we explain that the Vancouver *Sun,* a leading Liberal paper, announced in July, 1937, that there had already been a refusal given a request by the British Government to establish air-training facilities here? I had not read the announcement until a year after. Are we asked to believe that it was based on a myth? Statements of that nature by friendly journals are not based on myths. What ground there was for the pronouncement I do not know, but there is every reason to think that the first approach, in whatever form it came, was made a year before 1938.

Hon. Mr. Dandurand: All we have here is the High Commissioner.

Right Hon. Mr. Meighen: There are other ways.

Hon. Mr. Dandurand: That is hypothesis.

Right Hon. Mr. Meighen: I know we have a Government who deny having a request unless it is put in writing—maybe under seal—and who say that an inquiry expressing a desire is not a request; and when we ask if there is anything further they can say, they tell us it is none of our business. I should like any honourable gentleman here to take that sentence and refute it. Again I ask: Is this to be the Government upon which Canada is to rely for conduct through this crisis?

Until the Administration is reorganized—

Hon. Mr. Dandurand: Until?

Right Hon. Mr. Meighen: Until is it reorganized or changed, until it can be recognized as representing every considerable war element of our people, it cannot have nation-wide confidence. Until it is reorganized or changed—and I do not want it changed and be again on a party basis, no matter what the party—it is not going to command that confidence. I ask the Government to move, and move now, to establish unity in this country. You can not do so by trying to destroy your political foes while the nation's foes flourish. This Government, though, can do much to bring it about. There is nobody in the Dominion more averse to office than I am; everyone knows that; but there is nothing, however subordinate, I would not labour to perform under any representative Government to unite and help our nation; and there is nothing any Canadian who is properly constituted could refuse to do.

SOME HON. SENATORS: Hear, hear.

RIGHT HON. MR. MEIGHEN: But do not conduct our affairs the way you have been conducting them. It will take a long while that way to bring us to real participation. How long a period we have left the leader of the Government does not know, and no one knows, but I ask him to act on the assumption that the time is brief. Do not be always looking years ahead. Try to get the utmost done in the next month, still more in the second, still more in the third. Only in that way can any government do its duty in the present state of our country and in sight of the dire and immediate peril which overcasts the world.

THE MOBILIZATION ACT, 1940

CONSCRIPTION

A Bill entitled The National Resources Mobilization Act, 1940, reached the Senate in June of that year. It provided for what was described as "mobilization" of men, money and materials for certain war purposes. So far as men were to be compulsorily enrolled under it, their service was to be confined geographically to Canada. The criticism appearing hereunder was made in the Second Chamber on June 20, 1940.

THIS MEASURE IS ONE OF THE MOST IMPORTANT and at the same time one of the most extraordinary ever presented to Parliament. It bears a euphonious and inoffensive title—which I doubt not was cautiously and skilfully chosen—"The National Resources Mobilization Act, 1940." This, frankly, is legislation for conscription of men, money and material for a war, and, as all of us know, it is in substance and intent legislation for conscription of men alone—for these other conscriptions the Government has ample powers already.

The Bill, therefore, brings to me many memories; and memories it summons back must be indeed poignant to members of the present Administration, particularly to those long associated with our public life.

I take definite and positive exception to the form and character of the Bill which this Government now presents, and for which it seeks approval. First, I am not in accord with its limited scope. The Bill invokes conscription and makes it law. True, it changes the word to "mobilization" and thus seeks to suppress harrowing thoughts of years gone by; but it confines its application to a home area where there can be no fighting—none, at least, until by defeat on decisive theatres the war has

384

already been lost. Second: As now drawn up, it provides no machinery, no tribunals for making selections of men: this Bill merely sets up Order in Council Government at its worst.

Nevertheless, with its object, as far as it goes—a poor and miserable distance—and with the principle of compulsion on which it rests, we on this side are in fullest agreement. The House may be surprised that we do not propose an amendment enlarging the measure into more ample and far more logical scope and demanding that the Government include in it, and thus submit to Parliament for review, principles to be applied in selecting these men, and, as well, their plan for constituting tribunals to apply those principles and see that fairness is done. Such surprise is natural because all that is put before us here is an invitation to keep quiet and dutifully authorize this omniscient Cabinet to do everything just as it pleases. Very emphatically it is Parliament which should decide on what conditions, with what safeguards and by what machinery of administration the liberty of the subject is to be so relentlessly invaded as it is by this measure. But we shall not move such an amendment, and I will tell hon. gentlemen why.

Assuming that a Motion along the lines I have outlined would be passed in this Chamber—and there is no reason to think it would not be, for it would be an eminently right step to take—we have to consider where we should be then. We should have a measure greatly improved in two very important features, but one which we know from what has occurred lately in the other Chamber would not be accepted by the Government and its huge majority there. Consequently, nothing but delay and perhaps serious friction would result, and this in the direst stresses of war. I am, therefore, going to content myself with lodging a distinct and most vigorous protest against these lamentable features and giving reasons therefor.

Let us consider closely the primary object of this Bill, its scope, and its consistency. It provides that the persons of all Canadians shall be placed without reservation at the disposal of Government for such duties as Government may assign to them. Though much has been talked about allocating men to this function and to that—merely to give apparent warrant for the word "mobilization" instead of "conscription"—any allocation apart from that to our armed forces, in the air, on water and on land, amounts to nothing. Once assignment to the armed forces has been effected, further assignment follows of itself. Give industry work to do—planes, tanks, munitions to produce; refuse to take into the services men who cannot be spared from specific industries and those not taken will find their places in those industries. Similarly, women will fall into their proper duties when work is waiting to be done. Though we talk a lot about putting this man here and that man there, and the real object of the measure is somewhat confused thereby, the one purpose which amounts to anything is to see that we do not fail in our supreme military duty, the imperious demand of this hour.

The Bill provides that men be conscripted for service throughout the Dominion, but it adds that no one upon whose shoulders the Government places its hand can, after he is required to join, be sent out of Canada or beyond the three-mile limit. As already stated, I am one hundred per cent in agreement with a decision that we should at last use common sense in the gathering of our armed forces. To leave this major duty of a citizen to whimsies and pure caprice in a day of the nation's peril is the veriest folly and grossly unjust. The Bill in this essential principle is right. But the Government, in limiting its application to local defence of Canada, provides that conscripted men stay in this country. If they fight by sea and pursue an enemy, they stop at the three-mile limit. Then, presumably, they come back, and volunteers must be found to take up the chase. Again, again and again I ask, what other defence is there but defence of Canada?

SOME HON. SENATORS: Hear, hear.

RIGHT HON. MR. MEIGHEN: Have we up to now been defending other people and not ourselves? Is this country content that its sons be compelled to engage in any form of defence so long as we know it is not a defence of value, and certainly not of maximum value, to the Dominion? We go through a hollow mockery of assuming that we have been unselfish idealists in sending our soldiers to the help of Britain and of her allies in Europe. Why not be honest with ourselves and say we sent them there because there they defend Canada best, because there is our first line and what ought to be made our strongest line. Are not men whom we are sending to England now going over yonder in the defence of Canada? There is not one hon. member who has the slightest doubt but that at this hour, and at every hour up to now, the way best to secure the defence of Canada is and has been to strengthen the Allied line.

SOME HON. SENATORS: Hear, hear.

RIGHT HON. MR. MEIGHEN: And there are none who should be more definitely certain of it than the members of this Government. The Prime Minister himself is quite certain; he told us only a few days ago that we should not wait until the enemy reached here, but we should go out and defeat him. These were his words:

> The way to meet an aeroplane or submarine attack is not to wait until the enemy reaches your shores, but to go out and meet him and try to prevent him from ever reaching your shores.

Every common-sense person agrees. That is what we have in our leisurely way been doing. And I wonder if there is anybody who believes that service where it can be of greatest effect is of less importance to our country than is service where it can be of least effect.

But the restraints this Government feel themselves under— the ugly memories that plague them—bend and compress their war energies into the narrow, inconsistent terms of this Bill. That narrowness and that inconsistency result from an attempt to fit the necessities of the perilous present into the contortions of the tragic past.

HON. MR. HAIG: Hear, hear.

RIGHT HON. MR. MEIGHEN: Everyone in this House knows the truth of that statement just as he knows his name.

The honourable leader of the House (Hon. Mr. Dandurand) read a few moments ago a speech which came originally from the lips of the Prime Minister, and in which it was said there had been no difficulty in obtaining plenty of volunteers for service overseas. I do not dispute the correctness of that assertion: but the numbers required were meagre, and the reason for their being meagre is very plain. We came into this conflict utterly unprepared either in spirit or in deed, although we had had abundant notice. We were lethargic and slow in getting equipment and becoming prepared: so we could not absorb many men. That is the most generous interpretation we can put upon our conduct up to now. That we have had enough men to answer the call for overseas service is, I suppose, correct, within the narrow limits of that call.

I do not, however, follow the logic of a contention that compulsion is not necessary to get men to fight outside this country, but that we must apply compulsion to get them to fight inside our own domain.

Hon. Mr. Dandurand: And to cover far more services than that.

Right Hon. Mr. Meighen: The intent cannot be confused in that way. The object of the Bill is to implement the necessities of the army, navy and air force. You will never need to compel men to work for wages. You cannot do so if you try—not in this country. Once you have your military, your air and your naval requirements attended to, the allocation of those left to other spheres will follow automatically: to this the Administration has not the smallest notion of applying compulsion. So the position the Government find themselves in is illogical and senseless, and this makes it necessary for them to submit to us the most preposterous of reasoning. Who would with any sincerity suggest that the sons of Canada are more ready to fight in Europe than they are to fight in Ontario or Quebec? We are told there are plenty of men volunteering to fight overseas—that no compulsion is necessary to enrol them for overseas service. How then can it be even whispered to sensible people that if the sons of Canada are thoroughly ready to go overseas to fight for this nation, they are not also ready without compulsion to fight within our own land? But that monstrous absurdity is just what Cabinet Ministers are now compelled to utter; such are the penalties of a guilty past.

The Government know even better than we do that at this hour clouds are hovering over the hills of our nation, and they fear they cannot depend long on hazard or caprice of any kind. That is why they are before us with this measure; they like this manner of approach. But implicit in their larger plan is the illogical character of this preliminary proposition; and behind it can be seen clearly, as through a glass, the conscience-smiting record of years that are gone but not forgotten.

Well, here is a beginning of compulsion, newly christened as mobilization. I will not stand in the way of action, however fathered, however deformed, if only it is vigorous. Still more, I will help the Government in every manner within my power. And I have helped them. Can any hon. senator point to another in this Dominion who has laboured harder and longer than my humble self to rouse Canadians to some appreciation of the peril which has been coming upon us? Can anyone be named who started to warn of this calamity sooner, both in and outside this House, and continued to do so over a period, not of months, but of years? The culmination has come. The more virile the means proposed for facing it, the more eager I shall be to support them.

But again what is the nature of this measure? I said it was unprecedented. It is unprecedented in those features which rob Parliament of its inherent rights and assert those rights on behalf of the Government. We have had compulsory military service statutes in Canada before, not after a few months of war, but after years of war. The Government of that day, though, did not come to hon. members and ask that a blank cheque be given them by way of a Bill of this character, which, though invading the subject's most precious liberties to a greater degree than has all other legislation we have passed in years, deprives Parliament of the right to define the safeguards and principles which are to govern its operation.

The Military Service Act of 1917 set out all the various classes who were to be called, and the order in which they must be called. No other order could afterwards be substituted. The constitution of those tribunals who were to do the selecting was defined. It was stipulated that they should be local, each one consisting of two members, and the choosing of those members was provided for in the fairest way that the wit of men could devise. The Government did not take power to choose them directly or indirectly. The Act provided that one member should be named by a Committee of Selection, a committee established by joint resolution of both Houses, and thus all members of Parliament of all parties had something to say in its composition. And, as many will remember, that Committee of Selection was in no sense partisan. The other member of each local tribunal was to be named by the local judge of the district, whoever he might be, by whomsoever appointed. Thereby it was made clear that there would be the utmost fairness as between parties, races and creeds in the determination of what men should go and what men should stay. Further, the Military Service Act went on to provide for appeals and the determination of those appeals, and for their removal from everything in the nature of Government interference, and particularly of political interference. And the party Government which had been in power decided as well that a measure of such character should have sponsorship of an Administration as thoroughly national as could be got together. Before it was called into effect, such an Administration was found. If it had been possible to select a Cabinet more widely representative than the one which was obtained, the heart of the Prime Minister of that day would have rejoiced.

Now we are asked to place the lives and property of every Canadian in the hands of a party Government, and to authorize that Government to decide by Order in Council principles, if any, to be applied in making selection, and by Order in Council to nominate tribunals, if indeed there will be any tribunals; by Order in Council to decide on the classes which are to be called and the order of their calling; by Order in Council to specify the nature of appeals, if any, and the courts or officials to whom they may be made. Passing this Bill gives the Government power to restrict where they want to restrict, to widen where they want to widen, to protect where they want to protect, to control the whole gigantic operation in harmony with their own sweet will. Parliament is asked kindly to step aside, to abandon its functions and leave them to the Cabinet. I wonder if any honourable members have at this moment in mind that loud champion of the rights of Parliament who thundered on this subject through Canada during all his years of opposition. I do not need to mention his name. He is now the author of the most flagrant defiance of parliamentary rights ever addressed to any free Parliament in the civilized world. Such defiance is the very essence of this Bill. It is the solemn duty of Parliament to lay down principles, safeguards, and a complete mechanism for operation of a measure which invades things so sacred as those invaded in the one now before us. That duty the Government call on us to abandon. This House is helpless by itself: it can only delay. It must surrender or be accused of obstructing the making of war.

What is the answer of the Administration? We are told, "This is an emergency." Certainly it is an emergency. An emergency fell from the skies of Britain when war broke on the first of September. Did the British Government in excited arrogance cry out, "We want Parliament to let us seize the persons of the men of this kingdom and force them into the army along our way of thinking; we want Parliament to have nothing whatever to say about the principles and methods of selection"? They did not. Within two days they introduced a Bill embodying rules, regulations and selective machinery placing safeguards around the rights of the subject. These were considered, debated, amended if necessary and finally passed by Parliament, and these the Government had to follow. That Bill provided that there could be no favouritism anywhere, that there must be fair and honest methods both in the calling out of men and in appeals therefrom—methods approved by the people's representatives. Why is such a course not followed here?

Hon. Mr. Dandurand: It has been.

Right Hon. Mr. Meighen: It has been? This Bill follows it?

Hon. Mr. Dandurand: The Bill carried in the other House by, I think, a vote of 156 to 2.

Right Hon. Mr. Meighen: It will be carried here—unanimously. But that does not change the character of the Bill.

Hon. Mr. Dandurand: But it affirms the principle of the authority of Parliament.

Right Hon. Mr. Meighen: Yes! to pass the Bill or reject it. I am going to vote for this measure, but that does not affect its character. The Government should submit to Parliament, for Parliament's review and decision, all these vital provisions and the whole scheme of operation. There is nothing of that nature here. Cannot the Administration prepare such a measure? With help of a capable draftsman they should be able to do so in half a day. They would not have one-tenth of the work we had to perform when the ground had to be pioneered in Canada twenty-three years ago. We now have the precedents of British laws of twenty-four years ago and of today. We have the precedent of our own law of 1917. Perhaps any one of them could be improved. A measure thus framed should be submitted to us. Parliament should review it and decide whether the safeguards therein proposed are fair and right, whether the principles of application are just, whether the classification is sound, what class should be called first, what second, third, fourth, fifth and tenth. This is the business of legislators. This business we are forbidden to enter into; or rather, this business we are called upon by the Government not to enter into, which means that to attempt to do so is futile. The Government demand that we vote them authority to do these things and do them on the high Privy Council plateau and in their own majestic way. I protested about this yesterday to a member of the Cabinet—a Minister well known to the leader opposite. "Oh," he said, "we will do all that, and we will tell you about it afterwards." That Minister frankly told the truth. Such is the spirit and purpose of this Administration, the purpose printed right here. Orders in Council are to enact what Parliament alone should enact.

We have sat now for some weeks and have tried to do our best with measures before us. What kind of material have we had? Just petty peanut legislation—amendments to the Yukon Act, amendments to the Northwest Territories Act, recurrence for the nth time of a Farmers' Creditors Arrangement Act, some little thing about agricultural products—just legislative chicken-feed, as everyone in this House has noted. But when there is something of moment to which we could address ourselves; matters than which there has never been anything of more consequence in Canada for a quarter of a century, the Government say: "We have neither time nor inclination to prepare for you a Statute. We want you to give us blanket authority, and we will pass the real legislation by Order in Council." I tell them it is just as easy to prepare for Parliament as to prepare for the Governor in Council. It is in truth easier because the same detail is not required. It does not take a moment longer to draft and submit legislation to the people's representatives than it does to draft and submit it to the high and mighty Governor in Council.

Why, then, is Parliament affronted? Why, then, is this Government asking for powers reserved to itself alone in respect of the liberty of the subject such as have never been asked for in any Parliament of Britain, in any Parliament of this Dominion, or of any other Dominion? I protest against the denial of parliamentary rights embedded in this legislation, and I warn the country against the application of this law, inasmuch as its entire application and the governing principles which control have been here and now torn from the hands of the people's representatives and gathered under the wing of a party Administration.

I have made my protest. To this Bill, notwithstanding its abhorrent features, I will give support. There is no purpose in moving amendments; they would only cause delay. We would all of us rather have what is here than nothing. But from the indictment I lay against the Administration I venture to say there is no escape in the minds of honourable members, even those across the floor, and I am certain there will be no escape in the minds of the people of Canada.

THE HOME ARMY—A COLOSSAL WASTE

Delivered in the Senate, Ottawa, November 13, 1940, during debate on the Address in reply to Speech from the Throne.

IT IS FITTING AT THIS TIME that reference be made to the universal feeling of sympathy in Canada for the family of the late Prime Minister of Great Britain, the Right Honourable Neville Chamberlain. I am not one of those who felt it their duty to criticize Mr. Chamberlain in respect of those major features of policy which, though applauded at the time by his own countrymen, by ourselves and our Prime Minister, brought upon him later severe rebuke at home, where right or wrong it was quite legitimate, and in other lands, including our own, where it was not legitimate at all; rebuke and derision which, I fear, resulted in undermining that confidence in British might and British honour which was even then so vital to all mankind. I recognized in him, as surely most of us do now, a typical Englishman in every fibre; a man of stern rectitude and elevation of character, and as well a man of marked ability, particularly in matters of administration and of business. I recognized in him one who by hard toil achieved much, and who suffered unjustly and cruelly, mainly at the hands of those whose policies of the past had made imperative those steps the taking of which was ultimately to bring upon him severe castigation and dethronement from his high place in Britain.

While we lament his passing and the undoubted suffering of body and mind which he endured, we all, I am sure, with one accord welcome as his successor Right Honourable Winston Churchill. I cannot by any stretch of aspiration claim to be Mr. Churchill's personal friend, but for a quarter of a century I have been his ardent admirer. In the dark days of Gallipoli I defended him and his momentous proposal. There is throughout the world now a sentiment very different from that which greeted him then. Through all vicissitudes of one of the fullest and most abundant careers that any human being has ever carved out for himself, I have looked with hope to the prospect of his reaching the pinnacle; indeed have never been able to understand how a government of his own party or any national government could justify leaving him out of its councils. Today he is leader of the British Empire, he is leader of civilization, and, so far as any one man can hold the title, he is the hope of mankind.

I mention next the pleasure which we all feel at the recovery of the honourable leader of this House (Hon. Mr. Dandurand)—

HON. SENATORS: Hear, hear.

RIGHT HON. MR. MEIGHEN: —from a rather serious illness which befell him in the autumn. His rugged strength and abounding vitality have triumphed again, and all of us know it is to the advantage of Canada that he is with us once more.

HON. SENATORS: Hear, hear.

RIGHT HON. MR. MEIGHEN: I regret that temporary absence last evening prevented my hearing the mover and the seconder of the Address, consideration of which is now before us. This regret was felt still more on reading their speeches today. I congratulate first the seconder of the address (Hon. Mr. Hayden) for the very practical and, on the whole, wise consideration he is giving to affairs of high domestic importance at this time. He has possibly been misled by none too accurate statements of the press and of others in certain of his conclusions as to our war effort, but for the most part his speech was a credit to himself and one which this House will remember.

I come particularly, with pride as a Canadian, to the address delivered by the honourable senator from Sorel (Hon. Mr. David). I read it today with admiration and with personal joy. The hand which he extends from the province of Quebec I should like to grasp; it is doubtful whether there is anybody in his province with higher authority to extend that hand. We well recall his distinguished father, once a member of this House, as he was in the habit of listening, from his place in the Commons gallery, to some of us with more or less impatience, but to his political idol[1] always with pride; and I am sure that father would have been proud to hear his son's speech of yesterday.

As a citizen of this Empire and of Canada, I thank the honourable senator for the just appreciation and splendid comprehension which he evidenced towards the might, the majesty and the honour of Britain—towards the service she is rendering mankind at this awful hour. We all follow him without reservation in the picture he has drawn of that other Motherland of Canada, France, and ardently I join in his hope that the resurrection of that nation may not be far away, and that the world may again be blessed with her contribution to its culture, to its gallantry and to its wealth.

SOME HON. SENATORS: Hear, hear.

RIGHT HON. MR. MEIGHEN: If one reference may be permitted to a mere passing phase of his speech, it is done for the purpose, the sincere purpose, of explanation, and in no spirit of recrimination. He will believe me when I say that there is nothing I have more anxiously sought in my public life, or more persistently sought, even though in vain, than the confidence of the Province of Quebec. He called attention to the schism which arose in 1917, and contrasted that situation with the absence of serious schism today. The contrast I quite admit. That schism arose over the belief, as conscientious a belief as ever men held, a belief reached with as great reluctance as ever characterized the approach to any conclusion, that the time had come when there was but one means of maintaining our forces at the scene of war commensurate or nearly commensurate with Canada's strength and honourable part in a terrible and doubtful conflict. I ask him to reflect that if the facts had not been present to warrant our conclusion, it is most unlikely that a very large section of those who had opposed us throughout our political history, and indeed had opposed us throughout the struggle, would have been not only of one mind with us on the issue, but, if possible, more insistent on effective compulsory action than we were ourselves. It is doubtful if Canada as a whole even today realizes the facts of that time. Our ranks overseas were depleted to a perilous, one might almost

[1] Sir Wilfrid Laurier.

say a shameful, degree. All arts and energies and all contrivances to add to their strength by voluntary response to our appeals had been applied and had failed. We were driven either to acquiesce in the abandonment of our gallant army or else to bring them by compulsion the necessary aid and face whatever consequences might ensue. Had the leaders of the hon. gentleman's party in those days conducted themselves with credit, there would have been no schism.

It is said that very few reinforcements reached our army under conscription. Of those who had been compulsorily enrolled, the number who actually got to the fighting line, though totalling several thousand, was not large. Had the war lasted three, four or five months longer, it would have been very large. The number, however, who reached those depleted ranks in good time under the shadow of conscription was gratifying to a high degree. Regiments reduced, some of them over half, some, indeed, almost to extinction, were restored to strength. Only a few months ago I spoke to one who had been in command. He told me of the gallant record of his own unit—only sixty-five men left. Before one man reached them under the Military Service Act, the whole regiment, just because that Act was passed, or certain to be passed, was brought up to strength. Thus Canada marched abreast of other nations of this Empire and of her allies, ranging the decisive forces at the decisive point, and the world was saved.

The honourable senator from Sorel feels happy at the fact that we have had to resort to no such means in this war. My only suggestion to him is this. Do not be premature; do not seek to forge the future too far ahead. We learned last night that the total of all men out of Canada is only fifty-two thousand. We have had very few casualties, almost none. Had our overseas force in the present struggle encountered the casualties which we suffered in the same period of time in the last war, there would be a great many fewer of those soldiers overseas today. We are not through with this war yet. A long, I fear, a dark, and certainly a very hazardous, road lies ahead. Without resort to any compulsion at all we sent in the last war many, many times the number we have sent in this. By the compulsory plan we augmented our efforts. There is not a human being in Canada who dare say we cannot by any possibility reach the same pass again.

The voluntary system, for a while anyway, avoids or evades schism; but withal it is most unjust, cruelly unjust; and that truth every one of us knows. We cannot look forward to conditions which will insure its permanency to the end of this war. Notwithstanding its infirmities we might like to, but we cannot. We do not know. The vision of man is short, but the range of events is long, and I ask that so sincere and honest-minded a man as the senator from Sorel should not feel in his heart too strongly, too bitterly, towards those who sustained the responsibility and endured the heartbreaking pangs of those last months of the first Great War.

We are meeting now to study a Speech from the Throne. There is little in it that can be the subject of study. It is true that while it does not foreshadow legislation, though to do so is the historic function of a Speech from the Throne, it opens the door to discussion, which, if proper information is not withheld, is a vital, and ought to be a valuable, part of Parliament's duty. I know—surely I ought to know—that in time of war governments must have huge and extraordinary powers. We had such powers in the last conflict and we exercised them; but we sought to exercise them only to the extent which was essential because of emergencies between sessions, or in the event of an absolutely quick decision being required on a matter not of first-ranking consquence during the session itself. We did not employ them as such powers are being employed today. As they are being employed today, Parliament is little better than a mockery.

In the absence of substance in the Speech itself, I wonder what will be before us for review. Apparently we are expected to give attention to so little that it would have looked insignificant, and even cynical, to put it into a Speech from the Throne. But does that mean that important things are not being done, that policies of moment are not being adopted? It does not. There never was a time when matters more fit for the consideration of Parliament were being dealt with; matters to which parliamentary consideration is peculiarly essential.

May I give but one example? I read yesterday a quotation from a speech made by Mr. Brockington, whom the Prime Minister describes as his adviser, and who, I fancy, is even of more importance than an adviser. The speech was delivered in Philadelphia on September 12th, and from it I read the following paragraph:

A few weeks ago the idealism of our two people—

Canada and the United States—

—met the realism of our two governments. They met in a pact between your country and mine, by which you agree to defend us in certain eventualities, and we agree to defend you.

The reference is to a much-heralded Ogdensburg arrangement. I should like to ask the leader of the Government whether that quotation is true. Has Canada entered into an agreement or pact with the United States to defend that country in certain eventualities? Has the United States entered into a corresponding agreement with us? These are words of a spokesman for or adviser of the Prime Minister. I am not discussing the merits or wisdom of such an agreement. We know, however, that for long years our Prime Minister has boasted of being successful in avoiding any similar commitment with Great Britain. I want to know, has he now undertaken an international pact, with heavy obligations, behind the back of Parliament, without even so much as submitting it after completion to representatives of the people of Canada? Apparently he has. Sometimes, this Ogdensburg performance is pictured as of relatively small consequence, not warranting consideration by Parliament; as providing for mere staff talks between experts as to what to do in certain vicissitudes of attack—staff talks like those which very frequently occur between nations with similar defensive necessities. If the arrangement is such and no more, it is strange that it is elevated to the dignity of a pact; strange that a spokesman for the Prime Minister should say it is an agreement placing heavy responsibilities upon us. If it is only an arrangement for staff talks, why was it attended with all the suits and trappings of photography, and publicity, with a showman on one side and a showman on the other, and photographers in between, and heralded as a great consummation? If it is, on the contrary, what Mr. Brockington describes it to be, then the ignoring of Parliament is a shocking contempt of our constitutional rights and can never be forgiven. If it is the other, lesser thing, then the publicity is wholly out of place. In fact, the less publicity the better.

Hon. Mr. Dandurand: Would my right honourable friend consider discussing this matter from the point of view of the statements made by the Prime Minister himself?

Right Hon. Mr. Meighen: I have read them and I am discussing the matter from that point of view at this moment.

Hon. Mr. Dandurand: My right honourable friend is discussing what was said by a gentleman who made a speech in Philadelphia some time ago. But the Prime Minister spoke for an hour and a half yesterday.

Right Hon. Mr. Meighen: Very well. I am discussing the matter as it has been understood in Canada, as it has been represented by the press time and time again. Those words of Mr. Brockington's have never been repudiated. I want to know what the truth is.

Hon. Mr. Dandurand: My right honourable friend has read Colonel Biggar's statement on this matter?

Right Hon. Mr. Meighen: I have read a lot from Colonel Biggar. I have read reports of interviews given by this Joint Commission on Defence, of which Colonel Biggar is one of two members. They fly to this coast and that. They look at harbours and aerodromes on the Atlantic, and in the evening that master of publicity, Mr. LaGuardia, gives a statement: "You people," he says, "do not need to fear anything here in the province of Nova Scotia. We will see to your defence. We are going to make proposals—and indeed we have them formulated now—under which no enemy can set foot on your shores." And Colonel Biggar adds, in much more modest terms: "We have had a successful day." What twilight twittering this is! We are to be defended by the work of a Joint Commission! There is one thing, and only one, as you can read in yesterday's speech of the honourable senator from Sorel, which can ever defend this continent until such time as the American Navy is doubled and the American Air Force is fifty times what it is today, and that is the British Fleet.

All this inspecting of aerodromes and harbours on the Atlantic coast and putting up of some guns on the Pacific, and Mr. LaGuardia's speeches, can only have one result and that is to induce our people to seek refuge under a delusion, to turn their eyes from unpleasant and forbidding truths. Of what value would these local defences be if the British Navy should lose control of the Atlantic? Of what value would be any defence produced by thirty days' training of the 30,000 or, for that matter, 300,000 men here, if the British Navy goes down? If Britain falls, at least before our strength—not our speeches, but our strength—on this continent is multiplied, and that means years hence, our fate is settled. No man can grasp the logical inference from the speeches of every allied leader and even of Mr. Roosevelt himself and come to any other conclusion. However hampered by inevitable political considerations Mr. Roosevelt may be, that conviction he plainly reveals. I do not take any comfort out of newspaper interviews of Mr. La Guardia or Colonel Biggar. I know where our defence is, as we all know. And we know where the decisive theatres of this war are, and not one of them is in Canada.

HON. MR. DANDURAND: We all know that.

RIGHT HON. MR. MEIGHEN: Surely we do. Then why make these statements to delude our people?

I come now to the main matter which I rose to discuss. What I fear is that we are not directing our efforts to the essential, vital end; that we are dissipating our toil and our substance in activities which sound fine and are popular, but which will never win this war. If the history of national conflicts has taught us anything it is that there is only one way to win a war, and that is by having decisive forces at decisive points at the decisive time. Are we contributing to that only way of achieving victory by sending to vital theatres somewhat less—far less—than 50,000 men? Those theatres are not in the West Indies or in Newfoundland. At some time one of them may be in Iceland. Others may develop; possibly the next one will be in Palestine. But just now the great theatres are in Britain, Greece and the Middle East. There is where the war may be won or lost. There is where our fate may be decided. And what have we there? We have two divisions abroad. The number of our men overseas is said to be 52,000, but, so far as I know, they are in none of the actual theatres I have mentioned, save in England. That is not a very ponderous force for this Dominion. I do not think that focussing that relatively small army in the real theatres, and gathering here many thousands of men one-half or one-quarter or one-tenth trained, and stationing of one division on the Pacific and another on the Atlantic, and all the paraphernalia we call home defence, is doing justice to Canada's power to win.

In emphasizing that victory overseas is the supreme end, I cannot refrain from reading words addressed a few days ago to the people of the United States by the late Prime Minister of Poland:

> Britain is suffering terribly, and while she is bloody she has no friends, or no friends who are strong enough, or bold enough, to offer her help.
>
> Without Britain the world will be a monstrous and dark place in which to live.
>
> I have fled here for sanctuary because only here and in besieged England, or the places controlled by England, is such sanctuary possible. My own nation of Poland is being systematically exterminated by brutes.
>
> Do not be deceived.

Let these words ring through Canada.

> Do not be deceived. Do not think you can escape because you are far away. If Britain dies, so dies America. Perhaps mine is an old, small voice in the wilderness, but its message is a vital message. Help Britain, help Britain now, help Britain with all you have.

Someone may ask: Are we to do nothing about home defence? I do not say so. But I read the Prime Minister's speech, where he says that at Imperial conferences, dating back for twenty years, it has been agreed that each Dominion will prepare its own defence, and after that will give all the help it can spare to Britain. And this, he says, is what we are doing. Now, in all sincerity I say, let us forget the resolutions of peacetime Imperial conferences. By making certain preparations at home you may be able to do something against a sporadic attack here in Canada, but even a sporadic attack of any significance is most unlikely in the present war, because if one of importance were made on us, the enemy well knows he would in all probability bring into action the United States. Of Australia a similar statement would not be true. Anyway, all these scores of thousands of men who are being trained or half trained—some of them, I fear, to be hothouse soldiers, because of the way they are treated in those thirty-day camps—these men would not be useful against sporadic attack, even if it came. No invasion can come while Britain lives. Consequently, the whole performance is a waste of money, of substance and of human energy. The object to which our every effort should be directed is as plain as the sun in heaven: to build up and train an army of men on land, in the air and on the sea, and send them to the theatres of war so equipped that with their comrades and allies they will be able to win.

If the United States feel that, having regard to public opinion in their country, they cannot enter this conflict, that is their own affair, though it may some day lead to their destruction. They seek to gather the great mass of their forces behind the lines, at home. To the extent that we take of our substance to build fortresses on our shores, and to hold our men in Canada, we are certainly fitting into the pattern of American defence. Yet we should know, and we do know, that if Britain falls we fall, and that at present we are not contributing as we should to that victory so essential to the whole of this continent, which alone can save our nation and our lives. From the selfish standpoint of Canada, our business now is to pattern our policy into the British effort, and, to the utmost of our strength, make certain of Britain's victory. Those words uttered so eloquently by the honourable senator from Sorel embody an immortal truth. I beg this House and the Government to act in the light of that truth, even if their doing so entails, which I do not think likely, a risk of schism at home. Speaking for myself, let me give assurance that if any of the Conservative party set about to instigate trouble, a happening to me inconceivable, I will oppose them and support the Government.

SOME HON. SENATORS: Hear, hear.

RIGHT HON. MR. MEIGHEN: Let us do what is vital to the life of this country. We can easily take care of any possible trouble here. The honourable senator from Sorel pleaded eloquently for union—union of heart and union of effort. Of his sincerity I have not a shadow of doubt, and will help without ceasing to bring it to pass. But I do offer to his mind this thought which comes to me every hour: Would union not be better achieved in this nation if the Dominion Government itself represented that union and thus enabled all Canadians loyally to express themselves within its compass and so contribute to its efficiency and its success?

We are spending uncounted millions on this much-touted training scheme for home defence. I have been told, and I think some figures were given in the other Chamber to show, that merely up to now, including structures for all these camps, the cost has been approximately $35,000,000 to $45,000,000. We have taken from the ranks of skilled labour and other labour men essential to the industrial contribution of our country. We are getting little or nothing for this sacrifice. Concentrate, I implore you, on training airmen, sailors and soldiers to send to the theatres where the conflict is going to be decided, and as well, concentrate on keeping workers at their posts making machines and munitions with which the fighting men can win. That should be the policy of Canada.

Under this rather enticing title of home defence we are, I am afraid, committing a grave and indelible sin. Home defence, so called, originates in selfishness. It is blind to truth; it is distinguished by insularity and not by foresight; it shrinks from realities that are unhappy and forbidding, but are overwhelming all the same. The spirit which dominated the policy of Belgium, of Holland and of Norway before these countries folded up and fell, is the spirit behind home defence appeals in Canada. I fear it is the spirit which too far controls the policy of this continent; and if the day comes—no, if the night comes, the dark, unending night when the world crashes into ruin, it will be just because that spirit prevailed too long.

The importance of this overshadows all other subjects. I cannot agree that we are doing our part; I cannot agree that we have used good judgment and forethought. The main reason is that we have been mesmerized and chloroformed by this popular appeal about home defence, and have kept the big, the life-or-death, objective shut away from our minds; and if we continue with our heads in the sand, we shall not take steps direct and certain to reach that supreme culmination. Therefore, for a policy which alone can save us I make my single appeal.

SIR JOHN A. MACDONALD

Address delivered on June 7, 1941, at a commemoration service held at Kingston, Ontario, to mark the fiftieth anniversary of the death of Sir John A. Macdonald, June 6, 1891.

THE FOOTSTEPS OF TIME MOVE FAST, and how short the term of life—very brief it is to those who are eager to toil and to achieve.

The thought now, though, deepest in every mind must be—how short, how narrowly bounded is human vision. Here in this place, hallowed by every Canadian, we meet fifty years after his death to do honour to the man who more than any other founded our country, and we meet under the shadow of the blackest clouds that ever overcast this world; we meet amid the fires, the thunders of war, distant perhaps in space but not in meaning, threatening all we possess and all we are. Sir Wilfrid Laurier ascribed to Macdonald as his highest attribute a far-reaching vision beyond the events of his time; but not to Macdonald, nor to any statesman of his era, did there come into contemplation any such tide of tragedy as rages in our day. We ourselves, let us confess, cannot pierce the future even as far as our fathers did, for events become swifter and bigger as man's mastery over nature becomes more and more supreme.

We turn aside for a mere moment to pay tribute where tribute is due and to gain inspiration if we can, courage if we can, wisdom if we can, at the fountain of history.

If it had been given to the penetrating mind of Sir John A. Macdonald to see beyond the veil and to foreshadow those strains and perils which now surround his country, I am not sure that his course at any stage of his career could have been different from what it was. He was a Canadian, struggling with the diversities and jealousies of far scattered people. With him it is true Canada was first. Sir John Thompson said that his chief's daily thought was expressed in Webster's words: "Let our object be our country, our whole country, and nothing but our country." His true and deep Canadianism was to him "a pillar of cloud by day and a pillar of fire by night." But with him Canada was first not in any narrow sense of singleness or priority but only in the sense of his own immediate duty. Never at any time did he lose sight of or subordinate to a selfish Canadian purpose the oneness of our interest, the oneness of our security, and the oneness of our destiny with the British Empire. From the first message to his people, delivered in this City of Kingston in 1844, to his last great appeal in the year of his death, he never ceased to affirm his conviction that our prosperity rested on the permanence of our place in that Empire and that our freedom as a nation depended on its unity and its strength. In this he was powerfully supported by his colleagues from French Canada, who loved him and shared his faith. They knew well what we all know in our country and what the crashing events of this hour are driving home to every quarter of this continent—that the corner stone of liberty must not be broken if liberty is to survive; and that corner stone is Britain. We do honour to him here as the father of our Canadian Confederation, but right in the heart of England, in the Cathedral of St. Paul's honour has been rightly done him as one whose services to the Empire deserved to be ranked with those of Wellington and Nelson.

Legend and biography are full of tales which illumine the personal life and reveal the personal charm of Macdonald. Those qualities we describe as human were his in almost incomparable degree. Of these we have heard today. We have read of them for half a century. Never have they found expression in terms so graceful, so memorable and so generous as in that immortal tribute paid him in the House of Commons by Sir Wilfrid Laurier. Not even the rich and stately eulogy delivered by Sir John Thompson at Hamilton in 1893 can last as long as Laurier's great speech. We are not likely ever to forget that salute to "Canada's most illustrious son," the story of the devotion, ardent devotion, and affection with which he was followed, of the "inner, subtle, and indefinable graces of soul which win and keep the hearts of men," of the angel of death touching him with his wing, of his struggle against enfeebled health and declining strength, until the hand of fate pinned him to his bed to die. We read in many places of his tact and his urbanity, of the amiability and gentleness of his nature, of the kindness, humour and forbearance which seemed the only weapons he would turn to attacks from those who should have been his friends. From every source we learn of his patience, his unbounded and unending patience. These are virtues possessed by a few—a very favoured few—but possessed in equal degree by Sir John's great rival and successor. They are virtues in public life of almost unbelievable importance, virtues valued most by those to whom they are denied.

The gifts I have just described helped him tremendously—they helped him to office, they helped him stay in office, they helped him in the supreme art of governing men. But do not make the mistake too often made of thinking that these talents stood alone, or that they were the basic and enduring talents which accounted for his usefulness to Canada. The truth is he was the most practical of men, a toiler, a builder devoted indefatigably to getting things done. No one can read his history, his letters, and especially his speeches in Parliament, without realizing the comprehensive grasp of facts, the order with which, under his hand, those facts fell into position, and consequently the firmness of conviction with which he could drive home his conclusions. Contrary to the general belief, he could reason just as well as he could appeal. His mind was quick, clear and vigorous, his nature earnest and tenacious; without these solid qualities he never would have reached the place he occupies in history as a Parliamentary leader.

A reading of Hansard, or of discussions outside Parliament, shows a marked difference between the methods of Macdonald's day and of our own. Into the causes I will not enter except to say that universal suffrage may be one. Whatever the reason, you will search in vain among the speeches of Macdonald or of his contemporaries including, of course, his opponents, for anything in the nature of a class appeal. He assumed and they assumed that the good of the State was the only talisman, that, next to the safety of the nation, the main objective of legislation must be to help those who need help most, to give opportunity to the unadvantaged, to encourage and assist those who are down to rise. They knew, and they assumed everybody else knew, that as soon as it could be shown that any article of policy would contribute to this end, that moment a case for such policy was made. From this point of view they argued the merits of whatever legislative step was in issue. They did not consider it the part of necessity or the part of honour to attribute other designs to their foes. Never will you find in the speeches of Macdonald or of his Opposition those attacks on the successful few and that flattery of the many, accompanied by portraits of heaven, which abound now in the orations of more countries than our own.

When the time came to Macdonald for an appeal, he made it; and it was a manly appeal and a very effective appeal. Sir John Thompson quoted one of these efforts, made at a time of great difficulty and danger. It may not be a finished literary production but it would be hard indeed to conceive of anything more admirably designed to rouse the loyalty of his friends and recover wanderers back into his fold:—

> "I have fought the battle of Confederation, the battle of Union, the battle of the Dominion of Canada. I throw myself upon the House. I throw myself upon this country, I throw myself upon posterity, and I believe that, notwithstanding the many failings of my life, I shall have the voice of this country and this House rallying round me. And, sir, if I am mistaken in that, I can confidently appeal to a higher court—to the court of my own conscience and to the court of posterity. I leave it with this House with every confidence. I am equal to either fortune. I can see past the decision of this House, whether for or against me, but whether it be for or against me, I know, and it is no vain boast for me to say so, for even my enemies will admit that I am no boaster, that there does not exist in Canada a man who has given more of his time, more of his heart, more of his wealth, or more of his intellect and power, such as they may be, for the good of this Dominion of Canada.

Sir John Macdonald does not stand alone in the galaxy of our eminent men; but his greatest rival, to his eternal credit, has awarded him the primacy among the founders and builders of our nation. For the heavier tasks of today there is more to be learned from him than from any other. If we govern ourselves, each one of us, by the principles which governed him; if we work as he worked; dare as he dared; and follow the star that lighted his life, we will serve our country as we ought to serve it and, with God's help, we will save it.

THE LAST HUNDRED YEARS

Address at St. Marys, Ontario, September 13, 1942, on the occasion of the hundredth anniversary of the town.

IT IS AN HONOUR TO BE INVITED and a happiness to come back to resume the role of fellow-townsman. This role, I can assure you, was long ago much enjoyed, and this afternoon fond memory brings around one the light of those earlier days.

A century is but a moment of history. In these times, however, such moments are vibrant with great events. Mankind has travelled far and witnessed much in the past hundred years. Some think we have learned but little, especially of the true purpose and principles of living. If so, the conclusion is lamentable beyond expression or conception, because without any doubt at all, the penalties of failure either in thinking or in character become heavier as the complexities of civilization multiply.

In 1842 Canada was emerging from the animosities of an unfortunate Rebellion, and was struggling with problems very similar to those which beset us still. In Europe nations were seething with social unrest—just the same thing that is all around us now. Poverty and want were rampant, far worse than we have ever known them on this continent. Britain had just launched herself on a journey toward universal suffrage, and very many believed that along that path was social salvation. They fondly hoped that with everybody voting the day of their worries would be over. Prophets of a millennium of social security were almost as numerous and just as confident as they are in our own time. Hope springs eternal—but somehow or other troubles never stay long away.

In the same year, 1842, India was the seat of Britain's anxieties. There were wars on her frontiers just as there are

411

now, but oh, how small was the sum of the perils faced by Melbourne and Peel compared to those which today flame before the eyes of Churchill! Then it was a matter mainly of tactics; now it is a strain, and the very uttermost strain, on the man-power and willpower of the British nation. Then it was a choice of the wisest diplomacy and the least suffering; now it is a choice of life or death.

It was in that year that an English historian wrote his famous essay on "Frederick the Great," from which most of us have derived our impressions of that not very admirable man. One wonders what Macaulay would have written had he known that the creed of blood and iron pumped through German veins by that ruthless tyrant would harvest out since in the massacre of millions and the scourging of humankind for a century.

True enough, your hundred years of life have been only a moment, but how crowded that moment has been with wisdom for all who will try to learn. It has been crowded with lessons and it has been charged and supercharged with interest. The years have been prolific with inventions, with discoveries, with events, which to the end of time will grip the human mind.

In that period man has entered the majestic arsenal of Nature and there has captured and brought forth for the service of his fellows her mighty forces—forces which for long ages had been hidden and unknown and which only Nature could call into being. In that period we have seen those mighty forces set to work with high efficiency in tremendous mechanisms. We have seen these mechanisms naturally and necessarily falling into place in great units of production which absorb the savings of and help to support, millions of people. And we have watched those great units of production adjust themselves slowly and cum-brously into an economy of free enterprise—the same economy of free enterprise to which they owe their birth and under which alone a free civilization can survive. In the midst of this adjust-ment, with its inevitable and serious imperfections, we find ourselves today. But the ills which flow from those imperfections we can take care of and steadily remove, if only we keep our feet on the ground and our common sense intact.

In this same century the restless, buoyant human intellect has peered into the mysteries of that astounding spectacle we call the world. It has penetrated far and toiled with amazing energy and patience. It has brought back to us tales of wonders bewildering. It has told us of a universe of staggering immensity and incredible antiquity, beyond the powers of human language to portray or human imagination to conceive. No map will ever disclose to us even a segment of the heavens, because any map upon which a speck the size of this earth could be seen with the naked eye would have to be as large as Europe. And yet, notwithstanding myriads of constellations, followed by myriads more and multiplied by myriads again, stretching wherever we look into endless space, we are told that only one, this little grain of dust we call the earth, is at all likely to be the home of man or of any form of life as we understand life to be—indeed, that before such life could exist on any other star, not only must a miracle have taken place but two miracles must have happened together. The all but indomitable intellect has reached out and examined the starry occupants of heaven and confidently informs us of the temperature of far-distant planets and even of their chemical components—all this of planets so far away that light travelling from them at the rate of one hundred and eighty-six thousand miles per second takes thousands of years to reach us.

The scientific mind returns from its journey through space to bend its light on the incomprehensible minuteness of an atom. The atom is held before us and we are told its character and conduct, and even composition, though the thing itself is so small as to be as far beyond our capacity to see as the Milky Way is beyond our capacity to reach.

Then, within the compass of these two extremes, which for want of better terms I call the infinitely large and the infinitely small, there has been revealed to us a biography of life in this our earthly home. And what a biography it is! We learn of its humble beginnings, its long struggle, its endless complexities, its abounding diversities, its pitiful frailties, its cruel strength. Over the ages we are carried in a recital of throbbing interest documented by evidence found in the footprints of onward-marching time, and in the end we are left in amazed wonderment by it all and more than anything else by the perfect conformity, throughout the universe of means to ends, a conformity which only Nature can achieve.

When one lifts his head from the contemplation of these things, he feels himself prostrate before the unimaginable grandeur of it all and the all-pervading Providence presiding within, without and around.

The more we learn the more there is left to learn. The vista of the unseen at once intrigues and appals. Macneile Dixon, whose book, "The Human Situation," is one of the great productions of this century, reports to us, after long biological study, that it is just as impossible for a man to understand a moth as for a moth to understand a man. "Before the mystery of memory"— for memory seems to be the deepest of enigmas—"Before the mystery of memory," he says, "all the sciences flee in despair." Yes, although what we now know is much and precious, and we salute men of science for conquests they have won and light they have shed, the whole seems to reveal more than anything else the vastness of the great unknown—the great unknown whose farther boundary recedes with every advance of knowledge, and still again recedes. Our learning, like our experience, is an arch "wherethrough gleams that untravell'd world whose margin fades for ever and for ever" as we move.

During this period, far from your peaceful town but within sight of every observant mind, tremendous events have taken place. In the middle of the nineteenth century, when you were just started on your journey, you saw the rise of democratic institutions in many lands—that is, of government by the people through Parliaments freely elected. In Britain, in the United States, in France, and in the expanding British Dominions, you saw these institutions grow into every appearance of maturity and permanence. Throughout nearly all of Europe and our own continent, through some of Africa, and through much of South America they took form as the years passed, and in varying degrees acquired substance as well.

Those of us who are old enough remember how sanguine we were as we passed into the twentieth century that mankind at long last was coming into its own. But no such millennium was near. The people of a nation can make success of government by Parliament only if education is general and the level of honesty high. I mean honesty both of Parliament and of people, honesty of character and of thinking. Without these the path downward is a Gadarene slope. Prejudice takes the place of reason; the demagogue finds himself with the handiest weapons, and too easily reaches power. It is an obligation of every citizen to read and ponder the last quarter century of French history. What lessons it has for us! We can think, as we look back, of nation after nation whose Parliament degenerated and passed away or became only a shell. Others could not sustain the shattering impact of war, and at a time at which in earlier days we had hoped to see the flowering of free institutions over civilized humanity, we witnessed instead their melancholy disappearance and the resurgence of selfish despotism. Even before the outbreak of this worst of wars, one could travel from the Atlantic seaboard in Europe all the way East to the shores of the Pacific in the Orient and never set foot in a country where democratic institutions had survived. They had been just houses built on sand.

Parliamentary government! Freedom! In the very hour in which you are gathered here to start your second century, what remains of this thing, this finest product of human aspiration and human toil, this hope, this last hope for the emancipation of mankind, is under the test of war. In Britain, its ancient home, in Britain, Mother of Freedom, in British Dominions, in the United States—for these are its only strongholds left—it is going through a furnace of fire. Its fate hangs on an issue which at this moment wavers in the balance, and with it your fate and my fate and our children's fate. If the light that lit the century goes out, there is nothing left for us.

This is the hour to be true to ourselves, true to our history and our lineage, true to our friends and our Allies. Remember, we are in the fourth year and we have not yet started to win. We in Canada have to fight this war as if to win or lose depended on ourselves. Once a nation is in a fight like this, there is no other way to behave. The more our Allies do, the more we must do. Look at the United States: there is an example of a giant aroused. What they accomplished in the last war was not a circumstance to what they are doing now. Their huge industrial machine is rolling swiftly to the top of its might, and what is far more significant, within three, four or five months of the day they threw the gauntlet down, their guns, their tanks, their ships, their men were fighting in every quarter of the globe—no privileges, no preferences, no reservations. The nation was in it for its life and all men were servants of the State.

And what of Britain! What of Britain! When that great and ancient country, in the crash of 1940, in the blackest hour that ever enveloped this planet—when Britain shook her lone fist in the face of Germany, shook her lone fist in the face of the master of Europe, she made herself again the standard-bearer of human liberty; she made herself a shining beacon and the world's hope.

I cannot give you any recital of Britain's part in the conflict, taken from British propaganda, from literature poured forth to impress her great effort on other countries. I cannot do so, because they send out no such literature. From a circular published by the American Government I find this:

> Britain's armies have fought ten campaigns and garrisoned strategic bases such as Iceland, Malta, Gibraltar, India and the Middle East. Britain's fighting forces have suffered 183,500 casualties, 71 per cent of all the Empire's dead and wounded. Britain's navy, with never less than 600 ships at sea, has sunk 5,520,000 tons of enemy merchant shipping, and convoyed 100,000 United Nations' ships with loss of only one half of one per cent. of those convoys. Britain's air force fought and won the greatest air battle in history; its coastal command has flown more than 50,000,000 miles.

The old land has four and a half million men in her armed forces. She has four times as many serving out of Britain as have her four Dominions together serving outside their countries. She has five and a half millions more in vital war work, and of these, one million are women. Women are being taken from their homes and put into essential war work at a rate of twelve thousand per week, and three-quarters of those women are married. The age of conscription for her men runs from eighteen and a half years to fifty-one. She has poured out the great bulk of her production to her allies, mainly to Russia, and to battle areas overseas. Her fighter planes and her bombers are as yet unmatched.

I lose patience with people who talk about Britain emerging wrecked and bloodless from this war and sitting powerless in the councils of peace, while others of the United Nations will sit there supreme. It is too soon to talk about councils of peace, but Britain has fought wars before. Stripped she will be of her wealth, drained she will be of her blood, but her abounding spirit will have soared to heights untouched in other centuries. The leader in victory will be leader of the rescued nations.

The century you have been through thrilled with interest from its opening year to this Anniversary Day. It was warmed and illuminated by the triumphs of peace: it was scourged by the brutalities and ennobled by the sacrifices of war. The cycle you enter now? . . . its key hangs by a sword. But, come what will, come the best, its aftermath will be heavy. The air is full of talk of new eras and new orders. There is no man fit to live who does not long for happier days for the masses of mankind, and there is no man worth very much who would not toil his utmost to bring better things about. But better things come only by clear thinking and hard work—not by dreams, demonstrations and resolutions. The road upward has always been steep and thorny; it has never been a primrose path and not likely ever will be. Keep in mind, though, this eternal truth: Difficulties do not crush men, they make men. All these things we are ready to face and we will face them cheerfully just as soon as we have made certain that this Nation is going to live. Make sure of that and there is solid ground for hope that sunshine serene and abundant will one day light the coming century. It may indeed, as decade follows decade, provide for our children a great deal more of warmth and happiness than we ourselves have seen. If the Allied Nations can not only succeed in striking down the wicked authors of this crime, but can accomplish man's greatest task and make a conquest of war itself, closing it like a tamed beast within the encircled nations, then our future will in very truth be better than our past. Let us not, however, strain to pierce the veil of tomorrow. Our day's work is here, and now.

I must close. Permit me to express what you all feel, sincere sympathy for those among you whose families already have suffered. The scythe of time swings swiftly in these days. Week by week, hour by hour, we must fortify ourselves with new resolve and new courage. We are on the threshold of tremendous events. The stoutest hearts, the clearest minds, the tireless toilers—to them will come the victory.

THE C. B. C.—A PARTY INSTRUMENT

WAR LETHARGY

Spoken at the opening of the Conservative Convention at Winnipeg on December 9, 1942. On this occasion the speaker handed over leadership of the Conservative Party to the Convention's choice, the Hon. John Bracken.

IT HAS NOT BEEN MY PURPOSE, nor am I now attempting to make what has been foreshadowed in the press as a keynote address. Such an undertaking did not seem to me appropriate for one who must soon pass from the stage. This duty has, indeed, been well performed already and I am glad to accept the very excellent speech which Mr. Hanson has just delivered as reflecting the spirit of this multitude and the resolve of the great party in whose name we gather.

When, sixteen and more years ago, I retired from active politics, I expressed an intention of remaining so retired, and now ask you to believe that that statement of intention was sincere. There are those who have a love of public life for its own sake. Of these I am not one. Many a time have I wished that love were mine. Some five years later, however, in the winter of 1931-32, our leader of that day, Mr. Bennett, now the Viscount Bennett—and a very able man he is—urged me strongly and repeatedly to accept a seat in the Upper House, that I might be chosen as leader there. It was Mr. Bennett's view that there was a worthwhile, long-term work to be done in that Chamber, and, as well, an immediate task of no small importance. I responded to our leader's appeal and devoted several years to an endeavour, in co-operation with my colleagues—and many of them on both sides were very competent—to make of that House a truly valuable part of our Constitutional machinery and a real service to our nation. To the credit of Mr. Bennett I want to add

that no man ever gave another freer scope than he gave me; no
Prime Minister ever before committed to the Senate constructive
work of such consequence, or ever accepted from it with so good
a grace such a formidable catalogue of amendments to legislation
initiated in the House of Commons. Whatever was our success
in raising that Chamber to a stature of real national worth, it was
in no small degree due to him.

Years passed, and not long after Mr. Bennett's defeat one could
plainly see that the usefulness of the Senate was doomed to
diminish. It was contemptuously ignored by the Government of
Mr. King, and condemned in its legislative sphere to desuetude
and idleness. The House of Commons has been steadily
manoeuvred into almost the same position, so much so that parliamentary government in this Dominion has become little more
than a memory.

Under circumstances which many of you recall, I found
myself in a situation, about a year ago, where after dissolution
of a Conservative Conference at Ottawa and return of its members to their distant homes, I was asked, on the authority of a
vote which was reported to me as unanimous, to take upon myself again the duties of leader. There were difficulties about any
decision; my earnest wish was to be left alone, and such wish in
the form, indeed, of a definite negative decision had been previously expressed to the Conference. I decided finally that there
could be just criticism, in that very peculiar juncture, if I failed
the party, particularly in time of war; and accordingly an acceptance was later despatched and I addressed myself to the task of
performing those functions of opposition leadership vital in all
democracies, and imperatively essential when a party government
with partisan practices persists in remaining in power in war.
By a combination, by a common resolve of not one, not two, but
three party leaders—the Liberal, the C.C.F. and the Communist—I was denied admission to the House of Commons.
News of my defeat was received with gloatings and coarse re-
joicings by ministers who at the time were leading this country
in war!

I have accepted the verdict of South York[1] and have not

---

[1] Where the author was defeated Feb. 9, 1942.

sought another seat. This is due in no small degree to an irremovable reluctance to ask favours again, or what appear as favours, from an elected member or from a constituency, and to vend myself from riding to riding in the hope of being accepted. I have, instead, devoted my time since, with what intelligence and energy may be mine, to an endeavour to guide the party along lines, or rather into lines, which seem to lead to a broadening of its outlook and an enhancement of its opportunities, and to enabling it, when called upon by the people of Canada, to provide a representative, a constitutional and a truly progressive government for this Dominion—a government which, surely, if ever in history, the nation longs for and needs at this very hour.

Rightly or wrongly, I have felt that to give such guidance according to my lights is my bounden duty, so long as I am leader and up to my last hour in this high office. With that thought in mind, the call for this Convention was worded in the wide terms in which it appeared. I express my gratitude to the National Convention Committee for having unanimously endorsed those terms, and at this point welcome, and welcome warmly, those who, believing in the principles embodied in that announcement, have come from other affiliations, or no affiliations at all, to join with us in the great work which is now ahead.

We are assembled here from all provinces, from all creeds and races. We include in our numbers descendants and near-of-kin of the great men who founded our country; and we include, perhaps more than any other assembly could include, outside of an assembly of veterans themselves, those who have given of their all and given of their blood for the triumph of our nation in its hour of need. We are gathered in no spirit of joviality; we are not here to thump drums and sound slogans; we are not here to debate personalities of other years, or to thrash over quarrels of other times. We are here because we see in front, and very near in front, a tremendous task to perform—a task which is recognized as momentous and immediate by all divisions of the press and by all schools of thought, by men and women of all parties and all sections of our country.

We at this Convention have an opportunity to do big things for Canada. Nothing less than big things must be done. I beg of you to sink all other thoughts and join together to do those very things.

My resolve was, until persuaded otherwise a few hours ago, to confine my words to a statement of intentions and of the hopes I had for this party, and then to leave the Convention open and free from all restraint. I speak at this time only under the prerogative which derives from my position as leader. No one can follow me. Therefore, it is not for me to invade territory which might be controversial as among ourselves. To that rule I shall strictly adhere.

I have been asked to present my views upon two issues, which today protrude into immediate and far-reaching significance and which stand out, or ought to stand out, with tremendous appeal to the people of our country. This shall be done with all the brevity and clarity in my power.

You will observe that the instrument on my left is a loud speaker; it is not a radio. This Convention, recognized universally by all classes of the Canadian people as of definite and outstanding significance, has been denied by the Canadian Broadcasting Corporation of Canada coverage over their lines—denied the right to carry its speeches, its arguments and decisions, or any of them, into the homes of our country. It has been forbidden access to millions of Canadian listeners, by an authoritarian Commission appointed by a Government constituted from a single party. Our Convention Committee appealed for the privilege of having the speeches of their leader and of the chairman of this Convention, outlining the purposes of this assembly, carried over C.B.C. lines throughout Canada. They were peremptorily refused by the Commission, every member of which is an appointee of the Government of Mr. King. They were not only refused free use of this radio, which is granted to every Cabinet minister on demand, but, after offering to pay regular charges for time, they were again repulsed.

As you will have seen in the press, the Chairman of the Commission has assured us that in this conduct they could not possibly have been moved by any party bias or by any pressure from above, because in a White Paper—how important that it was white—in a White Paper they had announced many months ago that there would be no political controversies allowed over the radio in time of war. Therefore, he said, that closes the issue, and intimated that we might apologize for having protested to the people of Canada the autocratic discrimination handed out to a large section of this nation by a Commission of Mr. King's.

No political controversy in time of war? They would not countenance such a heinous thing! True, they did not countenance it on this occasion; they did not allow it; and the method by which they prevented it has at least the merit of simplicity; they prevented it by allowing one party on the radio, and one alone. But has anyone listened since the war began, or for years before, to a radio address by the Prime Minister, or by any of his ministers, which was not charged and replete with political appeal; whose purpose was not from first to last to boost the stock of the King Government, to show the people what wonderful things it was doing, what a grand success it was making, how beloved it was by the whole country, and what great and immortal men were at the head of our affairs; which was not designed especially to demonstrate their conspicuous superiority over those bungling incompetents who had led us to victory in the last war? These men, month after month, week after week, day after day, have gone on delivering messages to the people of Canada, the central purpose of which was to build themselves up, to popularize themselves and thus to be ready for a trial of strength when an appeal to the electors comes. And the Radio Commission says that is all right; that is in the national interest; that only contributes to loving harmony which must prevail in time of war! That, according to Chairman Thomson, is a great patriotic purpose; but if we who think differently seek to upset those contentions, if we seek to show the other point of view, he tells us that to do so is to inject political discord into a happy atmosphere, and he turns the button against millions of people whom we want to reach, and who are waiting to hear.

Believe me, radio reaches virtually all. The press is still a mighty factor, but radio gets to more than the press; it is easier to sit and listen than it is to direct one's energies to reading.

Radio has advanced to a status of influence and power hard indeed to exaggerate. By radio Hitler rose to office and to domination. Give a single party the radio between elections, and it won't matter much whether there is an election or not. Just continue a single party monopoly of radio and you might as well sit up and recognize that fascism is here to stay. This Commission has given the Liberal party a monopoly and they are using that monopoly with their eyes on the ballot morning, noon and night.

We are told that we must bow before the majesty of a White Paper, and that we are denied a hearing only because we would create political controversy. Listen; if political controversy is to be forbidden, was there nothing controversial in Mr. Ilsley's radio speech of last week? Are we to assume that that speech is fully accepted by the people of this nation, by you people here? Mr. Ilsley told about the fine civil policy of the King Government, explained to us that tea was going to be two or three cents cheaper by higher taxes, and went on to draw a contrast between the magnificent efficiency of the present War Prices Board and the sad stupidity of the Administration of the 1914-18 war which allowed farm prices and other prices to go up seventeen odd per cent! Nothing controversial about that speech? It was a subtle attack on the Conservative party from beginning to end. But if Mr. Ilsley could have contrived to make it worse in the way of partisanship, he would still have been given the radio free. If he could have been very much worse, he would not only have had free broadcast through the nation, but would have been paid a fee by the Commission for his services to Canada!

Why do I use those words? You have in your midst, here in Winnipeg, a gentleman known as Professor Watson Thompson. He is on the pay-roll of the Commission. I have in my hand, received from the Commission, a verbatim report of his address delivered on the fourth of last month, and I am going to read to you one paragraph and ask this assembled multitude if there is anything of partisanship, anything politically controversial about it: and there are worse things to come. What he had been talking about just before matters not, but this he said:

> And I would like to tie that in with the whole record of Canada's war effort—

The issue between the parties in this nation since the war began has been this war effort—here is what he said about it:

> In any fair comparison with Britain or the United States, one discovers that we grossly underestimate ourselves. It is true, of course, that in Britain air raids and the closeness of people on a small island have induced a remarkably high sense of unity, and the kind of morale which comes only under fire.

An astonishing thing that there should be high morale in Britain! He thought it necessary to explain that people there had the advantage of being under fire.

> But Canada has quietly taken—

Think how quietly!

> —quietly taken the necessary steps.

Now, here is our record as against the British record of high morale assisted by fire:

> Canada has quietly taken the necessary steps introducing price control, manpower regulations—

Did you hear it?

> —and such things, which put her on a par with Britain in internal efficiency, and without benefit of bombs. . . .

Imagine the super-wisdom of a government of this nation, which is able to bring about internal efficiency in war prices without the "benefit of bombs,"

> and without all the disadvantages of a disturbance to the normal population, and have made her a model which the United States has at almost every point only belatedly followed.

And the other Professor Thomson, head of this Commission, tells you people sitting here, and other millions of this nation, that there is nothing controversial about an assertion that Canada "without benefit of bombs" has become a model nation which others follow; and follow—we are sorrowfully told—too far behind, because they are not blessed with such a government as ours!

Wholly uncontroversial! All this!—and I come to what is worse. In this speech Professor Thompson went the length of besmirching, in the middle of war, the fair name and honour of Britain; left no inference other than this, that Britain was an oppressor and exploiter of India, and that Canada—Canada— should take her place in the ranks of those who are going to set the United Kingdom right, who are going to strike down the iron hand of Britain from the neck of Indian natives whom she is exploiting for her own benefit! He went on speaking over a government broadcasting system, under the auspices and under pay of a government commission—he went on to point his finger at men in high position who, he said, had betrayed Czecho-slovakia, Spain and China, and to reprimand the people of Britain for leaving some of them in office to this day!

I ask you, citizens of Canada, to put yourselves for a moment in the position of listening to a broadcast by the government-owned system in England and imagine you hear a talk from some hireling of that system in which he addresses to the world a criticism of the people of Canada and tells them what they ought to have done and have not done; and demands, for example, to know why the man who rejected requests of the British Govern-ment in 1937 and 1938 to be permitted to establish a Training School of British airmen in this Dominion is still at the head of our affairs! It is true that Mr. King rebuffed the British Govern-ment when they wanted, in good time, to train their airmen in Canada, but let anyone over a national radio of Britain attack Mr. King on that ground and I, as a Canadian, will rebuke him. If a speaker who does not pay our taxes and is not a Canadian citizen should be provided with the national network of Britain and should use it to dictate to us as to whom we should have in office and whom we should not have in office, I certainly would resent it. Have you any idea that Mr. King himself would not resent it? Would he not be off on another anti-Downing Street-domination campaign, and would he not rejoice in springing to his opportunity, and doing so with infinitely more warrant than he ever had before? But this Thompson stuff is what Mr. King permits over the government radio of Canada—permits—ought I to use that word? This is what he pays for with our money, for I have a letter from the Broadcasting Commission of this Government acknowledging that they handed Thompson twenty-five dollars for that address. And we of the Conservative Convention of this Dominion cannot be heard and we cannot pay to be heard.

Finally the Commission Chairman, as if to expose the grossness of his discrimination, announced that while he will not permit Canadians to listen to your leader of today, he will under certain conditions permit them to listen to your leader of tomorrow, and then dares to tell us that in order to be heard, our future leader must not attack and must not abuse—in other words, he must speak under the directions of the Chairman of the Radio Commission!

Do you realize what that means in this country? Did you not hear a speech about ten days ago from New York, by Mr. Mackenzie King, spread free across this Continent by the C.B.C., to the effect that the great principle moving his Government is equality? Equality! Do you grasp now the equality dealt out to us under his Government in the matter of radio, the most powerful franchise known to man?

Did you not, as well, hear something from the same Mr. King about forsaking paths of privilege and monopoly, which he had never before admitted following, and about casting his eyes, from this time onward, to one guiding-star, human welfare? These words, of course, according to Chairman Thomson, were not intended to help the Liberal party! Can you not, though, sense something of the nature of monopoly in the radio practice of Canada? The radio of Canada has been for years, is today, and Mr. King intends it will continue to be, the effective monopoly, tool and instrument of a partisan Government headed by himself.

Not long ago, just before the war, there were two great political Conventions in the United States—one Democratic and one Republican. The big national network systems of that country—not government-owned and controlled monopolies—gave free distribution over this continent to proceedings of those Conventions, the same to the one as to the other. They did this because, in their enlightened judgment, subjects discussed were of moment and of value to people who wanted to hear. Contrast that course with the Gestapo methods in matters of radio, under which we live in Canada.

I was admitted over the radio once. I was able to listen the next day to the broadcast, because it had been delayed, and when it came through I found they had mutilated and butchered a speech of twenty minutes. They took out everything in the nature of criticism and left a shapeless, truncated mess, which they paraded far and wide as a speech of Mr. Meighen's. I wrote a letter of protest and would like to read it to you.

VOICES: Read it, read it.

It is not here.

You ask what reply was sent me. I got an acknowledgment from the General Manager that my letter was received and would be laid before his Board of Governors at their next meeting. That was a year ago last July and I have heard nothing since from the multiplied $14,000-a-year salaried Commission.

My information now is that the King Government prize this radio monopoly so highly that they are giving, under Orders in Council, priorities to radio employees ahead of priorities granted to workers on the press. Radio under their own charge must be supreme; it must have right of way.

I have enlarged upon this subject because there is nothing more momentous to the freedom of our people than this threatening situation in which we are already far engulfed, and into which we are being driven deeper and deeper day by day.

We talk about freedom of speech—it is one of the four freedoms of the Atlantic Charter—but where is freedom of speech if one political party seizes for itself dictatorial powers over carrying speech among the masses? Where is equality, if there is dictatorship on one side and silence imposed on the other?

There is a second subject, and one of still greater immediate concern, upon which I wish to dwell. It is regrettable that some speaker with military experience, who understands military organization, who lives in the atmosphere, could not present this subject. There are those present—you know them—two men prominently mentioned for the leadership—who would be much better equipped to expound the case than I am, but it falls to me to give you my own convictions on the manpower situation of our country.

I do not know, and I am absolutely certain that none of you know, how many men we have overseas in any theatre of war, or in any portion of the overseas world, liable and ready for service in this terrible conflict.

We are not winning the war. It can only be won by fighting. Where Canadians have had a chance to fight, they have revealed all the courage, all the tenacity, all the heroism with which they are so abundantly endowed, and which was exemplified in the grandeur of their performance in the last war. On sea our numbers are naturally and inevitably greater than they were then at a corresponding time. In the air the same words apply. Our men when they have had opportunity to meet the foe have been the equal of the best, whether in the air or on the sea. But do not let us flatter ourselves. Have we really in the fighting fronts taken the fair share of this Dominion in insuring victory? Have we taken any share comparable for a moment with that taken by the Motherland of Britain, with that taken by Australia, or New Zealand, having regard to the proportion of our numbers and our strength? You know, the Government knows, we all know that, relative to them, we are still far behind, and we are well on in the fourth year of war.

The time is approaching when a great test must come. But before any nation, or rather, before any commander has a right to throw his divisions into battle, he is bound to make certain that behind those divisions are reinforcements. To these every man of those divisions is entitled before he can justly be called on to face the guns of an enemy and offer his life. Have we those reinforcements? How many have we altogether? I have tried to ascertain by many routes. I finally received word, while sitting here, that we have upwards of a hundred and sixty thousand overseas. I am informed also that we have in Canada in our home army, our draftee army, upwards of fifty thousand. I was refused information as to the number of our reinforcements, or rather as to the proportion of the hundred and sixty thousand which constitutes reinforcements. I want to know what those reinforcements are and cannot learn. Are the people of this Dominion not entitled to know? Are those whose kin and whose blood are over there ready for the foe at any hour—are they not entitled to know whether reserve supplies of troops and vehicles and guns are adequate or not? Are they not entitled, as well, to such facts as will enable them to be sure that this country has provided trained and equipped reinforcements which will justify their boys in entering the fray? But we are told this information is not for us; "it is against the public interest." What! Against the public interest! The line of division of our men, as between reinforcements and normal strength, cannot be divulged for fear the information would help Hitler? Think of it! We have one hundred and fifty thousand plus—no doubt many less in the British Isles alone—among the millions of Britain's fighting men, and we are asked to believe that if the Canadian people are given information as to per-centage of this small army which constitutes and is qualified as reinforcements, the news will be helpful to Hitler! Believe me—if those reinforcements were ready and adequate, we would not be denied the facts. I charge now that they are not adequate, that they are very far from adequate, and that the Government is afraid to give us the truth. Not a man of us, least of all those who have most at stake, want in any way to help the foe, but the people of Canada have a right to the truth and to assurance they never yet have been given as to the extent, condition and suf-ficiency of those reinforcements. Everything precious to us on earth depends on that extent, condition and sufficiency. All we are ever permitted is to be submerged in collective figures which mean little.

We are aware that we have here a reserve army. All honour to those men. I think the proper course is to have a reserve army in Canada; it is necessary and right. In addition we are assured that we have a home, a draftee, army of more than fifty thousand.

A few comments are now in order about this home army. Remember, it is composed of draftees under no liability whatever to fight outside this country. What I am about to say now was openly declared as soon as the home army scheme was announced. My view has not changed, and has been repeated time and again. It takes more penetration than my mind is capable of to see the value of this home army. Australia and New Zealand may well be invaded while Britain stands in her present strength. With them invasion is a real peril; but while the armies of Britain and the overseas forces of our great ally to the south remain undefeated, while the Atlantic and the Pacific are for all practical purposes under our control, Canada cannnot be invaded. Australia and New Zealand are near Japan. There is no protecting barrier between them and Japan—a powerful enemy which is at their side. We are comparatively near to Britain; we are very near to our great American ally. Can anybody believe that there is danger of invasion of our country until the forces of Britain meet the forces of the foe and have lost the battle, and until the Atlantic or the Pacific is under control of our foes? Can we be actually invaded until then? And if that Allied collapse occurs—if that Allied collapse occurs because of procrastination on our part or for whatever cause—what does our draftee army amount to?

True, there may be sporadic attacks; there may be spasmodic attacks from the air or from the sea, and defences appropriate to such attacks should be provided. But that is a different thing from keeping up a land army here of fifty thousand draftees.

Why are they here? I never could, nor can anyone else, logically justify two classes of armies; one with a right to keep itself geographically in a defined area at home, and the other obliged to fight where the enemy is and where alone a war can be won. Are we not all citizens of the same country? How then can we have two standards of obligation? And how can we recognize the claim of any individual to say, "I will determine where I am going to be stationed and where I am going to fight, if I fight at all. The military, the naval authorities of the nation have no right to direct me. I know best myself." That right, that claim of right, I never for the life of me could understand, but that right and that claim of right have been preached by Mr. Lapointe and Mr. Cardin and all their fellow-travellers, on behalf of Mr. King, for a quarter of a century, in the Province of Quebec. Would that I had the eloquent tongue of Mr. Monette and could reveal to you the state of mind into which they roused the good people of his province by telling them of their un-doubted privilege to stay right here in time of war, and by telling them that it was an infringement of their God-given manhood to be sent anywhere save within their own land. After twenty-five years, after the harvests of those twenty-five years, the harvests of Mr. King and his confederates in election after election, boasted of by themselves and by their organs far and wide—and by none more loudly than by one right in this city of Winnipeg—they now find themselves in a position where, having so long falsified facts for their own political advantage, they dare not tell their people the truth; they dare not tell them that the true, logical obligations of war compel service wherever the nation decides that the nation can best be saved. They dare not tell them that truth. So they build up a home army of draftees. They take them out of industry; they take them out of agriculture; they sterilize them from real service of any kind by drafting them to rust in idleness in Canadian camps. The numbers of that fos-silized army fill the speeches of ministers of the Crown and clutter the radio week after week. For such purposes they were drafted and for such purposes the monstrous farce was conceived. Naturally this information does not matter to Hitler. We, at home, are implored to look with pride at the scores of thousands being equipped and mobilized, gathered for an imaginary defence in the interior of Canada, and to forget about reinforce-ments overseas. In other words, the Government of our country shelters itself behind a deceitful paper façade.

This is an illuminating indication of the country's manpower war effort under Mr. King; and the reason we are in this con-dition, the reason we are bound in these shallows, is that the party now in office is the heir of its own discreditable past. Its leading members and its first minister are entangled in the meshes of a sorry history. Today they dare not do the right, and Canada must take the consequences.

What are those consequences? What is all this costing our country, even if total draftees remain at only fifty thousand men? They tell me officially the cost per year is two thousand dollars per man, so that on a basis of fifty thousand men, the cost is one hundred million dollars per year. There goes the money that you raise in $50, $10 and $5 war savings certificates—one hundred million per annum to support this home army of draftees—draftees who never can fight until after the war is lost. But far worse than any cost in money, this political army means a subtraction from our forces on the fighting fronts in the crucial stage of war.

Now, I ask you: Is that holding the obligation of victory singly and alone in front of us? Is that evidence of throwing aside party interests and party compulsions in a great united drive for victory?

I speak with earnestness. I feel it. There are those around me—men from the Province of Quebec—who have lived even nearer these things than I have, who, themselves, have been victims of the performances I have described to you today. Their position has been far more difficult than mine. They are those who have witnessed at close range the disunity, the chaos, the manpower impasse which political chicanery has brought upon our Dominion. The responsibility for these calamities is as plain as their occurrence is deplorable.

Gentlemen, I am through. It is just thirty-five years ago this month that I was honoured with nomination in Portage la Prairie for the House of Commons. The intervening three decades and a half have been crowded with events, including two wars, and they have been strenuously lived. Those words apply in the public as in the private sphere. For about twenty-eight years I have served as a member of parliament in one House or the other. For something over twelve I was a minister of the Crown; for more than sixteen I have been honoured with the position of leader in either House, and at different times have led both sides of both Houses. Please do not think I am relating this by way of boasting; it is recalled only to indicate that I have worked hard and done my best. It has fallen to me to lead this party through three general elections, and that in pre-radio days. Fortune came and fortune fled; but, believe in my sincerity when I say that this is no reason for sympathy. It is only the lot of all of us, at least of all who strive—the joy of the upward struggle, the successes, disappointments and defeats. Perhaps it has been my fate to have had more than the average on both sides of the account, but I promise you there is going to be nothing of bitterness carried forward after the page is turned. As a matter of truth, health and happiness have been better in adversity and no man need feel that he has failed unless, in looking back, the retrospect is blank, or unless time and events have proved that he was wrong. Whether now judged right or wrong, whatever I have said, whatever I have done, is going to remain unrevised and unrepented. As it is, it will await whatever verdict may come. The future can assess it or forget it, and it will be all right with me. It is some satisfaction to know that on certain subjects history has already made its finding.

When this Convention closes, my days of leadership are over. I take my place cheerfully in the ranks and without a touch of sadness, of remorse, or of envy, and will hope still to be able to do something for causes in which I believe and which mean much to our country. Chiefly—and overshadowing and overmastering all others—there is this war to win, and to win this war no one old or young can turn away from either danger or toil. Our other troubles, however threatening, we can take care of in their turn, and, if we keep our feet on the ground and our common sense at command, we can surmount and survive them all. Canadians have something to live for. Through the fogs and confusions which surround us we can see grand things ahead, and though the short future may be heavy, the long prospect beckons brightly once this great cloud has passed.

SOCIALISM

Spoken before the Kiwanis Club, Vancouver, British Columbia, on October 21, 1943.

THIS FOR ME, IS A HAPPY OCCASION, for the reason that I find myself among so many friends of other days.

We are well on in the fifth year of a very fateful war. In consequence and challenge it still demands the best of our thinking and our energy, for likely the road ahead is long and painful. But on this subject I do not intend to speak. From the beginning I have not been associated in any way with Canada's management of the conflict and there is nothing I could tell you that would be new or carry any special authority. We all believe that the exceeding darkness of the first three years has been in great measure dissolved, and that at last our confidence in ultimate victory is intelligent and justified.

If so, there surely can be no disagreement as to those to whom we owe these brighter days. To thousands, of course; to tens of thousands. To the few dauntless airmen of 1940, only a remnant of them left, who saved the British Isles and the citadel of freedom; to the Navy once again, which defied the foe on every Sea and piloted unnumbered convoys that saved the lives of millions; to the brave hosts of Russia; to the brilliant generalship of the Mediterranean campaigns, and to our own fine lads who have fought and died. These we shall never cease to honour.

But there is one who stands, in very truth, alone. Never in the long history of human conflict has any nation had such leadership as Churchill has given this Empire. His incredible exertions; his iron courage; his ringing, rousing eloquence, classic in form but aflame with present-day life and fire—these, and more than all, the shining wisdom of his judgment have com-

manded as of right the admiration of all free peoples, and for
our own race will light its pathway down the centuries. In the
blackest crisis of human annals he has displayed not just some,
but a full galaxy of these talents which make men great, and has
gloriously earned his place in the first ranks of the immortals.

What I shall discuss today is more prosaic, but I am going to
link it with his name.

Back in the first half of the 1920's, Great Britain was con-
vulsed by class schism and socialist threatenings of the same
character as pervade this country now. Developments in the
Old Land came to a head in the General Strike of 1926. The
British people then decided the issue and by their verdict they
re-wrote their charter of liberty. Old contests, of course, continue, but the General Strike cleared the air and from that time
on danger of anything in the nature of revolution had passed.
Not very long before the great culmination of '26, the Earl of
Birkenhead, a close friend and lifelong associate of Winston
Churchill, wrote a sketch of his friend's career. I give you its
last few sentences, because they disclose not only Birkenhead's
estimate of Churchill, but also the seriousness with which he
contemplated the impending crisis of the British people. He
said, referring to Churchill:

> Every fibre of his being is individualistic, and in office or out
> of office, in Parliament or out of Parliament, his sword will
> be flashing in the struggle which awaits us all. And as I
> survey the combative qualities of those who, equally with
> himself, are pledged to march in that crusade, I can find
> none possessed of more formidable weapons in the battle
> which is so soon to decide the genius of our race and the
> future of civilization.

Winston Churchill has not changed his mind; his radio
speech of some months ago on post-war principles, makes that
very plain. He has always stood for freedom and he stands for
freedom still—political freedom, religious freedom, economic
freedom—freedom in every creative sphere of human life. Of
these principles Churchill is the stoutest champion in all the
world.

You have noted the impressive language in which Birkenhead described the emergency which had overtaken his country. We, in Canada, are in very much the same position today. Our very air is filled with clamorous cries for a New Order. The class appeal, the demand indeed that the nation be split in twain on a class basis, is heard on every side. Those free institutions which for generations we have been taught to cherish are held up to contempt. Some call for revolution, and others more discreet in their language demand revolutionary results without any revolution. Clearly we have a portentous decision to make and none can decide this thing but the whole people. We people of Canada have to respond to this challenge; we have to get down to clear, hard thinking and find where lies the right.

We are told that our economic system is wrong. We have the same economic system as all countries in the world, except totalitarian nations. There are, in fact, and there can be, only two systems, the totalitarian and our own, and right there is the issue that must be joined. Those who uphold a free economy in Britain, in the United States, in Canada, indeed in almost all the world, make no claim that their laws are beyond improvement. Far from it! There is now, and always will be, much to be done. No one has any excuse for indifference, complacency or smugness, in the face of social evils. We must never be satisfied; we must carry the banner excelsior, and battle on and on for better things. But this does not mean the upheaval of free institutions.

The great evil complained of is unemployment. Recurrent unemployment is by far the most complex social problem of our age. There seem to be myriads of people who think that what we call business cycles and the unemployment which goes with them can be cleared away very easily if we only try. Categorical pledges to abolish unemployment are scattered far and wide, but mere pledges get us nowhere. What really count are practical policies and action. To say that society will no longer tolerate unemployment is just as vain and just as senseless as to say that society will no longer tolerate disease. We have been attacking both these evils for generations with what we thought was the best intelligence we possessed, but both of them still persist. We have to keep on and try harder, profit by experience and, above all, keep our feet on the ground.

On every side you hear it said that unemployment has been abolished in Germany and in Russia and that we have abolished it ourselves in British countries in time of war. From this, people hastily conclude that now we know it can be done. It is not so simple as that. Certainly in a totalitarian nation where a Fuehrer rules and forces the whole nation to obey—in such a nation everybody can be put to work. But that means all freedom is gone; the citizen ceases to exist; he becomes a slave in the hands of government; an overlord stands above and with pistol and baton makes all decisions and tells everybody what to do. Not only is everyone told what to do, but everyone is made to do as he is told at the price of his life. The result wherever we are allowed to see it is a sorry toll of human suffering. Unemployment at any time is bad—it is very bad—but there are things which are worse!

True, we ourselves have banished unemployment by war production. A new school of noisy economists cries out: "If we can do this in war, we can do it in peace." The trouble with that theory is that what we produce for war does not have to be sold; it does not have to find a market; it goes at once into the ghastly work of destruction. What we produce in peace has to find a market; it must be produced at a cost that others can afford to pay. If a Government sets about to buy what it cannot sell, just for the sake of making work, that Government is at once on the Gadarene slope, and the calamitous precipice of inflation is very near ahead. Inflation makes misery unanimous; it is universal poverty.

Very certain it is, unemployment—especially this severe cyclical unemployment—is a stupendous problem. It is the summation of difficulties with which our democratic world must cope. You ask: Why is it so difficult? Why is it so baffling? I counter with the question: Why is disease still unconquered? Scientists in the medical world have striven and struggled for centuries, but even what are called preventable diseases still abound and weigh heavily and bitterly on human happiness and progress. In very large measure unemployment also arises from human infirmities, and those infirmities affect every class of our species. One can conceive, and be confident, of progress; it is hard to conceive of anything like an unqualified triumph. If those weaknesses of mankind which find their expression in unreasoning optimism when things go well, so that we easily become convinced that prosperity knows no limit, and so that the almost universal urge is to eat, drink and be merry today and eat, drink and be merrier tomorrow—if those could be doctored and cured, then the major cause which precipitated the last depression would be gone and there would be more hope. The public itself, in good times, seems bent on making depression inevitable. Then again if it were possible to adjust ourselves more quickly to the conditions of bad times when they do come, by producing finished goods at such lower costs as would enable primary producers to purchase, both in our land and in other lands, the wheels of trade would soon start again and unemployment would be far less severe. A too great rigidity of wage levels contributes much to the severity and bitterness of depression. Labour is entitled to all it can secure under just and equitable laws; it is entitled to fair collective bargaining rights in every free economy. But labour costs are around eighty-five per cent of all production costs and there comes a point where primary producers who want to buy just cannot buy. Plants are, therefore, compelled to curtail or to close. Students of Canadian statistics report that farmers and labour—about equal in numbers—comprise together three-quarters of our population and receive about three-quarters of our national income. They tell us also, though, that of the 74.2% earned by both these classes in the fifteen years 1926 to 1940, 62.4% went to labour and only 11.8% to farmers. This arresting contrast is of great and far-reaching significance. An unbalanced economy is the fruitful mother of unemployment.

What I have said is intended only to indicate factors inherent in our nature, which have always made this problem difficult and, up to now, insuperable. But there is no cause for discouragement. Never lose sight of the thoroughly-established truth that human ingenuity, though barren and lifeless under dictation or constraint, in a free world knows no limits. What is of overwhelming importance is to make sure that we do not go wrong.

There are an incredible number in these days who have the idea that all such troubles can be cured by the simple process of the Government distributing money here, there and everywhere, wherever it is needed, under all sorts of attractive formulas. Our ears are assailed with slogans:—"Production for use, not for profit"; "Human rights, not property rights." Such are some modern creeds. All these slogans can be exploded by the magic of a little thinking. Every product is, and always has been, brought into the world for use. There could not be any profit in producing it if it were not for use. Then again, property rights do not exist, and most emphatically never should exist, except insofar as they serve human rights. There can be no betterment in the standard of living by any distribution of unearned money. Nothing but a distribution of goods needed by humanity can help the standard of living, and these goods must first be brought into being. You cannot Beveridge a country into prosperity any more than a lawyer can make his client rich by drawing up his Will. The first and basic essential is greater and ever greater volume of goods. The aggregate of production today over this world, even if everything were distributed without any distinction between those who work and earn and those who do not or will not—that aggregate would still mean a very low standard of living spread over the masses of mankind. Most careful students of this subject tell us, after long and thorough investigation, that the income of the average family, measured in terms of the necessaries of life that a dollar will buy, was, before the war, only $10.00 per week for 81% of the earth's population. They mean by that what $10.00 a week would buy in the United States of America on an average over the period from 1925-35. Remember, it is not dollars that count. What counts is what dollars will buy. In the very richest countries embracing ten per cent of the earth's people the average was only $20.00 per week. Those countries were Great Britain, the United States, Canada, Australia and New Zealand, Switzerland and the Argentine. It is worth observing that these are all democratic nations. Not one of them is totalitarian. Clearly then, on the basis of aggregate production, even in these later years of power and machinery, no change in the distribution system, however hostile to justice, to common sense and reason, can bring about even a glimpse of that paradise which thoughtless people are predicting. The first essential is an enlargement of total production.

What I have said makes clear, just as a mere matter of adding and dividing, that over the whole population of even the richest ten per cent of this world, the total output of consumers' goods will provide only a very modest living per person; that over the entire world it will provide only a very meagre living, close to the line of want. It follows that if any system were adopted which would tend to reduce this total output, hunger and want would immediately prevail and no system of distribution could prevent it. A reduction of ten per cent would be fatal to millions; a reduction of twenty per cent would make a poorhouse of most of the world. Surely then it is apparent that one thing we cannot dare to do is to reduce the urge to toil and enterprise.

What is the urge which for hundreds of years has brought about a constant advance of productive effort, a constant elevation of the standard of living? What is the driving power which accounts for the fact that whereas at the opening of this century not one in a hundred of the urban population of the United States had a horse and buggy, by 1940 one in five had an automobile? What is the energizing force that has drawn out the virility and fertility of human genius, that has stirred men out of idleness and indifference, that has kept hands at the forge and brains at the desk, resisting all temptations to frivolity and ease? Everyone knows what it is: it is the living, vitalizing principle under a free economy which insures that every person works for himself and has to work for himself. It is the incentive of reward, bigger earnings, pay in the measure of toil, remuneration in the measure of results, profit in the measure of efficiency, the prize of property ever ahead as the reward of industry and thrift. We have had a system under which success is personal and failure is personal.

We are told now we must change all that. John Smith and everyone else is to be allotted his place by a power above, and all work for the State; we are going to be fixed into a regimented national corpus and do as we are told. This is what Churchill has described as a world where nobody will amount to anything except the politician. Can you think steadily just for a few moments and fail to see where such a system would carry us? Take away the main, the universal, incentive to toil; smother out the craving for possessions natural to all mankind; yes, just keep on in that direction more and more, as we are every day commanded to do, and down goes the aggregate product of toil and down goes the standard of living. You know, and I know, and every person knows, who will allow his own experience to enlighten his mind, that you cannot lift from the great mass of men responsibility each for his own destiny and thereafter get the same contribution from those men. That applies not only to wage-earners, but to you and to me and the whole body of mankind. There is nothing you can substitute, with the same impelling power and the same universal appeal.

There are some who tell us that men in any sphere will work their best just for love of country or love of occupation. These, it is true, are collateral motives which help with many; with a few they are supreme. But tell me! How strong and how wide is their power and reach over the whole range of human kind? Surely we must in our hearts acknowledge that these reeds left alone would never support the world. Depend on them and stalking Want would decimate our species. Others say that workers will be more willing and faithful as soon as they know that profits are gone. When you get a chance, take a good, long look at some Government-operated undertaking, and then ask yourself: Where would this plant end up if it had to pay taxes and meet competition like others? Britain nationalized her coal mines in the last war and the rate of production per worker went down from 258 tons per man per year to 176 tons, even though wages were maintained or increased. When the mines were handed back to their owners the rate came back to 316 tons per man per year. Meantime the Government lost £44,000,000 on its experiment, which loss the taxpayers had to shoulder. Coal miners are just as good as gold miners and both are just as good as factory workers or clerks or accountants, or dock-workers or lawyers. Human nature is human nature, and it is with human nature that we have to deal.

But there is a consequence which is still worse. The betterment of our race depends on character; it depends on morale. Which system do you think is going to make the strong and self-reliant man—the system under which the State takes charge of his life, or the system under which he takes charge himself; the system under which a Fuehrer above directs his destiny, or that under which he is captain of his own soul and master of his fate? The struggle of life is in harmony with our nature. Rivalry and struggle under equitable laws are the glory of living. Men become strong by defying defeat, by grasping the skirts of happy chance and beating back the blows of circumstance, by cheering in the face of discouragement and shaking off the yoke of inauspicious stars, by steering for the lights ahead, singing in the fray with fate, turning loss to gain and failure to success. Never toy with the notion that these things have to pass from life.

Who wants to substitute force for reward as the power behind human toil? You must have one or the other. Force has to come if the higher incentives go. In every socialist country today the Gestapo, the Ogpu or some other incarnation of sword and gun stands behind the whole population. Why would it be any different here? It just cannot be. Remember, with every surrender of the functions of the citizen to the hands of government, the powers of government over the citizen are enhanced; government grows, the citizen declines. Keep on with that process and the citizen becomes helpless. Freedom of enterprise is the very essence of our system of reward. Freedom of enterprise and political freedom live together and never can live apart. They never have lived apart and never will. In the great field of human enterprise let this plant and that plant, this institution and that institution pass one by one over to the State and very soon the procession cannot be stopped. A Government that directs the radio will very soon direct the press. A Government, indeed, that directs industry, inevitably directs the press, because the press is nourished by industry. No one whose eyes are open can even dream that political freedom can survive where government pervades and determines every movement of life. Such an idea in the light of reason is a fantasy, and experience is in line with reason.

"Power corrupts," said Lord Acton, "and absolute power corrupts absolutely." That is why German National Socialism became a despotism, and that is why Russian Socialism or Communism—whatever you call it—became a despotism. Power piled on power drives democratic processes to the woods. Force becomes essential when other incentives are gone, and force is applied universally and without remorse.

Surely it is not necessary to follow the invasion of force over the whole field of Russian economy. We all recognize the armed strength of Russia; we all acknowledge her tremendous contribution to this war; we all admit her right to choose her own form of government and to a potent voice in the Councils of peace. But do not let us get confused. A great army and a brave army— and Russia has both—a great army and a brave army does not necessarily come from a healthy economic system. Germany, too, has a great army and a brave army, but Germany's National Socialism is hateful to the soul of free men. Genghiz Khan had the mightiest and best-led army the world had ever known. It was built from a nation of slaves. But in civilian life ruthless force, applied for over twenty years to the brave, industrious Russian people, failed to produce anything comparable to the achievements of free nations.

What I shall give you on this subject comes in large part from books written by Communists themselves, who spent years in the Soviet and who were disillusioned, and in part as well from other careful and thorough students of economic results and statistics. Colin Clark, a highly-regarded authority, in his book, "A Critique of Russian Statistics," has affirmed that the standard of food consumption, which since the days of the revolution of 1917 had improved in other lands, actually went down in Russia and was, in 1934, about 25% lower than where it stood before World War I. Aggregate production had apparently reached pre-war levels, but so large a proportion was taken to build and purchase armaments that the balance left for consumption was cruelly small. Indeed, Sir John Orr finds that the average level of food consumption in Russia in the 30's was thirty per cent below the level of the poorest fed ten per cent of the British population. Such was the consequence of exterminating the incentive to cultivate and toil. The tragedy of Russian famines can never be concealed. Some writers say the most terrible one was a man-made famine. Whether it was or not, the Soviet was totally unable to relieve its sufferers, and this notwithstanding the fact that it had confiscated all property and repudiated all debt. Men, women and children died in millions. Undoubtedly, more died of famine than the whole population of Canada. In this country we had drought continuously in our Western Provinces over a tremendous area, but the nation was able to relieve and there was no starvation in our land. There are things that despotic direction can accomplish—and some of them worth while—but it cannot keep alive and alight the spirit of a nation, and it cannot sustain the store of life's necessities on which the well-being of the masses of people depends.

There are some who, although they shudder at the thought of a socialist transformation, seem to harbour an idea that we can have a sort of semi-socialism, a blend, and that Government, by a programme of public works, can protect us from unemployment. I dare to say that this is a delusion, and in so daring I ask to be judged by the outcome, if such an experiment on a big scale is ever tried. There are, of course, projects which a Government can wisely launch. There are necessary and fruitful public works and especially conservation works—those which can earn profits on the investment in one form or another and which, quite properly, a Government can undertake. These should be reserved in good times against darker days of lower industrial activity, but the projecting of public works at any time just for the sake of employment is vain and fallacious. Capital is timid, and a government programme of spending for spending's sake is a threat to industry and a harbinger of higher taxation. Three or four dollars in the hands of thrifty people may run to cover for one which the Government spends. An atmosphere of threat to private enterprise is itself prolific of unemployment, no matter what professions and slogans may rend the air.

Let us study recent experience in two countries, and profit by what facts reveal.

On the advent of the Roosevelt regime in the United States, there was heavy unemployment in that country. A wave of depression, had, indeed, overswept the world. With the best of intentions President Roosevelt launched his New Deal. A very prominent feature of his plan was a large programme of public works. Results show that its purpose was to make work and that it had little or no other justification. In a few short years— all years of peace—the national debt of the United States was almost trebled. Debt is still debt, and the service charges of their forty-five billions at the outbreak of World War II will be a burden on their industries for decades.

On the other hand, Great Britain stood loyal to the principle of private enterprise and sound finance. She launched a housing programme on a well thought-out plan of initial public assistance, but on the base of private and building-society enterprise, and with a reservation that, later, public assistance constantly diminishing was to vanish. She re-built the homes of one-third of her population and made England over anew. Through it all she balanced her budgets and, indeed, reduced her debt. The service charges on her unparalleled obligations following World War I were no less than £350,000,000 per year; but before World War II started, those service charges were down to £230,000,000 per year.

Now, let us look for a moment at comparative social results. Taking the year 1929 as a base with respect to each country, it is a fact that on the score of total industrial production the United States, recovering from the depression, had reached, by 1938, 72% of that country's level in 1929. Britain in 1938 had reached 116% of her industrial production in 1929. On the score of employment, the United States, recovering from the depression, had reached an employment level, in 1938, 82% of where the country stood in '29. Britain had reached 104% of her employment figures of 1929. There is another test probably even more decisive—national income. By 1938 the United States had restored her annual national income to 85% of where it stood in 1929. By the same year Britain had restored her national income to 120% of where it stood in 1929.

Those figures reveal a truth which surely demands today the attention of a distraught and groping world. The field of investment in Britain was maintained bright and promising, and expansion was in evidence on almost every side. The atmosphere was healthy and confidence was high. Let no one say that the years between the two Wars were shameful years for Britain. They were perhaps the most resilient and at the same time the most humanitarian in the whole history of that island nation. Gustave Stolper, an American who lived long in Europe, a thorough and enlightened student, is authority for the statement that no country in the world took care of her unemployed as well as did Britain. The annual cost of her social services rose to £360,000,000, or more than the entire service charge of her debt at the close of the last war. But still her debt went down and the condition of her people improved. These things are written for our instruction.

A favourite fable which one often hears recited, though never supported, is that what are called capitalistic rivalries or struggles for markets are the main cause of wars. This proceeds on the glib hypothesis that governments are the creatures of exporters. All this is possible but very unlikely. Hunger and want over large populations will breed discontent and even hatred of wealthier nations, but those are very different things from capitalistic rivalries for markets. A careful analysis of the factors which have brought about major wars of the last one hundred and fifty years shows that in not one of them was any question of markets or of capitalistic economic rivalries of the least influence or importance, and that in most cases such considerations did not even exist. Under the economies of free countries, individuals and individual units trade with individuals and individual units of other lands. A man or a company in Canada does friendly business with a purchaser or a seller in a foreign field. He competes with some; he co-operates with others. This is the kind of relationship that brings nations together and does not drive them apart. But what is to be the order of trade under socialism? The State becomes the producer; the State becomes the exporter. Individuals no longer compete with individuals, companies no longer compete with companies, but nation competes with nation. Commercial rivalry of government with government is piled on top of international rivalries of every other kind. Can one think of an atmosphere more charged with the peril of war? Those myriad communications between the people of one country and the people of another, which arise from trade between those peoples and which contribute so much to friendships across the boundaries of nations—those things are gone and rivalry of State with State reigns supreme in every sphere. This is the condition of affairs which we are asked to believe will conduce to world peace!

There seem to be many who think that there is some vast pool of wealth into which rivers of profit have been flowing and which can be captured and spread all round to the nourishment and sustenance of a needy world. There is no such pool. There never was such an ocean as people imagined, and there is less now than ever. Taxations on a huge scale and capital levies in the form of succession duties have brought down its dimensions and have been redistributing possessions of the successful at a swift and constantly accelerating pace. These taxations and levies will have to continue. At the present time if the total aggregate income of all those in, say, the United States of America, enjoying more than ten thousand dollars per year after taxation, were to be taken from them in toto and distributed among the poorest third of their population, no one would get enough to fill the hollow of his hand. United States' Government statistics show that for a period of ten years preceding 1937, average earnings of capital in the form of profits over the whole field of American industry amounted, after taking account of losses, to about four per cent per annum. Keep in mind we have never had a profit system. What we have had was a profit and loss system, and the meaning of that system is that efficiency is rewarded and inefficiency pays the penalty. That four per cent— or make it five or make it six if you like—is the prize which rewards the man or company that does a job better than others, makes the best products which sell the best, and eliminates waste of human energy and human resources. We hear a lot in these times about Freedom from Want. The best way to get freedom from want is to get freedom from waste, and there is no way of getting freedom from waste except by rewarding the energy and brains which bring about that result, and by penalizing those who fail. That four per cent or five per cent or six per cent is the base and life-blood of the great insurance companies and other institutions which sustain the fabric of free civilization. It is the prize that inspires the able and the enterprising to take risks and to make themselves of real value to their fellowmen. It is the prize that constitutes the incentive which builds up that huge mass of production upon which the standard of living of every man and woman depends.

I said some time ago that no one would contend that all is now perfect in a perfect world. Such a happy state of affairs never was and never will be. Indeed, it is my belief that there is more to be done now in the way of reform than there has been for many years. The adjustment of an industrial system where, in a mechanized age, some units of enterprise necessarily become tremendously large—the adjustment of such a system into a free competitive economy is difficult, and as yet cannot be said to be happily achieved. We hear a lot about monopoly and "monopoly finance," whatever that means, just because the word "monopoly" is supposed to have vote-catching power. The design is to spread an impression that almost every large business is a monopoly. Such talk is dishonest nonsense. Indeed, it is doubtful if a real monopoly can exist or can long exist. There is always a rival product or a substitute product on hand or on the way. That there must be more active control of larger units is, I think, generally true; that there must be definite control of anything in the nature of monopoly is unquestionably true. Control, however, is one thing and Government operation is another. The theorist talks as if control were something new, but the truth is the State in a democratic country has always been the master. Control is the very essence of its being. The problem is what controls to apply, how to apply them and to enforce them in the interests of the nation. Well thought-out and salutary regulation is healthful and helpful. Unnecessary interference is a bane, a burden and a curse. The greater the interference, the greater the bureaucracy, and the larger you make a bureaucracy the harder other people have to work. Neither politician nor bureaucrat ever produced an ounce of food. They regulate, they distribute, they divide, and very often they diminish and destroy, but they never produce or increase the necessities of life.

One truth, though, that needs to be driven home now is a sense of personal responsibility. That sense is weakening—without a doubt it is weakening. It is far harder to sustain than a sense of personal rights. Just before leaving Toronto I read in a paper of large circulation a statement that everyone in a democratic country had a right to social protection from the State. Something of the same doctrine has come to my notice in Vancouver. I stand before you and declare—whether it is popular or not—that such an assertion is false. There comes a time when calamity or old age robs the individual of his power; there comes a time when the individual has done his utmost and exhausted every resource, and the State comes to his help. But the primary responsibility, the full responsibility, is on the individual himself. The creed of "something for nothing" as a matter of right is fatal to the fibre of a people. We have been witnesses in our own time to the spectacle of countries destroyed from within. Those who preach this doctrine of a universal right to social protection from others are sowing the bacilli; they are spreading the bacteria, scattering the drug, which spells the decadence of a nation. If you want your country to travel the sure road to dissolution, keep on dilating on the sweet parenthood of the State and keep on luring young manhood into visions of rights without responsibilities, of idleness without suffering and of a livelihood without toil.

Just a word, and a very earnest word, in conclusion. Betterment of our laws, making them more equitable and more just, more encouraging to the hard worker in whatever sphere, to the man who is struggling upwards—this has been the first function of legislatures ever since legislatures were known. It has been the first object of public men ever since Parliaments were free. It has not been performed as we would like, but to its performance have been devoted the lives of many good and faithful men.

What we need is not a new dispensation. As a matter of fact there is no such thing. It is a case of freedom or the loss of freedom; it is a case of making enlightened use of the heritage our fathers won, or going back to the crudities and bondages of long ago. What we need is not a new political system; it is not some new and fantastic scheme of economics or of money. What would help a lot would be a re-invigoration of the institutions we have—and not only our political institutions, but those which have their temple in the home, in the Church and in the school. What we need more than anything else is a learning again of the old lessons of toil, of honesty and thrift. One thing is certain: It is not an intense cultivation of the inveterate habit of looking to the Government, dreaming evermore of "a nursemaid State that will spoon us out our food"; it is not a noisy facility in demanding help from others, accompanied by a multitude of blue-prints and a standing army of bureaucrats to make sure that we get it; that is not what we need. It is, rather, the old tonic, the old discipline of self-reliance and self-help. Without these verities which were thundered into our ears and burned into our hearts vastly more a generation ago than they are today—without them, all the laws of Christendom or heathendom will never make a nation, because they never will make men. Basic truth does not change and basic principles are eternal. These, the simple ones, are still the mighty ones and they decide everything for us for weal or woe—these have to be enthroned again as in the days of our youth, in the homes and the schools and the Churches, for surely it can be said that in not one of them, the home, the school nor the Church, are they taught today with the power of the olden time.

The real issue at the heart of all this controversy over socialism and citizenship, over the State on the one hand and the free man on the other, the real issue is this, and on its answer hangs our destiny:—Are we going to build on the sterner virtues on which civilization has been made, or are we going to relapse into the soft and easy habits and hypnosis on which from earliest times civilization has decayed?

Let the guns be turned on those last words of mine by whomsoever will! Those words are true, and men and angels know they need to be spoken. They are true today to the last syllable of expression and they will still be true to the last syllable of time.

UNIVERSITIES AND THE NATION

*From an address before London Branch, Toronto Alumni Association,
January 27, 1948.*

THE SCIENCES AND THE HUMANITIES are recognized everywhere as
fitting studies for serious and aspiring youth. The instrument of
language, or rather, of languages, is the equipment which opens
gates to these dual fields, and for that reason certain languages
are mastered and this mastery, if complete, becomes a prized and
useful possession. All possible under those headings the educated
man should possess and with that huge empire or as much of it
as he can explore, his mind should keep in converse while it grows
in discipline and power. In earlier times there was apprehension
that science, especially in the field of natural science, was
resolved to oust its rival claimant, the humanities, and take the
University curriculum to itself. This apprehension I hope is
passing away. A major place, a vast territory, the physical sciences
must always occupy, and from it they can never be dislodged.
But the other realm of human evolution has large dimensions
too and has values as large as its dimensions. We should not even
think of these two groups of studies as rivals. In the simple
words of Lincoln, they are not enemies, but friends. The great
Huxley, at a meeting in London back in the last century, said
that in his concept Science and Art were the obverse and the
reverse of nature's medal, one seeking to express the eternal
order of things in terms of feeling, the other in terms of thought.
In thus speaking, Huxley was thinking of Art as not so much a
skill as a kingdom of ideas endowed with simple beauty, sanity
and healthiness—qualities inherited so abundantly from ancient
Greece. "When man no longer loves nor hates"—this is how he
phrased it—"When man no longer loves nor hates, when suf-

453

fering causes no pity and the tale of great deeds ceases to thrill, when the lily of the field seems no longer more beautifully arrayed than Solomon in all his glory, when the awe has vanished from the snow-capped peak and from the deep ravine, then, indeed, Science will have the world to itself, not because the monster has devoured Art, but because one side of human nature is dead and mankind has lost the half of its precious and eternal heritage."

These two broad departments shade somewhat into each other. A study of the sciences may summon forth those qualities which the humanities more directly encourage, but that does not subtract from the case I wish to present. The curricula of Universities have been for years more and more invaded by subjects which I dare to suggest have no proper place in either category. Whether the Western Ontario is free from this development I do not know, but, undoubtedly, it is one of the freest. At Toronto's recent Convocation, Mr. Massey, the new Chancellor, in a penetrating and scholarly address, emphasized with great force that the one fundamental purpose of a University is cultivation of the mind. To this end the gifts of an education, he said, are, first, intellectual integrity—(to that I would add as a corollary integrity of words, suspicion of catch-words and scorn of slogans which deceive the hearer and debase the language—to debase its language is more dangerous to a nation than to debase its coinage)—and so, to return:—clarity of thought and precision of expression, mental alertness, a critical sense which enables one to distinguish the real from the spurious, the excellent from the second-best; and then, on the side of the humanities, an awakening of the imagination, a development of a sense of beauty and a power to enjoy beauty of thought, of vision and of words.

What has taken place has been, in the first instance, an accession of subjects under the name of Science which are not sciences, and in my judgment, never can be. Science is accumulated and accepted knowledge directed toward the search for truth, and, one might add, unchallengeable truth. The subjects of whose prevalence I complain are in the nature of excursions into the world of affairs, and deal with a vast variety of events and circumstances always changing and shifting, with a multitude of conditions, some departing, some arriving. The wisdom of any decision to be made on the basis of such variable facts and events must be dictated by common sense applied to the situation of the hour as such situation stands between its background and its prospect. It cannot be assisted much by philosophical disquisitions in advance. The best equipment for wise executive action, upon such living and moving foundations as I have described, is practical contact with affairs and such understanding of human nature as comes from experience and experience alone.

Then, again, there has been witnessed an introduction of ever-increasing occupational studies—studies very useful in their place and some of them worthy of public assistance, but not contributing, or contributing very little, to the higher mission for which, as we all know, Universities exist. As Mr. Massey puts it, the lines leading toward higher objectives are obscured and confused, and the essential purpose is lost to sight.

True, the great professions have been traditionally included in, and are still a large sector of, academic work. But does it follow that all occupations should be similarly included? Admittedly they should be, if all of them—that is, the training for all of them—can fit equally well into the great design for which Universities are founded. Everyone knows they cannot, and I earnestly impress upon you this principle, that nothing in the way of occupational or professional training should be enfolded in a University curriculum unless the subject matter covered by the training lends itself to truly scientific thinking and to cultural growth. To bring others into the ambit is to deflect the institution from its predestined and exalted purpose, to dissipate its energies and to confuse its task. There are activities carried on under the aegis of some Universities, whose passport of admittance can only be justified on a theory that anything worth discussing should have a professor to open the debate.

Both tendencies of which I have spoken have the effect of forcing abnormal growth in these centres of higher learning. Some have multiplied their students until they have from five to ten times what they had when Canada's population was half what it is today. Can it be honestly argued that this country is, on the whole, a better-educated country than it was thirty, forty or fifty years ago? I do not think so. Bigness, of itself, is a curse and not a blessing. It forbids, on the score of cost alone and for other reasons as well, that close intimacy between pupil and teacher so precious to those who are rightly in College halls, an intimacy that arose from the old conception of a University as a community of masters and students. As the Toronto Chancellor has said, anything in the nature of mass education is impossible. An alma mater must know her children one by one, and can never become a mint or a factory or even an army. There are, it is plain, reasons for abnormal attendance just now because of special obligations we owe war veterans. But anyone can see that when these obligations are discharged there will still be unwieldy thousands—larger attendances by far than before the war. By no means should our College halls become a mere refuge for high-brows. Their doors must be opened to the brilliant student if he has shown his worth, even though handicapped in funds, and, conversely, they should be closed to the unfit applicant even though smothered in wealth. But the tendencies I have spoken of result in the admission of large numbers who clog the processes, and have not that intellectual equipment and sternness of purpose which can make them leaders. The standard of quality so important to places of higher learning is impaired.

I am against mere bigness for another reason, a reason which I think goes to the very roots of our whole social organization. It has to do with the social teaching—yes, the political teaching—of our time. As our academic halls multiply and diversify, a University becomes more and more dependent on the State, and dependence on the State is becoming a veritable epidemic, a spreading pestilence, in every department of life. Certainly the essentials of at least some occupations must be taught. The University, though, must be a place of higher learning and of highest standard of student and of faculty. True, even in this work the public is right in demanding that the University come to the people. But it must answer that demand while still retaining its quality and remembering its mission, by producing leaders of thought who go among the many and carry the first fruits of education, the true values they have acquired, to all who can listen and learn. The State, by higher training, can develop leaders. It can make leaders of those who show they have the stuff to qualify. It can help with special generosity those who specially help themselves, those who by extraordinary effort demonstrate that they have capacity and will to get to the front. But beyond that the State, for the good of the Nation, for the good of its youth, cannot dare to go.

There has spread through the world in recent times a creed that Governments must be the director and protector of everybody, and in some way bring about equalization by destroying self-reliance and self-responsibility. To this doctrine democracies are peculiarly exposed because of the power of the ballot. The weakening of democratic institutions in many lands, and their disappearance in some, can be traced to this disease. We make education free—that is elementary education. Public schools for the young are open and free. What is taught there is necessary for the tasks of life, and children cannot take care of themselves. Our High Schools and Collegiate Institutes are all but free. We are rightly generous with them. We ought also to be more generous than we are to many of our people, who, because of disability, are handicapped in life. But the open door of the University for higher education on a mass scale is a symptom of the malady which is eating at the vitals of society. Step by step we are substituting a so-called social security for self-reliance; Government direction for self-adventure, self-experience and self-responsibility.

What is this social security we have been hearing so much about? In a factual sense there is no such thing. It does not belong to this world. This is a world of danger and adventure. It is only by going through danger and adventures that we acquire capacities to face them and to master them. Certainly there can be no such thing as social security handed out by the State. The only thing of the name that is worth anything is what we provide for ourselves. The more the State aims to provide it, the farther we will be from it. Coming as a gift it is unreal; it is empty, and besides, it debilitates morale; it corrupts and impoverishes the human spirit. Safety without the power of self-protection and self-sustenance is not safety at all. What Government should do is to establish and enforce laws, and so frame its laws as to provide the maximum of opportunity. It is for man, within the law, to make his way, to pay the penalty for his failures, to grow strong by his struggles, to give employment by his enterprise, to inspire others by his victories and to help the unfortunate by his success. Too much Government means little men. It is only by battling with burdens and dangers that self-reliance becomes a reality, and without self-reliance no human being is in moral health and no life is worth while.

My last thought is this:—"With malice toward none, with charity for all" was the wise precept of Lincoln. It is a wholesome teaching for all mankind, and its appeal the State itself must heed. But charity does not mean protection through life's storms. It does not mean shelter from the battle and a withering of the wrestling thews. It does not even mean benefaction, or bounty, or paternalism; and anyway, benefaction, or bounty, or paternalism are hardly ever of value. Very certain it is that these things are not a function of Government whose money is not its own—and that, no matter who or what the favoured beneficiary may be.

The vicissitudes and perils of our journey on this earth are not getting less; they are increasing as years advance, even though opportunities are greater. Paternalism can produce only greenhouse plants, and a greenhouse generation will surely go down in the battle of the strong. These are simple, homely truths— simple, homely truths that a few years ago hardly any would dispute. But we are losing our hold on them; we are drifting away from them under the spell of slogans and the passion for votes and power.

The greatness of a nation, its value to humankind, is measured by the stature of the men and women who make it. This must never be forgotten. And so, whatever the complexities of our bewildering age, whatever its perils, whatever the need for larger union and organization wide as the world, we must in our own domain so fashion our polity that every one of us will feel that to the very utmost he is master of his fate and author of his woes; that he is still at the helm of his own life and that on his captainship depends his destiny. Not under the totalitarianism of centuries ago, not—a thousand times not—under the totalitarianism of today, but only when and where the principles just recited were paramount, has there been witnessed, even in smallest measure, an onward march of the masses of mankind.

TRIBUTE TO DR. J. R. P. SCLATER

Spoken on behalf of the Congregation of Old St. Andrew's United Church, Toronto, at a Memorial Service for Dr. Sclater held in the Church on Sunday, September 18, 1949.

It has been my privilege—a truly valued privilege—to be one of Dr. Sclater's congregation for more than twenty-two years of his Ministry in this Church. And I am one of thousands who have been impressed by the shining integrity of his character and his intellect, by the rare richness of his talents and, as well, by the ingratiating human appeal of his person and his presence. These attributes which make men respected and esteemed he possessed in bountiful measure. As time moves on, the thought of them and of their manifold illustrations while he was among us will never cease to be helpful.

But fundamentally and preëminently Dr. Sclater was a preacher. What is more, or should I rather say what is of first importance, he was a preacher of the gospel, and to the task of preaching the gospel with unwavering devotion he adhered. Beyond its ample and benign circumference he was not tempted to wander, and within its domain he was supreme. For this we honour him; for this we are grateful.

An estimate of the man would, however, be inadequate if it failed to reveal the wider area of his interests and his learning. No one was more at home than he in the currents of modern thinking. Very certainly no one was more appreciative, more intelligently appreciative, of the achievements of Science, indeed, of the conclusions of Science and of the impact of these things on mankind. But on his own life work he never permitted himself to be mistaken. His duty was never obscured. It was to hold before his people the exalted mission of the Christian Church,

460

the glory of the world's greatest Teacher, and to extol Him as the Way, the Truth and the Life on our journey from the finite to the infinite.

All of us, especially those who, like myself, number their years in scores, have heard other great preachers. We have listened to many good sermons. Some of them have clung to memory all the way from youth to age, and these even now we would be sorry to forget. Comparisons have their frailties; they are said to be odious, and none would wish them shunned more than our departed friend, but surely one may be forgiven, now that he is no longer with us, in offering him a tribute which, if it has no other value, is sincere: From no other man at any time have I heard sermons which in power, inspiration and practical worth were, in my humble opinion, equal to some of those which fell from Dr. Sclater in the pulpit of Old St. Andrew's.

We are all of us oppressed now with a feeling of sadness and loneliness. He whom we revered has toiled till he could toil no longer. For some months the shadow of an approaching fate had been visible on his kindly face, and yet, as one talked with him, he could not fail to observe an accompanying brightness which denoted generous, courageous acceptance of whatever might befall.

No word can ever come to us of his last moments of life, but we may be certain they were serene and peaceful, and we are comforted by the assurance that they were free from pain. If consciousness still was his, we can believe that even then he was breathing in silence a message to this troubled world, a message of lofty and unclouded purport, a message to which humanity, however weary and preoccupied, must needs listen and attend.

APPENDIX

Opinion from the Department of the Privy Council

(See p. 172).

July 1, 1926.

Dear Mr. Meighen:

Replying to your inquiry on the subject of oaths taken by ministers and acting ministers, I beg to inform you that upon a member of the Privy Council being called to take a portfolio and preside over a certain department, he is required in all cases to take the oath of office.

The wording of this oath, a copy of which is attached, is not prescribed by any statute, in so far as I have been able to discover, but would seem rather to be dependent upon custom and usage.

Regarding the appointment of acting ministers, this is generally done by order in council, but it has not been customary for an acting minister to subscribe to any oath and no acting minister in the past twenty-five years has been asked to do so.

Ministers without portfolio have in several instances been called upon to temporarily preside over departments as acting ministers, but in no case, in at least the period of time mentioned above, was an oath administered to them.

Such was the opinion which I gave you two days ago, after consultation with Mr. Kezar, the assistant clerk of the Privy Council, who has an experience of over thirty-five years in this office.

During the last administration three ministers without portfolio were at different times appointed as acting ministers, namely, the Hon. E. M. Macdonald, Acting Minister of National Defence, appointed 28th April 1923.

The Hon. R. Dandurand, appointed acting Minister of

Justice, 27th August, 1923; no oath was administered. The Hon.
H. B. McGiverin, appointed Acting Secretary of State, 26th
November, 1924. No oath was administered save that of a privy
councillor. Mr. Macdonald was appointed Minister of National
Defence on the 17th August, 1923, and was sworn in as such on
the 18th of the same month, but was never sworn in as acting
minister; nor was either Senator Dandurand or Mr. McGiverin.
In the case of Mr. Macdonald, he was appointed as Acting
Minister of National Defence when that position was vacant,
the former minister, the Hon. George P. Graham having resigned as such and appointed Minister of Railway and Canals.

I may also inform you that there have been other cases in the
past of ministers without portfolio being appointed as acting
ministers after the resignation of the regular minister, or the post
was otherwise vacant.

Yours very sincerely,
(Signed) E. J. LEMAIRE,
Clerk of the Privy Council.

Form of Oath

I,   do solemnly and sincerely promise and swear
that I will duly and faithfully and to the best of my skill and
knowledge execute the powers and trusts reposed in me as
Minister of   . So help me God.

Opinion from the Justice Department

(See p. 172).

July 1, 1926.

By section 11 of the British North America Act it is provided
that:

"There shall be a council to aid and advise in the government
of Canada, to be styled the Queen's Privy Council for Canada;
and the persons who are to be members of that council shall be
from time to time chosen and summoned by the Governor

General and sworn in as privy councillors, and members thereof may be from time to time removed by the Governor General."

I understand that the Prime Minister and all the members of the present acting ministry have been at one time or another chosen and summoned by the Governor General and sworn in as privy councillors and have never ceased to be members of the Privy Council. In these circumstances I am of opinion that upon their being summoned to attend meetings of the Privy Council, no oath other than that already taken is required of them.

With regard to the question whether a meeting of members of the Privy Council, summoned upon the advice of the Prime Minister, has power to appoint acting ministers of departments, I am of opinion that this question should be answered in the affirmative. It is a well known principle of constitutional government in Canada that the Governor General may act upon the advice or with the advice and consent of or in conjunction with the Privy Council of Canada or any members thereof. I know of no provision which creates any limitation upon the exercise of this power in connection with the appointment of acting ministers, and I am of opinion that the orders in council in question appointing acting ministers of departments were validly passed and are as effective as if made upon the recommendation of any committee of council.

(Signed) W. STUART EDWARDS,
Deputy Minister of Justice.

INDEX

Abbreviations

f. n.—Footnote
pré.—Précis at the beginning of each speech
et seq.—And on following pages of the same speech
Sen.—Senator